JAPAN

FOR BUSINESSMAN & JOB-HUNTER

BORGNAN

JAPAN – FOR BUSINESSMAN AND JOB-HUNTER

First Edition: April 1993

Compiled by James Rickman and
Toshishige Kusunoki

Published by Borgnan Corporation,
Dai-san Taihei Building, 1-25-3 Higashi Ikebukuro,
Toshima-ku, Tokyo 170, Japan.
Tel. 03-3983-7151

Distributed by Yohan (Western Publications Distribution Agency),
3-14-9 Okubo, Shinjuku-ku, Tokyo 169, Japan.
Tel. 03-3208-0181

ISBN 4-938749-00-9

Printed in Japan

PREFACE

This project has been undertaken with the aim of smoothing the way a little for those who are interested in doing business with Japan or in living here for a while in order to find out more about the country whilst working at the same time.

Basically this is a list of companies which have shown interest in being approached about overseas business opportunities or in employing non-Japanese members of staff, or both. The list is supplemented by what we hope are useful comments on each industry and even some personal experiences. We believe that the strength of this book lies in its lists, for we think that no other work has attempted such a lengthy listing of companies which are interested in business and employment opportunities (as opposed to simply making a list of companies without regard to their inclinations).

Borgnan Corporation has already established its reputation in the English teaching and job-placement fields, but this is its first publication aimed at the non-Japanese reader. The writer wishes to express his sincere appreciation of the assistance and advice which has been given by so many people in the organization.

The professed aim of our publisher is to try to bridge the gap which exists between Japan and western cultures and to play some little part in reducing the frictions and misunderstandings which have sometimes occurred in recent years. It is the hope of all who have worked on this book that it will be well received and that its success may enable and encourage us to continue to follow the principles under which it has been created, perhaps by compiling a work aimed at tourists and travellers next, or one dealing with the cultural differences between Japan and the west.

We should welcome your comments and suggestions, favourable or to the contrary, regarding this book and hope that you will consider it to have been a worthwhile purchase. If it helps your business to prosper or assists you in your search for remunerative employment — and thereby helps you to understand and value this complex nation a little better — then our efforts will not have been in vain.

CONTENTS

KEY TO ABBREVIATIONS

Each of the chapters 2 to 18 in this book contains listings of companies and associations. Some explanation of the abbreviations used is necessary.

Company Name: Immediately following the name of a company, one of the following notations may appear.

①	Company listed on first section of Tokyo Stock Market.
②	Company listed on second section of Tokyo Stock Market.
(L)	Company listed on local market in Japan.
(OTC)	Company not listed but shares traded on 'over the counter' basis.
K.K.	*Kabushiki Kaisha*, Japanese equivalent of 'limited company'.

Association Name: Immediately following the name of an association, one of the following notations may appear.

(SG)	Semi-Governmental organization.
(F)	Non-profit foundation.
(C)	Non-profit corporate body.
(IM)	Association offering individual membership.

The Boxes: After each entry, there is a series of thirteen boxes. The headings at the top of the page refer to these boxes, but here follows a more detailed guide to deciphering the notations.

Size (Box 1): Size of company has been determined according to the number of employees, using the following rankings.

A: Over 1,000 employees.
B: 101 - 1,000 employees.
C: 11 - 100 employees.
D: 1 - 10 employees.

Overseas Branches (Box 2): Number of overseas branches.

Overseas Experience (Box 3): Our questionnaire asked, "Do you have experience of overseas business, for example by importing or exporting?" Y = yes; N = no.

In Future (Box 4): Our questionnaire asked, "Do you wish to have such experience in the future?" Y = yes; N = no.

Country (Box 5): Our questionnaire asked, "If you answered yes to question 4, is there any particular country or area with which you are interested in doing business?" US = U.S.A., Can = Canada, Eur = Europe, UK = U.K., Rus = Russia, F = France, G = Germany, It = Italy, Aust = Australia, Indo = Indonesia, Ch = China, All = all or most countries.

Non-Japanese, Full-Time (Box 6): The number of non-Japanese full-time employees working for the company in Japan.

Non-Japanese, Part-Time (Box 7): The number of non-Japanese part-time employees working for the company in Japan.

Increase (Box 8): Our questionnaire asked, "Do you wish to increase the number of non-Japanese working for you, or have a need for replacement non-Japanese employees?" Y = yes; N = no.

Language (Box 9): Our questionnaire asked, "If you answered yes to question 8, for what foreign language(s) do you have a need?" E = English, F = French, G = German, S = Spanish, It = Italian, P = Portuguese, Eur = European languages, Ch = Chinese, Kor = Korean, All = all or most languages.

Answer in English (Box 10): Our questionnaire asked, "Are you able to answer enquiries made in English?" Y = yes; N = no.

Answer Job-Hunters (Box 11): Our questionnaire asked, "Are you willing to respond directly to enquiries made by job-hunters?" Y = yes; N = no.

Answer Businesses (Box 12): Our questionnaire asked, "Are you willing to respond directly to enquiries made by those seeking business opportunities?" Y = yes; N = no.

Answer Researchers (Box 13): Our questionnaire asked, "Are you willing to respond directly to enquiries made by researchers?" Y = yes; N = no.

Where there was insufficient space for an answer in Box 5 or 9, an asterisk (*) or similar mark appears and the information is printed to the left of the boxes.

Where boxes are empty, either the company did not repond to that question, or the question was inappropriate in the circumstances, due to a previous answer or to the type of business conducted.

Please note that the boxes in Chapter 19 contain different categories of information. The system used in that chapter only is explained in the introduction to the chapter, on page 142.

CHAPTER 1. INTRODUCTION

OUR PURPOSE

This modest work is aimed at three types of reader. Firstly, it is for those in overseas companies who wish to open a route for trade with Japan, but do not know where to start. Secondly, it is for the increasing numbers who wish to work in Japan either temporarily or on a more permanent basis. And thirdly, it is for those who may wish to study or carry out research related to this country.

Of course, these three groups are very different and we need to deal separately with each in a moment, but first a few general words about how we have arranged our book. This work is divided by type of industry or institution. Each chapter commences with a general introduction with some advice for approaching that type of company or other body. Then follows a list of organizations which might be of interest to our readers.

We have written to all of these organizations and sent a questionnaire to ascertain whether they have an interest in overseas business or in employing non-Japanese, as well as asking questions concerning their size, experience, location and willingness to deal directly with enquiries.

In addition, near to the end of the book, there is a list of all the companies on the Tokyo Stock Exchange. In general, companies listed here do not appear elsewhere in the book, unless they responded to the questionnaire. Those Stock Market companies which did answer us are clearly marked and may be of particular interest to our readers, since this is a strong indication of their willingness and ability to become involved in overseas business.

In addition, we have marked in our listings each company which appears on the Tokyo Stock Exchange. The symbol ① indicates that a company is listed in the first section of the market. The symbol ② shows that it appears in the second section. The notation (L) identifies a company listed on a local Japanese market, while (OTC) appears after the names of companies which are not listed but whose shares are sold on an 'over the counter' basis. Non-profit foundations are shown by the mark (F) and non-profit corporate bodies by (C). Associations with individual membership are marked (IM) and semi-government organizations are identified by the letters (SG).

For each organization in the main part of the book we have listed the type of business in which it engages or specializes. Then follows its address and its telephone number. Where space is limited, the telephone number has been moved to the line above or below. In addition, we have mentioned the nearest railway station and the line on which that station is located. Where the line is operated by the national Japan Railways system, the abbreviation JR appears before the name of the line. Where this abbreviation does not appear, the line is part of a city subway system or is operated by a private railway company, of which there are many in Japan. Sometimes it has not been possible to mention all lines on which the station is situated. In such cases, we have included the names of what seemed to be the most useful lines, always assuming that our readers would be going out of a city, rather than into it. Then there is the name of a contact person within the company and his extension number or direct telephone number, if these differ from the company's switchboard number. Where these or any other details are absent, it is because the company did not offer us such information.

We venture to suggest that this contact is perhaps the most useful single feature of this book, for, when one telephones a Japanese company, it is always important to know for whom to ask. The caller who has no contact, and, moreover, does not speak much or any Japanese, is not likely to make much progress, even though there may, in fact, be somebody lurking somewhere in the quiet recesses of one of the offices who is interested in what he has to say. In some cases, the name of a position or section or department, rather than a person, appears as the contact. Unless the company actually uses an English title, we have given such information in Japanese, since the switchboard operator is unlikely to speak much English, and have placed it in brackets, so that the reader can distinguish that it is the name of a position, section or department, rather than of a person. Where there is insufficient space in our entry for two telephone numbers, we have included the contact person's number in preference to the company number.

At the end of this information appears a series of boxes, beneath brief headings at the top of the page. A key to these boxes, providing additional information about each company or organization, appears on page (iv), immediately preceding this introduction. Although the headings may appear somewhat cryptic, we considered that this was the most concise way to offer as much information as possible. The reader will, we hope, soon become familiar with the headings, and can easily refer to the key in case of doubt. An empty box indicates that the organization did not provide an answer or that the question was irrelevant in view of a previous response or of the type of business.

Finally, following these organizational listings, there is a chapter of practical advice for those who need to visit Japan. This contains such useful material as a guide to the transportation system and an explanation of the address system. It is not aimed at the long-term visitor, nor at the tourist, but at the businessman, job-hunter or student whom we envisage (optimistically?) as the purchaser of our little book. Incidentally, it is our hope that we might, in the future, produce books for the tourist and for the person who opts to make Japan his home.

THE JAPANESE COMPANY

It is a modern misconception that Japan is synonymous with Utopia and that everything in the country is highly efficient and superbly organized. If you approach Japan with these ideas in mind, you are due for a surprise, for, like all other nations, Japan is an amalgam of favourable and unfavourable points and it is rather odd that recent press reports, for example, have tended to concentrate on making readers feel that Japan has developed the ideal social climate. At the same time, it is strange that the world has also been persuaded that Japan is an 'unfair' trader and that no contrary case can possibly be made. So let us begin with a look at the Japanese company, which is an institution with which most of our readers will have to deal.

We are often told that the western system is a 'top down' system, while the Japanese system operates 'bottom up'. This writer is not convinced that that is necessarily the case. Certainly in smaller companies bosses tend to make arbitrary decisions without consulting the workers even in cases where one might think that their opinions deserved to be heard. In larger companies it is true that the people right at the top often feel that there are few decisions which they can make by themselves. They rather tend to regard themselves as representatives, almost in the same way as the emperor might regard his functions as ceremonial and advisory rather than legislative. The real decision-making process is based upon the *ringi* system. Whenever a person does a piece of work or makes a proposal he puts his *hanko* (rubber or wooden stamp used instead of a signature) on it and passes it to his superior who, if he approves it, adds his own *hanko* and passes it up the chain until all necessary approvals have been obtained. Final decisions are usually made by general managers of departments for routine matters, but higher approvals will be required for really important decisions.

This system does have some advantages. For a start, it means that everybody in the chain of command knows what is happening. It also makes it clear who has taken responsibility for a certain course of action by attaching his approval. On the other hand, it has the disadvantage of being slow, especially when somebody in the chain of command is away from the office. It also leads to the repetition of the same work many times over, because, in practice, each superior usually feels duty bound to make some 'improvement' to each piece of work which passes through his hands. Since his inferior rarely feels that he can argue with such amendment, even though really he may not agree, in fact the final product is often not improved by its passage through the process.

A Japanese office is a very conservative place and a very hierarchical one. The first thing that you will notice is that nearly all offices look exactly the same. All furniture is a uniform grey and made of metal and plastic. It is arranged in blocks, typically a double row of desks facing each other with a single desk cross-wise at the head. This permits the hierarchy to be seen as well as felt. The manager sits at the head with his assistant immediately on his right. Others follow in descending order down the line. Only the most senior person in the office is likely to have his own room, and even he may just have an isolated desk. Everybody else is usually condemned to work elbow to elbow and eye to eye.

One of the favourite office games is moving desks. This may take place as often as every three months or so and involves great excitement. First there is the period of subdued fighting to get the best positions. Then the Grand Plan is revealed and a plan of action developed. Finally, on the appointed Friday afternoon, chaos breaks out as desks are emptied, moved and replenished, floors swept, places discovered with months or even years of accumulated dust, long-lost documents found hiding in unexpected places and various minor injuries given first-aid attention. Nor is this the end of the story, for, on Monday morning, the telephone company has to be called in to rewire all of the extensions and on Tuesday the electrician comes to replace the cables which no longer reach the equipment. On Wednesday the plasterer repairs the places where electrical installations had to be changed and on Thursday the venetian blinds have to be moved because the boss's desk is no longer protected from the sun. At the end of all this, you may observe that the office looks very similar to its original state. However, we digress.

The hierarchy is so strict and has so many distinctions of rank that it is often difficult to render them in English. Thus you may find that the English version of somebody's business card bears a dazzling title such as 'Acting Deputy Vice Assistant General Manager' and it may then continue with several layers of group, section, department, division and headquarters. These ranks, however, are important, for they clarify who can make suggestions to whom and whether such suggestions can be disputed or not, as well, of course, as a host of other relationships.

Another office game is the Office Meeting. In a western company this would be the opportunity for each person to express his opinions, particularly if they happened to disagree with those of the majority, and, if necessary, to have recorded his opposition to a plan. A course of action might be decided by a vote or it might simply be decided by the person in charge after listening to the various views. This is not the purpose of the Japanese Office Meeting. Disagreement is not appreciated, so anybody who wishes to make any proposal will already have carried out a process known as *nemawashi*. That is to say that he will have talked to all the other people involved and ascertained that they are in agreement with him, or, at the least, not opposed to him. If necessary, he will have modified his proposals to obtain general agreement. You may think that the meeting is, therefore, unnecessary, but, in fact, it is the formal ratification of what has been done behind the scenes. Well, you might think that at least it would be quick, but that is not so either. Much explanation and discussion takes place — usually regarded as rather boring, even by the Japanese participants — and that is thought to be healthy, just as long as no argument occurs. Interestingly, and as a slight digression, it is revealing to notice that the success of a company's annual general meeting is generally measured by its length, and the shorter the better. Such meetings are carefully timed and times are reported as a gauge of the company's success. Under thirty minutes is regarded as acceptable, as long as there are no embarrassing questions, and preferably no questions at all.

There are, of course, some very agreeable features to the Japanese office. One of these is the group spirit. People always seem to be aware that they are part of a larger entity, the company, not just individuals, and so they work together in a way which is rare in the west. Thus, when a mistake is made, it is the mistake of the group, not of an individual, which is very reassuring if you happen to be the one who made it!

It is also well known that work in Japan often includes after-hours festivities. Going for a drink after work is thought to cement the group spirit, and indeed it does do so, even if occasionally one may come to feel that the time used in this unpaid — and sometimes even costly — socializing might be better spent. However, it often enables those who are obliged to spend many hours together in the office to become real friends, or, at least, better acquaintances, and begin, just a little, to understand what their fellow workers are really feeling behind those façades of compliance with instructions received. Sometimes larger companies may use their cafeteria as a cheap drinking place in the evening once or twice a week. This writer was fortunate enough to work for the International Operations Department of a company for some years. Whenever somebody was dispatched overseas on some business errand, he was duty bound to return with at least one bottle of suitable lubrication, which was then consumed at the evening festivities, making for remarkably cheap conviviality. Luckily, the number of business trips made was very substantial, so demand was hard pressed to keep up with supply.

Some other features of the Japanese management system have also been given much publicity. One is the philosophy of promotion by seniority (i.e. number of years with the company). This gives the employees the feeling of security, both mentally and financially. They usually join their chosen organization immediately after graduating from university or college and stay for life. Salaries at the start are comparatively low, but the employees know that, in time, if they stay, their loyalty will be rewarded. It is not necessary to be brilliant, only to be diligent, and, as the years pass, their status and salary will increase. In the end they can look forward to an honourable retirement at a relatively early age — typically 55 or 60 — with a comfortable pension and the pleasant house, although perhaps still mortgaged, which they have managed to acquire as a result of their years of conscientious labour.

The Japanese company thus becomes a type of family in which the workers try to do their best for the organization and the organization tries to do its best for the employees. To be sure, this family has its conflicts and disagreements, its jealousies and rivalries, like any other family, but it tries to keep family problems within the family and to offer a united front to the outside world. The employees thus come to have the desired feeling of security and loyalty and, after a few years, it becomes very difficult for them to leave the company even if they wish to do so. By that time they will probably have domestic responsibilities and a mortgage and they know that any change would mean a loss of seniority and security. So the system tends to perpetuate itself.

From our readers' point of view, the best points about Japanese companies are likely to be their reliability and continuity. A change of management, for example, does not usually mean any major change of policy. Moreover, Japanese companies usually regard deadlines as deadlines, particularly in respect of delivery dates. Their bad points are likely to be their conservatism and slowness in decision making. This means that they may not readily respond to new ideas, particularly from overseas, and that it may take a surprisingly long time to get any definite answers.

The last point to make, however, in this section, is that things are constantly changing. The Japanese company of this decade is not like the Japanese company of last decade. Japan does not rush to make changes, but modifications are constantly considered. If it is seen that a western policy is more efficient, it will gradually be adopted. More people than ever before are changing jobs these days, for example, even if it is still only a small minority of the total workforce. More companies are adopting western management policies, particularly for emergency decision making where speed is essential. So generalizations may not always prove to be accurate in relation to any individual company. However, hopefully generalizations are better than no information at all.

THE BUSINESSMAN

Let us look first at the requirements of the businessman reading this book. He wants to make contact with Japanese companies with some proposition in mind. How should he proceed?

The best way is to have somebody known to a company to introduce you. This will establish your credentials from the start. However, the introducer will be expected to take some responsibility for your actions thereafter, so is unlikely to wish to perform this service unless he knows you well. There are various companies in Japan willing to do this go-between work — for a fee, of course. Alternatively, your embassy may be willing to provide some assistance if it thinks you a worthwhile cause.

Another useful source of information is JETRO — the Japan External Trade Organization. This is a semi-governmental organization with offices throughout the world. The Japanese embassy in your own country will be able to give information about local branches. Contrary to popular belief, Japan is very interested in importing as well as in exporting. The government is concerned about the bad publicity created by its trade imbalance, while the consumer regards high-quality imported goods as status symbols. JETRO distributes a weekly newsletter offering information about companies hoping to establish business contacts in Japan, for example, and also has a library of useful reference books at each of its branches. In its domestic offices, it offers to Japanese companies similar reference material about overseas business opportunities and will display requests received from abroad. So JETRO is a very useful source of information and can also help you to advertise yourself, but it cannot, of course, get involved in the actual business relationship.

Next there are trade associations which can provide information about member companies. We sent questionnaires to many such associations and have listed those which responded in Chapter 18 of this book. If your industry is included, you should find the relevant association responsive to trading opportunities.

It is also possible to purchase lists produced commercially of all the companies in a particular industry, including the name of the president and various other useful information. Often these can be custom-made to suit your requirements, but usually they are not cheap and, of course, the price depends upon the amount of research which had to go into the production. Generally, lists are in Japanese. Further information regarding such lists can be obtained from the publisher of this book, who can also arrange for translation upon request.

Assuming that you have found some potential business partners, from JETRO, from the appropriate trade association, from a commercial listing or from the long lists of names and addresses in this book, you had better start writing. At this stage you must be prepared for some frustrations and, whichever way you go about the matter, you must be prepared to invest a great deal of time, as things move slowly in Japan. Probably this considerable investment of time, and therefore money, is what deters most companies from trying to penetrate the 'impenetrable' Japanese market.

Now, the companies in this book have nearly all indicated an interest in doing overseas business, so they are the ideal companies for you to write to. Even so, you should not expect too much. Patience is essential! You might believe that, with those who are not interested apparently eliminated already, a high response rate could now be anticipated. Let us hope that it will be so. Realistically, however, you might expect a maximum of ten per cent of the companies to which you write to answer. Refusals will be few. Companies in Japan do not usually refuse; they simply do not respond.

Again, this writer used to feel uncertain whether companies were not interested or whether the letter had just been lost in the bureaucracy. My policy was to send the same letter three times, at monthly intervals, without any hint of recrimination, marked to the attention of different departments or officers, then to follow up with further letters mentioning that I had written before. I have to confess, however, that this hardly seemed to improve the chances of receiving a reply.

Moreover, if you do get an answer, it is likely to be a slow one. This is due to the basic differences in the Japanese office system which were mentioned previously. You could, perhaps, think of a month as being the practical minimum response time from a big company. Or you could, of course, just be lucky. Who knows?

The addressing of the letter is very important. Good advice is not to send a letter simply addressed to a company. If this little book has listed a contact, be sure to mark it to his attention, for he has indicated a willingness to hear from you. If there is no contact available, address it to the manager of a suitable department. 'Overseas Department' is a good bet. If you address it to the president, it is not likely to reach him, nor will anybody else want to take responsibility for dealing with it. If, on the other hand, you address it to the president *by name,* it probably will reach him, but he may not be the correct person to deal with it. We considered giving the names of the presidents of companies listed, but decided against it, as, in many cases, they are not the ideal contacts and because presidents, particularly of the larger companies, tend to change regularly in Japan, perhaps so that they do not stamp their marks too indelibly on the organizations of which they have been appointed temporary custodians.

It is not a very good idea to try to establish initial contact by fax. The Japanese company is likely to regard this as rather too informal. After relations have been established, it will be fine, but not to try to introduce yourself.

In fact, if you are serious about doing business here, you must face the fact that you will have to visit Japan at some stage. The Japanese transportation system seems almost to be kept in operation by businessmen rushing hither and thither across the country to do what one would think could perfectly well be done by telephone. To mention just a single example, after New Year half of the employees of each company seem to be on the move, often to quite remote locations, to render the compliments of the season to those with whom they have business relationships, of course bearing appropriate little gifts with them. The other half of the employees presumably have to stay in the office to receive those who are visiting them! Personal contact is taken very seriously in Japan and if somebody does not know you and has not got drunk with you once or twice and found out that, on the whole, you are a pretty good fellow, why, how can he possibly do business with you?

Whether you converse in person or establish contact by writing, but particularly in the former case, you will need a working knowledge of Japanese business terms. To avoid your wasting too much time, you simply need to understand that "Well, it may be rather difficult," or some similar phrase means, in translation, "I'm sorry, but that is absolutely impossible," while "We shall have to consider the matter," can be succinctly interpreted as "Probably not." If you do not get the hang of these linguistic complexities at an early date, you may find yourself expending a lot of effort unnecessarily, when somebody familiar with the manner of speech could have told you from the start that there was no hope. The point to remember is that in oriental thinking it is not very polite to utter the actual word "No," if the other party is hoping for a yes, so euphemisms are sought. Such a way of speaking is, of course, by no means unique to Japan. It is just that Japan seems so westernized that one tends to forget that this type of thinking persists.

Open argument too is more or less forbidden, so getting hot under the collar is never going to help. A typical situation which may arise is that your Japanese counterpart may sense that your mood is becoming explosive and will take steps to calm it by offering nebulous concessions of the "Well, it might be possible to" type. When you calm down, you need to consider what was said and take it very literally. Well, it might be possible — and it might very well not be possible too. By pressing too hard, you are only going to end up with misleading responses, and very likely soured relations into the bargain.

The approved approach is to put your proposition quietly and gently, with a sprinkling of mirth and maintaining good humour throughout, without any pressuring. If possible, then present it in writing as well as orally, because it may well turn out otherwise that your hosts, who listened attentively throughout, have understood barely a word, but cannot dare to say so. Then go away and leave them to consider — and that may well take a surprisingly long time. If you want to make your continued interest known, it may be by informal means such as a follow-up letter thanking them for their hospitality, a seasonal greetings card, an invitation to visit you when they next happen to be in your country, or whatever other pretext you can devise. If none of this seems to be having any effect, the time may eventually come for you to assume the worst! Even then, be careful to do nothing to sour the non-existent relationship, for there is no knowing when it might come in handy.

One day Mr. Suzuki may chance to go out drinking with his acquaintance Mr. Yamaha from another company and the latter may mention that he has heard from you with a business proposition, about which he is now hesitating. Mr. Suzuki replies, "Oh yes, I know him. We had a meeting a couple of years ago. Nice chap, although we didn't manage to do any business. You know how our boss is about new ideas. Had a splendid evening together though. Some of the stories he told were really hilarious." And that may be just the recommendation which Mr. Y needs. You have been around Japan for a few years now and a person as well respected as Mr. S is prepared to vouch for your character. In many cases, it may be not your business proposition, but you yourself, about which there are doubts. Being a 'good bloke' counts for an awful lot in Japanese society.

Another event which may occur is that you may give up the idea that anything will ever come of a suggestion made to a particular company and forget about it. Three years later, perhaps, there will be a telephone call and the voice at the other end will say urgently, "This is Kurosu Brothers Industry Company, Incorporated." (Japanese companies seem to enjoy such tautology in their titles, as if believing that the longer the title, the bigger and better the company will become.) "Who?" you will be thinking, as you respond with an ambivalent "Oh, yes." "We have considered your proposition," the voice will continue, "And have decided to accept your offer. Can you deliver next week?" One thing is certain. Japan is never short on surprises.

A few more words about the inevitable meetings with Japanese companies. Whilst the way of speaking is a type of subdued informality, there is a definite standard of decorum which must be observed, even by eccentric foreigners. After all, it was from them that most of these rules were stolen a century or so ago. First of all, one should wear a conservative suit, or correspondingly conservative fashionable attire for women, even in the overpowering heat and humidity of Tokyo's summer. Next, you must, of course, present your business card upon first meeting each important person in the company. No respected businessman would be without a good stock of cards in this part of the world. Even if you do not work for a company, you still need business cards or else you are nobody. These cards are truly very important, for they determine your relative rank. If your opposite number can establish that you are a director of a moderate-sized company, for example, while he is a general manager of a larger organization, he can work out to his own satisfaction who should defer to whom. The fact that you do not know is unimportant. It makes *him* feel more at ease.

Now when you meet, should you bow or shake hands? Your host may well feel that he should do both, but the answer is that shaking hands is totally acceptable. If you feel like giving a little bow as well, it is quite permissible, but not at all an essential.

Sit down when bidden, but do not relax too much. If new people come into the room to take part in the meeting, you will be expected to stand up each time and present your business card. You are supposed to offer it using both hands and with a slight bow, murmuring the pertinent details at the same time with a formula such as, "I'm Tom Smith. Pleased to meet you." In general, however, it will not be held against you if you do something fairly acceptable, as a result of which a business card gets transferred. It is not a bad idea to line up the cards which you have been given on the table to correspond with the positions of those opposite you. You may see Japanese do this too. It helps you to remember who is who. The cards are usually written in Japanese on one side and in

English on the other, so, if you think that a card is rather hard to understand, try turning it over. If your own card were similarly inscribed, it would probably be thought a politeness, but it is not essential. When the meeting finishes take the cards with you, putting them very carefully and visibly in a place where they will suffer no damage, perhaps in a special holder made for the purpose. Not only may these cards be useful to you at a later date, but if you start mutilating them during the meeting it will be taken as a personal affront, as perhaps an indication of what you might like to do to the donor if you got him outside for five minutes, so be careful of what your nervous twitching fingers are getting up to while you are not watching them.

A meeting will usually start with tea or coffee. At this point, small talk is expected, typically some sort of topical comparison with conditions in your own country. Maybe something like, "Do you play much baseball in your own country, Mr. Gromyko?" or "Do you have flies in Australia too, Mr. Hawke?" You are not expected to get down to business at this stage, so this phase may continue for several minutes. In any case, those present probably are genuinely interested in your country and also want to get to know you as a person, that being such an important part of the business relationship. Now, can we really trust this man? What is his character? You will find out when it is time for business, either by being told to go ahead or by there being an uncomfortable silence which presents you with the opportunity to move the topic in a different direction. One thing to remember, however, about this comparatively civilized way of doing business is that it will almost inevitably take about twice as long as you had anticipated, so be sure not to plan your meetings too close together.

Now, how should you address your opposite number — Mr. Tomisawa or Tomisawa-*san*? Of course, it is only an opinion, but this writer finds the latter method rather pretentious. You should be aware, also, that it is not even very polite, in fact somewhat the opposite. Almost nobody in his company would refer to this man as Tomisawa-*san*. His inferiors would all call him by rank, thus, "Excuse me, General Manager," without any name mentioned. His superiors might well refer to him as Tomisawa-*kun*, but on no account should you ever think of doing that, of course. Only his equals might refer to him as Tomisawa-*san*, but, even then, *-san* is most often used within the company for speaking to ladies. If somebody wanted to refer to this gentleman when speaking to another person who was not a member of the same company, he would become plain Tomisawa, with no honorific at all. For meetings with other companies, those who feel their rank inferior would probably adopt the course of addressing superiors by rank and name, but might use *-san* for speaking to inferiors. So you see how useful that business card has become. Best, however, not to get involved in such difficult matters. *Mr.* Tomisawa is safe, clear and polite. Why not stick with that? You will find that the Japanese quite like it that way in any case.

One comparatively pleasant feature of business in Japan, especially if you happen to come here in a somewhat undernourished state, is the almost overwhelming hospitality of those whom you meet, particularly if they take a liking to you. You are quite likely to be invited to lunch — usually a very good lunch too — if your meeting happens to end at around that hour. If you are still around at the close of play, you may be invited for a quick drink, that which may keep you busy until the wee hours if you allow it, although better not if you have any thoughts of doing anything constructive on the morrow. If you are given any choice in the matter, the cheapest drinking establishments are the most fun. The atmosphere is usually thick with appetizing aromas and the range of little dishes available is quite an educational experience. Your hosts, though, may think that a somewhat classier establishment is needed, but it will still be enjoyable. When it comes to time to pay for the evening's entertainment, you can offer if you wish, but you certainly will not be allowed to contribute. The company will usually foot the bill and it will be regarded as a normal business expense in a land where private life scarcely exists and socializing is such an intrinsic and essential part of business.

There is one more caution to put in this section, and that is, perhaps surprisingly, against blowing your nose. Nose-blowing is just not a Japanese custom — indeed not an Asian custom. If an irresistible urge overcomes you, you must apologize in advance, turn away and deal with the necessary business as quietly as possible, using a tissue, but never, on any account, a handkerchief. In Japan, handkerchiefs are *hand*kerchiefs, used for drying the hands, not for such dirty purposes as blowing the nose. As somebody once said to the writer in another country, "Whatever do you want to keep *that* for?" So the soiled tissue should be disposed of at the first convenient opportunity. When blowing cannot be avoided, remember to be both inconspicuous and quiet. A quick dab may go unnoticed, but trumpeting is absolutely forbidden. Noisy sniffing, you will find, together with sickening throat-clearing at most impressive volume, usually followed after a dramatic pause by well-practised expectoration (not on the office floor, please!) is quite acceptable, although not necessarily advisable for visitors. Nose-blowing, however, no!

THE JOB-HUNTER

Now what about the job-hunter? How should he, or she, of course, go about finding profitable employment? The first point to answer is the doubt which assails many who feel that they might like to work in Japan. No, you do not need to speak Japanese to work here. In some jobs, it will be regarded as an advantage, but usually only for the purpose of communication with other staff, so, even in such positions, an everyday conversational level is sufficient, except for very skilled professions such as interpretation and translation. For most of the opportunities available, however, Japanese ability is not a necessity at all.

Until just a decade ago, nearly all of those who came to work in Japan regarded English teaching as the main industry of interest to them. An industry it is too, rather than the educational experience for which one might hope. In the last few years many other employment opportunities have opened up, but teaching is probably still the largest employer of foreign labour. Moreover, it is basically an employer of unskilled labour, which is not really to its credit when the matter is considered carefully. However, the fact is that you need no qualifications to obtain employment teaching in Japan, although you will need some to obtain a visa for doing so legally, about which more anon.

The next profession which has been available for a long time is, of course, translation. You may be surprised to find that it is not a profession particularly highly regarded in Japan. Maybe this is because the work is often done so badly. Translations from Japanese to English are usually made by a Japanese and the results leave much to be desired. Following the translation process, the work may be proofread and improved by a native speaker of English. Presumably this policy is followed because it is cheap, for *real* translators, although not held in high regard, are paid well. So, if you can speak Japanese or English and another language, there may be opportunities for you. Perhaps it is surprising that English and another language might be sufficient, but it is often thought cheaper or more efficient to translate into English first and then into another language than to do the whole job in a single process. Of course, the results can be imagined. It is also worth noting that translation machines have recently been invented and that some companies are now using such devices as a cheaper alternative than real humans. It remains to be seen to what extent the translator will find himself out of a job.

Interpretation demands even better developed language skills, but, if you have them, work is certainly available — and very well paid work too. It is well paid, though, because one is likely to be gainfully employed for only one or two days in each week.

Connected with the translation profession is the art of proofreading and correction. The language skills necessary for becoming a translator take years to acquire. Proofreading is much less demanding, however. Basically, you are given a chunk of translated work and asked to make it intelligible. This often requires highly developed powers of clairvoyance. The work is moderately paid but, as often in this area, rates vary surprisingly and, naturally, one tends to start with the poorer paid work and move gradually up the scale by developing contacts or even, perhaps, by doing the job well.

Then there is narration, for videos, public relations films or slide shows. Again this is the type of work which is well paid but occasional.

The remaining area which has existed for a long time is modelling, including television and film work. Again it tends to be well paid, but offers limited availability. Television programmes and films often require non-Japanese extras and these will be paid more for close-up appearances or for speaking parts. Models are needed for such activities as advertising and fashion shows.

These, then, are what might be termed the traditional industries. But in the last few years a whole new range of opportunities has opened up and now people with all types of skills can find employment in Japan. Particularly in demand are those whose abilities relate to computers. As these opportunities have developed suddenly, so a new type of business has grown with them. This is the 'placement company', which, only ten years ago, was almost unknown in Japan.

Basically, there are two types of activity involving the placement company. One is the introduction of members of staff to the employer. The other is the dispatching of people actually employed by the placement company itself. These are not exactly what the west terms 'temps', since they are usually employed on at least a semi-permanent basis. Although placement companies may handle both Japanese and non-Japanese staff, this book concentrates on aspects concerned with non-Japanese. More about such companies follows in the introduction to the chapter devoted to such organizations, but they should not be neglected by the job-seeker, because they often have access to positions which the individual is unable to discover on his own.

The other, and more traditional way, to obtain employment is to look in the advertisements in the 'Japan Times' on Monday morning. There are also advertisements on other days and in other of the four newspapers printed in English, of course, but the best crop is found in the 'Japan Times' on Monday, or on Tuesday if Monday happens to be one of the eight annual newspaper holidays. Then start telephoning at 9.00, and be aware that competition is keen these days, with fifty applicants for a single position being not uncommon.

In fact, the most effective way to find employment in Japan is through connexions. Friends, or even acquaintances, in the right places should never be overlooked. If you can get somebody to recommend you for something, you are half-way there. So never be afraid to ask for help, if you know a person appropriately positioned. However, if that person is Japanese, do not press. Asking once will be enough. If the friend thinks that he can help you, he will, because he will be well aware of the value of his recommendation. If he does not help, that means that, for one reason or another, he did not feel that he could.

People often ask, "Should I apply for positions before I come to Japan?" The answer is that there is generally not much advantage in doing that. Most prospective employers seem to want people immediately and they also want to see them, to judge their characters, not just see their paper qualifications, for character is such an important consideration in Japan. So, if you try applying from afar, you probably will not even get an answer, and, if you do get one, it is most likely to invite you to make a further approach upon arrival. In any case, you should beware of accepting a position offered to you before you reach Japan, since you will have little idea of appropriate rates of pay and conditions. What seems appealing from afar may well appear in quite a different light when you arrive and see the cost of living here and the generally accepted levels of remuneration. Moreover, you will probably have used the contract which you signed to obtain a visa, so you will be stuck with it for at least one year and could even find yourself working for a less than reputable organization which does not even feel it necessary to honour the conditions of the contract too closely. So beware! Usually it is better to come here and see what conditions are like for yourself before accepting a position.

One exception to the above is if you can obtain employment with an overseas company which has offices in Japan. Such positions are often very lucrative and sometimes include accommodation far above the standard which you could expect to live in on your own resources.

If, however, you decide to come to Japan to search for employment and if you decide that your preference is for one of the new-style non-teaching positions, you are likely to be working either for, or at least with, a Japanese company. A section of this chapter has already been devoted to a few comments about that unique organization and the job-hunter should have read that section. However, a little more detail is perhaps necessary on the features which will particularly affect the person who is looking for employment in the company.

The first thing to realize is that, even though you are working in a Japanese company, in most cases you will never be accepted as a normal part of the system. You may as well realize this and use it to your advantage, rather than try to become what you are not. This is not a suggestion that one should ask for special favours, merely that one should accept that there are differences between one's own position and that of a Japanese worker.

Most of the positions available to non-Japanese are office-based, so let us concentrate on that type of work. There are two ways in which you may be employed. The first is as a regular full-time employee, just like all the Japanese around you. This type of employment is rare. Not only is the company reluctant, in most cases, to make a permanent commitment to somebody who may not fit into the system well, but most non-Japanese feel that it would not really be to their advantage, unless they intend to stay for the rest of their working lives, not least because of the fact that salary would be paid at Japanese rates. The alternative usually adopted is a short-term contract, most commonly for one year, but renewable annually. This gives advantages to both parties, but does, of course, mean that you always remain something of an outsider to the company.

So you can expect a higher rate of pay than Japanese staff. The difference is often very great indeed and, perhaps surprisingly, this is one condition which will usually be accepted without question by the employer. There are reasons, of course, for paying you more. The most important of these is the Japanese 'bonus' system. Japanese basic salaries, although quite adequate for everyday living, even at the relatively high rates which prevail in the major cities, are not perhaps quite as generous as one might expect from the world's economic leader. And this is because of the bonus which is paid every six months. The bonus depends upon the company's prestige and profitability, but, in general, bonus payments account for a quarter to a third of an employee's annual income. As an outsider to the system, you will not usually be paid bonuses, although this alternative, with a lower salary, may sometimes be offered if you prefer it. Generally, however, the extra quarter to third will be included in the regular monthly payment which you will receive, virtually all salaries being paid monthly in Japan, usually on the twentieth or twenty-fifth day of the month, in respect of the complete calendar month, with overtime being paid a month later.

Consideration will also be made for other benefits which Japanese will receive, but which you will not. These include, for example, pensions, a life-long career and the use of various company facilities. Even when you have taken account of all these factors, you might still think that your salary is high, and that seems to be because being a non-Japanese in a Japanese company is, in many ways, prestigious. Or perhaps it is because the country works on precedent and precedent has established that non-Japanese are a rare commodity requiring high salaries. Whatever the reason, if your salary offer does not seem attractive, examine it carefully and, if necessary, look for something better. It might be that the company has no experience and is merely offering you the same as it would to a Japanese of your age and sex.

Generally all office staff will be expected to clock in and out. The idea of 'flex-time' has recently been introduced in Japan, but most offices still work to fixed hours. If 'flex-time' is used, it is generally a rather inflexible 'flex-time' which recognizes only half-hour intervals and insists on certain rest times. The morning often starts, even in the office, with those exercises which you have seen Japanese doing on television. These are performed to taped music superimposed with spoken instructions and are carried out with varying degrees of enthusiasm, but usually mildly disliked by the majority of performers. There may be a second opportunity to demonstrate physical agility in the middle of the afternoon. The morning exercises are likely to be followed by the 'morning meeting', which is merely an opportunity for the department manager to give a pep talk and issue any notices. It generally lasts for five to ten minutes.

Lunchtime is usually from 12.00 until 1.00. Since everybody takes lunch at the same time, all eating places tend to be crowded. Large companies may have their own cafeteria, therefore, but those who work for smaller organizations just have to battle the masses, which they are pretty accustomed to doing anyway.

Work will finish at a reasonable time in the evening, say 5.30 or 6.00, but readers will already know that almost nobody goes home at that time. That is not to say that everybody remains working hard, however. It is just that it is not seemly to go home before the boss, so even those who have nothing to do will pretend to be performing some useful function until the coast is clear to escape. This is one area where attitudes have been changing recently, however. Not only is there a new generation in the ordinary clerical positions, a generation more aware of its own worth and expectations, but also there has been a decline in economic prosperity, which has caused the companies to be careful about overtime payments. The working rules may state that after normal working hours all employees must take a fifteen minute break (during which they are usually expected to continue working!) and that thereafter only complete hours of overtime work will be paid. Thus somebody who stays for one hour extra, for example, will receive no additional payment, because the first fifteen minutes was a compulsory break and he failed to work for a full hour after that. Overtime is usually paid at slightly higher rates than normal time, although part-time workers, which category may often include non-Japanese employees, may be paid at just the normal rate. Recently there has been discussion of enacting legislation to increase overtime pay rates. There has also been talk of reducing the total number of working hours to 1,800 per year, a figure more in line with the hours worked in western countries.

Another well-known feature of the Japanese system is that employees do not feel free to take all of their leave entitlement. This should not be taken to mean that they do not have such entitlement. Typically, a company may grant eight days of annual leave to new entrants, plus national holidays, with the entitlement increasing by one day for each year of service to a maximum of about twenty days. A few of the days may have to be taken on pre-ordained company holidays. Unlike in western countries, there is usually no distinction between sick leave and annual leave, so those who have the misfortune to be sick simply consume their annual leave. When it is all used up, the company will usually be generous enough to grant a further period of unpaid leave, but taking such leave is likely to affect the employee's bonus and annual salary increment. Ladies are often granted one additional day of leave per month. It is expected that it will be taken, if at all, at approximately the same time each month. Usually leave entitlement cannot be carried forward into subsequent years beyond a maximum entitlement of twenty days, except for a brief period of three or four months. Then it is simply lost to the system. Recent statistics suggest that about a half of the leave entitlement of senior workers is lost this way, and about a third of the entitlement of junior members of staff. What most companies really seem to disapprove of is the taking of extended periods of leave, which is to say more than a week at a time at the very most. Maybe this is because of the *ringi* system, mentioned in more detail in the section on Japanese companies, which ensures that piles of documents will accumulate on the desk of an absent worker and that, if he does not return fairly soon, the system will grind to a halt. However, it is odd that Japanese ingenuity cannot learn to circumvent this difficulty.

For the non-Japanese employee, leave can be a problem, for it is difficult for the management of some companies to appreciate the different circumstances in which the non-Japanese finds himself. Although the Japanese are reluctant to use their holiday allowances, they do feel an obligation to return from the big cities to their 'home-towns' at certain times of the year, particularly at New Year and at '*o-bon*' (equivalent to what we might call 'All Souls' Festival'), as well as for family events such as funerals and memorial services. No matter how busy a person is, no company would ever dream of refusing an employee permission to attend such ceremonies. Typically, allowing for weekends, the employee may need to take three or four days off work, and this is absolutely acceptable. Should some calamity happen in your family, you will find the company equally compassionate and there will be no objection to your taking three or four days off either. However, it may need you to explain that, in your case, three or four days is not really enough. For a start, you will hardly have time to go home and come back in that time. Moreover, the economics of the matter make it logical to stay a little longer, having gone all the way to wherever it is. This is not special treatment. It is merely a difference in circumstances. Most Japanese companies will reluctantly appreciate that non-Japanese staff really have to be allowed, for the reason of economics, to take their holidays in larger clusters than Japanese do, but it may not be automatic appreciation. Moreover, at the time when most Japanese are expected to take holidays, domestic transportation is packed beyond belief and international airfares may double, so the non-Japanese finds himself asking to take extended holidays at times which are regarded as inconvenient. This can easily be interpreted as a failure to display the proper spirit of putting the company first. Probably the best approach is to include the Japanese holiday period within the period of leave requested but to set off early before the prices go up. That way everybody is relatively satisfied and the additional leave is reduced to a minimum.

It should be noted that legislation recently passed gives everybody in Japan the right to paid holidays, a minimum of eight days per year for full-time workers at the time of writing, to increase to ten days in 1994. Part-time workers are entitled *pro rata.*

Since everybody is supposed to work as a group, it follows that one rarely feels alone, even less ostracized, as one might perhaps expect, one being, after all, something of a square peg. Your workmates are likely also to be extremely kind, their kindness often extending far beyond the office. If you need any help — personally, as well as in your work — you usually have only to ask, although, of course, one should always be careful not to impose upon others.

Before one starts work in a Japanese enterprise, one is expected to sign a contract. Such documents vary considerably, but, since the immigration officials will want to see your contract before issuing a visa, there are some conditions which it must contain. It must be for at least a year and must offer an acceptable salary. It should also contain a stipulation that the company will repatriate you at the end of your employment if you are not able to pay your own way back to your country. If this condition is not included, Immigration will want a separate document to the same effect. This, of course, should not be taken to mean that you will be paid an airfare at the end of your employment, although some companies are willing to make such an offer. It is merely a guarantee to the government that you will not become a burden to Japan. If your employer were obliged to repatriate you, there would be nothing to stop him from reclaiming from you the cost of doing so. Once signed and presented to Immigration, this contract is not usually referred to ever again!

When you start to work in a company, you will usually be introduced to everybody in the office, but told that one person in particular is your boss, or, if a euphemism is thought more appropriate, that he "will take care of any problems which you might have". You will probably be told who his boss is too. This should be interpreted as meaning that if you have anything to say, you say it to one of those two people, and preferably not to your boss's boss without saying it to your boss first. As a foreigner, you may be allowed a little latitude, but basically you are not expected to circumvent the chain of command.

Now, what sort of work might you be expected to perform in a Japanese office? Well, you may have some special skill which can be offered, in which case you can look for a company in the appropriate listing in the ensuing pages. But whether you have a special skill or not, you may well find that quite a large proportion of your duties pertains to checking and correcting materials written in English — letters, brochures, manuals and academic papers. You may find it odd that you are not usually invited to write any of these materials yourself, only to check them. The English used is frequently so convoluted and imprecise that it is difficult to understand the real meaning and really you may think that it would be better and quicker to let you write the piece yourself. However, that is not usually how it is done, unfortunately.

You will encounter a variety of other frustrations in this work too, especially if you have an inner urge to have things done well. Often letters will be sent without any check at all, because "there was no time" or "I thought that it had been checked already." Often, in such cases, the truth is that the writer suspected that it would be full of mistakes, but felt that he would lose face if the typist were to see his effort covered in red ink, since he was considered to be the resident English expert. It requires a good deal of tolerance and patience to overcome these situations, qualities which this writer has to admit that he does not possess in abundance. Employed to check and rewrite English in a large company, I used to find (too late!) unchecked and incomprehensible letters being sent even to Prime Ministers.

On other occasions, you may rewrite a piece of English and then find that your effort has been discarded and the original used instead. When I questioned such a case, I was told that I had misunderstood the writer's intention. My reply was that if I had misunderstood, so probably would the recipient and that it would have been better to come and explain my mistake to me and get me to write what was intended. This response was mulled, but I realized that the writer was probably afraid to do that because he feared that I would take his return as an insult to my writing and that a disagreement would ensue. A common variation on this theme is that the corrected product is used, but that the writer changes his mind over one paragraph or decides to insert an extra paragraph, having realized that some important detail was omitted. It quite genuinely never occurs to him that the revised version needs any further checking, so it is sent, or printed, in quite acceptable English, with one paragraph of gibberish in the middle.

Truly, if one takes a pride in one's work, these are great frustrations and they are not unique to this writer. Almost everybody who has worked in Japan will tell such stories — and worse. Two techniques which I tried to improve the situation were these. Whenever I returned a piece of checked work, I always requested that it come back to me for a final check, since, if nothing else, the typist or printer would introduce a few — or more than a few — mistakes. However, only rarely did people bring back work for this final check, despite my plea. Secondly, instead of correcting in red ink, which makes the changes very obvious, I used pencil and when I could see that the original was just full of mistakes, I tried rewriting it, instead of correcting the original, claiming, euphemistically, that "you did not leave me enough space." Although I thought that this would be a good idea to save the writer from losing face, in fact it was another failure, since the whisper would go round that "Mr. Sawamura's letter had to be completely rewritten because it was so bad!" A little more successful was making a point of returning any work personally to the writer when there was nobody else around him. He would then rewrite it all in his own handwriting before giving it to the typist.

It seems that these difficulties are caused because of the Japanese theory, mentioned in more detail in the introduction to the chapter on language schools, that, "We can read and write English, but we cannot speak it," whereas, in reality, Japanese tend to be able to communicate, at least, in English, and the best can speak really quite well, but very few can write grammatically. Thus they lack confidence when speaking, but have quite unjustified confidence when writing. They also fail to understand the different standards required of the two skills and to realize that mistakes which can pass almost unnoticed in speech are absolutely unacceptable in print. This too is odd, because basically the same criteria apply in Japanese as in English. In any case, trying to analyze the reasons does not provide solutions to the problems. Since this writer does not have the solutions, please be warned that this type of work is certainly likely to have its frustrations and to demand tolerance, patience and probably compromise.

Finally, a brief look at the characteristics which will fit you best for life in a Japanese office. Perhaps the three qualities which your company will appreciate most of all are competence, willingness to do whatever is necessary to finish a job on time, and conviviality. Competence, first. Nobody requires you to be brilliant. Indeed, brilliance may well cause conflicts. If you work checking English, for example, and you keep finding mistakes in the addresses of letters, people are likely to get irritated, rather than praise you for your resourcefulness. On the other hand, if you keep making spelling mistakes, you are likely soon to get a reputation for incompetence. Good all-round above average ability is what is needed.

More important, however, is willingness to do whatever is required and to make yourself available whenever needed — in short to put the company first. This writer's experience includes, by way of example, receiving telephone calls from those at the company as late as 1.00a.m. and as early as 7.00a.m. on Sunday, as well as being asked to "come in a bit early and perhaps stay a few minutes extra if necessary," on which occasion I worked from 7.20a.m. until 11.15p.m., with one twenty-minute break for lunch, and had to beg to be allowed to catch my last train home. It is not uncommon for Japanese employees to work all night, if necessary.

And conviviality. As mentioned previously, having a "quick" drink after work once in a while to lubricate human relations is regarded as an important part of business. You do not have to attend every such occasion, of course, but getting a reputation for being anti-social is a problem, whereas getting a reputation as a drunkard is not quite such a handicap! Of course, something in between is best of all. There will also be official company social events, which may include welcome and farewell parties for members of staff who are retiring or being transferred, sports days and company trips. Although these are not quite compulsory, you are expected to attend if possible and to have an excuse ready if you do not do so. Especially if you are a part-time worker, being invited to join in these events is an indication of your being accepted as part of the office and should not be scorned.

As to the specialist positions, it is less easy to make generalizations. The introduction to each chapter contains a few words on each profession and it is suggested that the reader refer to those for any further information which we may be able to offer.

THE RESEARCHER OR STUDENT

Although the number of students from overseas has been increasing recently, it should be noted that the bulk of these are from Asian countries. Opportunities for western students are available, but they are limited. A few universities or colleges offer Japanese language courses for students from overseas, but there are many more private language schools offering such opportunities. One of the problems in this area is that some such schools cater mainly for those who wish to 'study' in order to obtain a visa, and wish to obtain a visa in order to stay in Japan and earn some money. As a result, little emphasis is placed on the standard of instruction at such institutions.

On the other hand, one needs a visa to stay in Japan, so one has to make sure that a school is recognized by the immigration authorities before one hands over money and commences studies.

This is not to deny the existence of plenty of good quality language schools in Japan, just to warn that there are pitfalls and that some preliminary investigation is advisable.

There are various other opportunities for study too, of course. Courses are offered by universities and colleges, most of which require proficiency in Japanese, but a few of which are geared for non-Japanese speakers. In addition, there are private schools which offer courses in various aspects of Japanese culture. As long as the course is a genuine one, and occupies a reasonable proportion of the student's time, it is usually possible to obtain a visa for studying at such institutions.

As for research, it is difficult, though not absolutely impossible, to obtain positions in academic institutions. There are plenty of Japanese wishing to carry out research who will be given priority, reasonably enough. Companies often carry out industrial research in their own facilities and there may be opportunities there. However, such positions are also difficult to obtain because most companies are concerned that by using a researcher from outside their organization, they will be leaking their valuable know-how. Therefore, to gain an opportunity of this type one usually needs not only some special skill but also an introduction and more than a modicum of luck. Note also that if a project is in any way related to national security, it will require government approval before a non-Japanese can work on it, which approval might take very many months to obtain, if it could be obtained at all.

Those who are interested in studying Japanese language or culture should look in Chapter 4 — 'Language and Other Schools'. Japanese language schools are listed under their own heading. Schools teaching other aspects of Japanese culture are included in the heading of 'Other Schools'. For those who wish to study at a university or college, Chapter 19 gives a listing of those, mentioning how many overseas students are currently studying at each (but remember that, in most cases, the majority of those are Asian students) and showing which can offer scholarships either themselves or in co-operation with some other body. For those who would like to undertake industrial research, please refer to the appropriate industry chapter.

VISAS

The immigration rules have changed several times recently and are quite likely to change again, so anybody thinking of coming to Japan should check that what is stated in the next few paragraphs is still correct.

Some nationalities need visas to visit Japan and some do not. Those who do not include citizens of the U.S.A., the U.K., Canada, New Zealand and most European countries. However, on arrival, assuming that the visa has been obtained by those who require it, all nationalities are usually treated the same and given a ninety-day stay as a 'temporary visitor'. This category seems to include anybody who is not earning money here. Thus, while most people so admitted are tourists, the businessman is also allowed to enter under this heading as long as he is not employed in Japan. For the job-hunter, it is possible to look for work whilst here as a temporary visitor but not, officially, to perform it. It used to be possible to obtain one ninety-day extension, but now it seems to be more difficult to do so. For citizens of the U.S.A., it appears to be impossible. If one wants to stay longer under this status, one usually has to leave the country and come back. There are relatively cheap air tickets, particularly to Seoul, which seem designed specifically for this purpose.

If you want to work in Japan, you will need either a working visa or a working holiday visa. The latter are issued only to young people who are nationals of countries with reciprocal arrangements with Japan. At present, this means Australia, New Zealand or Canada. The age limit used to be 26, but now seems to have been raised to thirty. The period of stay granted is initially six months. One extension is relatively easy to obtain and a second extension is possible but more difficult. One is expected to combine part-time work with sightseeing, but there is little check on what proportion of each one does.

The working visa needs much more formality. It can be obtained before one comes to Japan, or one can apply for a 'Certificate of Eligibility to a Status of Residence' inside Japan once one has found an employer. However, in the latter case it is necessary to leave Japan to obtain the visa and then return using it. It does not have to be obtained in one's home country. Any place outside Japan will do. To obtain a working visa, one requires a university degree, where it seems an appropriate qualification for the work to be performed, and a contract for at least one year from an acceptable employer to perform an acceptable job. Basically, an acceptable job means one which a Japanese could not perform adequately. English teacher is, of course, the most common such position, but there are plenty of other possibilities. An acceptable company means one which is big enough (size often being equated with quality in Japan) and which has not got into any trouble with the immigration authorities for dubious conduct. Recently, however, the immigration authorities have seemed more willing to accept smaller companies for the purposes of obtaining a visa than they were previously. If you want to know whether a company is acceptable or not, the obvious test is whether it is already acting as the official employer of those with working visas. One also needs to produce one's *curriculum vitae* and one's academic qualifications (originals to be sighted and copies to be retained by the authorities). Certain other documents are required from your employer, including his business registration, his annual financial report, a letter giving his reason for wishing to employ you and letters offering certain guarantees regarding his new employee. It may take up to three months before the visa or Certificate of Eligibility is ready, although the applicant is usually told that it will not be as long as that. The working visa is generally granted for one year initially and is extendable annually thereafter.

When it is time to extend a working visa, one needs a letter from one's employer to state that one is still employed and why, as well as the guarantee letters again. One also needs one's tax statement so that the authorities can see not only that one is paying taxes properly, but also that one worked sufficiently over the previous year to justify one's continued presence in the country. If one leaves Japan for any reason, one must first obtain (buy!) a re-entry permit if one wishes to retain one's current status. This applies to any type of status, in fact.

If one wishes to change one's employment, it is necessary to obtain a letter of release from one's current employer, even though all one's contractual obligations have been fulfilled. Then one needs all the documents and guarantee letters as before from the new employer and one's own tax statement.

Those who are studying can obtain a cultural visa. This needs various documents from the institution where one is studying, including one to state that all fees due have been paid. The institution must be one recognized by the immigration authorities. Importantly, one also needs a guarantee letter from a private sponsor, preferably a Japanese. This letter is to say that the guarantor will take responsibility for any debts which one may incur, for repatriation if it becomes necessary and for ensuring that one's conduct remains within the limits of the law. (How is he supposed to do that, one wonders?) Cultural visas are usually granted initially for six months and are extendable until the authorities think that one has been studying for long enough. One year visas are also available. If one studies Japanese, one will usually be expected to demonstrate some proficiency in the language when applying for a visa extension. Those with cultural visas are permitted to do some part-time work to help to support themselves. This is not an automatic right. Permission must first be obtained from the authorities. It seems, incidentally, to be becoming more difficult to obtain a cultural visa. The authorities are examining the services offered by the schools more carefully now and scrutinizing the true purposes of the applicants. In particular, it seems that a request to change from temporary visitor status to cultural activities status is regarded with suspicion. Those with a cultural visa will also need to purchase a re-entry permit if they wish to leave the country and return with the same status.

There are other types of visa too, of course. If one is married to a Japanese, one will qualify for a spouse visa, these days available to males as well as females. Then there are visas for entertainers, missionaries and trainees. Most of those reading this book, however, will be interested in one of the types already dealt with.

In connexion with visas, it should be mentioned that there are plenty of people in Japan without the correct visa. The majority of these are from Asian countries. They arrive in Japan and are permitted short stays, following which they obtain employment, often involving manual labour for men or 'hostess' work for women, and then they stay until they feel that they have earned enough. When they leave the country, they are usually fined for overstaying, although they can also or alternatively be imprisoned, and are blacklisted from returning. There are also those with western backgrounds who work in the teaching or other industries without working visas and leave the country and return every three or six months. One point to make is that these people leave themselves open to exploitation, more particularly the Asians, but the westerners too to some extent. There are criminal organizations waiting to exploit the Asians, but there are also unscrupulous schools who know how to take advantage of the visaless westerner. So do the right thing and get the proper visa for what you want to do in Japan, even if it does involve some paperwork. The chances of your getting caught working without a proper visa are, in fact, quite slim if you behave reasonably, since the immigration authorities are not usually searching for people such as you when they have many more serious cases to worry about. Nevertheless, you will feel much better if you have the proper documentation. In any case, there is a limit to the time for which you can keep popping in and out of the country without anybody noticing that there is anything odd, whereas with a proper visa you can stay as long as you wish.

Those who stay in Japan for more than three months, or have permission to stay for more than three months, must obtain a 'Certificate of Alien Registration' from the local government office in the area where they are residing and must carry this certificate at all times. Those who are staying for less than three months are required to carry their passports at all times. Police and certain other officials are entitled to ask to see such documents and, if one does not have either the certificate or the passport, one is likely to find a lot of one's time being wasted at the local police station.

On the following page is a list of various types of status of residence, activities permitted with each and period of stay allowed, with the most common period granted listed first. Please note that this is not a comprehensive list. We have included only the categories most likely to be of interest to our readers and have summarized the types of activities permitted. For complete information, a book succinctly entitled 'A Guide to Entry, Residence and Registration Procedures in Japan for Foreign Nationals', published by the Japan Immigration Association is available in Japanese and typical Japanese English (both languages in the same volume) for ¥1,500.

STATUS OF RESIDENCE LIST

Status of Residence	Activities Permitted	Period of Stay
Investor/Business Manager	Activities to commence or continue international trade	1 year, 6 mths., 3 years
Legal/Accounting Services	Activities required by attorneys or certified public accountants recognized under the Foreign Lawyers' Law or the Accountant Law	1 year, 6 mths., 3 years
Researcher	Research on basis of contract with public or private organization in Japan	1 year, 6 months
Instructor	Language instruction or other education	1 year, 6 mths.
Engineer	Engineering work on basis of contract with public or private organization in Japan	1 year, 6 months
Specialist in Humanities/ International Services	Activities requiring knowledge of jurisprudence, economics, sociology, human science or foreign culture on basis of contract with public or private organization in Japan	1 year, 6 months
Intra-Company Transferee	Work permitted for Engineer or Specialist in Humanities/ International Services, but as temporary transferee to an office legally established in Japan	1 year, 6 months
Skilled Labor	Activities requiring industrial techniques or skills belonging to special fields on basis of contract with public or private organization in Japan	1 year, 6 months
Cultural Activities	Academic or artistic activities providing no income, studying Japanese culture or arts	6 months, 1 year
College Student	College or equivalent education	6 mths., 1 year
Dependent	Daily activities for spouse or unmarried minor child of person legally residing in Japan under one of above categories	1 year, 6 mths., 3 mths., 3 yrs.
Trainee	Learning technology, skills or knowledge at public or private organizations in Japan	6 mths., 1 year, 3 months
Spouse or Child of Japanese National	Unrestricted	1 year, 6 mths., 3 years
Temporary Visitor	Sightseeing, recreation, sports, visiting relatives, inspection tours, lectures, meetings, business contact, similar activities	90 days, 15 days

CHAPTER 2. JOB-PLACEMENT COMPANIES

This first category of businesses is one likely to be of interest mainly to the job-hunters of course. We mentioned in our introduction that this type of company is a recent phenomenon, one which has expanded rapidly in the last decade to meet a sudden demand, the demand for non-Japanese labour of a skilled variety and in fields other than teaching and translating.

Why, one may wonder, should job-hunters use such a company rather than applying for employment directly? The answer is that many Japanese companies would rather have it that way. Typically, they have no experience of dealing with 'foreigners' and are frightened of trying. They need a buffer, a Japanese middleman whom they can trust. Usually they have no idea of how to select, since the principles which apply to choosing Japanese staff do not seem to relate well to picking non-Japanese. And what should they do if things go wrong later and they have nobody to whom to turn for advice? So these intermediaries have sprung up, companies which are already familiar with dealing with difficult foreigners, to take care of all the problems which may arise. If you are new to Japan, therefore, these companies should not be disregarded, for they will have opportunities which you may never even hear about otherwise.

First, of course, you need to check the authenticity of these middlemen. Although they need a government licence to engage in such business, it is not perhaps a good start to ask whether they have one, although it is something to bear in mind later if you start to have doubts. An initial test is whether somebody is available to speak to you in reasonable English on the telephone. That is always an indication that the company is accustomed to dealing with non-Japanese and is a professionally-minded company.

Although, of course, the middleman must make his profit somehow, it is not customary for him to make it from you, but this is something which you need to check in an initial interview, assuming that you are granted one. The usual way for a placement company to obtain its margin is for it to charge a substantial fee to the client company for any successful introduction. Alternatively, if you work for the placement company and are dispatched to the office of a client, you should be offered a reasonable income for the work involved and the client will be charged that amount plus the intermediary's fee. It is not usual for you to have to pay any fee yourself and you should be wary of any company which asks for one.

Just in case the point has not already been made, we here repeat that things move slowly in Japan. Do not expect to submit your *curriculum vitae* to a placement company one day and be offered a position the next. First of all, the placement company will want to examine the information submitted to it. Next it will probably want to interview you to find out how your character, as well as your abilities, would fit into a Japanese company. Only then will the process of looking for a position for you begin.

When something which seems suitable is found, a representative of the placement company will go along to the client company and present your file, maybe with those of several other people as well. Then the process of decision-making will start in the client company and you should already be aware that decision-making takes a long time in Japan. The person who wants to recruit you, usually the manager of the department in which you are to work, will not have the final say. He will almost certainly have to consult the Personnel Department and the approval will probably have to be verified through the *ringi* system. You will be called for interview not just once but two or three times. It is almost like an endurance test. If both prospective employer and prospective employee survive without any altercations or feelings of friction, then the marriage may well be solemnized in due course. Bear in mind that the company will be looking during these interviews at two points which you can easily adjust to suit the occasion. One is your appearance. It is important that you appear neat and tidy in personal appearance (for example with short hair and clean-shaven or, failing that, with a neatly trimmed beard, for men and with tidy well-groomed hair for women). Men, of course, should never think of appearing other than in a suit, while women should wear conservatively fashionable attire. The second point is that you must display infinite patience and good humour and never let this long drawn-out and sometimes apparently superfluous interview system get to you. In reality, it may prove to be quite an appropriate test, for your patience is likely to be tried quite often in the position which you are hoping to take up. So never, never display any hint of irritation at the length of time which the whole procedure is taking. Smile through it all and show the best side of your character, for it is at your character that your interviewers will be looking at least as much as at your abilities.

As this recruitment process continues, you are quite likely to be given misleadingly optimistic feed-back, such as being told that, "the client is just making the final decision, but it is 90% certain." Do not be fooled. This will take time — weeks, maybe months. And just when you have given up hope, the telephone call will come, asking, as usual, "Can you start the day after tomorrow?"

The lesson to learn from this is not to take on, in the meantime, other work which will preclude your accepting the position which you really want. In fact, the placement company and the client company are going to be willing to accept some reasonable compromise. They, especially the placement company, will not want to invest so much time and effort for no result, so if you say that you must give two weeks' notice to your current employer and can then accept the position offered, that will probably be regarded as reasonable. Therefore, while you are waiting, make sure that you do accept only work which can be given up on two weeks' notice, otherwise you will be earning a bad name not just for yourself but for all non-Japanese.

It is, of course, very pleasant that the placement company usually requires no fee from you. However, it is important to remember that this affects the priorities of the situation. One would like to feel that the placement company was acting as an honest broker, feeling equal responsibilities towards employer and employee. Unfortunately, economic realities mean that this may not be so. When working through a placement company, this writer made some suggestions to the placement company as to how the effectiveness of the work at the client company might be improved, which improvements would lead to my being much more enthusiastic about renewing the contract at the appropriate time. When that time came, some while later, I found that my suggestions had never even been mentioned to the client company and, when I asked why, the person in charge brought home to me the reality which I should, of course, have appreciated long before. "It is not my job to tell the company what you think," I was told, in a manner which left no doubt about the priorities in this person's mind. "My job is to tell you what the company thinks." So do not make the mistake which I did. The client company pays, so is the customer, and the customer always comes first. Remember and beware!

Fortunately, some placement companies have now started to realize that a dis-satisfied employee in the client company may damage their own reputation, so some of the better ones may now be a little more willing to listen to polite suggestions these days, but there is still no real guarantee that suggestions will actually get back to the client company.

So placement companies have some shortcomings, but, because of the lack of confidence of Japanese organizations in their own ability to select employees directly, such companies seem likely to continue in business for a while yet. They usually have a wide range of opportunities, so, if you have some special skills to offer, this is one of the places where you should start your job-hunting activities. Note that such companies can deal only with those who have proper visas and that, although there are many placement companies now in existence, only a few cater for non-Japanese. Start with the companies in our list and look also for advertisements in the newspapers, particularly in Monday's 'Japan Times'.

					← Non-Japanese		→			← Answer		→
Size	Overseas Branches	Overseas Experience	In Future	Country	Full-Time	Part-Time	Increase	Language	Answer in English	Job-Hunters	Businesses	Researchers

AMIDAS

Job placement. Consulting. Vocational training.
18F Imperial Tower Bldg., 1-1-1 Uchi Saiwai-cho, Chiyoda-ku, Tokyo 100
JR Yamanote Line, Yurakucho. 03-3507-2441 No contact

Size	Overseas Branches	Overseas Experience	In Future	Country	Full-Time	Part-Time	Increase	Language	Answer in English	Job-Hunters	Businesses	Researchers
C	0	Y										

ASIK CO., LTD

Job placement for tour conductors.
4-12-9-202 Nagai Higashi, Sumiyoshi-ku, Osaka 558. 06-699-1614
Midosuji or JR Hanwa Line, Nagai. Contact: Ms. Okada (Kaigai Jigyo-bu)

Size	Overseas Branches	Overseas Experience	In Future	Country	Full-Time	Part-Time	Increase	Language	Answer in English	Job-Hunters	Businesses	Researchers
C	0	Y	N		0	10			Y	Y	Y	Y

BABEL INC.

Job placement. Translation. Schooling.
NS Bldg., 2-2-3 Sarugaku-cho, Chiyoda-ku, Tokyo 101. 03-3295-2305
JR Chuo Line, Ochanomizu. Contact: Mr. Toshiki Hotta 03-3295-6302

Size	Overseas Branches	Overseas Experience	In Future	Country	Full-Time	Part-Time	Increase	Language	Answer in English	Job-Hunters	Businesses	Researchers
C	2	Y	Y	US	0	3	Y		Y	Y	Y	Y

BORGNAN HUMAN DEVELOPMENT INSTITUTE , LTD. (BHDI)

Job placement. Dispatching and out-placement of personnel.
Dai-san Taihei Bldg., 1-25-3 Higashi Ikebukuro, Toshima-ku, Tokyo 170.
JR Yamanote Line, Ikebukuro. Contact: Mr. Yamada 03-3989-8153

Size	Overseas Branches	Overseas Experience	In Future	Country	Full-Time	Part-Time	Increase	Language	Answer in English	Job-Hunters	Businesses	Researchers
C	1	Y	Y	All	1	1	Y	E,Ch	Y	Y	Y	Y

BOYDEN INTERNATIONAL LTD.

Executive search and consulting.
Suite 1307 Aoyama Bldg., 1-2-3 Kita Aoyama, Minato-ku, Tokyo 107.
Ginza or Hanzomon Line, Aoyama I-chome. 03-3478-5477 No contact

Size	Overseas Branches	Overseas Experience	In Future	Country	Full-Time	Part-Time	Increase	Language	Answer in English	Job-Hunters	Businesses	Researchers
D	51	Y	Y	US	2	0			Y	Y	Y	Y

CASTERS JAPAN INC.

Placement of top company executives. 03-3238-0341
1st Fl. Nakagawa Building, 2-13-4 Iidabashi, Chiyoda-ku, Tokyo 102.
Tozai, Hanzomon or Toei Shinjuku Line, Kudashita. No contact

Size	Overseas Branches	Overseas Experience	In Future	Country	Full-Time	Part-Time	Increase	Language	Answer in English	Job-Hunters	Businesses	Researchers
D	9						Y	G	N	N	Y	Y

GLOBAL BRAIN CORPORATION

Job placement. 03-3593-0351
Hibiya Kokusai Building, 2-2-3 Uchi Saiwai-cho, Chiyoda-ku, Tokyo 100.
Toei Mita Line, Uchisaiwaicho. Contact: Mr. Christoph Lohse

Size	Overseas Branches	Overseas Experience	In Future	Country	Full-Time	Part-Time	Increase	Language	Answer in English	Job-Hunters	Businesses	Researchers
C		Y			2	0			Y	Y	Y	Y

INTERNATIONAL INTERCHANGE CORPORATION

Job placement. Translation and interpretation. Tour conductors.
SN Kurosu Bldg., 3-33-20 Nakano, Nakano-ku, Tokyo 164. 03-3380-3201
Tozai or JR Chuo Line, Nakano. Contact: Mr. Tetsuro Nishi

Size	Overseas Branches	Overseas Experience	In Future	Country	Full-Time	Part-Time	Increase	Language	Answer in English	Job-Hunters	Businesses	Researchers
D		Y	Y	Asia					N	Y	Y	Y

INTERNATIONAL TRANSACTION CENTER LTD .

Job placement. Language services. International business co-ordination.
Senbikiya Bldg., 1-1-9 Kyobashi, Chuo-ku, Tokyo 104. 03-3274-0655
Ginza Line, Kyobashi. Contact: Mr. Yoshinori Omata 03-3561-1057

Size	Overseas Branches	Overseas Experience	In Future	Country	Full-Time	Part-Time	Increase	Language	Answer in English	Job-Hunters	Businesses	Researchers
C		N			1	4			Y	Y	Y	N

INTER PACS CORPORATION

Job placement for translators and interpreters.
2-15 Kakuta-cho, Kita-ku, Osaka 530. 06-373-3976
JR Tokaido Line, Osaka. No contact

Size	Overseas Branches	Overseas Experience	In Future	Country	Full-Time	Part-Time	Increase	Language	Answer in English	Job-Hunters	Businesses	Researchers
D	0	N	N		0	0	N			N	N	N

Size	Overseas Branches	Overseas Experience	In Future	Country	Non-Japanese: Full-Time	Non-Japanese: Part-Time	Non-Japanese: Increase	Non-Japanese: Language	Answer in English	Answer: Job-Hunters	Answer: Businesses	Answer: Researchers

I.S.S. INC.

Job placement for translators, interpreters, travel guides, etc.
13-5 Obase-cho, Tennoji-ku, Osaka 543. 06-761-7838
Tanimachi, Sennichimae Line, Tanimachi Kyu-chome. Contact: Mr. Vancampen

Size	Overseas Branches	Overseas Experience	In Future	Country	Full-Time	Part-Time	Increase	Language	Answer in English	Job-Hunters	Businesses	Researchers
C	0	Y	Y	*	3	20	Y	All	Y	Y	Y	Y

* U.S.A., S.E. Asia, Europe

JAPAN CONVENTION SERVICES, INC.

Planning and operation of international conferences. Job placement.
2-2-1 Uchi Saiwai-cho, Chiyoda-ku, Tokyo 100. 03-3508-1211
Marunouchi, Hibiya or Chiyoda Line, Kasumigaseki. No contact

Size	Overseas Branches	Overseas Experience	In Future	Country	Full-Time	Part-Time	Increase	Language	Answer in English	Job-Hunters	Businesses	Researchers
B	0	Y	N									

J K C RECRUITING CO., LTD.

Job placement for managers, specialists and engineers. 03-3502-3781
Yamagata Bldg., 1-14-7 Nishi Shinbashi, Minato-ku, Tokyo 105.
Ginza, Toei Asakusa or JR Yamanote Line, Shinbashi. Contact: Mr. Sekii

Size	Overseas Branches	Overseas Experience	In Future	Country	Full-Time	Part-Time	Increase	Language	Answer in English	Job-Hunters	Businesses	Researchers
C	0	N	N		0	0	N		Y	Y	N	N

J. P. S.

Job placement for managers and engineers.
Oka Bldg., 2-1-16 Kyomachi-bori, Nishi-ku, Osaka 550. 06-441-7341
Yotsubashi Line, Higobashi. Contact: Mr. Ryuzo Honda

Size	Overseas Branches	Overseas Experience	In Future	Country	Full-Time	Part-Time	Increase	Language	Answer in English	Job-Hunters	Businesses	Researchers
D									N	Y		

JUST SERVICE CO., LTD.

Job placement. Translation. Interpretation.
Tsubaki Bldg., 3-15-16 Shinjuku, Shinjuku-ku, Tokyo 160. 03-3225-5511
JR Yamanote or Chuo Line, Shinjuku. Contact: Mr. Kohata or Mr. Osawa

Size	Overseas Branches	Overseas Experience	In Future	Country	Full-Time	Part-Time	Increase	Language	Answer in English	Job-Hunters	Businesses	Researchers
C		N	Y		0	50	Y		Y	Y	Y	Y

K & M PROMOTION CO., LTD.

Job placement for foreign fashion models.
201 Villa Aoyama, 2-10-25 Kita Aoyama, Minato-ku, Tokyo 107.
Ginza Line, Gaien-mae. Contact: Ms. Masako Saito 03-3404-9429

Size	Overseas Branches	Overseas Experience	In Future	Country	Full-Time	Part-Time	Increase	Language	Answer in English	Job-Hunters	Businesses	Researchers
C	0	Y	Y	*	0	2	Y	All	Y	Y	Y	Y

* U.S.A., Canada, Australia

MARUBENI PERSONNEL SUPPORT CO., LTD.

Job placement. Language training. Consultation for management.
3-25 Jimbo-cho, Kanda, Chiyoda-ku, Tokyo 101. 03-3234-1324
Tozai, Hanzomon or Toei Shinjuku Line, Kudanshita. Contact: (Koshi Jinji-bu)

Size	Overseas Branches	Overseas Experience	In Future	Country	Full-Time	Part-Time	Increase	Language	Answer in English	Job-Hunters	Businesses	Researchers
B	0	Y	Y	*	20	40	Y	All	Y	Y	Y	Y

* U.S.A., Canada

MIK INTERNATIONAL

Job placement for tour conductors and translators.
Maison Bunkyo Sekiguchi, 1-7-5 Sekiguchi, Bunkyo-ku, Tokyo 112.
Yurakucho Line, Edogawabashi. 03-3269-6858 No contact

Size	Overseas Branches	Overseas Experience	In Future	Country	Full-Time	Part-Time	Increase	Language	Answer in English	Job-Hunters	Businesses	Researchers
D	0	N	N									

NIHON CONSULTANTS CO., LTD.

Job placement. Various types of consultation.
Tokiwa Building, 1-21-11 Yoyogi, Shibuya-ku, Tokyo 151.
JR Yamanote Line, Yoyogi. 03-3370-7719 Contact: Mr. Otsuka

Size	Overseas Branches	Overseas Experience	In Future	Country	Full-Time	Part-Time	Increase	Language	Answer in English	Job-Hunters	Businesses	Researchers
D	0	Y	Y	*	0	0	N		Y	Y	Y	Y

* U.S.A., Europe

PERSONA JAPAN, INC.

Temporary personnel services. 03-3409-9361
Shibuya Nomura Shoken Building, 1-14-16 Shibuya, Tokyo 150.
Ginza, Hanzomon or JR Yamanote Line, Shibuya. Contact: Ms. Oliver

Size	Overseas Branches	Overseas Experience	In Future	Country	Full-Time	Part-Time	Increase	Language	Answer in English	Job-Hunters	Businesses	Researchers
C	16	Y	N		3	0			Y	Y		

PRONET CO., LTD.

Job placement. Training. Sales promotion.
11th Fl. Togeki Bldg., 4-1-1 Tsukiji, Chuo-ku, Tokyo 104. 03-3543-2611
Hibiya or Toei Asakusa Line, Higashi Ginza. Contact: Mr. Yoshinori Naito

Size	Overseas Branches	Overseas Experience	In Future	Country	Non-Japanese Full-Time	Non-Japanese Part-Time	Increase	Language	Answer in English	Answer Job-Hunters	Answer Businesses	Answer Researchers
C	0	N	N		1	3			N	Y	N	N

TEMPORARY CENTER CORPORATION

Job placement. 03-3506-8021
Nihon Press Center Bldg., 2-2-1 Uchi Saiwai-cho, Chiyoda-ku, Tokyo 100
Marunouchi, Hibiya or Chiyoda Line, Kasumigaseki. Contact: (Kaigai Kanri)

Size	Overseas Branches	Overseas Experience	In Future	Country	Non-Japanese Full-Time	Non-Japanese Part-Time	Increase	Language	Answer in English	Answer Job-Hunters	Answer Businesses	Answer Researchers
A	2	Y	Y		10	0			Y	Y	Y	

TOKYO EXECUTIVE SEARCH CO., LTD.

Job placement. 03-3230-1881
Kioicho TBR Bldg., 5-7 Koji-machi, Chiyoda-ku, Tokyo 102.
Hanzomon or Yurakucho Line, Nagatacho. Contact: Mr. Watanabe (R&D)

Size	Overseas Branches	Overseas Experience	In Future	Country	Non-Japanese Full-Time	Non-Japanese Part-Time	Increase	Language	Answer in English	Answer Job-Hunters	Answer Businesses	Answer Researchers
C	0	N	N				Y	E	Y	Y	Y	Y

YOSHINO CO., GROUP

Job placement. Various types of consultation (especially Kansai area).
1-2-2-1200 Umeda, Kita-ku, Osaka 530. 06-341-8031
JR Tokaido Line, Osaka. No contact

Size	Overseas Branches	Overseas Experience	In Future	Country	Non-Japanese Full-Time	Non-Japanese Part-Time	Increase	Language	Answer in English	Answer Job-Hunters	Answer Businesses	Answer Researchers
C		Y	Y	*	1	1			Y	Y	Y	Y

* Taiwan, Korea

CHAPTER 3. BUSINESS CONSULTANTS

For our businessmen readers, one method of reaching new markets may be through the mediation of those already familiar with the necessities for doing business in Japan.

There are, in fact, many companies and individuals capable of acting as go-betweens for the inexperienced. The problem lies in locating these mostly small concerns and in choosing a good one.

Although these businesses are likely to have useful contacts within various industries and can save unnecessary expenditure by their clients by doing the initial spadework for them in Japan, it is suggested that the assistance of JETRO (the Japan External Trade Organization — see introduction) and one's own embassy or chamber of commerce be sought first.

There are also, of course, the trade associations which are listed in Chapter 18 and which can usually provide listings of member companies and can indicate which particular companies might be interested in any particular proposition.

Those who are attempting to market in Japan usually encounter three types of problem in particular. The first is the difficulty of making contact with users and buyers. JETRO, the trade associations and embassies or chambers of commerce may provide the best solutions to that initial stumbling block.

Next comes the difficulty of understanding the complex Japanese distribution system. Western countries tend to streamline their systems to keep prices as low as possible and offer the best value in competition with their rivals. That is not the way in Japan. Agreements, tacit or even openly expressed, are tolerated which would certainly be thought to be in restraint of fair trade in other nations. And rather than streamlining operations, it often seems as though the Japanese are trying to ensure that goods pass through as many hands as possible on their way to the consumer, each pair of hands, of course, adding another margin to the final price. There is little incentive to circumvent this system, for the consumer will pay and, as long as cut-throat competition is not introduced, everybody can benefit (except the poor consumer, of course). Sometimes Japanese companies accused of 'dumping' overseas can reply truthfully that they are not 'dumping'. It is simply cheaper to sell in the overseas market, despite the cost of international freight and import duties, because the profits of so many middlemen can be eliminated.

Anybody trying to avoid this elaborate distribution system is not going to be popular so, although it is not absolutely impossible, it will be difficult to find anybody willing to help, since bread is not buttered on that side. At the same time, using the system may well prove to be impossibly expensive, so this can indeed be a dilemma.

The third and related problem is the understanding of Japanese business customs, for Japanese business tends to function less on questions of economics than on relationships established over the years. And probably you do not know anybody, so you need some help.

A typical scenario is that of the businessman who comes to Japan and carries out a feasibility study regarding the marketing of his product. He encounters the difficulties mentioned above, gives up and goes home. He may be right, of course, but there are people who could help in a basic but practical way.

These are the little companies, some of which are listed below. They can, for example, make telephone appointments and arrange meetings, for it is getting to the right people which is often so difficult and these little but vital tasks which become so frustrating sometimes. If things go well, the scope of their services can be widened, and, if not, well, at least the path may have been smoothed a little.

These small companies are often quite bashful about advertising their services, but those listed below responded to our questionnaire.

					Non-Japanese					Answer		
Size	Overseas Branches	Overseas Experience	In Future	Country	Full-Time	Part-Time	Increase	Language	Answer in English	Job-Hunters	Businesses	Researchers

BARCLAYS DE ZOETE WEDD INVESTMENT MANAGEMENT (JAPAN) LTD.

Consultation regarding investment. 03-5255-0030
Urban Net Otemachi Building, 2-2-2 Otemachi, Chiyoda-ku, Tokyo 100.
Various subway lines, Otemachi. Contact: Mr. Kazuyuki Suzuki

Size	Overseas Branches	Overseas Experience	In Future	Country	Full-Time	Part-Time	Increase	Language	Answer in English	Job-Hunters	Businesses	Researchers
C	0	Y	Y	*	3	0			Y	N	N	N

* U.K., U.S.A. and others

EAST WEST CONSULTING K.K.

Personnel and management consultation for foreign companies.
Sagamiya Honsha Building, 6 Ichiban-cho, Chiyoda-ku, Tokyo 102.
Hanzomon Line, Hanzomon. Contact: Mr. Takeda 03-3222-5531

Size	Overseas Branches	Overseas Experience	In Future	Country	Full-Time	Part-Time	Increase	Language	Answer in English	Job-Hunters	Businesses	Researchers
C	0	Y			20	0	Y	E	Y	N	N	N

EGON ZEHNDER INTERNATIONAL COMPANY LTD.

Management consultation.
Ichibancho NN Building, 15-5 Ichiban-cho, Chiyoda-ku, Tokyo 102.
Hanzomon Line, Hanzomon. 03-3239-8791 No contact

Size	Overseas Branches	Overseas Experience	In Future	Country	Full-Time	Part-Time	Increase	Language	Answer in English	Job-Hunters	Businesses	Researchers
C	36	N	N		3	0	Y		Y	Y	Y	N

FAR EAST ENTERPRISES

Representation of and consultation for foreign companies.
3-6-18 Kita Aoyama, Minato-ku, Tokyo 107. 03-3407-8100
Ginza, Hanzomon or Chiyoda Line, Omote Sando. No contact

Size	Overseas Branches	Overseas Experience	In Future	Country	Full-Time	Part-Time	Increase	Language	Answer in English	Job-Hunters	Businesses	Researchers
D		Y	Y							N	Y	N

INTERNATIONAL INVESTMENT CONSULTANTS LTD.

Financial, investment and managerial consultation. Market research.
Shuwa Kioicho TBR Bldg., 5-7 Koji-machi, Chiyoda-ku, Tokyo 102.
Yurakucho Line, Kojimachi. Contact: Mr. Robert Hitchner 03-3239-2841

Size	Overseas Branches	Overseas Experience	In Future	Country	Full-Time	Part-Time	Increase	Language	Answer in English	Job-Hunters	Businesses	Researchers
D		Y	Y		2	0			Y	Y	Y	Y

INTERNATIONAL TRANSACTION CENTER (ITC)

International business co-ordination. Interpretation. Translation.
Senbikiya Building, 1-1-9 Kyobashi, Chuo-ku, Tokyo 104. 03-3274-0655
Marunouchi or JR Yamanote Line, Tokyo. Contact: Mr. Omata 03-3561-1057

Size	Overseas Branches	Overseas Experience	In Future	Country	Full-Time	Part-Time	Increase	Language	Answer in English	Job-Hunters	Businesses	Researchers
C	1	N	N		3	5			Y	Y	Y	N

JAPAN ASSIST INTERNATIONAL

Various information and services related to foreign countries.
Southern Castle Building, 2-19-3 Minami Aoyama, Minato-ku, Tokyo 107.
Ginza Line, Gaien-mae. 03-3497-8670 No contact

Size	Overseas Branches	Overseas Experience	In Future	Country	Full-Time	Part-Time	Increase	Language	Answer in English	Job-Hunters	Businesses	Researchers
C	3	N								N	N	N

JAPAN COUNSELORS INC.

Public relations and management consultation.
3-13-16 Mita, Minato-ku, Tokyo 108. 03-3457-0311
JR Yamanote Line, Tamachi. Contact: Mr. Victor Shrenzel (Kokusai-bu)

Size	Overseas Branches	Overseas Experience	In Future	Country	Full-Time	Part-Time	Increase	Language	Answer in English	Job-Hunters	Businesses	Researchers
C	42	Y	Y		1	0	Y	E	Y	Y	Y	Y

JAPAN MARKET RESEARCH BUREAU, INC.

Market research.
2-13-2 Kami Osaki, Shinagawa-ku, Tokyo 141. 03-3449-8711
JR Yamanote Line, Meguro. Contact Mr. Nobuo Isoda (Jinji-bu) Ext. 877

Size	Overseas Branches	Overseas Experience	In Future	Country	Full-Time	Part-Time	Increase	Language	Answer in English	Job-Hunters	Businesses	Researchers
C	6	Y	Y	*	5	0	Y	E	Y	Y	Y	Y

* U.S.A., U.K., Germany, France

KEPNER TREGOE INC.

Consultation and education.
Moto Akasaka Kikutei Bldg., 1-7-18 Moto Akasaka, Minato-ku, Tokyo 107
Marunouchi or Ginza Line, Akasaka Mitsuke. 03-3401-9521 No contact

Size	Overseas Branches	Overseas Experience	In Future	Country	Full-Time	Part-Time	Increase	Language	Answer in English	Job-Hunters	Businesses	Researchers
C	0	N	N									

KLEINWORT BENSON INVESTMENT MANAGEMENT K.K.

Investment consultation.
3-1-1-930 Marunouchi, Chiyoda-ku, Tokyo 100. 03-3212-6681
Yurakucho or JR Yamanote Line, Yurakucho. No contact

					Non-Japanese					Answer		
Size	*Overseas Branches*	*Overseas Experience*	*In Future*	*Country*	*Full-Time*	*Part-Time*	*Increase*	*Language*	*Answer in English*	*Job-Hunters*	*Businesses*	*Researchers*
C	5				1	0				N	N	N

CHAPTER 4. LANGUAGE AND OTHER SCHOOLS

As mentioned in the introduction, teaching English is the traditional occupation of non-Japanese in Japan. So famous has this industry become that many travellers passing through Asia use it as their refuelling stop. Nowadays, of course, it is not only Japan which can be used for this purpose, but also South Korea, Taiwan, Hong Kong and even China. However, the financial rewards still remain greatest in Japan. The cost of living is high here, so salaries are correspondingly high. Therefore, if one manages to save, say, 30% of what one earns, one will have more by working in Japan than by working in another land where costs, and so salaries, are lower. And, as all travellers know, what one can save in a month in Japan can last for three months or even longer in other parts of Asia — and so the influx of refuellers continues undiminished.

Nowadays there is competition, though. The numbers have been augmented by students looking for somewhere remunerative and interesting to spend their summer vacations and, not least, by those with a genuine interest in Japan who want to come and find out about this country of their dreams, but who need to earn some money at the same time.

And so the market has gradually become saturated. English schools which used to accept anybody who came along can now afford to be choosy. Nor is that a bad thing either, for it has put some pressure on those who used to make easy money by turning up and chatting to actually think about teaching. At this point it is worth saying that, despite the supposed decline in Japan's economic fortunes, the situation has not yet been reached when it is impossible to obtain a job teaching English. It is just more difficult than it used to be, but turn up here and start applying and it is just a lottery as to when your number will come up, although there are several things which you can do to improve your chances, about which more in a few paragraphs.

At this stage, we should consider why the English teaching industry exists at all. Virtually all Japanese complete a high school education and a large proportion of them continue to some form of further education. By the end of high school they have studied English for six years — all of them. By this time nearly all have mastered the complexities of the English language to the level of being able to say "yes" and "no", although not necessarily in the right places.

There is fairly general agreement as to why this low standard persists. You can find the reasons in various books about Japan and the Japanese themselves can tell you what the defects of the system are. Ask any of your prospective students when you start a teaching job and you will hear something like this. "I studied grammar at school and I understand that fairly well. I can read and write English, but I cannot speak it, because I never had any practice." This is a particularly articulate student, but the content is what every person would want to tell you, and it is, if this writer may express his personal opinion, nonsense. It is a case of the basic facts being correct, but the conclusion being erroneous. To prove this, you only have to ask that same student to write a few sentences for you. They will be full of the most basic grammatical errors, riddled with spelling mistakes and quite possibly almost totally incomprehensible. And yet, he is right. He has studied English grammar for many years. One detail which he omitted to mention, though, is that he has never before been asked to write anything down by himself, only to translate or paraphrase Japanese sentences given to him. Even the examinations mainly asked him only to choose among a, b, c and d.

So what has happened in the educational system? Well, for a start, all of the teaching has taken place in classes of forty students or more, so the claim that the student has never had a chance to say anything in English is probably correct. More importantly, though, what is taught is dictated by the need to follow a prescribed curriculum and to pass certain examinations. Emphasis is on the memorizing of a large number of rules rather than on developing any particular ability to use English as a language. The pace demanded is a very brisk one indeed, so what usually seems to happen is that the student is borne along on the wave of fast-paced teaching until he reaches a point where he does not understand. In the mass-production system this passes unnoticed and the lessons rush on. But now that he is lost, he is lost. There is no time for review and he never really learns much more. The universally low standard seems to suggest that this point of no further learning occurs relatively early in the process in most cases. This writer's opinion is that the system of English education might be much more successful if it tried to teach half as much in an effective and reasonably-paced manner instead of insisting that students should fail to understand every conceivable intricacy of the language. But then, nobody asks him.

In any case, the result of this system's shortcomings has been the development of the English Conversation industry. Teachers, note, are generally required to teach 'English Conversation', as if such a subject could exist in isolation, not English itself. This means that grammar, the very area in which the failure of basic understanding has its roots, is almost taboo. Maybe this attitude has been fostered by itinerant teachers who are themselves not too strong on grammar. And, above all, this is an industry. The student is a customer and, in the opinions of many of the conversation schools, customers have to be pleased and are always right. Teachers, however, especially these days, are expendable.

Against this background, it is only fair to say that there are some fine schools, ethical in their dealings and sincere in their teaching of English, but, if you want to be an English teacher in Japan, you should decide which type of school you want to work for and be careful to choose accordingly.

First, let us suppose that you feel that teaching is genuinely your vocation. Then you should be looking for one of the schools which makes demands of its prospective teachers such as a qualification in teaching English as a Second Language or a B. Ed. degree or a teaching qualification or experience. Not many schools make such demands and, unfortunately, those that do sometimes seem to be excessively rigid in the application of their rules. For example, a friend with 28 years of experience in teaching English as a second language was rejected without interview on the grounds that he did not have a TESL qualification, when, in fact, such qualifications probably had not been invented when he trained to become a teacher. However, if you have an appropriate qualification or experience, together with the university degree which you are going to need to obtain a visa, you should be able to get some interviews.

Appearance is very important. Males should always wear a suit to an interview. You have little chance of obtaining a good job without a suit and tie, if you are a man, or suitable respectable apparel, preferably a skirt, if you are a woman. Take along your typed *curriculum vitae*. And remember, at the interview, that pushiness is not highly valued in Japan. A quiet but alert manner will probably be best if your interviewer is Japanese. You should listen attentively to what he or she has to say and not interrupt. An important point to make in your favour will be your intention of staying for a long time in Japan. If you can say truthfully that you are thinking of staying for at least two years, that will probably be thought a good recommendation.

If, however, you do not think of yourself as a teacher by profession, but wish to earn some money anyway in the English Conversation industry, there are still some ways in which you can improve your chances. First you should understand that the most important factor is appearance, because your appearance will be marketed by the school. Youth is important (so if you are not so young you had better try to disguise the fact or offer something in lieu!). The clients of conversation schools tend to like young teachers. Anywhere in your twenties or thirties is quite acceptable. If you are in your forties, you are going to find it more difficult and if you are older than that you will have a distinct disadvantage.

If you are female, you will have an advantage, especially if you are obviously female, for male students tend to prefer young women teachers! However, of course, sex is a factor beyond your control and there are plenty of jobs for men too. Unfortunately, race and nationality will be other considerations. North Americans are preferred, but not, regrettably, black Americans, because they do not fit the Japanese image of the English teacher well. If you are not North American, British, Australian or New Zealand will be acceptable, approximately in that order, but anybody else will have a hard time, even though he or she may have English as a first language and may have been brought up in an entirely English-speaking environment. If your colour is not pure white, in addition, it will be even more difficult to find a job. Although we feel some embarrassment in having to report such facts, it is preferable for our readers to be aware of the situation. This writer is, of course, not approving of any of these stereotypes, merely stating that they exist.

Again clothing will be important. It will do no harm for men to wear suits for interviews at schools of this type too, although conservatively fashionable clothes might be an acceptable alternative — but not the T-shirt and jeans in which you have been touring Asia for the last six months, even if you did manage to wash them last Thursday week! For women, less formality is required, but a skirt is definitely preferably to trousers. Men should note that long hair is a good way not to get a job and that, if you insist on retaining your beard, it should be relatively short and neat. These matters are very important.

This type of conversation school is not likely to insist on any particular qualifications, except a university degree if you require sponsorship for a working visa, as that is a requirement imposed by the immigration authorities for the issuing of such a visa. The degree can be in any subject. Surprisingly, a teaching qualification is not usually thought relevant, although, of course, teaching experience may well be a help in keeping a job, as opposed to getting one.

There are some other matters which you need to consider when searching for an English teaching appointment. One important one is your visa status. If you have not already read the visa section in the Introduction, it is suggested that you do so now. As stated there, it is illegal to teach English in Japan without a working, working holiday or other suitable visa and you might, just possibly, get caught. More serious, though, is the fact that you leave yourself open to exploitation, since it is difficult to complain if you get cheated. Also, you will have to leave the country every three or six months, which is an inconvenience, and your total stay will probably be limited to about nine months. Now, if you decide, therefore, that you should get a working visa, you need to think carefully before accepting any employment. As soon as you accept a part-time teaching position on one evening, however appealing the pay for that evening's work may be, you make it very difficult for another company to sponsor you for a working visa, because that company needs you to be available virtually all the time for its own work. Note that it is evening work which is important, for that is when English Conversation schools do the bulk of their business. If you accept a morning job on one or two days a week, it might not be so serious. However, if you want a full-time position with a working visa, you must be careful to obtain that first, before succumbing to the temptation of other lucrative part-time offers.

You should also beware of the schools which offer a three-months trial, after which, assuming that all is satisfactory, you will be sponsored for a working visa. It is not unknown for such schools, at the end of the three months, to decide that you are not suitable for the position after all and to look for a new person for the next three months trial. This leaves you in a rather awkward position, with your time in Japan expiring and no sign of a full-time job. It may even turn out that the company was not recognized as qualified in the view of the immigration officials to sponsor a non-Japanese teacher. To guard against this happening to you, you could enquire whether there is any other person being sponsored by the school or, failing that, whether there is evidence that somebody has been sponsored in recent times. In any case, it is within the law —

and, indeed, quite common — to make a contract allowing for a trial period. Then the sponsorship process can begin immediately.

The question of whether it is worthwhile to try to obtain employment before coming to Japan has been mentioned before in the Introduction, but it is worth making a further comment here in connexion with teaching positions. Usually, it is rather dangerous to try to get a job before you arrive, for it is easy to be tricked into signing a contract with a school which then changes its mind over the conditions or exploits them in ways which you had not previously thought of. For example, you may have to work only 25 hours per week, but if those hours range from 7.00a.m. until 11.00p.m., as they sometimes do, and require you to work six or even seven days every week, the proposition becomes less attractive. Or housing may be provided at a low rental, but you have not had a chance to inspect the housing and, if you do not find it habitable, you may still find the rent being deducted from your salary. The immigration authorities are not likely to be terribly sympathetic with your dilemma and be aware that, before you can change your job in Japan you must have a letter of release from your employer, even if you have fulfilled all your contractual obligations to him. Moreover, before you come to Japan, you will not have a good idea of salary levels. So be careful of accepting a position from afar, unless you know that the school has a good reputation.

In case you are not persuaded by the arguments in the previous paragraph, and still want to obtain a teaching position before you arrive, at least check on the following conditions. Discover beyond doubt the actual work hours, the work place or places, the duties involved, the salary and the teaching principles of the school. It might also be relevant to ask about living conditions and, if the school is not in a major city, about the area in which it is situated. If a contract is presented for your signature, make sure that it includes most of these points.

There are at least a couple of exceptions to this *caveat*. Universities often have arrangements to recruit teachers from certain institutions abroad. You can be reasonably assured that you will be treated fairly by well-known seats of learning, for they have reputations to maintain. However, you should be aware that Japanese university students are not renowned for studying hard. They have done all the studying they ever want to do to get into the university. Now they have four years to relax, before starting the drudgery of company life. They will gain their degrees all right unless they do something very stupid indeed, so they are not much inclined to bother about little matters like studying English. However, university lecturers' pay is good and the hours are short and the holidays long, so if it is not intellectual stimulation for which you are searching, these are very good jobs indeed. Of course, remember that, when universities recruit teachers, qualifications are important. There is a list of universities and colleges in Chapter 19, but the majority of university teachers are recruited outside Japan, in fact, or through connexions, and such positions are not easy to obtain.

The second exception is the Japan Exchange and Teaching Program (JET), whereby teaching assistants are recruited in North America, Australasia and the British Isles to work in government schools throughout Japan. Note that they are only assistants, to do as instructed by the teachers. They may work in a single school, but are more usually required to visit a number of schools in an area. People selected for this scheme are usually young and inexperienced. One fears that that may be because the authorities suspect that experienced teachers would be too critical of the Japanese English teaching system, but perhaps there are other reasons too. Most people who participate in this scheme, however, feel that it has some rewards, including, incidentally, a very reasonable salary, and, in particular, that they have learned a lot about Japan from the experience, especially as they are frequently sent to areas of the countryside where they would never have had the chance to live otherwise and where traditional lifestyles still exist. Contracts are for one year, and usually extendable for a further year and information and application forms can be obtained from Japanese embassies. It is difficult to be accepted for this scheme from inside Japan, although it is not completely unheard of for a few last-minute vacancies to be filled here.

What most people want to know is what a reasonable salary level is, bearing in mind the relatively high costs of living in Japan. Just as a guide, and, in particular, to avoid anybody from being deceived by offers made overseas, the immigration authorities set ¥250,000 per month as the lowest level acceptable for a teaching position. Remuneration at this level should not involve more than about twenty-five hours of work per week. For part-time work, or for overtime, the minimum acceptable rate should be about ¥3,000 per hour. One should also consider where the duties are to be performed. If one has to teach on the premises of several different companies, which is sure to involve a considerable amount of travelling time, this should be taken into account in the pay rates. It is normal in Japan for all travelling expenses to be refunded, including those to and from one's home. Please note that the rates quoted above should be considered to be minima. Really professional teachers should be able to earn considerably more than that.

There are possibilities for teaching languages other than English, of course, but they are much more limited. Many of the schools listed in this chapter claim to teach other languages, but, in fact, for most of them the primary demand is for English. You can apply to teach French or German, or whatever your native language is, but many people end up teaching English despite the fact that they are not native speakers of that language. After all, they look the part and for some schools that is the most important criterion. If English is your first language but you also speak another well, that might be considered an advantage.

A few last words on teaching English. You will already have gathered that there are some schools around whose ethics are none too pure. Unfortunately, there are also teachers around who do not treat the schools fairly, for example by leaving without warning to take up a more lucrative offer, a move which they justify with a comment such as, "Well, they would have done it to me too." In such an atmosphere, mutual suspicion and intolerance grows, until teachers feel that they can never trust schools and schools feel that they are justified in doing as they wish to these unreliable foreigners. Please do not accelerate such distrust. Be suspicious before you join a school. Try to speak to one or two of the teachers there if possible. But once you have accepted the offer, carry out your obligations in a responsible manner. If you do decide to leave the school, have a good reason and give proper warning.

Now this section of our book should also be the most valuable for those who wish to study in Japan, obtaining a cultural visa. You need to look under the sections dealing with Japanese language schools and other schools. Before you make any commitment, and particularly before you part with any money, ascertain that the school is authorized for the purposes of obtaining a cultural visa. Although we have *tried* to list only fairly reputable schools, we cannot guarantee that all are so authorized. You must check. Remember that there are schools which sponsor for cultural visas, but do little in the way of education. We did not intend to list such establishments, but it is very difficult to be sure, as, understandably, they do not advertise such facts. If, on the other hand, that is the type of school which you want, ask around at typical places of accommodation for non-Japanese, for example the '*Gaijin* Houses'. Those who wish to study seriously should bear in mind that schools run by non-profit organizations are likely to be more reliable than those which are operated with profit as their main purpose. The notation '(F)', indicating 'non-profit foundation' appears after the names of such schools in our list. Those who wish to study at an advanced level should also look at Chapter 19 — 'Universities and Colleges'.

It should be noted that it seems to be becoming more difficult to obtain a cultural visa now. The immigration authorities examine the performances of the schools more carefully these days and are much more inclined to reject the applications of those who request visas for study at schools which do not meet the expected standards, so make sure that the school to which you are applying is a reputable one.

ENGLISH AND OTHER LANGUAGE SCHOOLS

					Non-Japanese					Answer		
Size	Overseas Branches	Overseas Experience	In Future	Country	Full-Time	Part-Time	Increase	Language	Answer in English	Job-Hunters	Businesses	Researchers

INTERNATIONAL EDUCATION CENTER (F)

English and Japanese language.
1-21 Yotsuya, Shinjuku-ku, Tokyo 160. 03-3359-9621
Marunouchi or JR Chuo Line, Yotsuya. Contact: Mr. Mori Ext. 222

Size	Overseas Branches	Overseas Experience	In Future	Country	Full-Time	Part-Time	Increase	Language	Answer in English	Job-Hunters	Businesses	Researchers
B	0	N	N		55	50	Y	E	Y	Y	N	N

THE ENGLISH LANGUAGE EDUCATION COUNCIL INC. (ELEC) (F)

English conversation and Japanese language.
3-8 Jimbocho, Kanda, Tokyo 101. 03-3265-8911
Hanzomon, Toei Mita or Shinjuku Line, Jimbocho. Contact: Mr. Enomoto

Size	Overseas Branches	Overseas Experience	In Future	Country	Full-Time	Part-Time	Increase	Language	Answer in English	Job-Hunters	Businesses	Researchers
C		N	N		31	12	Y	E	Y	Y	Y	Y

ALEC SCHOOL OF LANGUAGES

English and Japanese language. 03-3400-4515
No. 2 Kobayashi Building, 1-14-13 Shibuya, Shibuya-ku, Tokyo 150.
Ginza, Hanzomon or JR Yamanote Line, Shibuya. Contact: Mr. Mimaki

Size	Overseas Branches	Overseas Experience	In Future	Country	Full-Time	Part-Time	Increase	Language	Answer in English	Job-Hunters	Businesses	Researchers
D		N	N		1	5	Y	E	Y	Y	Y	Y

AMERICAN HOUSE ENGLISH CENTER

English language. Translation.
634 Grande, 5-4-1 Honcho, Tanashi-shi, Tokyo 188. 0424-64-0930
Seibu Shinjuku Line, Tanashi. Contact: Ms. Matsuzaki 0424-64-7686

Size	Overseas Branches	Overseas Experience	In Future	Country	Full-Time	Part-Time	Increase	Language	Answer in English	Job-Hunters	Businesses	Researchers
C	0	N	N		0	3	Y	E	Y	Y	Y	Y

BABEL INC.

Various languages. Translation.
2-2-3 Sarugaku-cho, Chiyoda-ku, Tokyo 101. 03-3295-6300
JR Chuo Line, Ochanomizu. Contact: Mr. Hotta

Size	Overseas Branches	Overseas Experience	In Future	Country	Full-Time	Part-Time	Increase	Language	Answer in English	Job-Hunters	Businesses	Researchers
C	2	N	Y	US	0	3	Y	E	Y	Y	Y	Y

BES INTERNATIONAL

English language. 03-3982-6651
Royal Building, 1-9-24 Minami Ikebukuro, Toshima-ku, Tokyo 171.
Marunouchi, Yurakucho or JR Yamanote Line, Ikebukuro. Contact: Mr.Furumura

Size	Overseas Branches	Overseas Experience	In Future	Country	Full-Time	Part-Time	Increase	Language	Answer in English	Job-Hunters	Businesses	Researchers
D	0	N	N		6	2	Y	E,Ch	Y	Y	Y	Y

BORGNAN ENGLISH SCHOOL

English language. Overseas study. Translation. 03-3983-7151
Dai-san Taihei Bldg., 1-25-3 Higashi Ikebukuro, Toshima-ku, Tokyo 170.
Marunouchi, Yurakucho or JR Yamanote Line, Ikebukuro. Contact: Ms. Iwahashi

Size	Overseas Branches	Overseas Experience	In Future	Country	Full-Time	Part-Time	Increase	Language	Answer in English	Job-Hunters	Businesses	Researchers
B	1	Y	Y	UK	0	4	Y	E,Ch	Y	Y	Y	Y

BUSINESS EDUCATION SOCIETY INC.

English conversation. Translation.
2-8-10 Iwamoto-cho, Chiyoda-ku, Tokyo 101. 03-3663-8774
Toei Shinjuku Line, Iwamotocho. Contact: Mr. Kawai Ext. 404

Size	Overseas Branches	Overseas Experience	In Future	Country	Full-Time	Part-Time	Increase	Language	Answer in English	Job-Hunters	Businesses	Researchers
C	1	Y	N		2	3	Y	E	Y	Y	Y	N

CREATERS CORPORATION

English conversation. Sales of computer software. 03-3546-8838
Matsumoto Ginza Bldg., 3-11-13 Ginza, Chuo-ku, Tokyo 104.
Ginza, Marunouchi or Hibiya Line, Ginza. Contact: Mr. Miyazaki

Size	Overseas Branches	Overseas Experience	In Future	Country	Full-Time	Part-Time	Increase	Language	Answer in English	Job-Hunters	Businesses	Researchers
C		N	Y	US	1	3	Y	E	Y	Y	Y	Y

Size	Overseas Branches	Overseas Experience	In Future	Country	← Non-Japanese Full-Time	Part-Time	Increase	Language →	Answer in English	← Answer Job-Hunters	Businesses	Researchers →

DEN HOUSE INTERNATIONAL LANGUAGE SCHOOL

Various languages.
7-19-9 Okusawa, Setagaya-ku, Tokyo 158. 03-3704-7636
Oimachi Line, Kuhonbutsu. Contact: Ms. Yoko Kimura

* English, French, Spanish, German, Italian, Chinese, Korean, Thai

Size	Overseas Branches	Overseas Experience	In Future	Country	Full-Time	Part-Time	Increase	Language	Answer in English	Job-Hunters	Businesses	Researchers
C		N	N		3	30	Y	*	Y	Y	Y	Y

DEUTSCHES SPRACHKOLLEG HEIDELBERG

German language. Translation.
1-59-1 Yoyogi, Shibuya-ku, Tokyo 151. 03-3374-4863
JR Yamanote Line, Yoyogi. Contact: Ms. Yamanaka

Size	Overseas Branches	Overseas Experience	In Future	Country	Full-Time	Part-Time	Increase	Language	Answer in English	Job-Hunters	Businesses	Researchers
C		Y	N		9	8	Y	G		Y	Y	Y

ENGLISH O'S FARM

English conversation.
1-14-20-201 Tomioka, Koto-ku, Tokyo 135. 03-3643-7308
Tozai Line, Monzen Nakacho. Contact: Ms. Masako Okazaki

Size	Overseas Branches	Overseas Experience	In Future	Country	Full-Time	Part-Time	Increase	Language	Answer in English	Job-Hunters	Businesses	Researchers
C	0	N	N		0	5	Y	E	Y	Y	Y	Y

GET ENGLISH ACADEMY

English conversation.
Tonbo Building, 2-1-18 Hara Machida, Machida-shi, Tokyo 194.
Odakyu Line, Machida. Contact: Ms. Midori Takahashi 0427-21-5434

Size	Overseas Branches	Overseas Experience	In Future	Country	Full-Time	Part-Time	Increase	Language	Answer in English	Job-Hunters	Businesses	Researchers
	0	N	N		0	5	Y	E	Y	Y	Y	N

GREGG INTERNATIONAL COLLEGE OF LANGUAGES

English conversation.
1-14-16 Jiyugaoka, Meguro-ku, Tokyo 152. 03-3724-0552
Tokyu Toyoko or Oimachi Line, Jiyugaoka. Contact: Ms. Hiromi Henmi

Size	Overseas Branches	Overseas Experience	In Future	Country	Full-Time	Part-Time	Increase	Language	Answer in English	Job-Hunters	Businesses	Researchers
B	2	N	N		0	100	Y	All	Y	Y	Y	Y

HELLO GUIDE ACADEMY

Language school for tour guides and STEP (national test) examinees.
Kitaguchi Ekimae Bldg., 2-13-2 Asagaya Kita, Suginami-ku, Tokyo 166.
JR Chuo Line, Asagaya. Contact: Mr. Tsuboi 03-3223-8691

Size	Overseas Branches	Overseas Experience	In Future	Country	Full-Time	Part-Time	Increase	Language	Answer in English	Job-Hunters	Businesses	Researchers
D		N	N		0	4	N		Y	N	N	Y

I C C LANGUAGE SCHOOLS

English and various other languages.
4th Fl. Maison Raffiné, 1-6-24 Hara Machida, Machida-shi, Tokyo 194.
Odakyu Line, Machida. Contact: Mr. Armand Knafo 0427-28-6535

* English, French, German, Spanish

Size	Overseas Branches	Overseas Experience	In Future	Country	Full-Time	Part-Time	Increase	Language	Answer in English	Job-Hunters	Businesses	Researchers
C		N	N		11	8	Y	*	Y	Y		

INTEC JAPAN INC.

English language (on premises of client companies). Cultural education.
7-5-27-618 Akasaka, Minato-ku, Tokyo 107. 03-3224-1812
Chiyoda Line, Nogizaka. Contact: Mr. Yasushi Kobayashi

Size	Overseas Branches	Overseas Experience	In Future	Country	Full-Time	Part-Time	Increase	Language	Answer in English	Job-Hunters	Businesses	Researchers
C	0	Y	Y	US	26	43			Y	Y	Y	Y

INTERNSHIP STUDY CENTER

English and Japanese language.
6-19-14 Hongo, Bunkyo-ku, Tokyo 113. 03-3812-5431
Marunouchi Line, Hongo San-chome. Contact: Mr. Nakamura

Size	Overseas Branches	Overseas Experience	In Future	Country	Full-Time	Part-Time	Increase	Language	Answer in English	Job-Hunters	Businesses	Researchers
					0	16			Y	N	N	Y

JAL COORDINATION SERVICE CO., LTD.

English and Spanish conversation. Japanese lang. Business manners.
1-26-15 Ebisu Nishi, Shibuya-ku, Tokyo 150. 03-3477-2911
Hibiya or JR Yamanote Line, Ebisu. Contact: Mr. Rick Shelly

Size	Overseas Branches	Overseas Experience	In Future	Country	Full-Time	Part-Time	Increase	Language	Answer in English	Job-Hunters	Businesses	Researchers
B	0	N	N		0	40			Y	Y	Y	Y

KABUSHIKI KAISHA A.I.T.

Foreign languages. Translation.
3-20-1-401 Tamagawa, Setagaya-ku, Tokyo 158. 03-3700-8110
Shin Tamagawa Line, Futago Tamagawa-en. Contact: Mr. Arnold

Size	Overseas Branches	Overseas Experience	In Future	Country	Non-Japanese Full-Time	Non-Japanese Part-Time	Non-Japanese Increase	Non-Japanese Language	Answer in English	Answer Job-Hunters	Answer Businesses	Answer Researchers
C	0	Y	Y	*	4	8	Y	All		Y	Y	Y

* U.S.A., Europe

KENT SCHOOL OF ENGLISH

English conversation.
1-6-3 Ebisu Minami, Shibuya-ku, Tokyo 150. 03-3713-7046
Hibiya or JR Yamanote Line, Ebisu. Contact: Mr. Masami Asai

Size	Overseas Branches	Overseas Experience	In Future	Country	Non-Japanese Full-Time	Non-Japanese Part-Time	Non-Japanese Increase	Non-Japanese Language	Answer in English	Answer Job-Hunters	Answer Businesses	Answer Researchers
C	0	N	N		5	8			Y	Y	N	Y

THE LINGUA GAKUIN

English and French language. Translation.
1-11-8 Umesato, Suginami-ku, Tokyo 166. 03-3312-2377
Marunouchi Line, Shin Koenji. Contact: Mr. Seihachiro Arikawa

Size	Overseas Branches	Overseas Experience	In Future	Country	Non-Japanese Full-Time	Non-Japanese Part-Time	Non-Japanese Increase	Non-Japanese Language	Answer in English	Answer Job-Hunters	Answer Businesses	Answer Researchers
D	0				0	2	Y	E,F	Y	N	Y	Y

PEGASUS LANGUAGE SERVICES

English for adults. Translation.
c/o Mobil Oil, 1-7-2 Otemachi, Chiyoda-ku, Tokyo 100. 03-3244-4247
Various subway lines, Otemachi. Contact: Mr. James Moore

Size	Overseas Branches	Overseas Experience	In Future	Country	Non-Japanese Full-Time	Non-Japanese Part-Time	Non-Japanese Increase	Non-Japanese Language	Answer in English	Answer Job-Hunters	Answer Businesses	Answer Researchers
C	0	Y	Y	US	15	35	Y	E		Y	Y	Y

REPUBLIC ENGLISH SCHOOL

English conversation. Overseas study.
2-1 Kanda Surugadai, Chiyoda-ku, Tokyo 101. 03-3295-1144
JR Chuo Line, Ochanomizu. Contact: Mr. Nobuyuki Hosoki

Size	Overseas Branches	Overseas Experience	In Future	Country	Non-Japanese Full-Time	Non-Japanese Part-Time	Non-Japanese Increase	Non-Japanese Language	Answer in English	Answer Job-Hunters	Answer Businesses	Answer Researchers
D		N	N		7	0			Y	Y	Y	N

PROGRESS INTERNATIONAL

English language. Translation. Proofreading.
1-31-8-328 Takadanobaba, Shinjuku-ku, Tokyo 169. 03-3208-8805
Tozai or JR Yamanote Line, Takadanobaba. Contact: Ms. Tsurukawa

Size	Overseas Branches	Overseas Experience	In Future	Country	Non-Japanese Full-Time	Non-Japanese Part-Time	Non-Japanese Increase	Non-Japanese Language	Answer in English	Answer Job-Hunters	Answer Businesses	Answer Researchers
C	2				2	6	Y	E	Y	Y	Y	Y

ROBERT LANGUAGE ACADEMY

English and other languages.
3-61-7 Sendagaya, Shibuya-ku, Tokyo 151. 03-3401-0067
JR Yamanote Line, Harajuku. Contact: (receptionist)

Size	Overseas Branches	Overseas Experience	In Future	Country	Non-Japanese Full-Time	Non-Japanese Part-Time	Non-Japanese Increase	Non-Japanese Language	Answer in English	Answer Job-Hunters	Answer Businesses	Answer Researchers
					8	15	Y	*	Y	Y	Y	Y

* English, French, German, Italian, Spanish, Chinese

SHIBUYA LANGUAGE SCHOOL

Foreign and Japanese languages.
15-15 Sakuragaoka-machi, Shibuya-ku, Tokyo 150. 03-3461-8854
JR Yamanote Line, Shibuya. Contact: Mr. Sugawara (Jinji) 03-3461-9008

Size	Overseas Branches	Overseas Experience	In Future	Country	Non-Japanese Full-Time	Non-Japanese Part-Time	Non-Japanese Increase	Non-Japanese Language	Answer in English	Answer Job-Hunters	Answer Businesses	Answer Researchers
C		N	N		21	21	Y	All	Y	Y	N	Y

SONY ENTERPRISE CO.

English language.
Sukiyabashi Fuji Bldg., 4-2-11 Ginza, Chuo-ku, Tokyo 104. 03-3535-1211
Ginza, Marunouchi or Hibiya Line, Ginza. No contact

Size	Overseas Branches	Overseas Experience	In Future	Country	Non-Japanese Full-Time	Non-Japanese Part-Time	Non-Japanese Increase	Non-Japanese Language	Answer in English	Answer Job-Hunters	Answer Businesses	Answer Researchers
									Y	Y		

SYNCRITE TECHNICAL ENGLISH CENTER

Training for technical English translators.
203 Eru Aru Kasaru, 15-14 Maruyama-cho, Shibuya-ku, Tokyo 150.
Inokashira Line, Shinsen. Contact: Mr. Ikuo Nakano 03-3461-4472

Size	Overseas Branches	Overseas Experience	In Future	Country	Non-Japanese Full-Time	Non-Japanese Part-Time	Non-Japanese Increase	Non-Japanese Language	Answer in English	Answer Job-Hunters	Answer Businesses	Answer Researchers
	0	N	Y	US	0	2	Y	E	Y	Y	Y	Y

					←Non-Japanese			→		← Answer		→
Size	Overseas Branches	Overseas Experience	In Future	Country	Full-Time	Part-Time	Increase	Language	Answer in English	Job-Hunters	Businesses	Researchers

TOKYO HITOTSUBASHI INSTITUTE OF FOREIGN LANGUAGE

English language.
Palaceside Building, 1-1-1 Hitotsubashi, Chiyoda-ku, Tokyo 100.
Tozai Line, Takebashi. Contact: Mr. Watanabe 03-3213-0962

Size	Overseas Branches	Overseas Experience	In Future	Country	Full-Time	Part-Time	Increase	Language	Answer in English	Job-Hunters	Businesses	Researchers
C	0	N	N		3	7	Y	All	Y	Y	Y	Y

WILLBE CO., LTD.

English, French and German language.
KS 7 Building, 2-54-3 Ikebukuro, Toshima-ku, Tokyo 171. 03-3986-2477
Marunouchi, Yurakucho or JR Yamanote Line, Ikebukuro. Contact: Mr. Hanna

Size	Overseas Branches	Overseas Experience	In Future	Country	Full-Time	Part-Time	Increase	Language	Answer in English	Job-Hunters	Businesses	Researchers
D	0	N	N		6	12	Y	E,F,G	Y	Y	Y	Y

Y T C LANGUAGE SCHOOL

Foreign and Japanese languages.
1-15-1 Sugamo, Toshima-ku, Tokyo 170. 03-3946-5266
Toei Mita or JR Yamanote Line, Sugamo. Contact: Mr. Arima

Size	Overseas Branches	Overseas Experience	In Future	Country	Full-Time	Part-Time	Increase	Language	Answer in English	Job-Hunters	Businesses	Researchers
D	1	Y	Y	*	1	2	Y	¶	Y	Y	Y	Y

* Sri Lanka
¶ English, Chinese, Korean

ZEUS INSTITUTE OF LANGUAGES

Various languages. Translation. 03-3362-2321
2nd Fl. Daikan City 2, 7-20-16 Nishi Shinjuku, Shinjuku-ku, Tokyo 160.
Marunouchi, Toei Shinjuku or JR Yamanote Line, Shinjuku. Contact: Ms. Hirai

Size	Overseas Branches	Overseas Experience	In Future	Country	Full-Time	Part-Time	Increase	Language	Answer in English	Job-Hunters	Businesses	Researchers
D	1	N	Y		0	4	Y		Y	Y	Y	Y

YOKOHAMA Y M C A (F)

Japanese and English language.
2-25-1 Tsuruo-machi, Kanagawa-ku, Yokohama 221. 045-316-1881
Keihin Kyuko, Toyoko or JR Keihin Tohoku Line, Yokohama. No contact

Size	Overseas Branches	Overseas Experience	In Future	Country	Full-Time	Part-Time	Increase	Language	Answer in English	Job-Hunters	Businesses	Researchers
B	5000				20	100	Y	E	Y	Y		

KAWAGUCHI ENGLISH ACADEMY

English language.
5-18-48 Aoki, Kawaguchi-shi, Saitama 332. 048-255-6705
JR Keihin Tohoku Line, Nishi Kawaguchi. Contact: Mr. Ichiro Suzuki

Size	Overseas Branches	Overseas Experience	In Future	Country	Full-Time	Part-Time	Increase	Language	Answer in English	Job-Hunters	Businesses	Researchers
C		N			0	2	Y	E	Y	Y	Y	Y

KOUKUKOUEN COMMUNITY COLLEGE

English conversation. Translation. Printing.
2-26-16 Miyamoto-cho, Tokorozawa-shi, Saitama 359. 0429-23-2388
Seibu Shinjuku Line, Koku Koen. Contact: Ms. Tomoko Suzuki

Size	Overseas Branches	Overseas Experience	In Future	Country	Full-Time	Part-Time	Increase	Language	Answer in English	Job-Hunters	Businesses	Researchers
C	0	N	Y	US	0	10	Y	E	Y	Y	Y	N

EAST WEST COLLEGE OF FOREIGN LANGUAGES

Foreign languages.
18-10 Inagetai-cho, Inage-ku, Chiba 263. 043-243-7611
JR Sobu Line, Inage. Contact: Ms. Sasamoto or Ms. Sato

Size	Overseas Branches	Overseas Experience	In Future	Country	Full-Time	Part-Time	Increase	Language	Answer in English	Job-Hunters	Businesses	Researchers
					2	1			Y	Y	Y	Y

HELENA ENGLISH SCHOOL

English conversation.
Matsuken Dai-ni Building, 2-1-1 Tanaka, Tsuchiura-shi, Ibaraki 300.
JR Joban Line, Tsuchiura. Contact: Mr. Y. Matsumoto 0298-23-4622

Size	Overseas Branches	Overseas Experience	In Future	Country	Full-Time	Part-Time	Increase	Language	Answer in English	Job-Hunters	Businesses	Researchers
C	0	N	N		6	4	Y	E		Y	Y	Y

JOYCE & WAT ENGLISH SCHOOL

Various languages.
4-17-22 Konandai, Konan-ku, Yokohama-shi, Kanagawa 233.
JR Keihin Tohoku Line, Konanadai. Contact: Ms. J. Mukai 045-832-1057

Size	Overseas Branches	Overseas Experience	In Future	Country	Full-Time	Part-Time	Increase	Language	Answer in English	Job-Hunters	Businesses	Researchers
D	0	N	N		3	0			Y	Y	Y	

Size	Overseas Branches	Overseas Experience	In Future	Country	←Non-Japanese→ Full-Time	Part-Time	Increase	Language	Answer in English	←Answer→ Job-Hunters	Businesses	Researchers

NEW WORLD SCHOOL OF LANGUAGES

English language. 044-211-5721
Maruito Building, 2-11-25 Isago, Kawasaki-ku, Kawasaki·210.
JR Keihin Tohoku Line, Kawasaki. Contact: Ms. Toshi Yoshiwara

Size	Overseas Branches	Overseas Experience	In Future	Country	Full-Time	Part-Time	Increase	Language	Answer in English	Job-Hunters	Businesses	Researchers
C		N	N		10	5	Y	E,S	Y	Y	Y	Y

WATSON ENGLISH CONVERSATION CLASS

English conversation.
3259-3 Kami Miyata, Minami Shitaura-machi, Miura-shi, Kanagawa.
Keihin Kyuko Line, Miura Kaigan Contact: Mr. Watson 0468-88-5771

Size	Overseas Branches	Overseas Experience	In Future	Country	Full-Time	Part-Time	Increase	Language	Answer in English	Job-Hunters	Businesses	Researchers
D		N			1	2	Y	E	Y	Y		

ACADEMY EIKAIWA

English conversation.
Mari Building, 2-2-4 Juso Higashi, Yodogawa-ku, Osaka 532.
Hankyu Line, Juso. Contact: Ms. Takemura 06-302-1456

Size	Overseas Branches	Overseas Experience	In Future	Country	Full-Time	Part-Time	Increase	Language	Answer in English	Job-Hunters	Businesses	Researchers
C	0	N	N		0	15	Y	E		Y	Y	Y

COSMO CULTURAL EXCHANGE CENTER

English language. Overseas study. Travel planning.
Mitsui Seimei Building, 2-9-24 Chuo-cho, Oita-shi, Oita 870.
JR Nippo Line, Oita. Contact: Mr. Kunihide Ogasawara 0975-33-2388

Size	Overseas Branches	Overseas Experience	In Future	Country	Full-Time	Part-Time	Increase	Language	Answer in English	Job-Hunters	Businesses	Researchers
D	2	Y	Y	UK	4	0			Y		Y	Y

JAPANESE LANGUAGE SCHOOLS

Size	Overseas Branches	Overseas Experience	In Future	Country	← Non-Japanese → Full-Time	Part-Time	Increase	Language	Answer in English	← Answer → Job-Hunters	Businesses	Researchers

INTERNATIONAL EDUCATION CENTER (F)

English and Japanese language.
1-21 Yotsuya, Shinjuku-ku, Tokyo 160. 03-3359-9621
Marunouchi or JR Chuo Line, Yotsuya. Contact: Mr. Mori Ext.222

Size	Overseas Branches	Overseas Experience	In Future	Country	Full-Time	Part-Time	Increase	Language	Answer in English	Job-Hunters	Businesses	Researchers
B	0	N	N		55	50	Y	E	Y	Y	N	N

THE ENGLISH LANGUAGE EDUCATION COUNCIL INC. (ELEC) (F)

English conversation and Japanese language.
3-8 Jimbocho, Kanda, Tokyo 101. 03-3265-8911
Hanzomon, Toei Mita or Shinjuku Line, Jimbocho. Contact: Mr. Enomoto

Size	Overseas Branches	Overseas Experience	In Future	Country	Full-Time	Part-Time	Increase	Language	Answer in English	Job-Hunters	Businesses	Researchers
C		N	N		31	12	Y	E	Y	Y	Y	Y

THE JAPANESE LANGUAGE SCHOOL OF THE INTERNATIONAL STUDENTS INSTITUTE (F)

Japanese language. Housing service for foreign students.
3-22-7 Kita Shinjuku, Shinjuku-ku, Tokyo 169. 03-3371-7265
JR Sobu Line, Okubo. Contact: Mr. Hayao Muguruma Ext. 13

Size	Overseas Branches	Overseas Experience	In Future	Country	Full-Time	Part-Time	Increase	Language	Answer in English	Job-Hunters	Businesses	Researchers
C	0	Y	Y						Y	N	N	Y

THE ASIAN STUDENTS CULTURAL ASSOCIATION (F)

Operation of boarding house. Japanese language.
Asia Bunka Kaikan, 2-12-13 Hon Komagome, Bunkyo-ku, Tokyo 113.
Toei Mita Line, Sengoku. Contact: (Any section) 03-3946-4121

Size	Overseas Branches	Overseas Experience	In Future	Country	Full-Time	Part-Time	Increase	Language	Answer in English	Job-Hunters	Businesses	Researchers
C	0	N	N						Y	N	N	Y

ACADEMY OF LANGUAGE ARTS

Japanese language and teacher training. 03-3235-0071
No. 2 Tobundo Building, 2-16 Ageba-cho, Shinjuku-ku, Tokyo 162.
Yurakucho, Tozai or JR Sobu Line, Iidabashi. Contact: Ms. Himuro

Size	Overseas Branches	Overseas Experience	In Future	Country	Full-Time	Part-Time	Increase	Language	Answer in English	Job-Hunters	Businesses	Researchers
C	0				20	5	Y	E		Y	Y	Y

ALEC SCHOOL OF LANGUAGES

English and Japanese language. 03-3400-4515
No. 2 Kobayashi Building, 1-14-13 Shibuya, Shibuya-ku, Tokyo 150.
Ginza, Hanzomon or JR Yamanote Line, Shibuya. Contact: Mr. Mimaki

Size	Overseas Branches	Overseas Experience	In Future	Country	Full-Time	Part-Time	Increase	Language	Answer in English	Job-Hunters	Businesses	Researchers
D		N	N		1	5	Y	E	Y	Y	Y	Y

EAST WEST JAPANESE LANGUAGE INSTITUTE

Japanese language school.
2-36-9 Chuo, Nakano-ku, Tokyo 164. 03-3366-4717
Marunouchi Line, Nakano Sakaue. Contact: Mr. Mori

Size	Overseas Branches	Overseas Experience	In Future	Country	Full-Time	Part-Time	Increase	Language	Answer in English	Job-Hunters	Businesses	Researchers
C	0	Y			0	7	Y	E	Y	Y	Y	Y

INTERNSHIP STUDY CENTER

English and Japanese language.
6-19-14 Hongo, Bunkyo-ku, Tokyo 113. 03-3812-5431
Marunouchi Line, Hongo San-chome. Contact: Mr. Nakamura

Size	Overseas Branches	Overseas Experience	In Future	Country	Full-Time	Part-Time	Increase	Language	Answer in English	Job-Hunters	Businesses	Researchers
					0	16			Y	N	N	Y

I.T.S. LANGUAGE CENTER

Japanese language.
3F Garden Plaza Hiro-o, 4-1-29 Minami Azabu, Minato-ku, Tokyo 106.
Hibiya Line, Hiro-o. Contact: Mr. Sakairi 03-3448-0971

Size	Overseas Branches	Overseas Experience	In Future	Country	Full-Time	Part-Time	Increase	Language	Answer in English	Job-Hunters	Businesses	Researchers
C	0	N	N		0	2	Y	E	Y	Y	N	Y

	Size	Overseas Branches	Overseas Experience	In Future	Country	Full-Time (Non-Japanese)	Part-Time (Non-Japanese)	Increase (Non-Japanese)	Language (Non-Japanese)	Answer in English	Job-Hunters (Answer)	Businesses (Answer)	Researchers (Answer)
JET ACADEMY						2	2	N		N	N	N	Y
KAI JAPANESE LANGUAGE SCHOOL LTD.	D	0	Y	Y	Can					Y	N		Y
OHTSUKA GAKUIN	C	0	Y	Y	Ch	2	0			Y			
SHIBUYA LANGUAGE SCHOOL	C		N	N		21	12	Y	All	Y	Y	N	Y
WASEDA JAPANESE SCHOOL		1	N	N		1	0	Y	Ch	Y	N	N	N
Y T C LANGUAGE SCHOOL	D	1	Y	Y	*	1	2	Y	¶	Y	Y	Y	Y
YOKOHAMA Y M C A (F)	B	5000				20	100	Y	E	Y	Y		
OSAKA Y M C A JAPANESE LANGUAGE SCHOOL (F)	C	0	N	N						Y	N	N	Y

JET ACADEMY

Japanese language.
7-8-9 Takinogawa, Kita-ku, Tokyo 114. 03-3916-2101
JR Saikyo Line, Itabashi. Contact: Mr. Inoue (Kyomu-bu)

KAI JAPANESE LANGUAGE SCHOOL LTD.

Japanese language.
Miyuki Building, 1-15-18 Okubo, Shinjuku-ku, Tokyo 164. 03-3205-1356
JR Yamanote Line, Shin Okubo. No contact

OHTSUKA GAKUIN

Japanese language.
2-18-12 Higashi Komagata, Sumida-ku, Tokyo 130. 03-3625-5661
Toei Asakusa Line, Honjo Azumabashi. Contact: Mr. Cho

SHIBUYA LANGUAGE SCHOOL

Foreign and Japanese languages.
15-15 Sakuragaoka-machi, Shibuya-ku, Tokyo 150. 03-3461-8854
JR Yamanote Line, Shibuya. Contact: Mr. Sugawara (Jinji) 03-3461-9008

WASEDA JAPANESE SCHOOL

Japanese language.
No. 35 Kyoritsu Bldg., 4-45-2 Koenji Minami, Suginami-ku, Tokyo 166.
JR Chuo Line, Koenji. Contact: Ms. Takezoe 03-3318-6218

Y T C LANGUAGE SCHOOL

Foreign and Japanese languages.
1-15-1 Sugamo, Toshima-ku, Tokyo 170. 03-3946-5266
Toei Mita or JR Yamanote Line, Sugamo. Contact: Mr. Arima

* Sri Lanka
¶ English, Chinese, Korean

YOKOHAMA Y M C A (F)

Japanese and English language.
2-25-1 Tsuruo-machi, Kanagawa-ku, Yokohama 221. 045-316-1881
Keihin Kyuko, Toyoko or JR Keihin Tohoku Line, Yokohama. No contact

OSAKA Y M C A JAPANESE LANGUAGE SCHOOL (F)

Japanese language.
1-5-17 Dojima, Kita-ku, Osaka 530. 06-344-1717
JR Tokiaido Line, Osaka. Contact: (Nihongo Gakka)

OTHER SCHOOLS

AOBA INTERNATIONAL EDUCATIONAL SYSTEMS

International kindergarten.
2-10-34 Aobadai, Meguro-ku, Tokyo 153. 03-3461-1442
Tokyu Toyoko Line, Daikanyama. Contact: Ms. Koshikawa

Size	Overseas Branches	Overseas Experience	In Future	Country	Non-Japanese Full-Time	Non-Japanese Part-Time	Non-Japanese Increase	Non-Japanese Language	Answer in English	Answer Job-Hunters	Answer Businesses	Answer Researchers
C		Y			20	0			Y	Y		Y

THE CHUO ACADEMY

English stenography, accounting, business correspondence, etc.
7-4-7 Nishi Shinjuku, Shinjuku-ku, Tokyo 160. 03-3362-4191
Marunouchi, Toei Shinjuku or JR Yamanote Line, Shinjuku. No contact

Size	Overseas Branches	Overseas Experience	In Future	Country	Non-Japanese Full-Time	Non-Japanese Part-Time	Non-Japanese Increase	Non-Japanese Language	Answer in English	Answer Job-Hunters	Answer Businesses	Answer Researchers
C	0	Y	N		0	3	N			N	N	N

INTERAC CORP.

Language training for companies. Cross-cultural seminars. Publications.
1-12-5 Iidabashi, Chiyoda-ku, Tokyo 102. 03-3234-7841
Yurakucho, Tozai or JR Sobu Line, Iidabashi. Contact: Mr. Hideki Egawa

Size	Overseas Branches	Overseas Experience	In Future	Country	Non-Japanese Full-Time	Non-Japanese Part-Time	Non-Japanese Increase	Non-Japanese Language	Answer in English	Answer Job-Hunters	Answer Businesses	Answer Researchers
B	5	N			260	130	Y	All	Y	Y	Y	Y

INTERNATIONAL INTERNSHIP PROGRAMS

International vocational training.
6-19-14 Hongo, Bunkyo-ku, Tokyo 113. 03-3812-0771
Marunouchi Line, Hongo San-chome. Contact: Mr. Oda (North Am. Sect.)

Size	Overseas Branches	Overseas Experience	In Future	Country	Non-Japanese Full-Time	Non-Japanese Part-Time	Non-Japanese Increase	Non-Japanese Language	Answer in English	Answer Job-Hunters	Answer Businesses	Answer Researchers
C	3	N			5	0				Y	Y	Y

ISHIKAWA GAKUIN

Languages and music.
3-29-12 Tateishi, Katsushika-ku, Tokyo 124. 03-3697-2222
Kesei Line, Tateishi. Contact: Mr. Hironobu Ishikawa 03-3691-2189

Size	Overseas Branches	Overseas Experience	In Future	Country	Non-Japanese Full-Time	Non-Japanese Part-Time	Non-Japanese Increase	Non-Japanese Language	Answer in English	Answer Job-Hunters	Answer Businesses	Answer Researchers
					5	5	Y	E,G	Y	Y	Y	Y

SUN LIFE

Language education. 03-3367-4881
2nd Fl. Art No.1 Bldg., 4-11-13 Takadanobaba, Shinjuku-ku, Tokyo 169.
Tozai or JR Yamanote Line, Takadanobaba. Contact: Mr. Ichiro Saito

Size	Overseas Branches	Overseas Experience	In Future	Country	Non-Japanese Full-Time	Non-Japanese Part-Time	Non-Japanese Increase	Non-Japanese Language	Answer in English	Answer Job-Hunters	Answer Businesses	Answer Researchers
D	0	N	N		2	18	Y	*	Y	Y	Y	Y

* English, French, Chinese, Korean

TOKYO BUSINESS COLLEGE

Business school.
Palaceside Building, 1-1-1 Hitotsubashi, Chiyoda-ku, Tokyo 100.
Tozai Line, Takebashi. Contact: Mr. Watanabe 03-3213-4722

Size	Overseas Branches	Overseas Experience	In Future	Country	Non-Japanese Full-Time	Non-Japanese Part-Time	Non-Japanese Increase	Non-Japanese Language	Answer in English	Answer Job-Hunters	Answer Businesses	Answer Researchers
C		N	N		3	7	Y	All	Y	Y	Y	Y

NAGOYA INTERNATIONAL SCHOOL

American school.
2686 Aza Nanbara, Oaza Naka Shidami, Moriyama-ku, Nagoya 463.
JR Chuo Line, Jinryo. Contact: Mr. Gerald Craig 052-736-2025

Size	Overseas Branches	Overseas Experience	In Future	Country	Non-Japanese Full-Time	Non-Japanese Part-Time	Non-Japanese Increase	Non-Japanese Language	Answer in English	Answer Job-Hunters	Answer Businesses	Answer Researchers
C	0	N			28	0	Y	E	Y	Y	Y	Y

Size	Overseas Branches	Overseas Experience	In Future	Country	Non-Japanese Full-Time	Non-Japanese Part-Time	Non-Japanese Increase	Non-Japanese Language	Answer in English	Answer Job-Hunters	Answer Businesses	Answer Researchers

EDUCATIONAL ASSISTANCE

SETAGAYA INSTITUTE FOR STUDY ABROAD (S.I.S.A.)

Counselling regarding overseas study.
Sankei Heights, 2-31-18 Daizawa, Setagaya-ku, Tokyo 155.
Odakyu Line, Shimo Kitazawa. Contact: Mr. Kuki 03-3419-1009

Size	Overseas Branches	Overseas Experience	In Future	Country	Full-Time	Part-Time	Increase	Language	Answer in English	Job-Hunters	Businesses	Researchers
D	22	Y	Y	US	0	0	Y	E	Y	Y	Y	Y

T G A INC.

Cross-cultural orientation.
Nishi Azabu Sonic Building, 3-2-12 Nishi Azabu, Minato-ku, Tokyo 106.
Hibiya Line, Roppongi. Contact: Ms. Hirano 03-3408-5331

Size	Overseas Branches	Overseas Experience	In Future	Country	Full-Time	Part-Time	Increase	Language	Answer in English	Job-Hunters	Businesses	Researchers
C	0	Y	Y		1	2			Y	N	Y	N

CHAPTER 5. TRANSLATION, INTERPRETATION AND PROOFREADING

This is a chapter for our job-hunters again. Let us take translation first. There is no doubt that there is plenty of work available in this area, but, of course, it needs skill to be a translator. If you have Japanese ability, however, you need not feel too shy about using it, for the fact is that a large proportion of Japanese into English translation, for example, is done by Japanese translators without overwhelming ability and you could hardly do worse than some of them do.

Moreover, translation is a financially rewarding business, but not, unfortunately, a very highly regarded one. This is strange, but maybe it is because of the level of translation to which Japanese have become accustomed. You will find that the emphasis is much more on quantity and speed of translation than on quality. In any case, after you have finished your translation, somebody else is almost sure to tamper with it.

It is possible to find translation jobs with large Japanese companies, but they are not very common, because usually it is cheaper to employ Japanese, often ladies (because they are paid less), to do this relatively unimportant work. When a company does not have anybody who can translate, or wants a job done well, it gives it to a translation agency, and here it is much more likely that you will be able to find employment. We have listed those which responded to our questionnaire. One slightly demoralizing aspect of this type of work, however, is that you will tend to be told that it was "all right" if you do a good job, but be blamed for any little mistake, sometimes even if it was not your mistake!

However, perhaps you can put up with that if the pay is right. For translating from Japanese to English, you can expect to be paid about ¥3,000 per page of English, and to be able to average two pages per hour once you become accustomed to the work. For translating from Japanese to another language, rates should be somewhat higher, as they should also be if the work is highly technical. Major assignments are often paid on a lump sum basis, rather than on a per page basis.

There is also the possibility of translating from English into another language. If a company wants a piece of work translated into a number of languages, it quite often arranges for an English translation first and then gets further translations made from the English to the other languages. It is easier to find translators from English to other languages than from Japanese. The pay for this will be similar to that for Japanese-English translation, which means that, for the company, total expenditure will be somewhat reduced. The problem is obvious, though. The quality of all subsequent translations depends on the ability of the original Japanese-English translator — and too often that leaves much to be desired. Anyway, such work is available.

People who make really big money in the translation business are those who manage to cut out the middleman. Not only is this much more rewarding financially, but it usually leads to a better job being done, because the translator is much more likely to be able to ask a few questions of somebody who is in a position to answer them. Thus it may well prove to be more rewarding not only financially, but also mentally. However, in practice one cannot obtain a visa to work freelance as a translator, nor can one expect to approach companies for translation work without the right connexions. So those who do work in this way have almost inevitably been in Japan for some years and built up the necessary network of connexions, as well as finding some way of obtaining and maintaining a visa. This is often done by working with a company for some years and gaining its confidence, then arranging to work just the minimum number of hours necessary to obtain a visa. Some translators get married to a Japanese and can then work freelance, often keeping their former company as a major customer, of course on the understanding that its work will be put first on the list of priorities. In any case, working as an independent translator is bound to be a proposition for the long term. One should start by getting employment with a translation company and looking for the odd independent assignment.

In doing this type of work, a fax machine will prove invaluable and a computer or word processor, especially one compatible with that owned by your principal employer, will be a great advantage too. These days, translators are also expected to have a speciality, knowledge of computers being a particularly useful one.

Another problem with translation work is time pressure. Things are almost inevitably done at the last moment, as though it never occurred to anybody that a manual would be needed for a new product, for example, until two days before its release. Quality suffers, but so does the life-style of the translator drinking endless cups of coffee and working without sleep for two days and nights. This is no joke. In this line of business it happens all the time, and the translator's reputation is established by his never missing a deadline, rather than by his producing an impeccably translated manuscript.

One thing to remember if doing translation work is that it is very risky ever to agree to translate from another language into Japanese, as you may occasionally be asked to do. People will have little idea of your ability in your native tongue, and may think it not of vital importance, but they will certainly notice every little mistake in your Japanese, and may well get the idea that your translation in the opposite direction is no better, illogical though that may seem.

As mentioned in the introduction, in the last few years translation machines have made their appearance in Japan. Some claim that such technology will soon put professional translators out of work and that the results are already just as good as those produced by Japanese translators translating from Japanese into English, as well as being much quicker and more economical in the long run. In this writer's opinion that only emphasizes the low quality of the translations which are usually produced. It remains to be seen whether the professional non-Japanese translator will soon be found selling paintings on the Tokyo streets to augment his income or not, but a personal opinion is that that day is still far away.

Interpretation is for the really highly skilled in Japanese and pay is commensurate with the level of ability demanded. Usually interpreters, although much in demand, will not be able to work at their profession for more than two or three days in each week, since assignments tend to be short, which, of course, is part of the reason for the high pay. Clients are typically charged ¥70,000 per day for the services of an interpreter or ¥40,000 for half a day. Of this, the interpreter might expect to receive half, if working through an agency, and it will be difficult to do otherwise when first arriving in Japan. Gradually, however, one will make contacts and, if one is competent and affable and somewhat cheaper than the agencies, one will gradually be able to obtain work privately. Do not forget, though, that somehow one has to keep one's visa at the same time.

Although the hours for interpretation will be fixed and overtime will be payable if these are exceeded substantially, it is usually expected that an interpreter will turn up sufficiently early for a briefing before starting work, however unnecessary this may seem to be, and that he will be available after work for a little celebration, if required, during which, of course, he will probably find himself doing what he has been doing all day!

Proofreading and rewriting are less highly skilled than translation or interpretation. No knowledge of Japanese is required. The proofreader is usually given the results of a translation into his native language, most commonly English, by a Japanese translator and asked to make it readable. The quality of the translation will vary, but it is probably fair to say that it will not be very good. If it were, by any stretch of the imagination, acceptable, it would not get the luxury of a proofreading. One of the constant problems is that Japanese is a vague language, delighting in ambiguities and long grammatically uncertain sentences and the result is often a similar style of English. If you ask the translator exactly what a certain sentence is supposed to mean, the answer may well be that he or she did not know either, "so I translated it in a general way." Such problems are compounded by the fact that technical materials, as the pieces often are, will usually be written by engineers who do not think much about end users and tend to omit important details which are, to them, obvious. Moreover, they apply a highly technical form of logic which may not be that of the user of the materials, nor even that of the translator. And, if this is not bad enough, their skills usually lie in the engineering field, understandably enough, rather than in the area of Japanese prose composition. All this is to say that the Japanese original may not have been terribly clear to start with and that the English translation will be far worse.

The pay for proofreading varies a great deal, within the range of about ¥500 to ¥2,000 per page of English, perhaps a little more for other languages. The attitudes and speeds of proofreaders also vary quite a lot. Some think that their task is only to correct glaring grammatical and spelling errors. Others want to make sure that every fact and figure is correct and that there are no inconsistencies, mistranslations or inaccuracies. If the wrong type of person is assigned to a job, the client, and therefore the agency, will not be pleased. In general the client is no happier with somebody who points out every inconsistency when what was required was a quick check of the spelling, than with somebody who found the odd spelling mistake when quality was needed. Some proofreaders claim that they can get through about ten pages per hour. Other proceed at the rate of two or three. In general, however, you get paid for what you do. The more thoroughly you do the job, the more you can expect to receive per page. If the pay is low, on the other hand, that is an indication that a really thorough job is not expected. In general, agents will not welcome a multitude of questions, but you can try asking one or two where necessary and see what the reaction is. And, as with translation, one of the frustrating features of this work is that somebody is almost sure to mess about with it after it has left your desk, so taking a pride in what you do is not terribly rewarding.

Translation companies also need proofreaders, of course, so they are the best places to search for this type of employment. In fact, though, many people use it to supplement their income rather than as a main job. The possession of a fax machine will again be a considerable advantage in obtaining assignments. As with translation, time pressure is often intense — and frequently it is difficult to understand why everything is always left until the last minute, except that is just the way that life is in Japan. This writer, for example, was once involved in the translation of the soundtrack of a Bing Crosby film for showing with subtitles on television. When I asked why it was that a film which had been around for forty years suddenly had to be translated in three days, I was told that there was no time to think about that!

	Size	Overseas Branches	Overseas Experience	In Future	Country	←Non-Japanese Full-Time	Part-Time	Increase	Language→	Answer in English	←Answer Job-Hunters	Businesses	Researchers→
BABEL INC. Job placement. Translation. Schooling. NS Bldg., 2-2-3 Sarugaku-cho, Chiyoda-ku, Tokyo 101. 03-3295-2305 JR Chuo Line, Ochanomizu. Contact: Mr. Toshiki Hotta 03-3295-6302	C	2	Y	Y	US	0	3	Y		Y	Y	Y	Y
BORGNAN HUMAN DEVELOPMENT INSTITUTE LTD. (BHDI) Job placement. Translation and interpretation. Consultation. Dai-san Taihei Bldg., 1-25-3 Higashi Ikebukuro, Toshima-ku, Tokyo 170. JR Yamanote Line, Ikebukuro. Contact: Mr. Yamada 03-3989-8153	C	1	Y	Y	UK	60	40	Y	All	Y	Y	Y	Y
BUSINESS EDUCATION SOCIETY INC. Translation. Various training. 2-8-10 Iwamoto-cho, Chiyoda-ku, Tokyo 101. 03-3663-8774 Toei Shinjuku Line, Iwamotocho. Contact: Mr. Kawai Ext. 404	C	1	Y	N		2	3	Y	E	Y	Y	Y	N
CHINA ATTEND Interpretation and translation of Chinese. 03-3365-6965 102 Heights Mifune, 3 Funamachi, Shinjuku-ku, Tokyo 160. Marunouchi Line, Yotsuya San-chome. Contact: Ms.Sawaguchi (Kanri-ka)	D	0	N	N		2	0	Y	Ch	N	Y	Y	Y
DEUTSCHES SPRACHKOLLEG HEIDELBERG German language training. Translation. 1-59-1 Yoyogi, Shibuya-ku, Tokyo 151. JR Yamanote Line, Yoyogi. Contact: Ms. Yamanaka 03-3374-4863	C		Y	N		9	8	Y	G		Y	Y	Y
I C C LANGUAGE SCHOOLS Translation and interpretation. School operation. Maison Raffiné, 1-6-24 Hara Machida, Machida-shi, Tokyo 194. Odakyu Line, Machida. 0427–28–6535 Contact: Mr. Armand Knafo * English, French, German, Spanish	C	0	N	N		11	8	Y	*	Y	Y		
I L C C CO., LTD. Interpretation and translation. Nissanken Kaikan Building, 5-3-14 Toranomon, Minato-ku, Tokyo 105. Hibiya Line, Kamiyacho. Contact: (Personnel) 03-3431-9159	C	1	N			3	0			Y	Y	N	N
INTERNATIONAL CULTURAL INFORMATION CENTER (I.C.I.C.) Interpretation and translation of various languages. 1-17-11 Park Height Bldg., Higashi Ikebukuro, Toshima-ku, Tokyo 170. JR Yamanote Line, Ikebukuro. Contact: Mr. Hara 03-3987-0208	B	1	Y	Y	UK	0	0	Y	E,Ch	Y	Y	Y	Y
INTERNATIONAL INTERCHANGE CORPORATION Job placement. Translation and interpretation. Tour conductors. SN Kurosu Bldg., 3-33-20 Nakano, Nakano-ku, Tokyo 164. 03-3380-3201 Tozai or JR Chuo Line, Nakano. Contact: Mr. Tetsuro Nishi	D		Y	Y	Asia					N	Y	Y	Y
INTERNATIONAL TRANSACTION CENTER LTD. Job placement. Language services. International business co-ordination. Senbikiya Bldg., 1-1-9 Kyobashi, Chuo-ku, Tokyo 104. 03-3274-0655 Ginza Line, Kyobashi. Contact: Mr. Yoshinori Omata 03-3561-1057	C	1	N	N		3	5			Y	Y	Y	Y

Size	Overseas Branches	Overseas Experience	In Future	Country	←Non-Japanese→ Full-Time	Part-Time	Increase	Language	Answer in English	← Answer → Job-Hunters	Businesses	Researchers

JAPAN CONVENTION SERVICES, INC.

Planning and operation of international conferences. Interpretation.
2-2-1 Uchi Saiwai-cho, Chiyoda-ku, Tokyo 100. 03-3508-1211
Marunouchi, Chiyoda or Hibiya Line, Kasumigaseki. No contact

Size	Overseas Branches	Overseas Experience	In Future	Country	Full-Time	Part-Time	Increase	Language	Answer in English	Job-Hunters	Businesses	Researchers
B		Y	N									

JAPAN LINGUA SERVICES CO., LTD.

Translation.
2-9-14 Ginza, Chuo-ku, Tokyo 104. 03-3567-3815
Ginza, Marunouchi or Hibiya Line, Ginza. Contact: Mr. Kobayashi

Size	Overseas Branches	Overseas Experience	In Future	Country	Full-Time	Part-Time	Increase	Language	Answer in English	Job-Hunters	Businesses	Researchers
D	0	Y	Y	*	0	10			N	N	N	N

* U.S.A., Europe

JUST SERVICE CO.,LTD.

Job placement. Translation and interpretation.
Tsubaki Bldg., 3-15-16 Shinjuku, Shinjuku-ku, Tokyo 160. 03-3225-5511
JR Yamanote or Chuo Line, Shinjuku. Contact: Mr. Kohata or Mr. Osawa

Size	Overseas Branches	Overseas Experience	In Future	Country	Full-Time	Part-Time	Increase	Language	Answer in English	Job-Hunters	Businesses	Researchers
C		N	Y		0	50	Y	All	Y	Y	Y	Y

KABUSHIKI KAISHA A.I.T.

Foreign language training. Translation.
3-20-1-401 Tamagawa, Setagaya-ku, Tokyo 158. 03-3700-8110
Shin Tamagawa Line, Futago Tamagawa-en. Contact: Mr. Arnold

Size	Overseas Branches	Overseas Experience	In Future	Country	Full-Time	Part-Time	Increase	Language	Answer in English	Job-Hunters	Businesses	Researchers
C	0	Y	Y	*	4	8	Y	All		Y	Y	Y

* U.S.A., Europe

K D D TELESERV INC.

Interpretation service for 8 languages by telephone. Translation.
KDD Bldg., 2-3-2 Nishi Shinjuku, Shinjuku-ku, Tokyo 163-03.
JR Yamanote Line, Shinjuku. Contact Ms. Nakamura 03-3347-9241

Size	Overseas Branches	Overseas Experience	In Future	Country	Full-Time	Part-Time	Increase	Language	Answer in English	Job-Hunters	Businesses	Researchers
		N			0	3	Y	*	Y	Y		

* English, Italian, Spanish, Russian

KOUKUKOUEN COMMUNITY COLLEGE

Translation, English language teaching and printing.
2-26-16 Miyamoto-cho, Tokorozawa-shi, Saitama 359. 0429-23-2388
Seibu Shijuku Line, Koku Koen. Contact: Ms. Suzuki

Size	Overseas Branches	Overseas Experience	In Future	Country	Full-Time	Part-Time	Increase	Language	Answer in English	Job-Hunters	Businesses	Researchers
C	0	N	Y	US	0	10	Y	E	Y	Y	Y	N

THE LINGUA GAKUIN

Translation. Language teaching.
1-11-8 Umesato, Suginami-ku, Tokyo 166. 03-3312-2377
Marunouchi Line, Shin Koenji. Contact: Mr. Arikawa

Size	Overseas Branches	Overseas Experience	In Future	Country	Full-Time	Part-Time	Increase	Language	Answer in English	Job-Hunters	Businesses	Researchers
D	0				0	2	Y	E,F	Y	N	Y	Y

MARUBENI PERSONNEL SUPPORT CO., LTD.

Job placement. Language training. Consultation for management.
3-25 Jimbo-cho, Kanda, Chiyoda-ku, Tokyo 101. 03-3234-1324
Tozai, Hanzomon or Toei Shinjuku Line, Kudanshita. Contact: (Koshi Jinji-bu)

Size	Overseas Branches	Overseas Experience	In Future	Country	Full-Time	Part-Time	Increase	Language	Answer in English	Job-Hunters	Businesses	Researchers
B	0	Y	Y	*	20	40	Y	All	Y	Y	Y	Y

* U.S.A., Canada

PEGASUS LANGUAGE SERVICES

Translation. Schooling for businessmen.
c/o Mobil Sekiyu, Otemachi, Chiyoda-ku, Tokyo 100. 03-3244-4247
Various subway lines, Otemachi. Contact: Mr. James Moore

Size	Overseas Branches	Overseas Experience	In Future	Country	Full-Time	Part-Time	Increase	Language	Answer in English	Job-Hunters	Businesses	Researchers
C	0	Y	Y	US	15	35	Y	E		Y	Y	Y

PROGRESS INTERNATIONAL

Translation. English language teaching.
1-31-8-128 Takadanobaba, Shinjuku-ku, Tokyo 169. 03-3208-8805
Tozai or JR Yamanote Line, Takadanobaba. Contact: Ms. Tsurukawa

Size	Overseas Branches	Overseas Experience	In Future	Country	Full-Time	Part-Time	Increase	Language	Answer in English	Job-Hunters	Businesses	Researchers
C	2				2	6	Y	E	Y	Y	Y	Y

Columns: Size | Overseas Branches | Overseas Experience | In Future | Country | ←Non-Japanese→ Full-Time | Part-Time | Increase | Language | Answer in English | ←Answer→ Job-Hunters | Businesses | Researchers

SANSEI INTERNATIONAL INC.

Management of international conferences. Interpretation and translation.
No. 2 Fukide Building, 4-1-21 Toranomon, Minato-ku, Tokyo 105.
Hibiya Line, Kamiyacho. Contact: Mr. Echizen 03-3433-1560

Size	Overseas Branches	Overseas Experience	In Future	Country	Full-Time	Part-Time	Increase	Language	Answer in English	Job-Hunters	Businesses	Researchers
C	1	Y	Y		0	1			Y	Y	Y	Y

SUPER LANGUAGE SERVICE INC.

Translation and inerpretation.
1-7-1-201 Hirakawa-cho, Chiyoda-ku, Tokyo 102. 03-3262-1591
Hanzomon Line, Hanzomon. Contact: Ms. Umeda or Ms. Suzuki

Size	Overseas Branches	Overseas Experience	In Future	Country	Full-Time	Part-Time	Increase	Language	Answer in English	Job-Hunters	Businesses	Researchers
D	0	Y	N		0	20			N	Y	Y	Y

TECHLINGUA INC.

Translation. Language education.
1-10-3-206 Den-en Chofu, Ota-ku, Tokyo 145. 03-3722-5211
Tokyu Toyoko Line, Tamagawaen. Contact: Mr. Takai or Ms. Koyama

Size	Overseas Branches	Overseas Experience	In Future	Country	Full-Time	Part-Time	Increase	Language	Answer in English	Job-Hunters	Businesses	Researchers
D	0	Y	Y	*	1	0			Y	Y	Y	Y

* U.S.A., Australia

TRATECH INC.

Translation, interpretation and printing.
Tatsunaka Bldg., 3-13-17 Ginza, Chuo-ku, Tokyo 104. 03-3543-1076
Ginza, Marunouchi or Hibiya Line, Ginza. Contact: Mr. Tabei

Size	Overseas Branches	Overseas Experience	In Future	Country	Full-Time	Part-Time	Increase	Language	Answer in English	Job-Hunters	Businesses	Researchers
C		Y	N		1	0			N	Y	Y	Y

ZEUS INSTITUTE OF LANGUAGES

Language teaching. Translation.
2nd Fl. Daikan City 2, 7-20-16 Nishi Shinjuku, Shinjuku-ku, Tokyo 160.
JR Yamanote or Chuo Line, Shinjuku. Contact: Ms. Hirai 03-3362-2321

Size	Overseas Branches	Overseas Experience	In Future	Country	Full-Time	Part-Time	Increase	Language	Answer in English	Job-Hunters	Businesses	Researchers
D	1	N	Y		0	4	Y		Y	Y	Y	Y

I.S.S. INC.

Translation, interpretation, job placement. 06-761-7838
Nihon Sangyo Building, 13-5 Obase-cho, Tennoji-ku, Osaka 543.
Tanimachi or Sennichimae Line, Tanimachi Kyu-chome. Contact: Mr. Vancampen

Size	Overseas Branches	Overseas Experience	In Future	Country	Full-Time	Part-Time	Increase	Language	Answer in English	Job-Hunters	Businesses	Researchers
C	0	Y	Y	*	3	20	Y	All	Y	Y	Y	Y

* U.S.A., S.E. Asia, Europe

UNION SERVICES CO., LTD.

Translation, publishing and consultation regarding international business.
5-1-6 Nishi, Uehon-machi, Chuo-ku, Osaka 542. 06-763-5431
Tanimachi or Sennichimae Line, Tanimachi Kyu-chome. No contact

Size	Overseas Branches	Overseas Experience	In Future	Country	Full-Time	Part-Time	Increase	Language	Answer in English	Job-Hunters	Businesses	Researchers
D	0	Y	Y	*	1	2	Y	E	Y	Y	Y	Y

* E.C. Countries, U.S.A.

SUGAI TRANSLATION ATTORNEY

Translation of various languages.
3-16-1 Otani-machi, Nagata-ku, Kobe 653. 078-611-4144
Sanyo Dentetsu Line, Nishidai. No contact

Size	Overseas Branches	Overseas Experience	In Future	Country	Full-Time	Part-Time	Increase	Language	Answer in English	Job-Hunters	Businesses	Researchers
		N	Y	All					Y	Y		Y

FUJITA TRANSLATION OFFICE, INC.

Law-related translations.
3-18 Banzan-cho, Okayama-shi, Okayama 700. 0862-22-1115
JR Sanyo Line, Okayama. Contact: Mr. Miyake or Mr. Fujita

Size	Overseas Branches	Overseas Experience	In Future	Country	Full-Time	Part-Time	Increase	Language	Answer in English	Job-Hunters	Businesses	Researchers
D		N	N		1	7	Y	E,F,G	Y	Y	Y	Y

FITCEN, LTD.

Translations related to science and technology.
2-16-3 Nogami-cho, Fukuyama 720. 0849-21-2888
JR Sanyo Line, Fukuyama. Contact: Mr. Matsuba Ext. 31

Size	Overseas Branches	Overseas Experience	In Future	Country	Full-Time	Part-Time	Increase	Language	Answer in English	Job-Hunters	Businesses	Researchers
C	0	Y	Y	All			Y	E,F,G	Y	Y	Y	Y

CHAPTER 6. PUBLISHERS, PRINTERS, BOOK-DEALERS, MASS COMMUNICATIONS

Here is an area which might be of interest to all our readers, printing and publishing being a field in which there is opportunity for commerce and also for employment. Many materials are produced in English and other languages in Japan, both for commercial distribution and as publicity. With an increasing number of non-Japanese living in the country, there are also opportunities for importing books and magazines.

There are four English language newspapers published daily, and there are several periodicals in various languages. Television programmes are often broadcast in another language simultaneously with the Japanese transmission. Admittedly, this simultaneous transmission usually consists of the original soundtrack of a film, but there are also news broadcasts in English which have improved in quality in recent years and can now usually be understood, as long as the reader is not required to pronounce difficult names like Edinburgh.

As for employment, although there are plenty of opportunities, many of them are not directly for the publishers, but through agencies, either translation agencies, as in the previous chapter, or advertising agencies, as in the next. However, there are some direct opportunities. The newspapers take most of their news direct from the teleprinter, but still need proofreaders. They also need people to check, and, if necessary, assist with advertisements placed in English. From information received from a friend who worked for a newspaper, it seems that they do not generally encourage native English speakers to write news articles for them, but they do use some feature articles by native English speakers.

The periodicals use native speakers of the language of publication. It is hard work, but you do have the reward of feeling that you have produced something and of being able to see your name in print. There is a demand for short articles, but steady work is much more difficult to obtain in this area. As writers will already be aware, this is not a very good way to get rich, although it is possible to earn some pocket money if you already have some other steady work. Unlike the newspapers, many of the periodicals are run by non-Japanese.

PUBLISHING

Company	Details	Size	Overseas Branches	Overseas Experience	In Future	Country	Non-Japanese: Full-Time	Non-Japanese: Part-Time	Non-Japanese: Increase	Non-Japanese: Language	Answer in English	Answer: Job-Hunters	Answer: Businesses	Answer: Researchers
BORGNAN CORPORATION	Cross-cultural and educational publications. Translation. Interpretation. Dai-san Taihei Bldg., 1-25-3 Higashi Ikebukuro, Toshima-ku, Tokyo 170. JR Yamanote Line, Ikebukuro. Contact: Mr. Kusunoki 03-3980-2041	B	1	Y	Y	UK	6	4	Y	E,Ch	Y	Y	Y	Y
C C H JAPAN LIMITED	Commercial and legal publications. 6th & 7th Fl. Kyobashi MK Bldg., 2-8-2 Kyobashi, Chuo-ku, Tokyo 104. Ginza Line, Kyobashi. Contact: Ms. Mihoko Shiba 03-3563-4591	D	6	Y	N		2	0			Y	N	N	N
CORONA PUBLISHING CO., LTD.	Scientific publications. 4-46-10 Sengoku, Bunkyo-ku, Tokyo 112. 03-3941-3131 Toei Mita Line, Sengoku. No contact	C	0	Y	Y	Eur					N	N	N	N
DAISAN SHOBO PUBLISHERS	Specializing in German and French publications. Also importer. 106 Yarai-cho, Shinjuku-ku, Tokyo 162. 03-3267-8531 Tozai Line, Kagurazaka. Contact: Ms. Hiroko Sakiyama (Yosho-bu)	D	0	N	N		0	0	N		N	N	N	N
DIAMOND, INC. * U.S.A., E.C. Countries	Business publications. 1-4-2 Kasumigaseki, Chiyoda-ku, Tokyo 100-60. 03-3504-6381 Ginza Line, Toranomon. Contact: Mr. K. Saito (Shoseki Shuppan)	B	0	Y	Y	*	0	0	Y		Y	Y	Y	Y
FUKUINKAN SHOTEN, PUBLISHERS INC.	Juvenile publications. 6-6-3 Hon Komagame, Bunkyo-ku, Tokyo 113. 03-3942-0032 Toei Mita or JR Yamanote Line, Sugamo. Contact: Mr.Hozumi (Kaigai-bu)	B	0	Y	Y	Asia	1	0			Y	N	Y	Y
GAKUSEI ENGO-KAI INC.	Publication of job-placement magazines. 2-15 Hon Mura-cho, Ichigaya, Shinjuku-ku, Tokyo 162. 03-3226-3491 Marunouchi or JR Chuo Line, Yotsuya. Contact: Mr. Motoki Yoshimura	A	0	Y	N		8	0	Y	E	Y	N	Y	Y
GRAPHIC-SHA PUBLISHING CO., LTD.	Publication of works related to art, architecture, graphic design, etc. 1-9-12 Kudan Kita, Chiyoda-ku, Tokyo 102. 03-3263-4318 Tozai, Hanzomon or Toei Shinjuku Line, Kudanshita. Contact: Ms. Komanoya		0	Y	Y	All					Y	Y	Y	Y
GOKEN CO., LTD.	Linguistics publications. 2-7-17 Sarugaku-cho, Chiyoda-ku, Tokyo 101. 03-3291-3986 Toei Mita or JR Sobu Line, Suidobashi. Contact: Mr. Okumura 03-3291-6748	C		Y	Y	US					Y	Y	Y	Y

HIROKAWA PUBLISHING COMPANY

Natural science (pharmacy, chemistry, medicine, etc.) publications.
3-27-14 Hongo, Bunkyo-ku, Tokyo 113. 03-3815-3651
Marunouchi Line, Hongo San-chome. Contact: Mr. Haruo Hirokawa

Size	Overseas Branches	Overseas Experience	In Future	Country	Non-Japanese: Full-Time	Part-Time	Increase	Language	Answer in English	Answer: Job-Hunters	Businesses	Researchers
		Y	N						Y	N	Y	Y

INTERCONTINENTAL MARKETING CORPORATION

Publications in English.
Wako Bldg., 1-19-8 Kakigara-cho, Nihonbashi, Chuo-ku, Tokyo 103.
Tozai or Hibiya Line, Kayabacho. Contact: Ms. Kuniko Ito 03-3661-7458

Size	Overseas Branches	Overseas Experience	In Future	Country	Non-Japanese: Full-Time	Part-Time	Increase	Language	Answer in English	Answer: Job-Hunters	Businesses	Researchers
D		Y	Y	*	0	3			Y	Y	Y	Y

* U.S.A., Asia

KAMAKURA SHOBO PUBLISHING CO., LTD.

Publication of various magazines and books on cooking and sewing.
21 Sanai-cho, Ichigaya, Shinjuku-ku, Tokyo 162. 03-3268-2306 Ext. 218
Yurakucho, Toei Shinjuku or JR Sobu Line, Ichigaya. Contact: Mr. Kubota

Size	Overseas Branches	Overseas Experience	In Future	Country	Non-Japanese: Full-Time	Part-Time	Increase	Language	Answer in English	Answer: Job-Hunters	Businesses	Researchers
B		Y	N						Y	Y	Y	Y

KINKI NIPPON TOURIST CO., LTD., PUBLISHING DIVISION ①

Publications on travel and leisure.
19-2 Matsunaga-cho, Kanda, Chiyoda-ku, Tokyo 101. 03-3255-7126
JR Yamanote or Sobu Line, Akihabara. Contact: Mr. Taguchi

Size	Overseas Branches	Overseas Experience	In Future	Country	Non-Japanese: Full-Time	Part-Time	Increase	Language	Answer in English	Answer: Job-Hunters	Businesses	Researchers
A	23	N	N							Y	Y	Y

KODANSHA INTERNATIONAL LTD.

English publications.
Otowa YK Bldg., 1-17-14 Otowa, Bunkyo-ku, Tokyo 112. 03-3944-6491
Yurakucho Line, Gokokuji. Contact: Mr. Higuchi (Somu-bu) Ext. 602

Size	Overseas Branches	Overseas Experience	In Future	Country	Non-Japanese: Full-Time	Part-Time	Increase	Language	Answer in English	Answer: Job-Hunters	Businesses	Researchers
C	2	Y	Y		10	0	Y	E	Y	Y	Y	Y

LOOK JAPAN, LTD.

Monthly magazines in English and Spanish. 03-3291-8962
8F Center Crest Bldg., 2-2 Ogawa-cho, Kanda, Chiyoda-ku, Tokyo 101.
Chiyoda Line, Shin Ochanomizu. Contact: Mr. Kunio Nishimura

Size	Overseas Branches	Overseas Experience	In Future	Country	Non-Japanese: Full-Time	Part-Time	Increase	Language	Answer in English	Answer: Job-Hunters	Businesses	Researchers
C	3	Y	Y		3	0			Y	Y	Y	Y

MERIT 5 CO., LTD.

Publication of newspaper.
2-8-13 Shiba, Minato-ku, Tokyo 105. 03-3457-7541
Toei Mita Line, Shiba Koen. Contact: Mr. Shiroyama

Size	Overseas Branches	Overseas Experience	In Future	Country	Non-Japanese: Full-Time	Part-Time	Increase	Language	Answer in English	Answer: Job-Hunters	Businesses	Researchers
C	0	N	N		3	2			N	N	Y	N

MORIKITA SHUPPAN CO., LTD.

Scientific and technological publications.
1-4-11 Fujimi, Chiyoda-ku, Tokyo 102. 03-3265-8341
Tozai, Yurakucho or JR Sobu Line, Iidabashi. Contact: Mr. K. Tonegawa

Size	Overseas Branches	Overseas Experience	In Future	Country	Non-Japanese: Full-Time	Part-Time	Increase	Language	Answer in English	Answer: Job-Hunters	Businesses	Researchers
C	0	Y	N		0	0	N		N	N	N	N

NIGENSHA PUBLISHING CO., LTD.

Publications of works on calligraphy, art, motor vehicles.
2-42 Kanda Jimbo-cho, Chiyoda-ku, Tokyo 101. 03-3239-0141
Hanzomon, Toei Mita, Shinjuku Line, Jimbocho. Contact: Mr. Kobayashi (Somu-bu)

Size	Overseas Branches	Overseas Experience	In Future	Country	Non-Japanese: Full-Time	Part-Time	Increase	Language	Answer in English	Answer: Job-Hunters	Businesses	Researchers
B	0	Y	Y	All	0	1			N	N	Y	Y

NOBUNKYO

Publications on foods, education, health and agriculture and for juveniles.
7-6-1 Akasaka, Minato-ku, Tokyo 107. 03-3585-1141
Maunouchi or Ginza Line, Akasaka Mitsuke. No contact

Size	Overseas Branches	Overseas Experience	In Future	Country	Non-Japanese: Full-Time	Part-Time	Increase	Language	Answer in English	Answer: Job-Hunters	Businesses	Researchers
B												

	Size	Overseas Branches	Overseas Experience	In Future	Country	Non-Japanese: Full-Time	Non-Japanese: Part-Time	Non-Japanese: Increase	Non-Japanese: Language	Answer in English	Answer: Job-Hunters	Answer: Businesses	Answer: Researchers
NOVA INCORPORATED	D		N			0	4	Y	E	Y	Y	Y	Y
P H P INSTITUTE, INC.	B	2	Y	Y	*	3	1	Y	E	Y	Y	Y	Y
PIA CORPORATION	B	0	Y	N		0	0	N		N	N	Y	N
PUBLISHERS ASSOCIATION FOR CULTURAL EXCHANGE (C)	D	0	N	N							N	N	Y
RINSEN BOOK CO., LTD.	C	0	Y	Y	US,F					Y	Y	Y	Y
RON RHODES OFFICE Y.K.	D		Y	Y	US,G			Y	E	Y	Y	Y	Y
SAN-EI SHOBO PUBLISHING CO.	C		Y	N							Y		
THE CENTER FOR EAST ASIAN CULTURAL STUDIES OF JAPAN FOR UNESCO	D		N	N		0	1			Y	N	N	Y
TOKUMA SHOTEN PUBLISHING CO., LTD.	B	3	Y	Y	*	0	0	N		Y	Y	N	Y
TOKYODO SHUPPAN	C	0	N	N						N	N	N	N

NOVA INCORPORATED

English magazine.
2-5-18 Utsubo Hon-machi, Nishi-ku, Osaka 550. 06-445-7531
Yotsubashi, Midosuji or Chuo Line, Honmachi. Contact: Mr. Yamamoto

P H P INSTITUTE, INC.

Publication of English books, magazines and video tapes. Seminars.
3-10 Sanban-cho, Chiyoda-ku, Tokyo 107. 03-3239-6238
Hanzomon Line, Hanzomon. Contact: Mr. Sayama (Intersect Henshu-bu)

* U.S.A., S.E. Asia

PIA CORPORATION

Publication of entertainment magazine and sales of tickets.
2-5 Koji-machi, Chiyoda-ku, Tokyo 102. 03-3261-9111
Hanzomon Line, Hanzomon. No contact

PUBLISHERS ASSOCIATION FOR CULTURAL EXCHANGE (C)

Publication of 'Guide to Publishing Industry in Japan'.
1-2-1 Sarugaku-cho, Chiyoda-ku, Tokyo 101. 03-3291-5685
JR Chuo Line, Ochanomizu. No contact

RINSEN BOOK CO., LTD.

Academic publications. Import of foreign classical books.
Kawabata Higashi Iru, Imaidegawa Dori, Sakyo-ku, Kyoto 606.
Keihan Line, Demachi Yanagi. 075-721-7111 No contact

RON RHODES OFFICE Y.K.

Media services, consultation on publishing, editorial work, design, etc.
2-17-13 Unoki, Ota-ku, Tokyo 146. 03-3757-3286
Tokyu Mekama Line, Unoki. Contact: Mr. Rhodes

SAN-EI SHOBO PUBLISHING CO.

Magazines on automobiles.
4-8-16 Kita Shinjuku, Shinjuku-ku, Tokyo 169. 03-3364-3812
Tozai or JR Yamanote Line, Takadanobaba. No contact

THE CENTER FOR EAST ASIAN CULTURAL STUDIES OF JAPAN FOR UNESCO

English publications. Academic information. 03-3942-0124
Toyo Bunko, 2-28-21 Hon Komagome, Bunkyo-ku, Tokyo 113.
JR Yamanote Line, Komagome. Contact: Mr. Takeshi Oi Ext. 261

TOKUMA SHOTEN PUBLISHING CO., LTD.

Various publications.
4-10-1 Shinbashi, Minato-ku, Tokyo 105-55. 03-3433-6231 Ext. 661
Ginza, Toei Asakusa or JR Yamanote Line, Shinbashi. Contact: Mr. Hagiwara

* U.S.A., Europe

TOKYODO SHUPPAN

Dictionaries, encyclopedias and other publications.
3-7 Kanda Nishiki-cho, Chiyoda-ku, Tokyo 101. 03-3233-3741
Tozai Line, Takebashi. No contact

Column headings: Size | Overseas Branches | Overseas Experience | In Future | Country | ←Non-Japanese→ Full-Time | Part-Time | Increase | Language | Answer in English | ←Answer→ Job-Hunters | Businesses | Researchers

TOKYO TODAY MAGAZINE

Publication of magazine.
3-14-12-505 Roppongi, Minato-ku, Tokyo 106. 03-3423-0660
Hibiya Line, Roppongi. Contact: Mr. Allan Gruhl

Size	Overseas Branches	Overseas Experience	In Future	Country	Full-Time	Part-Time	Increase	Language	Answer in English	Job-Hunters	Businesses	Researchers
C	0	N	N		5	15	Y	E	Y	Y	Y	Y

TOYO KEIZAI INC.

Business publications.
1-2-1 Hongoku-cho, Nihonbashi, Chuo-ku, Tokyo 103. 03-3246-5655
Hanzomon or Ginza Line, Mitsukoshi-mae. Contact: (Kokusai Gyomu-shitsu)

Size	Overseas Branches	Overseas Experience	In Future	Country	Full-Time	Part-Time	Increase	Language	Answer in English	Job-Hunters	Businesses	Researchers
B	1	N			2	2			Y	N	Y	Y

UNIVERSITY OF TOKYO PRESS (F)

Scholarly publications (in both Japanese and English).
University of Tokyo, 7-3-1 Hongo, Bunkyo-ku, Tokyo 113. 03-3815-1900
Marunouchi Line, Hongo San-chome. Contact: Mr. Masami Yamaguchi

Size	Overseas Branches	Overseas Experience	In Future	Country	Full-Time	Part-Time	Increase	Language	Answer in English	Job-Hunters	Businesses	Researchers
C	0	Y	N		2	0			Y	Y	Y	Y

YUZANKAKU PUBLISHING CO., LTD.

Publications, especially on Japanese history.
2-6-9 Fujimi, Chiyoda-ku, Tokyo 102. 03-3262-3231
Tozai, Yurakucho or JR Sobu Line, Iidabashi. No contact

* U.S.A., Europe

Size	Overseas Branches	Overseas Experience	In Future	Country	Full-Time	Part-Time	Increase	Language	Answer in English	Job-Hunters	Businesses	Researchers
C		N	Y	*							Y	Y

DISTRIBUTORS OF PUBLICATIONS

JAPAN PUBLICATIONS TRADING CO., LTD.

Distributor. Also importer and exporter.
1-2-1 Sarugaku-cho, Chiyoda-ku, Tokyo 101. 03-3292-3751
Hanzomon or Toei Mita or Shinjuku Line, Jimbocho. No contact

Size	Overseas Branches	Overseas Experience	In Future	Country	Full-Time	Part-Time	Increase	Language	Answer in English	Job-Hunters	Businesses	Researchers
B	3	Y	Y		0	0	N			N	N	Y

MARUZEN COMPANY, LIMITED ①

Distributor. Also importer, exporter and retailer.
2-3-10 Nihonbashi, Chuo-ku, Tokyo 103. 03-3272-7021
Tozai, Ginza or Toei Asakusa Line, Nihonbashi. Contact: Mr. Hiraga Ext.2235

Size	Overseas Branches	Overseas Experience	In Future	Country	Full-Time	Part-Time	Increase	Language	Answer in English	Job-Hunters	Businesses	Researchers
A	3	Y	Y		0	0			N	Y	Y	Y

NAUKA LTD.

Distributor. Also importer, exporter and book retailer.
30-19 Minami Ikebukuro, Toshima-ku, Tokyo 171. 03-3981-5265
JR Yamanote Line, Ikebukuro. Contact: Mr. Yuichi Hirano (Export Dept.)

Size	Overseas Branches	Overseas Experience	In Future	Country	Full-Time	Part-Time	Increase	Language	Answer in English	Job-Hunters	Businesses	Researchers
C	0	Y	Y	Eur					Y	N	Y	Y

NIPPON SHUPPAN HANBAI INC.

Distributor of books, compact discs, video tapes.
4-3 Surugadai, Kanda, Chiyoda-ku, Tokyo 101. 03-3233-1111
JR Chuo Line, Ochanomizu. Contact: Mr. Ishikawa (Kokusai-bu)

* U.S.A., Europe
¶ French, Korean

Size	Overseas Branches	Overseas Experience	In Future	Country	Full-Time	Part-Time	Increase	Language	Answer in English	Job-Hunters	Businesses	Researchers
A	5	Y	Y	*	2	1	Y	¶	N	N	Y	N

TOHAN CORPORATION

Distributor.
6-24 Higashi Goken-cho, Shinjuku-ku, Tokyo 162. 03-3266-9593
JR Sobu Line, Iidabashi. Contact: Ms. Yuasa (Kaigai-jigyo Kaihatsu-ka)

* Asia, Europe, U.S.A.

Size	Overseas Branches	Overseas Experience	In Future	Country	Full-Time	Part-Time	Increase	Language	Answer in English	Job-Hunters	Businesses	Researchers
A	1	Y	Y	*	1	0			Y	N	N	N

Header groups: ⟵Non-Japanese⟶ (Full-Time, Part-Time, Increase, Language); ⟵Answer⟶ (Job-Hunters, Businesses, Researchers)

WESTERN PUBLICATIONS DISTRIBUTION AGENCY

Distributor of foreign books and periodicals.
3-14-9 Okubo, Shinjuku-ku, Tokyo 169. 03-3208-0184
JR Yamanote Line, Takadanobaba. Contact: Mr. Murayama (Shi-ire-bu)

Size	Overseas Branches	Overseas Experience	In Future	Country	Full-Time	Part-Time	Increase	Language	Answer in English	Job-Hunters	Businesses	Researchers
B	2	Y	Y	*	2	2	Y		Y	N	N	N

* U.S.A., U.K., Europe

BOOKSELLERS

ADDISON-WESLEY PUBLISHERS JAPAN LTD.

Importer and exporter. 03-3291-4581
Nichibo Building, 1-2-2 Sarugaku-cho, Chiyoda-ku, Tokyo 101.
Hanzomon or Toei Mita or Shinjuku Line, Jimbocho. No contact

Size	Overseas Branches	Overseas Experience	In Future	Country	Full-Time	Part-Time	Increase	Language	Answer in English	Job-Hunters	Businesses	Researchers
D					0	0	N			N	N	N

BAKER & TAYLOR INTERNATIONAL LTD., JAPAN BRANCH

Wholesaler for American publications.
5th Fl. Tamaya Building, 40-30-14 Honcho, Nakano-ku, Tokyo 164.
Marunouchi Line, Shin Nakano. Contact: Ms. Akemi Goto 03-5340-3561

Size	Overseas Branches	Overseas Experience	In Future	Country	Full-Time	Part-Time	Increase	Language	Answer in English	Job-Hunters	Businesses	Researchers
D		N	N		1				Y	Y	Y	N

DAI-ITI PUBLICATIONS TRADING CO., LTD.

Importer and retailer of electronic, electrical and other scientific books.
Shinjuku Q Flat Building, 5-4-1 Shinjuku, Shinjuku-ku, Tokyo 160.
Marunouchi Line, Shinjuku Gyoen-mae. Contact: Mr. Mitonoya 03-3352-4541

Size	Overseas Branches	Overseas Experience	In Future	Country	Full-Time	Part-Time	Increase	Language	Answer in English	Job-Hunters	Businesses	Researchers
D	0	Y	Y	*	0	1	Y	E	Y	Y	N	N

* U.S.A., U.K., Germany, Netherlands and others

HARPER COLLINS JAPAN INC.

Liaison office for sales promotion in Japan and Korea.
1-2-1 Sarugaku-cho, Chiyoda-ku, Tokyo 101. 03-3291-6343
Hanzomon or Toei Mita or Shinjuku Line, Jimbocho. Contact: Mr. Foley

Size	Overseas Branches	Overseas Experience	In Future	Country	Full-Time	Part-Time	Increase	Language	Answer in English	Job-Hunters	Businesses	Researchers
D		Y	Y	*	2	0	N		Y	N	Y	N

* U.S.A., U.K., Australia

HEINEMANN INTERNATIONAL

Branch office for sales promotion. 03-3294-0791
Shin Nichibo Building, 1-2-1 Sarugaku-cho, Chiyoda-ku, Tokyo 101.
Hanzomon or Toei Mita or Shinjuku Line, Jimbocho. Contact: Ms. Yamakawa

Size	Overseas Branches	Overseas Experience	In Future	Country	Full-Time	Part-Time	Increase	Language	Answer in English	Job-Hunters	Businesses	Researchers
D		Y	Y	Asia	2	1	Y	E		N		

KITAZAWA BOOKSTORE CO., LTD.

Importer and retailer of western literature.
2-5 Jimbo-cho, Kanda, Chiyoda-ku, Tokyo 101. 03-3263-0011
Hanzomon or Toei Mita or Shinjuku Line, Jimbocho. No contact

Size	Overseas Branches	Overseas Experience	In Future	Country	Full-Time	Part-Time	Increase	Language	Answer in English	Job-Hunters	Businesses	Researchers
C	0	Y	Y	*						N	Y	Y

* U.K., U.S.A.

LONGMAN PENGUIN JAPAN CO., LTD.

Sales and promotion of publications. 03-3266-0459
Gyokuroen Building, 1-13-19 Sekiguchi, Bunkyo-ku, Tokyo 112.
Yurakucho Line, Edogawabashi. Contact: Ms.Inaba 03-3266-1141

Size	Overseas Branches	Overseas Experience	In Future	Country	Full-Time	Part-Time	Increase	Language	Answer in English	Job-Hunters	Businesses	Researchers
C		Y			4	0				N	N	N

O E C D PUBLICATIONS AND INFORMATION CENTRE, TOKYO (SG)

Sales promotion and PR activities related to OECD. 03-3586-2016
Landic Akasaka Building, 2-3-4 Akasaka, Minato-ku, Tokyo 107.
Marunouchi or Chiyoda Line, Kokkai Gijido-mae. Contact: Mr. Amano

Size	Overseas Branches	Overseas Experience	In Future	Country	Full-Time	Part-Time	Increase	Language	Answer in English	Job-Hunters	Businesses	Researchers
		Y	Y	Asia	1	0			Y	Y	N	Y

Size	Overseas Branches	Overseas Experience	In Future	Country	Non-Japanese Full-Time	Non-Japanese Part-Time	Non-Japanese Increase	Non-Japanese Language	Answer in English	Answer Job-Hunters	Answer Businesses	Answer Researchers

OSAKA OVISS INCORPORATED

Importer of scientific books and journals. 06-352-7090
Higashi 6-go Kan, 7-22 Matsugae-cho, Kita-ku, Osaka 530.
Tanimachi or Sakaisuji Line, Minami Morimachi. Contact: Mr. Saito

Size	Overseas Branches	Overseas Experience	In Future	Country	Full-Time	Part-Time	Increase	Language	Answer in English	Job-Hunters	Businesses	Researchers
D		Y	Y	*					Y	N	Y	Y

* U.S.A., Europe

OXFORD UNIVERSITY PRESS, JAPAN BRANCH

Branch office.
2-4-8 Kaname-cho, Toshima-ku, Tokyo 171. 03-5995-3441
Yurakucho Line, Kanamecho. Contact: Mr. Stephen Ziolkowski

Size	Overseas Branches	Overseas Experience	In Future	Country	Full-Time	Part-Time	Increase	Language	Answer in English	Job-Hunters	Businesses	Researchers
C					3	0			Y	Y	Y	Y

PRENTICE HALL REGENTS CO., INC.

Importer, publisher and distributor of educational books, CDs, videos.
3rd Fl. Jochi Kojimachi Bldg., 6-1-25 Kojimachi, Chiyoda-ku, Tokyo 102.
Marunouchi or JR Chuo Line, Yotsuya. Contact: Mr. Ono 03-3238-1050

Size	Overseas Branches	Overseas Experience	In Future	Country	Full-Time	Part-Time	Increase	Language	Answer in English	Job-Hunters	Businesses	Researchers
C		Y	Y	US	2	0			Y	N	Y	Y

THOMSON PUBLISHING JAPAN

Branch office. Importer.
1-7-11 Hirakawa-cho, Chiyoda-ku, Tokyo 102. 03-3221-1385
Hanzomon Line, Hanzomon. Contact: Ms. Hisae Inami

Size	Overseas Branches	Overseas Experience	In Future	Country	Full-Time	Part-Time	Increase	Language	Answer in English	Job-Hunters	Businesses	Researchers
C		Y	Y	*	1	0	Y	E	Y	Y	Y	Y

* U.S.A., U.K.

WAKO YOSHO HANBAI K.K.

International publications.
2-22-16 Yagumo, Meguro-ku, Tokyo 152. 03-3717-9568
Tokyu Toyoko Line, Toritsu Daigaku. Contact: Mr. Hiroshi Fukuda

Size	Overseas Branches	Overseas Experience	In Future	Country	Full-Time	Part-Time	Increase	Language	Answer in English	Job-Hunters	Businesses	Researchers
D		Y	Y		0	0	N		Y	N	Y	

Column key (left to right): Size · Overseas Branches · Overseas Experience · In Future · Country · Non-Japanese: Full-Time · Part-Time · Increase · Language · Answer in English · Answer: Job-Hunters · Businesses · Researchers

MASS COMMUNICATIONS

AGENCE FRANCE-PRESSE

Gathering, editing and distributing news. 03-3545-3061
11th Fl. Asahi Shinbun-sha, 5-3-2 Tsukiji, Chuo-ku, Tokyo 104.
Hibiya or Toei Asakusa Line, Higashi Ginza. Contact: Ms. Shibata

Size	Overseas Branches	Overseas Experience	In Future	Country	Full-Time	Part-Time	Increase	Language	Answer in English	Job-Hunters	Businesses	Researchers
C	120	N	N		4	0	N		Y	N	N	N

BRITISH BROADCASTING CORPORATION

Distributing news. 03-3288-0011
Nihon TV Yonban-cho Bekkan, 5-6 Yonban-cho, Chiyoda-ku, Tokyo 102.
Yurakucho, Toei Shinjuku or JR Sobu Line, Ichigaya. No contact

Size	Overseas Branches	Overseas Experience	In Future	Country	Full-Time	Part-Time	Increase	Language	Answer in English	Job-Hunters	Businesses	Researchers

FOREIGN PRESS CENTER / JAPAN

Support for reporters from overseas.
2-2-1 Uchi Saiwai-cho, Chiyoda-ku, Tokyo 100. 03-3501-3401
Marunouchi, Chiyoda or Hibiya Line, Kasumigaseki. Contact: (Any officer)

Size	Overseas Branches	Overseas Experience	In Future	Country	Full-Time	Part-Time	Increase	Language	Answer in English	Job-Hunters	Businesses	Researchers
C	0	N	N						Y			Y

THE JAPAN TIMES, LTD.

English newspaper. Publication of English books.
4-5-4 Shibaura, Minato-ku, Tokyo 108. 03-3453-5314
JR Yamanote Line, Tamachi. Contact: (Henshu Kyoku-cho)

Size	Overseas Branches	Overseas Experience	In Future	Country	Full-Time	Part-Time	Increase	Language	Answer in English	Job-Hunters	Businesses	Researchers
B	1	Y	Y	All	45	0	Y	E		Y	Y	

KYODO NEWS SERVICE INC.

Gathering, editing and distributing news.
2-2-5 Toranomon, Minato-ku, Tokyo 105. 03-3584-4111
Ginza Line, Toranomon. Contact: Mr. S. Hiyama Ext. 3722 (Int'l Dept.)

Size	Overseas Branches	Overseas Experience	In Future	Country	Full-Time	Part-Time	Increase	Language	Answer in English	Job-Hunters	Businesses	Researchers
A	39	N	N		10	20	Y	E	Y	Y	Y	Y

THE MAINICHI NEWSPAPERS CO., LTD.

Publication of newspaper and books.
1-1-1 Hitotsubashi, Chiyoda-ku, Tokyo 100-51. 03-3212-0321
Tozai Line, Takebashi. Contact: Mr. Hikino Ext. 7510 (Eibun Mainichi)

Size	Overseas Branches	Overseas Experience	In Future	Country	Full-Time	Part-Time	Increase	Language	Answer in English	Job-Hunters	Businesses	Researchers
A	26	N	N		25	0			Y	Y	Y	Y

THE YOMIURI SHIMBUN-SHA

Publication of newspaper and books.
1-7-1 Otemachi, Chiyoda-ku, Tokyo 100-55. 03-3242-1111
Various subway lines, Otemachi. Contact: Mr. Sato Ext. 3750

Size	Overseas Branches	Overseas Experience	In Future	Country	Full-Time	Part-Time	Increase	Language	Answer in English	Job-Hunters	Businesses	Researchers
					50	10				Y	Y	Y

DAI NIPPON PRINTING CO., LTD. ①

Various kinds of printing.
1-1-1 Ichigaya Kaga-cho, Shinjuku-ku, Tokyo 162-01. 03-3266-2111
Yurakucho, Toei Shinjuku, JR Sobu Line, Ichigaya. Contact: Mr. Fujii 03-3266-3390

Size	Overseas Branches	Overseas Experience	In Future	Country	Full-Time	Part-Time	Increase	Language	Answer in English	Job-Hunters	Businesses	Researchers
A	12	Y	Y	*	1	0			Y	N	Y	N

* U.S.A., Europe, Asia and elsewhere

JAPAN TELECOM CO., LTD. (L)

Long distance telephone company.
4-1-7 Kudan Kita, Chiyoda-ku, Tokyo 102. 03-3222-6657
JR Sobu Line, Ichigaya. Contact: Mr. Yamamoto (Keiei Kikaku-bu)

Size	Overseas Branches	Overseas Experience	In Future	Country	Full-Time	Part-Time	Increase	Language	Answer in English	Job-Hunters	Businesses	Researchers

CHAPTER 7. ADVERTISING

Here is an area of great potential interest to our job-seekers, especially those with interest or experience in the field. As Japanese products become recognized throughout the world for their combination of quality and reasonable price, more and more companies take an interest in the export market. And advertising is one area where, fortunately, they feel that they cannot manage without help.

The major Japanese advertising agencies are huge and control the market almost entirely. They are very powerful politically as well as within their industry, which is a good reason for clients to continue to use their services. The two best known agencies are Dentsu and Hakuhodo. These agencies do employ some non-Japanese, but not, of course, in very important positions. To work for such influential companies, an appropriate background will usually be necessary, but then the employee is likely to be dis-satisfied by the rather mundane level of work required of him. These major companies tend to recruit directly from overseas or, as might be imagined from their background, through connexions which they have established.

What is perhaps surprising is that in this apparently monopolistic atmosphere so many tiny advertising companies also manage to survive, and indeed thrive. They do this by being cheaper than the big names and by having connexions. The advertising industry is so big in Japan that the larger concerns often cannot handle all that they have to do, so pass on segments of work down the line to sub-contractors. In fact, this style of business is common throughout Japan. It enables everybody to make a profit and, in the end, of course, it is the consumer who will pay for it.

It is these smaller concerns which often need the non-Japanese manpower, for overseas advertising is less prestigious work than that for the domestic market — and more difficult too — so it is one of the likely areas to be farmed off or to go to a smaller company in the first place. The opportunities are more far-ranging than one might realize at first. First of all there are the ordinary advertisements placed in newspapers and periodicals. Additionally, though, many companies have started producing public relations materials in English — magazines for their distributors or trade-related journals for their clients. Then there are advertising videos, Christmas cards, diaries, annual reports, brochures and a wealth of other propaganda. It is not just a question of writing ability. Good readers will be needed to record the soundtracks for videos, for example. Specialists may be used (and paid well), but a good all-round non-Japanese can be a very useful acquisition for a small advertising agency, where he is likely to have considerably more responsibility than he would for a larger company.

Even so, it is necessary to keep in mind that, in Japan, the client is the boss. Even though you may think that you know better about the western environment, your opinion is not necessarily going to be asked and even though ridiculous decisions are made by the client, you are not at liberty to comment on them unless asked, and even then only in a mild way. This, of course, is a remark which could be made about virtually all work in Japan, but those involved with advertising may feel particularly tempted to give their gratuitous opinions.

If another anecdote may be tolerated, the writer was once dealing with a large company which gave away annually to its international customers a diary. The diary had a series of maps at the back riddled with spelling errors. France, for example, was marked as 'Frence' on one page and 'French' on another. I suggested that some of the overseas customers would not find the mis-naming of their countries very polite and it was eventually agreed that a meeting would be held, with the producer of the diary as well as the client company present, and that I would be permitted to attend. At first the producer of the diary claimed that there could not possibly be any mistakes because the maps had the name of a famous professor of Tokyo University on them. When a large atlas was fetched, however, it became difficult to maintain this opinion. It also transpired that the professor in question had departed this mortal life nearly two decades earlier and might not, therefore, be overly offended if some necessary modifications were made. Finally, the client company, the name of which would appear on the diary, said that, as a compromise, it would like the names of the countries to be corrected, but that it would not bother about the mis-spelling of the names of cities and towns. (I am not making this up, honestly!) When I rashly expressed my opinion that this was one of the most absurd compromises that I had ever heard, especially as it would cost just as much as doing the job properly, an ominous silence descended over the meeting and I was never permitted to attend another one. The names of the cities and towns were never corrected.

Because there seems to be so much money available for advertising and related work, this industry offers reasonable pay. For a full-time position, one can probably expect something in the region of ¥300,000 per month as a starting salary, although small agencies may not necessarily be able to offer full-time work, at least initially. Remember also that this is another area in which pressure from time is likely to be intense. It is essential to keep deadlines, even at the expense of quality, as so often with paperwork in Japan.

Domestic advertising is quite different from the overseas type, which is one reason why client companies may seem to make very strange decisions. In Japan it is image which counts. One can watch advertisements on television, for example, and have no idea what they are for. Cuddly animals may be used to sell machinery or soft drinks, simply because Japanese like cuddly animals. A few years ago, a particular brand of beer became very popular simply because it had penguins on the can! Therefore, non-Japanese are not likely to be asked to do much in relation to the domestic market, except possibly to record a few words of nonsense English to be used in a fashionable television advertisement. However, merely working in an agency where such work is going on is likely to give experience which would be valuable to somebody returning to the advertising industry in his native land.

As for advertising in Japan by overseas companies, there are some advertising agencies from abroad, primarily from the United States, which have established offices here, despite the difficulties of entering a market which is already controlled tightly by the big names. These non-Japanese companies handle a large proportion of business from or for overseas. Of course, they need non-Japanese staff too, but they usually have their own, brought with them and paid rather handsome salaries. However, if you have a great deal of experience in the industry, you could try contacting such organizations.

For businesses which want to advertise themselves in Japan, the companies referred to in the previous paragraph would, no doubt, be delighted to handle your business, but any of the smaller agents listed below might be equally happy and should be capable of communicating in English if they already handle overseas advertising.

Company	Size	Overseas Branches	Overseas Experience	In Future	Country	Non-Japanese: Full-Time	Non-Japanese: Part-Time	Non-Japanese: Increase	Non-Japanese: Language	Answer in English	Answer: Job-Hunters	Answer: Businesses	Answer: Researchers
DAIKO ADVERTISING INC.	A	5	Y	Y	Asia	2	0			Y	N	Y	Y
DENTSU INC.	A		Y	Y	Eur			Y	*	Y	N	Y	Y
LEO BURNETT-KYODO CO., LTD.	B		Y	Y	*	26	0				N	N	N
PRAP JAPAN INC.	C	0	Y	Y	US					Y	Y	Y	N
SAATCHI & SAATCHI ADVERTISING	C		Y	Y	*	6	0	Y	E	Y	Y	Y	Y
STONE WELL CO., LTD.	C	0	Y	N							N	N	N

DAIKO ADVERTISING INC.

Advertising agent.
2-4-1 Shiba Koen, Minato-ku, Tokyo 105. 03-3437-8086
Toei Asakusa Line, Daimon. Contact: Mr. Hori (Kokusai Honbu)

DENTSU INC.

Advertising agent. Planning of various events.
1-11 Tsukiji, Chuo-ku, Tokyo 104. 03-3544-5937
Hibiya or Toei Asakusa Line, Higashi Ginza. Contact: Mr. Fujito (Kaigai Jigyo)

* English, French, German, Spanish, Chinese, Russian

LEO BURNETT-KYODO CO., LTD.

Advertising agent.
2-17-22 Akasaka, Minato-ku, Tokyo 107. 03-5563-8458
Marunouchi or Chiyoda Line, Kokkai Gijido-mae. Contact: Ms. Hata (Somu-bu)

* U.S.A., U.K., France, Australia, Hong Kong

PRAP JAPAN INC.

Advertising agent.
NES Bldg. 22-14 Sakuragaoka, Shibuya-ku, Tokyo 150. 03-3496-2351
Marunouchi, Hanzomon or JR Yamanote Line, Shibuya. Contact: (Kokusai-bu)

SAATCHI & SAATCHI ADVERTISING

Overseas advertising for Japanese organizations.
9-2-16 Akasaka, Minato-ku, Tokyo 107. 03-5410-8602
Hibiya Line, Roppongi. Contact: Ms. Yamaoki (Management)

* U.S.A., Europe, Asia

STONE WELL CO., LTD.

Advertising agent.
Fugetsudo Bldg., 6-6-1 Ginza, Chuo-ku, Tokyo 104. 03-3572-0355
Ginza, Marunouchi or Hibiya Line, Ginza. No contact

CHAPTER 8. FINANCE

In the last decade, the financial sector has been booming in Japan. The passing of new regulations in the 1980s opened up the market and allowed overseas institutions to do business relatively freely here. These regulations also persuaded Japanese companies of the necessity of introducing some non-Japanese members of staff into their organizations.

However, the situation changed suddenly in 1992 when, as one cannot avoid hearing again and again, "the bubble burst". Since then prices on the Tokyo Stock Exchange have declined dramatically and all companies concerned with finance have started to re-examine their operations, especially as several dubious practices amongst banks and securities companies have come to light recently.

One might think, therefore, that the days when jobs with financial institutions in Japan could be found are now gone. Indeed, this writer thought that that would be the case. However, I was told, to my surprise, that there is still a demand for financial specialists – and, of course, the financial market will recover, even if it is obliged to act with more prudence in future.

Job-hunters should not make any mistake about this sector, however. Positions here are not for amateurs or for casual employment. They are for those who want to make a career in finance, or, preferably, for those who have already started to do so.

There are, basically, two types of position – with Japanese companies or with overseas companies. The former are likely to be more interesting, but the latter are likely to be better paid. In general, good Japanese ability is required for any job, because of the need for communication with Japanese clients.

Japanese companies are most likely to accept applicants who have worked for overseas financial institutions and can provide information about how they are operating or, better still, of course, can offer connexions promising new clients. Specialized knowledge of a particular field of finance would be an acceptable alternative. Although companies might prefer non-Japanese to work as ordinary members of staff, at ordinary salaries, the prospective employees usually wish for much more lucrative short-term contracts. However, even the former method of employment would provide valuable experience which might help in the obtaining of an interesting post with a non-Japanese concern later.

Non-Japanese companies usually bring the majority of their staff from home, a costly business, so they may be interested in recruiting a suitable person locally, not, however, at the expense of sacrificing quality. Again the point needs to be made that this is a field for professionals.

Since high standards are required, a relatively high salary is to be expected, the only exception being for those who work with Japanese companies as ordinary members of staff.

Where should one look for a position in the financial sector? If it is to be with a non-Japanese company, it is probably best to apply directly to the company, either in Japan or overseas. If it is to be with a Japanese company, the best course might be to try to work through a placement company. A good alternative would be to get an introduction through a friend or acquaintance, which would be considered a very good recommendation. If you look in the newspaper, you will find advertisements for positions of this type and can apply for them. In reality, though, although it may often seem that the advertisements have been inserted by the institutions concerned, you may well find that many of them have actually been inserted by placement companies and it is with them that you will have to deal.

Financial institutions are looking for people from many different countries, including Asian nations, and M.B.A. degrees seem to be highly regarded. A degree of some sort is almost essential and particular regard is often paid to which particular university granted it.

Typical duties include writing financial documents, dealing with overseas communications, translation, rewriting, financial research, credit analysis, assessment of overseas financial proposals and portfolio management. Nobody is expected to perform all of these functions, of course, but experience or specialization in any one of them would probably be regarded as a merit.

BANKS

ARAB BANKING CORPORATION

Tokyo representative office. 03-3245-0415
Akiyama Building, 4-1-12 Nihonbashi Honcho, Chuo-ku, Tokyo 103.
JR Sobu (Kaisoku) Line, Shin Nihonbashi. Contact: Ms. Junko Hisano

Size	Overseas Branches	Overseas Experience	In Future	Country	Non-Japanese Full-Time	Non-Japanese Part-Time	Non-Japanese Increase	Non-Japanese Language	Answer in English	Answer Job-Hunters	Answer Businesses	Answer Researchers
		N			1	0			Y	N	Y	Y

BANK OF NEW ZEALAND

Banking business.
1-3 Kanda Ogawa-machi, Chiyoda-ku, Tokyo 101. 03-3291-5651
Toei Shinjuku Line, Ogawamachi. Contact: Ms. Wakasugi

Size	Overseas Branches	Overseas Experience	In Future	Country	Non-Japanese Full-Time	Non-Japanese Part-Time	Non-Japanese Increase	Non-Japanese Language	Answer in English	Answer Job-Hunters	Answer Businesses	Answer Researchers
C		N	N		2	0			Y	N	N	N

THE FUJI BANK, LTD. ①

Banking business.
1-5-5 Otemachi, Chiyoda-ku, Tokyo 100. 03-3216-2211
Various subway lines, Otemachi. Contact: (Kokusai Sokatsu-bu, Kikaku-ka)

Size	Overseas Branches	Overseas Experience	In Future	Country	Non-Japanese Full-Time	Non-Japanese Part-Time	Non-Japanese Increase	Non-Japanese Language	Answer in English	Answer Job-Hunters	Answer Businesses	Answer Researchers
A	17	Y							Y	Y		

Z-LÄNDERBANK BANK AUSTRIA AG

Tokyo representative office. 03-3501-8631
6th Fl. Imperial Tower, 1-1-1 Uchi Saiwai-cho, Chiyoda-ku, Tokyo 100.
Chiyoda, Hibiya or Toei Mita Line, Hibiya. Contact: Ms. Akiko Yagi

Size	Overseas Branches	Overseas Experience	In Future	Country	Non-Japanese Full-Time	Non-Japanese Part-Time	Non-Japanese Increase	Non-Japanese Language	Answer in English	Answer Job-Hunters	Answer Businesses	Answer Researchers
		N			2	0			Y	N	Y	Y

THE BANK OF IKEDA, LTD. ①

Banking business.
2-1-11 Jonan, Ikeda-shi, Osaka 563. 0727-51-3521
Hankyu Takarazuka Line, Ikeda. Contact: Mr. Kitamura 06-251-3175

Size	Overseas Branches	Overseas Experience	In Future	Country	Non-Japanese Full-Time	Non-Japanese Part-Time	Non-Japanese Increase	Non-Japanese Language	Answer in English	Answer Job-Hunters	Answer Businesses	Answer Researchers
A	0								N	N	Y	N

THE CHUGOKU BANK, LTD. ①

Banking business.
1-15-20 Marunouchi, Okayama-shi 700. 086-223-3111
JR Sanyo Line, Okayama. Contact: Mr. Tadahiko Inoue (Kokusai-bu)

Size	Overseas Branches	Overseas Experience	In Future	Country	Non-Japanese Full-Time	Non-Japanese Part-Time	Non-Japanese Increase	Non-Japanese Language	Answer in English	Answer Job-Hunters	Answer Businesses	Answer Researchers
A	1	Y	Y	Asia	0	0	N		N	N		

SECURITIES COMPANIES

Column key (Non-Japanese: Full-Time, Part-Time, Increase, Language; Answer: Job-Hunters, Businesses, Researchers)

BARING SECURITIES (JAPAN) LIMITED, TOKYO BRANCH

Securities.
New Otani Garden Court, 4-1 Kioi-cho, Chiyoda-ku, Tokyo 102.
Marunouchi or Ginza Line, Akasaka Mitsuke. 03-5210-1500 No contact

Size	Overseas Branches	Overseas Experience	In Future	Country	Full-Time	Part-Time	Increase	Language	Answer in English	Job-Hunters	Businesses	Researchers
B		Y			60	0				N	N	N

CHUO SECURITIES CO., LTD.

Securities.
3-8-1 Ningyo-cho, Nihonbashi, Chuo-ku, Tokyo 103. 03-3660-4758
Hibiya or Toei Asakusa Line, Ningyocho. Contact: Mr. Isawa (Kokusai-bu)

Size	Overseas Branches	Overseas Experience	In Future	Country	Full-Time	Part-Time	Increase	Language	Answer in English	Job-Hunters	Businesses	Researchers
B	1	Y	Y	*	0	0	N		Y			

* Europe

C S FIRST BOSTON (JAPAN) LIMITED

Securities and investment banking. 03-3508-4200
Asahi Seimei Hibiya Bldg., 1-5-1 Yurakucho, Chiyoda-ku, Tokyo 100.
Hibiya, Chiyoda or Toei Mita Line, Hibiya. Contact: (Jinji-bu)

Size	Overseas Branches	Overseas Experience	In Future	Country	Full-Time	Part-Time	Increase	Language	Answer in English	Job-Hunters	Businesses	Researchers
B		Y	Y	All	84	3	Y	E	Y	Y	Y	Y

MARUSAN SECURITIES CO., LTD. ①

Securities.
2-5-2 Nihonbashi, Chuo-ku, Tokyo 103. 03-3271-5808
Ginza, Tozai or Toei Asakusa Line, Nihonbashi. Contact: Mr. Nakamura

Size	Overseas Branches	Overseas Experience	In Future	Country	Full-Time	Part-Time	Increase	Language	Answer in English	Job-Hunters	Businesses	Researchers
A	1	N	Y	*	2	0			Y	Y	Y	Y

* U.K., U.S.A.

NEW JAPAN SECURITIES CO., LTD. ①

Securities.
3-11 Kanda Surugadai, Chiyoda-ku, Tokyo 101-03. 03-3219-1111
JR Chuo Line, Ochanomizu. No contact

Size	Overseas Branches	Overseas Experience	In Future	Country	Full-Time	Part-Time	Increase	Language	Answer in English	Job-Hunters	Businesses	Researchers
A	9	Y	Y		0	0	N					

UNIVERSAL SECURITIES CO., LTD. ②

Securities.
3-4-2 Marunouchi, Chiyoda-ku, Tokyo 100. 03-3284-3816
JR Yamanote Line, Yurakucho. Contact: Mr. Hase (Kokusai-bu)

Size	Overseas Branches	Overseas Experience	In Future	Country	Full-Time	Part-Time	Increase	Language	Answer in English	Job-Hunters	Businesses	Researchers
A	5	Y	Y	Asia	0	0	Y	E,Ch	Y	Y	Y	Y

FINANCE COMPANIES

CENTRAL FINANCE ①

Miscellaneous financing.
3-20-27 Nishiki, Naka-ku, Nagoya. 052-203-1111
Higashiyama or Meijiro Line, Sakae. No contact

Size	Overseas Branches	Overseas Experience	In Future	Country	Non-Japanese Full-Time	Non-Japanese Part-Time	Non-Japanese Increase	Non-Japanese Language	Answer in English	Answer Job-Hunters	Answer Businesses	Answer Researchers
		Y	N							N	N	N

ALL CORP. (OTC)

Real estate, securities, financing.
All Corp. Bldg., 1-12-1 Shibuya, Shibuya-ku, Tokyo 150. 03-5466-0365
JR Yamanote Line, Shibuya. Contact:(Kaigai Kakari) 03-5466-8836 Ext.3707

Size	Overseas Branches	Overseas Experience	In Future	Country	Non-Japanese Full-Time	Non-Japanese Part-Time	Non-Japanese Increase	Non-Japanese Language	Answer in English	Answer Job-Hunters	Answer Businesses	Answer Researchers
B	0	N	N						Y	N	Y	Y

THE TOKYO FOREX CO., LTD.

U.S.A., U.K., Hong Kong, Singapore and others

Foreign exchange and financing.
3-2-15 Nihonbashi Muro-machi, Chuo-ku, Tokyo 103. 03-3270-8801
Ginza or Hanzomon Line, Mitsukoshi-mae. Contact: Mr. Fukuhara (Somu-bu)

Size	Overseas Branches	Overseas Experience	In Future	Country	Non-Japanese Full-Time	Non-Japanese Part-Time	Non-Japanese Increase	Non-Japanese Language	Answer in English	Answer Job-Hunters	Answer Businesses	Answer Researchers
B	18	Y	Y	*	4	0	Y	E	Y	Y	Y	N

JAPAN LEASING CORPORATION

* U.S.A., Europe

Long-term large-scale leasing. 03-3214-0155
Shin Yurakucho Building, 1-12-1 Yurakucho, Chiyoda-ku, Tokyo 100.
JR Yamanote Line, Yurakucho. Contact: Mr. Yasuda (Jinji-bu) Ext. 2111

Size	Overseas Branches	Overseas Experience	In Future	Country	Non-Japanese Full-Time	Non-Japanese Part-Time	Non-Japanese Increase	Non-Japanese Language	Answer in English	Answer Job-Hunters	Answer Businesses	Answer Researchers
A	19	Y	Y	*	0	0	N		N	Y	Y	N

INSURANCE COMPANIES

MITSUI MUTUAL LIFE INSURANCE COMPANY

Life assurance.
1-2-3 Otemachi, Chiyoda-ku, Tokyo 100. 03-3213-2815
Various subway lines, Otemachi. Contact: Mr. Togashi (Kokusai-bu)

Size	Overseas Branches	Overseas Experience	In Future	Country	Non-Japanese Full-Time	Non-Japanese Part-Time	Non-Japanese Increase	Non-Japanese Language	Answer in English	Answer Job-Hunters	Answer Businesses	Answer Researchers
A	4	N	N		1	1	N		Y	N	Y	Y

TAISEI FIRE & MARINE INSURANCE ①

Accident insurance.
4-2-1 Kudan Kita, Chiyoda-ku, Tokyo 102. 03-3234-3111 Ext. 2657
Subway or JR Chuo Line, Ichigaya. Contact: Mr.Shinto (Kokusai-bu) 03-3222-3072

Size	Overseas Branches	Overseas Experience	In Future	Country	Non-Japanese Full-Time	Non-Japanese Part-Time	Non-Japanese Increase	Non-Japanese Language	Answer in English	Answer Job-Hunters	Answer Businesses	Answer Researchers
A	3	N							Y	N	Y	Y

CHAPTER 9. MANUFACTURING

We have divided this wide field into many areas as can be seen from the listing which follows. For those hoping to do business with Japan, this will, we hope, be one of the most useful chapters.

For those seeking employment, there are plenty of opportunities here too. Companies who are exporting or importing or doing business overseas need to communicate in foreign languages, principally English. In most cases, it has taken some time for them to appreciate their need for expert assistance. When they did, they turned to translation companies, but they are expensive and the work takes time to complete. Gradually, therefore, some have accepted the need to employ their own non-Japanese staff. One feels that such decisions have been taken with reluctance in many cases, as being a type of threat to the company's independence and, as a result, much of the work which needs doing by a non-Japanese is never actually submitted to his attention. This means, however, fortunately for the job-hunter, that the market is continuing to expand as companies gradually appreciate the importance of correct English, or other languages. In fact, for the future, maybe this wide field has the greatest potential of all.

The first to appreciate such a need were the electronics and motor vehicle industries (see Chapter 10 for electronics companies), for their products received international recognition relatively early. In many other types of company, the need has still not been recognized and letters are still sent, for example, which are completely incomprehensible.

The more progressive concerns have now realized that non-Japanese can be used in other areas too. They can be used as salesmen, for instance, overseas, and they can put together proposals in a foreign language just as effectively as Japanese members of staff and in only a fraction of the time. They can even help to carry out negotiations. Such realization has expanded the opportunities remarkably, although there is generally thought to be danger in giving too much power and authority to non-Japanese, so the trend is a slow one and has its limitations. Nevertheless, the opportunities are increasing all the time and now is perhaps a good time to become involved in such business, although, in this area too, the bursting of the 'bubble' has brought a deceleration in the rate of increase.

However, in an effort to reduce production costs and decrease Japanese exports, while still expanding world market share, many manufacturers are now trying to shift production to overseas plants and to become more involved in joint-venture projects. Thus even the smaller companies are starting to have a need for non-Japanese personnel and may respond favourably to enquirers.

This field is likely to be of particular interest to people with engineering backgrounds and opportunities are not limited to westerners. There is demand for those from other Asian countries also.

Those with good Japanese ability may be able to work as sales engineers, while there are other opportunities in the Overseas Department, as well as in sales, procurement and engineering. If the employer is a large company, there may also be the possibility of transferring, after a few years in Japan, to the branch office in the employee's own country.

As mentioned before, only those companies with considerable experience feel confident in selecting their own non-Japanese staff, so many turn to the placement companies to assist them. However, that is not to say that they would not necessarily be interested in a direct approach. Indeed, where our list shows a contact, this may be an indication that they would be interested. Those who speak Japanese will have an advantage, but, for most positions, a working knowledge of conversational Japanese will suffice. However, this situation may well change over the years as more fluent Japanese speakers become available. Of course, as usual, any connexions which you may be able to offer within a company will be most useful.

HEAVY INDUSTRIES

MITSUBISHI HEAVY INDUSTRIES, LTD. ①

Comprehensive heavy machinery manufacturer.
2-5-1 Marunouchi, Chiyoda-ku, Tokyo 100. 03-3212-3111
JR Yamanote Line, Tokyo. Contact: Mr. Hiramatsu (Kaigai Jinji-ka) 03-3212-9016

Size	Overseas Branches	Overseas Experience	In Future	Country	Full-Time	Part-Time	Increase	Language	Answer in English	Job-Hunters	Businesses	Researchers
A	29	Y	Y	*	11	0			Y	Y	N	Y

* U.S.A., E.C. Countries, S.E. Asia

AIRBUS INDUSTRIE, TOKYO LIAISON OFFICE

Aircraft manufacturer.
No. 9 Kowa Bldg., 1-6-7 Akasaka, Minato-ku, Tokyo 107. 03-3505-6521
Ginza Line, Toranomon. Contact: Ms. Sugimura (Secretary)

Size	Overseas Branches	Overseas Experience	In Future	Country	Full-Time	Part-Time	Increase	Language	Answer in English	Job-Hunters	Businesses	Researchers
D					1	0			Y	Y	N	N

INDUSTRIAL MACHINERY

AIDA ENGINEERING, LTD. ①

Manufacturer of presses and automatic feeding equipment.
2-10 Oyama-cho, Sagamihara-shi, Kanagawa 229. 0427-72-5231
Keio, JR Yokohama Line, Hashimoto. Contact: Mr. Yabe (Kaigai Jigyo-bu) Ext. 476

Size	Overseas Branches	Overseas Experience	In Future	Country	Full-Time	Part-Time	Increase	Language	Answer in English	Job-Hunters	Businesses	Researchers
A	3	Y	Y	Ch	6	1	Y	*	Y	Y	Y	Y

* English, German, Chinese

TOSHIBA MACHINE CO., LTD. ①

Manufacturer of industrial machinery.
4-2-11 Ginza, Chuo-ku, Tokyo 104. 03-3567-0511
Ginza, Marunouchi or Hibiya Line, Ginza. No contact

Size	Overseas Branches	Overseas Experience	In Future	Country	Full-Time	Part-Time	Increase	Language	Answer in English	Job-Hunters	Businesses	Researchers
A	8	Y	Y	*	1	0				N	N	N

* U.S.A., S.E.Asia

SHIN-KOBE ELECTRIC MACHINERY CO., LTD. ①

Manufacturer of storage batteries and resin-moulding products.
2-1-1 Nishi Shinjuku, Shinjuku-ku, Tokyo 163-04. 03-3344-2807
Marunouchi, Toei Shinjuku or JR Yamanote Line, Shinjuku. No contact

Size	Overseas Branches	Overseas Experience	In Future	Country	Full-Time	Part-Time	Increase	Language	Answer in English	Job-Hunters	Businesses	Researchers
A		Y	Y	US						Y	Y	Y

YAMAZAKI CO., LTD. (OTC)

Manufacturer of machine tools.
489-23 Aritama Kitamachi, Hamamatsu-shi, Shizuoka 431-31.
Entetsu Nishi Kashima Line, Sekishi. 053-434-3011 No contact

Size	Overseas Branches	Overseas Experience	In Future	Country	Full-Time	Part-Time	Increase	Language	Answer in English	Job-Hunters	Businesses	Researchers
B	0	Y	Y	*	0	0	N					

* China, Korea

SANKYO ENGINEERING CO., LTD. (OTC)

Manufacturer of liquid chemical disposal equipment for semiconductors.
1-25-12 Akebono-cho, Tachikawa-shi, Tokyo 190.
JR Chuo Line, Tachikawa. 0425-23-6686 No contact

Size	Overseas Branches	Overseas Experience	In Future	Country	Full-Time	Part-Time	Increase	Language	Answer in English	Job-Hunters	Businesses	Researchers
B		Y			1	0			N	N	Y	

RISO KAGAKU CORPORATION (OTC)

Manufacturer of copying machines for office and home use.
Shinbashi Eki-mae Building, 2-20-15 Shinbashi, Minato-ku, Tokyo 105.
JR Yamanote Line, Shinbashi. Contact: Mr. Hasegawa 03-3572-8532

Size	Overseas Branches	Overseas Experience	In Future	Country	Full-Time	Part-Time	Increase	Language	Answer in English	Job-Hunters	Businesses	Researchers
A	4	Y	Y	Asia					Y			

Size	Overseas Branches	Overseas Experience	In Future	Country	Full-Time (Non-Japanese)	Part-Time (Non-Japanese)	Increase (Non-Japanese)	Language (Non-Japanese)	Answer in English	Job-Hunters (Answer)	Businesses (Answer)	Researchers (Answer)

AIRTECH JAPAN, LTD. (OTC)

Manufacturer of cleaning equipment.
3-17-8 Higashi Ueno, Taito-ku, Tokyo 110. 03-3832-1731
Ginza, Hibiya or JR Yamanote Line, Ueno. Contact: Mr. Kawamata (Kikaku-shitsu)

Size	Overseas Branches	Overseas Experience	In Future	Country	Full-Time	Part-Time	Increase	Language	Answer in English	Job-Hunters	Businesses	Researchers
B	2	Y			2	0	Y	E	Y	Y	Y	Y

CHARMILLES TECHNOLOGIES (JAPAN) LTD.

Manufacturer of electric discharge machines.
1-14-11 Shin Yokohama, Kohoku-ku, Yokohama 222. 045-474-2641
JR Yokohama Line, Shin Yokohama. Contact: Mr. Hayakawa (Jinji-ka)

Size	Overseas Branches	Overseas Experience	In Future	Country	Full-Time	Part-Time	Increase	Language	Answer in English	Job-Hunters	Businesses	Researchers
C	7	Y	Y	*	3	0	Y		Y	Y	Y	Y

* U.S.A., S.E. Asia

CORONA CORPORATION

Manufacturer of air-conditioning equipment.
7-7 Higashi Shinbo, Sanjo-shi, Niigata 955. 0256-32-2111
JR Joetsu Shinkansen, Tsubame Sanjo. Contact: (Kaigai Jigyo-bu)

Size	Overseas Branches	Overseas Experience	In Future	Country	Full-Time	Part-Time	Increase	Language	Answer in English	Job-Hunters	Businesses	Researchers
A	1	Y	Y	Asia	0	0	Y	Ch	Y	N	N	N

TOYO SHOSHA

Manufacturer of machine tools.
2-28-24 Izumi, Higashi-ku, Nagoya 461. 052-931-7501
Sakuradori Line, Takadake. No contact

Size	Overseas Branches	Overseas Experience	In Future	Country	Full-Time	Part-Time	Increase	Language	Answer in English	Job-Hunters	Businesses	Researchers
B	0	N	N		0	0	N		N	N	N	N

MATSUMOTO KOSAN

Manufacturer of parts for numerical control equipment. 0494-75-0571
247 Shimo Ogano, Ogano-machi, Chichibu-gun, Saitama 368-01.
Seibu Ikebukuro Line, Seibu Chichibu. Contact: Mr. Matsumoto

Size	Overseas Branches	Overseas Experience	In Future	Country	Full-Time	Part-Time	Increase	Language	Answer in English	Job-Hunters	Businesses	Researchers
C	0	N	Y	*			Y	¶	N	N	Y	Y

* Korea, China
¶ English, Chinese, Korean

RUBBER AND SIMILAR PRODUCTS

NOK-MEGULASTIK CORPORATION ①

Oil seals for motor vehicles and other machinery.
1-12-15 Shiba Daimon, Minato-ku, Tokyo 105. 03-3432-4211
Toei Asakusa Line, Daimon. No contact

Size	Overseas Branches	Overseas Experience	In Future	Country	Full-Time	Part-Time	Increase	Language	Answer in English	Job-Hunters	Businesses	Researchers
B		N	N		1	0			N	N	N	N

NITTA CORPORATION (OTC)

Industrial belt maker.
1-8-12 Honcho, Chuo-ku, Osaka 541. 06-266-1771
Sakaisuji or Chuo Line, Sakaisuji Honmachi. Contact: (Global-ka Suishin-shitsu)

Size	Overseas Branches	Overseas Experience	In Future	Country	Full-Time	Part-Time	Increase	Language	Answer in English	Job-Hunters	Businesses	Researchers
B	6	Y	Y		3	0	Y	E,G		N	Y	Y

RHÔNE-POULENC SILICONE JAPAN K.K.

Silicone rubber products.
Fushide Bldg., 4-1-13 Toranomon, Minato-ku, Tokyo 105. 03-3459-1421
Hibiya Line, Kamiyacho. No contact

Size	Overseas Branches	Overseas Experience	In Future	Country	Full-Time	Part-Time	Increase	Language	Answer in English	Job-Hunters	Businesses	Researchers
C		Y	Y		0	0				N	N	N

BUILDING MATERIALS

MITSUI MINING & SMELTING ①

Non-ferrous smelter.
2-1-1 Nihonbashi Muro-machi, Chuo-ku, Tokyo 103. 03-3246-8090
Ginza, Hanzomon Line, Mitsukoshi-mae. Contact: Mr. Ohashi (Kokusai Gyomu-bu)

Size	Overseas Branches	Overseas Experience	In Future	Country	Non-Japanese Full-Time	Non-Japanese Part-Time	Non-Japanese Increase	Non-Japanese Language	Answer in English	Answer Job-Hunters	Answer Businesses	Answer Researchers
A	15	Y	Y		11	0	Y	E	Y	Y	Y	Y

SHIN NIKKEI COMPANY, LTD. ②

Producer of building materials.
2-7-23 Kiba, Koto-ku, Tokyo 135. 03-3820-2217
Tozai Line, Kiba. Contact: Mr. Yoshida (Kaigai Eigyo-shitsu)

Size	Overseas Branches	Overseas Experience	In Future	Country	Non-Japanese Full-Time	Non-Japanese Part-Time	Non-Japanese Increase	Non-Japanese Language	Answer in English	Answer Job-Hunters	Answer Businesses	Answer Researchers
A	4	Y	Y	Asia	10	0	Y	E	Y	Y	Y	Y

NIPPON FILCON CO., LTD. ②

Manufacturer of nets for paper and pulp-making. Also conveyor belts.
3-27-24 Ikejiri, Setagaya-ku, Tokyo 154. 03-3412-3141
Tokyu Shin Tamagawa Line, Ikejiri Ohashi. No contact

Size	Overseas Branches	Overseas Experience	In Future	Country	Non-Japanese Full-Time	Non-Japanese Part-Time	Non-Japanese Increase	Non-Japanese Language	Answer in English	Answer Job-Hunters	Answer Businesses	Answer Researchers
A	1	Y	Y	*						N	Y	Y

* N. America, S.E. Asia

OKAWA TRANSTEEL CORPORATION

Producer of steel fabrications, bridges, etc.
1523-3 Aza Yamanoshita Taro-dai Niigata-shi, Niigata 950-31.
JR Shinetsu Line, Niigata. 025-255-2171 No contact

Size	Overseas Branches	Overseas Experience	In Future	Country	Non-Japanese Full-Time	Non-Japanese Part-Time	Non-Japanese Increase	Non-Japanese Language	Answer in English	Answer Job-Hunters	Answer Businesses	Answer Researchers
B	0	Y	N		0	0	N			N	N	N

MARSIMA AQUA SYSTEM CORP.

Producer of water gates, bridges, etc.
1-6-15 Tsuruhashi, Ikuno-ku, Osaka 544. 06-716-8001
Sennichimae or JR Kanjo Line, Tsuruhashi. Contact:Mr.Anryu (Secretary)

Size	Overseas Branches	Overseas Experience	In Future	Country	Non-Japanese Full-Time	Non-Japanese Part-Time	Non-Japanese Increase	Non-Japanese Language	Answer in English	Answer Job-Hunters	Answer Businesses	Answer Researchers
B		Y	N	Asia			Y		Y	Y	Y	Y

MITSUI WOOD SYSTEMS, INC.

Housing and construction materials manufacturer.
3-8-4 Nihonbashi Honcho, Chuo-ku, Tokyo 103. 03-3663-3631
JR Sobu (Kaisoku) Line, Shin Nihonbashi. Contact: (Any section)

Size	Overseas Branches	Overseas Experience	In Future	Country	Non-Japanese Full-Time	Non-Japanese Part-Time	Non-Japanese Increase	Non-Japanese Language	Answer in English	Answer Job-Hunters	Answer Businesses	Answer Researchers
A	0	Y	Y	*	3	0			N	N	N	Y

* S.E. Asia, N. America, China

Column headings: Size | Overseas Branches | Overseas Experience | In Future | Country | ←Non-Japanese→ Full-Time | Part-Time | Increase | Language | Answer in English | ←Answer→ Job-Hunters | Businesses | Researchers

CEMENT AND CERAMICS

CHICHIBU CEMENT CO., LTD. ①

Manufacturer of cement and fine ceramics.
1-4-6 Marunouchi, Chiyoda-ku, Tokyo 100. 03-3812-7163
Marunouchi or JR Yamanote Line, Tokyo. Contact: Mr. Okabe (Koho-shitsu)

Size	Overseas Branches	Overseas Experience	In Future	Country	Full-Time	Part-Time	Increase	Language	Answer in English	Job-Hunters	Businesses	Researchers
A	0	Y	N		0	0	N		N	N	Y	Y

NIPPON HUME CORPORATION ①

Manufacturer of pipes, piles and wells.
5-33-11 Shinbashi, Minato-ku, Tokyo 105. 03-3433-4118
Ginza, Toei Asakusa or JR Yamanote Line, Shinbashi. Contact: (Kokusai Jigyo-bu)

Size	Overseas Branches	Overseas Experience	In Future	Country	Full-Time	Part-Time	Increase	Language	Answer in English	Job-Hunters	Businesses	Researchers
B	3	Y							Y	Y	Y	Y

NIPPON CRUCIBLE CO., LTD. ②

Manufacturer of refactories, graphite crucibles, etc.
1-21-3 Ebisu, Shibuya-ku, Tokyo 150. 03-3443-5554
Hibiya or JR Yamanote Line, Ebisu. Contact: Mr. Murata (Boeki-bu)

Size	Overseas Branches	Overseas Experience	In Future	Country	Full-Time	Part-Time	Increase	Language	Answer in English	Job-Hunters	Businesses	Researchers
B		Y	Y	Asia	1	0			Y	N	Y	Y

NIPPON RESIBON CORPORATION ②

Manufacturer of grindstones.
1-22-10 Kita Horie, Nishi-ku, Osaka 550. 06-538-0136
Yotsubashi Line, Yotsubashi. No contact

Size	Overseas Branches	Overseas Experience	In Future	Country	Full-Time	Part-Time	Increase	Language	Answer in English	Job-Hunters	Businesses	Researchers
B	2	Y	Y	All						N	Y	Y

FUKAGAWA PORCELAIN MFG., LTD. (L)

Manufacturer of tableware and chinaware for interior decoration.
Arita-machi, Nishi Matsuura-gun, Saga 844. 0955-46-2251
JR Sasebo Line, Arita. Contact: Mr. Sakai (Somu-bu)

Size	Overseas Branches	Overseas Experience	In Future	Country	Full-Time	Part-Time	Increase	Language	Answer in English	Job-Hunters	Businesses	Researchers
B	1	Y	Y	*	1	0			N	Y	Y	Y

* U.S.A., E.C. Countries

CHEMICALS

TOKUYAMA SODA CO., LTD. ①

Producer of caustic soda, cement, plastics, etc.
Shibuya Konno Building, 3-3-1 Shibuya, Shibuya-ku, Tokyo 150.
JR Yamanote Line, Shibuya. Contact: (Kokusai-bu) 03-3499-8937

Size	Overseas Branches	Overseas Experience	In Future	Country	Non-Japanese Full-Time	Non-Japanese Part-Time	Non-Japanese Increase	Non-Japanese Language	Answer in English	Answer Job-Hunters	Answer Businesses	Answer Researchers
A		Y	Y		2	0			Y	N	N	N

KOATSU GAS KOGYO CO., LTD. ①

Producer of industrial gases.
Osaka Godo Bldg., 1-5 Doyama-cho, Kita-ku, Osaka 530. 06-311-1371
JR Tokaido Line, Osaka. Contact:Mr.Nakai (Kaigai Jigyo Hon-bu) Ext.507

Size	Overseas Branches	Overseas Experience	In Future	Country	Non-Japanese Full-Time	Non-Japanese Part-Time	Non-Japanese Increase	Non-Japanese Language	Answer in English	Answer Job-Hunters	Answer Businesses	Answer Researchers
B	0	Y	Y	*	2	0	N		Y	N	Y	Y

* N. America, E.C.Countries, Asia

NOF CORPORATION ①

Oil and fats products. Paints. Foodstuffs. Explosives. 03-3283-7244
Yurakucho Building, 1-10-1 Yurakucho, Chiyoda-ku, Tokyo 100.
JR Yamanote Line, Yurakucho. Contact: Mr. Iyoda (Kokusai-bu)

Size	Overseas Branches	Overseas Experience	In Future	Country	Non-Japanese Full-Time	Non-Japanese Part-Time	Non-Japanese Increase	Non-Japanese Language	Answer in English	Answer Job-Hunters	Answer Businesses	Answer Researchers
A	4	Y	Y	All	1	0			Y	Y	Y	Y

TAIYO KAGAKU CO., LTD. ②

Materials for foodstuffs, drugs, cosmetics, etc.
9-5 Akabori Shin-machi, Yokkaichi-shi, Mie 510. 0593-52-2555
Kintetsu Nagoya Line, Yokkaichi-shi. Contact: Mr.Ito (Kokusai-ka) Ext.410

Size	Overseas Branches	Overseas Experience	In Future	Country	Non-Japanese Full-Time	Non-Japanese Part-Time	Non-Japanese Increase	Non-Japanese Language	Answer in English	Answer Job-Hunters	Answer Businesses	Answer Researchers
B	0	Y	Y	*		8			Y	N	Y	Y

* U.S.A., E.C. Countries

TAKI CHEMICAL CO., LTD. ②

Manufacturer of fertilizers and industrial chemicals. 0794-35-6133
2 Midori-machi, Beppu-cho, Kakogawa-shi, Hyogo 675-01.
JR Sanyo Line, Kakogawa. Contact: Mr. Kurosawa (Kaihatsu-bu)

Size	Overseas Branches	Overseas Experience	In Future	Country	Non-Japanese Full-Time	Non-Japanese Part-Time	Non-Japanese Increase	Non-Japanese Language	Answer in English	Answer Job-Hunters	Answer Businesses	Answer Researchers
B		Y	Y						Y	Y	Y	Y

TOHO CHEMICAL INDUSTRY CO., LTD. ②

Manufacturer of surfactants and special solvents.
1-2-5 Ningyo-cho, Nihonbashi, Chuo-ku, Tokyo 103. 03-3668-2279
Hibiya or Toei Asakusa Line, Ningyocho. No contact

Size	Overseas Branches	Overseas Experience	In Future	Country	Non-Japanese Full-Time	Non-Japanese Part-Time	Non-Japanese Increase	Non-Japanese Language	Answer in English	Answer Job-Hunters	Answer Businesses	Answer Researchers
B	0	Y	Y	All	1	0			Y	N	N	N

ROHM AND HAAS JAPAN K.K.

Manufacturer of chemical products.
1-8-10 Azabu-dai, Minato-ku, Tokyo 106-91. 03-3583-9461
Hibiya Line, Kamiyacho. Contact: Mr. Nakae (Somu-bu) 03-3224-3857

Size	Overseas Branches	Overseas Experience	In Future	Country	Non-Japanese Full-Time	Non-Japanese Part-Time	Non-Japanese Increase	Non-Japanese Language	Answer in English	Answer Job-Hunters	Answer Businesses	Answer Researchers
C	0	Y	N		1	0			Y	N	N	N

JOHNSON CO., LTD.

Manufacturer of detergents and waxes.
699 Kokufu Hongo, Oiso-machi, Naka-gun, Kanagawa 259-01.
JR Tokaido Line, Oiso. 0463-72-2111 Contact: (Jinji-bu)

Size	Overseas Branches	Overseas Experience	In Future	Country	Non-Japanese Full-Time	Non-Japanese Part-Time	Non-Japanese Increase	Non-Japanese Language	Answer in English	Answer Job-Hunters	Answer Businesses	Answer Researchers
B	0	Y	N		6	0				N	N	N

RIKA HERCULES INC.

Manufacturer of industrial chemical products.
2-5-17 Minami Aoyama, Minato-ku, Tokyo 107. 03-3423-7821
Ginza or Hanzomon Line, Aoyama I-chome. Contact: Mr. Kobayashi (Keiri-bu)

Size	Overseas Branches	Overseas Experience	In Future	Country	Non-Japanese Full-Time	Non-Japanese Part-Time	Non-Japanese Increase	Non-Japanese Language	Answer in English	Answer Job-Hunters	Answer Businesses	Answer Researchers
C		Y	Y	Asia					Y	N	Y	N

PAINTS

TOA PAINT CO., LTD. ①

Paints and acrylic rubber products (for automobile industry).
2-1-29 Dojimahama, Kita-ku, Osaka 530. 06-344-1371
Yotsubashi Line, Nishi Umeda. Contact: Mr. Taguchi (Kaigai-shitsu) Ext. 205

Size	Overseas Branches	Overseas Experience	In Future	Country	Non-Japanese Full-Time	Non-Japanese Part-Time	Non-Japanese Increase	Non-Japanese Language	Answer in English	Answer Job-Hunters	Answer Businesses	Answer Researchers
B	1	Y	Y						Y	N	Y	Y

NIHON TOKUSHU TORYO CO., LTD. ①

Maker of synthetic resin paints and soundproofing materials.
5-16-7 Oji, Kita-ku, Tokyo 114. 03-3913-6131
Nanboku Line, Oji Kamiya. Contact: Mr. Ito (Kaigai Jigyo-bu)

Size	Overseas Branches	Overseas Experience	In Future	Country	Non-Japanese Full-Time	Non-Japanese Part-Time	Non-Japanese Increase	Non-Japanese Language	Answer in English	Answer Job-Hunters	Answer Businesses	Answer Researchers
B	1	Y	Y	*	0	0	N		Y	N	Y	Y

* U.S.A., E.C. Countries

FUJIKURA KASEI CO., LTD. ②

Manufacturer of synthetic acrylic resin and other coating materials.
2-6-15 Shiba Koen, Minato-ku, Tokyo 105. 03-3436-1100
Toei Mita Line, Shiba Koen. Contact: (Jinji-ka)

Size	Overseas Branches	Overseas Experience	In Future	Country	Non-Japanese Full-Time	Non-Japanese Part-Time	Non-Japanese Increase	Non-Japanese Language	Answer in English	Answer Job-Hunters	Answer Businesses	Answer Researchers
B	0	Y	Y						N	Y	Y	Y

NIPPON GINSHA CO., LTD.

Manufacturer of coloured sand.
4-10-20 Funairi Minami, Naka-ku, Hiroshima 730. 082-234-9119
JR Sanyo Line, Hiroshima. Contact: Mr. Lai (Overseas Business Planning Dept.)

Size	Overseas Branches	Overseas Experience	In Future	Country	Non-Japanese Full-Time	Non-Japanese Part-Time	Non-Japanese Increase	Non-Japanese Language	Answer in English	Answer Job-Hunters	Answer Businesses	Answer Researchers
C	0	Y	Y		1	0	Y	E,Ch	Y	Y	Y	Y

TEXTILES

KATAKURA INDUSTRIES COMPANY, LTD. ①

Silk spinning. Manufacturer of clothing.
3-1-2 Kyobashi, Chuo-ku, Tokyo 104. 03-3281-6966
Ginza Line, Kyobashi. Contact: Mr. Kobayashi (Shoji-bu)

Size	Overseas Branches	Overseas Experience	In Future	Country	Non-Japanese: Full-Time	Part-Time	Increase	Language	Answer in English	Answer: Job-Hunters	Businesses	Researchers
A		Y	Y	*					Y	Y	Y	Y

* Asia, U.K., U.S.A.

DYNIC CORPORATION ①

Bookbinder. Producer of fabrics. 03-3986-3505
31st Fl. Sunshine 60, 3-1-1 Higashi Ikebukuro, Toshima-ku, Tokyo 170.
JR Yamanote Line, Ikebukuro. Contact: Mr. Nojiri (Kokusai-bu)

Size	Overseas Branches	Overseas Experience	In Future	Country	Non-Japanese: Full-Time	Part-Time	Increase	Language	Answer in English	Answer: Job-Hunters	Businesses	Researchers
A	6	Y	Y		1	0	Y	E,Ch	Y	Y	Y	Y

TAKA-Q CO., LTD. ①

Manufacturer of various clothing.
1-5-22 Shimo Ochiai, Shinjuku-ku, Tokyo 161. 03-3366-6853
JR Yamanote Line, Takadanobaba. Contact: Mr. Fujiwara (Kaigai Jigyo-bu)

Size	Overseas Branches	Overseas Experience	In Future	Country	Non-Japanese: Full-Time	Part-Time	Increase	Language	Answer in English	Answer: Job-Hunters	Businesses	Researchers
A	4	Y	Y	Ch	6	0			Y	N	Y	Y

SEIREN CO., LTD. ①

Processor of fibres.
1-10-1 Keya, Fukui-shi, Fukui 910. 0776-35-2111
JR Hokuriku Line, Fukui. Contact: Mr. Shibata (Kaigai Tokatsu) Ext. 223

Size	Overseas Branches	Overseas Experience	In Future	Country	Non-Japanese: Full-Time	Part-Time	Increase	Language	Answer in English	Answer: Job-Hunters	Businesses	Researchers
A		Y	Y	Asia			Y	E	Y	N	Y	N

TOKAI SENKO K.K. ①

Processing and printing of woven fabrics. 052-581-8141
Dai Nagoya Bldg., 3-28-12 Mei-eki, Nakamura-ku, Nagoya, Aichi 450.
JR Tokaido Line, Nagoya. Contact: Mr. Sakurada (Kaigai Jigyo-ka)

Size	Overseas Branches	Overseas Experience	In Future	Country	Non-Japanese: Full-Time	Part-Time	Increase	Language	Answer in English	Answer: Job-Hunters	Businesses	Researchers
A	4	Y	Y	All					Y	N	N	N

TOWA ORIMONO CO., LTD. ②

Carpet manufacturer.
737 Nishi Itamochi, Tondabayashi-shi, Osaka 584. 0721-34-1234
Kintetsu Minami Osaka Line, Tondabayashi. No contact

Size	Overseas Branches	Overseas Experience	In Future	Country	Non-Japanese: Full-Time	Part-Time	Increase	Language	Answer in English	Answer: Job-Hunters	Businesses	Researchers
C		N	N							N	N	N

OZAKI SHOJI CO., LTD.

Manufacturer of students' uniforms and training wear.
3-10-25 Kojima Tanokuchi, Kurashiki-shi, Okayama 711. 086-477-6111
JR Seto Ohashi Line, Kojima. No contact

Size	Overseas Branches	Overseas Experience	In Future	Country	Non-Japanese: Full-Time	Part-Time	Increase	Language	Answer in English	Answer: Job-Hunters	Businesses	Researchers
A	0	Y	Y	*							Y	

* Korea, Indonesia

MARUHISA CO., LTD.

Manufacturer of clothing.
72 Aza Hamabata Kita, Saita, Muya-cho, Naruto-shi, Tokushima 772.
JR Naruto Line, Naruto. Contact: Mr. Hiraishi (Kaigai-bu) 0886-85-0151

Size	Overseas Branches	Overseas Experience	In Future	Country	Non-Japanese: Full-Time	Part-Time	Increase	Language	Answer in English	Answer: Job-Hunters	Businesses	Researchers
B	1	Y	Y	Ch	11	0			Y	Y	Y	Y

NEGORO SANGYO CO., LTD.

Carpet manufacturer.
1-1 Nishiki Naka-machi, Kaizuka-shi, Osaka 597. 0724-31-5431
Nankai Line, Kaizuka. Contact: Mr. Kono

Size	Overseas Branches	Overseas Experience	In Future	Country	Non-Japanese: Full-Time	Part-Time	Increase	Language	Answer in English	Answer: Job-Hunters	Businesses	Researchers
B	1	Y	Y	*	35	0	Y	¶	N	N	Y	Y

* Middle East, Hong Kong, Korea, U.S.A.
¶ English, Thai, Spanish

PHARMACEUTICALS

S S PHARMACEUTICAL CO., LTD. ①

Producer of pharmaceuticals.
2-12-4 Nihonbashi Hama-cho, Chuo-ku, Tokyo 103. 03-3668-4511
Hibiya or Toei Asakusa Line, Ningyocho. Contact: (Jinji-bu) 03-3663-4324

* U.S.A., Europe

Size	Overseas Branches	Overseas Experience	In Future	Country	Full-Time (Non-Japanese)	Part-Time (Non-Japanese)	Increase (Non-Japanese)	Language (Non-Japanese)	Answer in English	Job-Hunters (Answer)	Businesses (Answer)	Researchers (Answer)
A		Y	Y	*	0	0	N		N			

YUKI GOSEI KOGYO CO., LTD. ②

Producer of pharmaceuticals, industrial chemicals, etc.
Hirakawacho CH Bldg., 2-3-24 Hirakawa-cho, Chiyoda-ku, Tokyo 102.
Hanzomon Line, Hanzomon. Contact: (Boeki Group) 03-5275-5067

Size	Overseas Branches	Overseas Experience	In Future	Country	Full-Time	Part-Time	Increase	Language	Answer in English	Job-Hunters	Businesses	Researchers
B	0	Y	Y		0	0	N		N	N	N	N

TAIHO PHARMACEUTICAL CO., LTD.

Producer of drugs and anticancer agents.
1-27 Kanda Nishiki-cho, Chiyoda-ku, Tokyo 101. 03-3294-4523
Various subway lines, Otemachi. Contact: Mr. Ito (Kokusai-bu)

* Europe, U.S.A.

Size	Overseas Branches	Overseas Experience	In Future	Country	Full-Time	Part-Time	Increase	Language	Answer in English	Job-Hunters	Businesses	Researchers
A	2	Y	Y	*	1	0			Y		Y	Y

OTSUKA PHARMACEUTICAL CO., LTD.

Producer of pharmaceuticals and foodstuffs.
2-9 Kanda Tsukasa-cho, Chiyoda-ku, Tokyo 101. 03-3292-0021
Marunouchi Line, Awajicho. No contact

Size	Overseas Branches	Overseas Experience	In Future	Country	Full-Time	Part-Time	Increase	Language	Answer in English	Job-Hunters	Businesses	Researchers
A	3	Y					Y					

NIHON SCHERING K.K.

Importer and manufacturer of pharmaceuticals and chemical products.
2-6-64 Nishi Miyahara, Yodogawa-ku, Osaka 532. 06-396-2311
Hankyu Takarazuka Line, Mikuni. Contact: Mr. Nakao (Jinji-bu)

Size	Overseas Branches	Overseas Experience	In Future	Country	Full-Time	Part-Time	Increase	Language	Answer in English	Job-Hunters	Businesses	Researchers
A	0	Y	Y	G	20	0	Y		Y	Y	Y	Y

REVLON KABUSHIKI KAISHA

Manufacturer of cosmetics.
6-9-12 Roppongi, Minato-ku, Tokyo 106. 03-3475-9005
Hibiya Line, Roppongi. Contact: Ms. Imanaka (Secretaries' Office)

* U.S.A., Asia

Size	Overseas Branches	Overseas Experience	In Future	Country	Full-Time	Part-Time	Increase	Language	Answer in English	Job-Hunters	Businesses	Researchers
B	0	Y	Y	*	2	0			Y	N	N	N

JANSSEN-KYOWA CO., LTD.

Manufacturer of pharmaceuticals.
3-1-5 Higashi Gotanda, Shinagawa-ku, Tokyo 141. 03-3445-2214
Toei Asakusa Line, Takanawadai. Contact: Mr. Chihara (Jinji Group)

Size	Overseas Branches	Overseas Experience	In Future	Country	Full-Time	Part-Time	Increase	Language	Answer in English	Job-Hunters	Businesses	Researchers
B	0	N	N						Y	Y	N	N

NOVO NORDISK PHARMA LTD.

Bio-technology company.
5-7 Odenma-cho, Nihonbashi, Chuo-ku, Tokyo 103. 03-3249-8408
Hibiya Line, Kodenmacho. Contact: Mr. Yamato (Jinji)

Size	Overseas Branches	Overseas Experience	In Future	Country	Full-Time	Part-Time	Increase	Language	Answer in English	Job-Hunters	Businesses	Researchers
B	50	Y	Y	All	9	0			Y	Y	Y	Y

AUTOMOTIVE AND RELATED PRODUCTS

TOYOTA MOTOR CORPORATION ①

Manufacturer of passenger cars, trucks, 'buses and other vehicles.
1 Toyota-cho, Toyota-shi, Aichi 471. 0565-28-2121 or 03-3817-7111
Aichi Kanjo Line, Mikawa Toyota. Contact: (Kaigai Shogai Koho-bu)

Size	Overseas Branches	Overseas Experience	In Future	Country	Non-Japanese Full-Time	Non-Japanese Part-Time	Non-Japanese Increase	Non-Japanese Language	Answer in English	Answer Job-Hunters	Answer Businesses	Answer Researchers
A		Y	Y		0	0			Y	Y	Y	Y

ICHIKOH INDUSTRIES, LTD. ①

Manufacturer of automotive lighting equipment, mirrors, etc.
5-10-18 Higashi Gotanda, Shinagawa-ku, Tokyo 141. 03-3443-7251
JR Yamanote Line, Gotanda. Contact: (Eigyo Kanri-bu) 03-3443-7781

Size	Overseas Branches	Overseas Experience	In Future	Country	Non-Japanese Full-Time	Non-Japanese Part-Time	Non-Japanese Increase	Non-Japanese Language	Answer in English	Answer Job-Hunters	Answer Businesses	Answer Researchers
A	4	Y	Y	US	2	0			Y	N	Y	Y

KOYO SEIKO CO., LTD. ①

Manufacturer of bearings and steering systems.
3-5-8 Minami Senba, Chuo-ku, Osaka 542. 06-245-6087
Midosuji Line, Shinsaibashi. Contact: Mr. Kamura (Kaigai Honbu) Ext. 543

Size	Overseas Branches	Overseas Experience	In Future	Country	Non-Japanese Full-Time	Non-Japanese Part-Time	Non-Japanese Increase	Non-Japanese Language	Answer in English	Answer Job-Hunters	Answer Businesses	Answer Researchers
A	22	Y	Y	All	2	0			Y			

SUMITOMO WIRING SYSTEMS, LTD. ②

Manufacturer of wire harnesses for automobile use.
1-14 Nishi Suehiro-cho, Yokkaichi-shi, Mie 510. 0593-54-6241
JR Kansai Main Line, Yokkaichi. Contact: (Somu-bu) 0593-54-6203

Size	Overseas Branches	Overseas Experience	In Future	Country	Non-Japanese Full-Time	Non-Japanese Part-Time	Non-Japanese Increase	Non-Japanese Language	Answer in English	Answer Job-Hunters	Answer Businesses	Answer Researchers
A	2	Y	Y	UK	8	0	Y	E	N	N	N	N

AISAN INDUSTRY CO., LTD. ②

Manufacturer of fuel-related automobile parts.
1-1-1 Kyowa-cho, Obu-shi, Aichi 474. 0562-47-1131 Ext. 232
JR Tokaido Line, Kyowa. Contact: (Somu-bu Koho-ka) 0562-48-6215

Size	Overseas Branches	Overseas Experience	In Future	Country	Non-Japanese Full-Time	Non-Japanese Part-Time	Non-Japanese Increase	Non-Japanese Language	Answer in English	Answer Job-Hunters	Answer Businesses	Answer Researchers
A	3	Y	Y	All					N	N	N	N

TOA VALVE CO., LTD. ②

Manufacturer of valves for electric power generation.
5-12-1 Nishi Tachibana-cho, Amagasaki-shi, Hyogo 660. 06-416-8865
JR Sanyo Line, Tachibana. No contact

Size	Overseas Branches	Overseas Experience	In Future	Country	Non-Japanese Full-Time	Non-Japanese Part-Time	Non-Japanese Increase	Non-Japanese Language	Answer in English	Answer Job-Hunters	Answer Businesses	Answer Researchers
B	0	Y	Y		0	0	N				Y	Y

OILES CORPORATION (OTC)

Manufacturer of oil-less bearings.
1-3-2 Shiba Daimon, Minato-ku, Tokyo 105. 03-5476-2016
JR Yamanote Line, Shinbashi. Contact: Mr. Shigenobu (Kaigai Kikaku-bu)

Size	Overseas Branches	Overseas Experience	In Future	Country	Non-Japanese Full-Time	Non-Japanese Part-Time	Non-Japanese Increase	Non-Japanese Language	Answer in English	Answer Job-Hunters	Answer Businesses	Answer Researchers
A	0	Y	Y	*					Y	Y	Y	Y

* U.S.A., Taiwan

Size	Overseas Branches	Overseas Experience	In Future	Country	←Non-Japanese→ Full-Time	Part-Time	Increase	Language	Answer in English	← Answer → Job-Hunters	Businesses	Researchers

CONTROL AND MEASURING EQUIPMENT

OMRON CORPORATION ①

Manufacturer of control equipment.
Nanajo Sagaru, Karasuma-dori, Shimogyo-ku, Kyoto 600. 075-344-7000
JR Tokaido Line, Kyoto. No contact

Size	Overseas Branches	Overseas Experience	In Future	Country	Full-Time	Part-Time	Increase	Language	Answer in English	Job-Hunters	Businesses	Researchers
A	65	Y	Y		21	0				Y	Y	Y

KYOSAN ELECTRIC MANUFACTURING CO., LTD. ①

Manufacturer of railway and other traffic signals.
2-29-1 Heian-cho, Tsurumi-ku, Yokohama-shi 230. 045-503-8100
JR Keihin Tohoku Line, Tsurumi. No contact

Size	Overseas Branches	Overseas Experience	In Future	Country	Full-Time	Part-Time	Increase	Language	Answer in English	Job-Hunters	Businesses	Researchers
A	0	Y	Y									

CHINO CORPORATION ①

Manufacturer of instrumentation and control equipment.
32-8 Kumano-cho, Itabashi-ku, Tokyo 173. 03-3956-2171 Ext. 2321
JR Yamanote Line, Ikebukuro. Contact:Mr.Yanagisawa(International Div.)

Size	Overseas Branches	Overseas Experience	In Future	Country	Full-Time	Part-Time	Increase	Language	Answer in English	Job-Hunters	Businesses	Researchers
B	46	Y	Y	US					Y	Y	Y	Y

HORIBA, LTD. ①

Manufacturer of analyzing and measuring equipment.
2 Miyano Higashi-cho, Kisshoin, Minami-ku, Kyoto 601. 075-313-8121
JR Tokaido Line, Nishi Oji. Contact: (Kaigai Eigyo-bu)

Size	Overseas Branches	Overseas Experience	In Future	Country	Full-Time	Part-Time	Increase	Language	Answer in English	Job-Hunters	Businesses	Researchers
A	4	Y	Y	US,G	1	0			Y	N	Y	Y

TATSUNO CORPORATION

Manufacturer of precision machinery and measuring equipment.
2-12-9 Shibaura, Minato-ku, Tokyo 108. 03-3452-6211
JR Yamanote Line,Tamachi.Contact: Mr.Mitsuishi 045-895-1661 Ext.910

Size	Overseas Branches	Overseas Experience	In Future	Country	Full-Time	Part-Time	Increase	Language	Answer in English	Job-Hunters	Businesses	Researchers
A		Y	Y	Asia	0	0	N		Y	N	Y	N

OPTICAL

OLYMPUS OPTICAL CO., LTD. ①

Manufacturer of cameras and endoscopes.
2-3-1 Nishi Shinjuku, Shinjuku-ku, Tokyo 163-09. 03-3340-2141
JR Yamanote Line, Shinjuku.Contact:Mr.Yamada (Jinji-bu) 03-3340-2002

Size	Overseas Branches	Overseas Experience	In Future	Country	Full-Time	Part-Time	Increase	Language	Answer in English	Job-Hunters	Businesses	Researchers
A		Y			17	0	Y		Y	Y	Y	N

PROCESS LAB. MICRON CO., LTD.

Manufacturer of various tools for image formation.
1-103-52 Yoshinodai, Kawagoe-shi, Saitama 350. 0492-26-3121
Tobu Tojo or JR Saikyo Line, Kawagoe. Contact: Ms. Kuboniwa (Kanri Block)

Size	Overseas Branches	Overseas Experience	In Future	Country	Full-Time	Part-Time	Increase	Language	Answer in English	Job-Hunters	Businesses	Researchers
B	2	Y	Y	Asia	8	3			N	Y	Y	Y

CHAPTER 10. COMPUTERS, ELECTRONICS AND ELECTRICS

Computers, electronics and electrics are entitled to a little chapter of their own because they have become so important to Japan. It seems to be generally agreed, however, that while Japanese industry has proven very successful at producing computers themselves, the 'hardware', it has not done quite so well at dealing with the programming, the 'software'. Moreover, apart from the question of quality, there has, in recent years, been a shortage of people to do this work. A few years ago, this industry was welcoming the services of any experienced non-Japanese who could assist, and paying good salaries too, as it could afford to do, for computers and all associated with them are expensive in Japan. Now, however, your credentials are likely to be more carefully examined than they would have been five years ago.

Nevertheless, there are still plenty of opportunities for those with skills in this field. Pay is good and work is not limited to those of any particular nationality. Many of those involved in this industry at present are from other Asian countries, especially as this is one area in which, due to the shortage of local labour available and the national necessity of keeping abreast of current developments, the immigration authorities seem to be a little kinder than usual when assessing applications for working visas. The 'software' companies are generally relatively small, yet it is not uncommon to find several non-Japanese at work in a single business enterprise.

The languages which are important here are computer languages and those who are specialists in any particular language or in a particular type of computer are likely to find themselves well received. Increasingly there is also a demand for those who are multi-media experts. In the field of computer 'software', Japan recognizes the need for new ideas and welcomes them.

The fact that everything associated with computers and electronics is so expensive in this country might give the businessman reader food for thought. Individuals who import their own computers from abroad find that they can buy them for considerably less than the Japanese price, even after duty and freight charges have been paid, but very few people do that because it is troublesome and just not a very Japanese thing to do. Also there may be problems with guarantees. However, somebody, somewhere, is making a good profit.

COMPUTERS

Company	Size	Overseas Branches	Overseas Experience	In Future	Country	← Non-Japanese			→	Answer in English	← Answer		→
						Full-Time	Part-Time	Increase	Language		Job-Hunters	Businesses	Researchers
CATENA CORPORATION ②	A	0	Y			2	0	Y	E	N	Y	N	N
CREATERS CORPORATION	C		N	Y	US	1	3	Y	E	Y	Y	Y	Y
CROSS-NET CO. LTD.	D	0	N	N		1	0	Y		Y	Y	N	Y
INTELEC CO., LTD.	C		N	N						N	N	Y	N
TOYOMURA ELECTRONICS CO., LTD.	C	0	Y	Y	*			Y	¶	Y	Y	Y	N

CATENA CORPORATION ②

Sales of personal and office-use computers.
2-10-24 Shiomi, Koto-ku, Tokyo 135. 03-3615-3211
JR Keiyo Line, Shiomi. Contact: Mr. Shimazu (Jinji-bu) 03-3615-9011

CREATERS CORPORATION

Computer sales and software development. 03-3546-8838
Matsumoto Ginza Building, 3-11-13 Ginza, Chuo-ku, Tokyo 104.
Ginza, Marunouchi or Hibiya Line, Ginza. Contact: Mr. Miyazaki

CROSS-NET CO. LTD.

Software development. 03-3735-4530
Kamata Maru Building, 2-29-6 Kamata Honcho, Ota-ku, Tokyo 144.
Keihin Kyuko Line, Keihin Kamata. Contact: Ms. Kamegawa (Somu-bu)

INTELEC CO., LTD.

Software development.
Nagao Building, 4-18-9 Shiba, Minato-ku, Tokyo 108. 03-3454-4946
JR Yamanote Line, Tamachi. Contact: Mr. Yamaguchi

TOYOMURA ELECTRONICS CO., LTD.

Sales of personal computers and wireless transceivers.
2-10-7 Soto Kanda, Chiyoda-ku, Tokyo 101. 03-3257-2672
JR Yamanote or Sobu Line, Akihabara. Contact: Mr. Komukai (Kanri-bu)

* Hong Kong, E.C. Countries
¶ English, Chinese, Korean

ELECTRONIC AND ELECTRICAL COMPONENTS

ALPS ELECTRIC CO., LTD. ①

Manufacturer of electrical components.
1-7 Yukigaya Otsuka, Ota-ku, Tokyo 145. 03-3726-1211
Tokyu Ikegami Line, Yukigaya Otsuka. Contact: (Kaigai Jinji-ka)

Size	Overseas Branches	Overseas Experience	In Future	Country	Non-Japanese: Full-Time	Part-Time	Increase	Language	Answer in English	Answer: Job-Hunters	Businesses	Researchers
A	8	Y	Y		10	0	N		Y			

IKEGAMI TSUSHINKI CO., LTD. ①

Manufacturer of broadcasting equipment.
5-6-16 Ikegami, Ota-ku, Tokyo 146. 03-5700-1111
Tokyu Ikegami Line, Ikegami.Contact:(Kaigai Eigyo Honbu)03-5700-1143

Size	Overseas Branches	Overseas Experience	In Future	Country	Non-Japanese: Full-Time	Part-Time	Increase	Language	Answer in English	Answer: Job-Hunters	Businesses	Researchers
A	4	Y	N		3	1			N	N	N	N

HITACHI DENSHI, LTD. ①

Manufacturer of broadcasting and communications equipment.
1-23-2 Kanda Suda-cho, Chiyoda-ku, Tokyo 101. 03-3255-8411
Marunouchi Line, Awajicho. Contact: Mr. Yamazaki (Kaigai Eigyo Honbu)

Size	Overseas Branches	Overseas Experience	In Future	Country	Non-Japanese: Full-Time	Part-Time	Increase	Language	Answer in English	Answer: Job-Hunters	Businesses	Researchers
A	11	Y	Y	Asia			Y	E,Ch	Y	Y	Y	Y

MATSUSHITA COMMUNICATION INDUSTRIAL CO., LTD. ①

Manufacturer of communications and automobile-related equipment.
4-3-1 Tsunashima Higashi, Kohoku-ku, Yokohama 223.
Tokyu Toyoko Line, Tsunashima. 045-531-1231 No contact

Size	Overseas Branches	Overseas Experience	In Future	Country	Non-Japanese: Full-Time	Part-Time	Increase	Language	Answer in English	Answer: Job-Hunters	Businesses	Researchers
A		Y	Y	*								

* U.S.A., Europe and other areas

SANKYO SEIKI MFG. CO., LTD. ①

Manufacturer of musical boxes and electronic components.
1-17-2 Shinbashi, Minato-ku, Tokyo 105. 03-3502-3711
Ginza, Toei Asakusa or JR Yamanote Line, Shinbashi. No contact

Size	Overseas Branches	Overseas Experience	In Future	Country	Non-Japanese: Full-Time	Part-Time	Increase	Language	Answer in English	Answer: Job-Hunters	Businesses	Researchers
A	9	Y	Y	All	2	0					Y	Y

SUMITOMO ELECTRIC INDUSTRIES LTD. ①

Manufacturer of electric wires and cables.
4-5-33 Kitahama, Chuo-ku, Osaka-shi 541. 06-220-4141
Midosuji Line, Yodoyabashi. No contact

Size	Overseas Branches	Overseas Experience	In Future	Country	Non-Japanese: Full-Time	Part-Time	Increase	Language	Answer in English	Answer: Job-Hunters	Businesses	Researchers
A	20	Y										

MATSUO ELECTRIC CO., LTD. ②

Manufacturer of capacitors.
3-5-3 Sennari-cho, Toyonaka-shi, Osaka 561. 06-332-0871
Hankyu Kobe Line, Kanzakigawa. No contact

Size	Overseas Branches	Overseas Experience	In Future	Country	Non-Japanese: Full-Time	Part-Time	Increase	Language	Answer in English	Answer: Job-Hunters	Businesses	Researchers
B	2	Y	Y						N	N	Y	Y

ENOMOTO CO., LTD. (OTC)

Electronic parts maker with precision metal-moulding technology.
2222 Uenohara, Uenohara-machi, Kitatsuru-gun, Yamanashi 409-01.
JR Chuo Line, Uenohara. Contact: Mr. Sugimoto (Keiri-bu) 0554-62-5112

Size	Overseas Branches	Overseas Experience	In Future	Country	Non-Japanese: Full-Time	Part-Time	Increase	Language	Answer in English	Answer: Job-Hunters	Businesses	Researchers
B	1	Y	Y	*					Y		Y	Y

* S.E. Asia, U.S.A.

NIPPON ANTENNA CO., LTD. (OTC)

Manufacturer of various kinds of antenna.
7-49-10 Nishi Ogu, Arakawa-ku, Tokyo 116. 03-3810-5521
JR Takasaki Line, Ogu. Contact: Mr. Takizawa (Jinji-bu)

Size	Overseas Branches	Overseas Experience	In Future	Country	Non-Japanese: Full-Time	Part-Time	Increase	Language	Answer in English	Answer: Job-Hunters	Businesses	Researchers
B	4	Y	Y	All	2	5			Y	N	Y	Y

					Non-Japanese					Answer		
Size	Overseas Branches	Overseas Experience	In Future	Country	Full-Time	Part-Time	Increase	Language	Answer in English	Job-Hunters	Businesses	Researchers

NEW JAPAN RADIO CO., LTD. (OTC)

Manufacturer of semiconductors and microwave-related equipment.
1-8-1 Shimo Meguro, Meguro-ku, Tokyo 153. 03-5434-8335
JR Yamanote Line, Meguro. Contact: Mr. Nomura (Kaigai Eigyo-bu) Ext. 2112

Size	Overseas Branches	Overseas Experience	In Future	Country	Full-Time	Part-Time	Increase	Language	Answer in English	Job-Hunters	Businesses	Researchers
A	1	Y	Y	*	6	0			Y	Y	Y	Y

* South Africa, India, Indonesia

PHILIPS JAPAN LTD.

General electronics manufacturer.
2-13-37 Konan, Minato-ku, Tokyo 108. 03-3740-5053
JR Yamanote Line, Shinagawa. Contact: Ms. Matsueda (Somu-bu)

Size	Overseas Branches	Overseas Experience	In Future	Country	Full-Time	Part-Time	Increase	Language	Answer in English	Job-Hunters	Businesses	Researchers
B		Y			37	0			Y	N	N	N

NIHON KOSUHA CO., LTD.

Manufacturer of microwave-related equipment and electronic products.
1119 Nakayama-cho, Midori-ku, Yokohama 226. 045-931-2621
JR Yokohama Line, Nakayama. Contact: Mr. Kawai (Somu-bu)

Size	Overseas Branches	Overseas Experience	In Future	Country	Full-Time	Part-Time	Increase	Language	Answer in English	Job-Hunters	Businesses	Researchers
B		Y	Y	*			Y	¶	Y	Y	Y	Y

* U.S.A., China
¶ English, Chinese, Korean

CHAPTER 11. CONSTRUCTION AND CIVIL ENGINEERING

Perhaps the most interesting characteristic of the construction industry for our readers is its recent interest in overseas projects, often in collaboration with manufacturing concerns. The manufacturer may offer the equipment for a power station, for example, while the construction company will offer to erect the buildings necessary. This type of joint work might be of interest to overseas ventures also.

For the job-hunter, it means that these companies have an ever-increasing need for foreign language services, as well as for overseas negotiators. Unfortunately, though, not all as yet appreciate that they have that need. Positions available include those dealing with technical re-writing, correspondence, writing proposals, writing tenders, making specifications, co-ordinating with sub-contractors or joint venture partners overseas, design work and preparation of drawings. A few companies are also willing to use exceptionally well qualified non-Japanese for management of overseas projects. The need is not restricted to English speakers. There are also opportunities for speakers of other languages, especially as many of the projects are carried out in other Asian countries.

It should be appreciated that the construction industry is rather a conservative one. It depends upon a large number of sub-contractors, in the Japanese tradition of sharing work around and, as usual, connexions are very important. For the non-Japanese working in this environment, it will mean an adjustment of priorities and ways of thinking. Of course, this is so with most types of employment in this country, but it is especially important in this area.

Although many small companies will be involved in a construction project, it is only the large companies, the principal contractors rather than the sub-contractors, who will usually be interested in employing non-Japanese.

CONSTRUCTION

Column key: Size · Overseas Branches · Overseas Experience · In Future · Country · Non-Japanese: Full-Time, Part-Time, Increase, Language · Answer in English · Answer: Job-Hunters, Businesses, Researchers

KAJIMA CORPORATION ①

Construction in general.
1-2-7 Moto Akasaka, Minato-ku, Tokyo 107. 03-3404-3311
Marunouchi or Ginza Line, Akasaka Mitsuke. Contact: (Kokusai-bu) Ext. 27111

Size	Overseas Branches	Overseas Experience	In Future	Country	Full-Time	Part-Time	Increase	Language	Answer in English	Job-Hunters	Businesses	Researchers
A	40	Y	Y	All	23	0			Y	N	Y	Y

TEKKEN CORPORATION ①

Construction in general.
2-5-3 Misaki-cho, Chiyoda-ku, Tokyo 101. 03-3262-3411
Toei Mita or JR Sobu Line, Suidobashi. No contact

Size	Overseas Branches	Overseas Experience	In Future	Country	Full-Time	Part-Time	Increase	Language	Answer in English	Job-Hunters	Businesses	Researchers
A	3	N	N		0	0	N			N	N	N

NISHIMATSU CONSTRUCTION CO., LTD. ①

Construction in general.
1-20-10 Toranomon, Minato-ku, Tokyo 105. 03-3502-7692
Ginza Line, Toranomon. Contact: Mr. Mizunaga (Kaigai Jigyo-bu)

Size	Overseas Branches	Overseas Experience	In Future	Country	Full-Time	Part-Time	Increase	Language	Answer in English	Job-Hunters	Businesses	Researchers
A	11	N	N		0	1			Y	Y	Y	Y

ISHIHARA CONSTRUCTION CO., LTD. ②

Construction in general.
25 Shinano-machi, Shinjuku-ku, Tokyo 160. 03-3355-3104
JR Sobu Line, Shinanomachi. Contact: Mr. Yoshida (Kaigai Jigyo-bu)

Size	Overseas Branches	Overseas Experience	In Future	Country	Full-Time	Part-Time	Increase	Language	Answer in English	Job-Hunters	Businesses	Researchers
B	2	N	N						Y	N	N	N

SATOHIDE CONSTRUCTION CO., LTD. (OTC)

Construction in general.
5-6-11 Shinjuku, Shinjuku-ku, Tokyo 160. 03-3225-0313
Marunouchi Line, Shinjuku Gyoen-mae. No contact

Size	Overseas Branches	Overseas Experience	In Future	Country	Full-Time	Part-Time	Increase	Language	Answer in English	Job-Hunters	Businesses	Researchers
B	0	N	N		0	0				N	N	N

FUKUI CONSTRUCTION CO., LTD.

Construction in general.
5-5 Naka-cho, Naka-ku, Hiroshima-shi, Hiroshima 730. 082-248-1877
JR Sanyo Line, Hiroshima. Contact: Mr. Konmura (Kikaku-bu)

Size	Overseas Branches	Overseas Experience	In Future	Country	Full-Time	Part-Time	Increase	Language	Answer in English	Job-Hunters	Businesses	Researchers
B	2	Y			28	0	Y		N	Y	Y	Y

CIVIL ENGINEERING

					← Non-Japanese			→		← Answer		→
Size	Overseas Branches	Overseas Experience	In Future	Country	Full-Time	Part-Time	Increase	Language	Answer in English	Job-Hunters	Businesses	Researchers

CHIYODA CORPORATION ①

Plant engineering.
Banzai Building, 2-31-19 Shiba, Minato-ku, Tokyo 105. 03-3456-1211
Toei Mita Line, Shiba Koen. Contact: Mr.Kanehira (Jinji-bu) 045-506-7101

Size	Overseas Branches	Overseas Experience	In Future	Country	Full-Time	Part-Time	Increase	Language	Answer in English	Job-Hunters	Businesses	Researchers
A	18	Y	Y	All	14	0	Y	E	Y	Y	Y	Y

J G C CORP. ①

Plant engineering.
2-2-1 Otemachi, Chiyoda-ku, Tokyo 100. 03-3279-5441
Marunouchi or JR Yamanote Line, Tokyo. No contact

Size	Overseas Branches	Overseas Experience	In Future	Country	Full-Time	Part-Time	Increase	Language	Answer in English	Job-Hunters	Businesses	Researchers
A	18	Y	N		10	0				N	N	Y

NIPPON DENTSU KENSETSU CO., LTD. ②

Communications and cable installations and other engineering.
2-21-1 Isoji, Minato-ku, Osaka 552. 06-575-3886 Ext. 350
JR Kanjo Line, Bentencho. Contact: Mr.Odashima (Tsushin Jigyo San-bu)

Size	Overseas Branches	Overseas Experience	In Future	Country	Full-Time	Part-Time	Increase	Language	Answer in English	Job-Hunters	Businesses	Researchers
B		Y	Y	Asia					N	N	Y	Y

CHAPTER 12. FOOD PRODUCERS

This is a section most likely to interest our businessman looking for import or export opportunities. However, although there are a few major companies dealing in such business, the majority of the concerns in this field are rather small.

Companies in this area do need assistance with foreign language work, of course, but, as usual, the problem is that often they do not appreciate that such assistance would be beneficial to them. Nevertheless, the job-seeker with experience in the area can try approaching companies, and can always hope that one will understand the potential benefits.

Opportunities are mainly for those who can offer assistance with import and export marketing, but the small size of most companies means that their demand for non-Japanese employees is somewhat limited. In this area, too, it should be noted that the market is by no means confined to English speakers. In fact, because a large proportion of food exporting and importing is to or from nearby countries, the demand, such as it is, in this area is often for speakers of Asian languages.

Column key: Size | Overseas Branches | Overseas Experience | In Future | Country | Non-Japanese: Full-Time | Part-Time | Increase | Language | Answer in English | Answer: Job-Hunters | Businesses | Researchers

MORINAGA & CO., LTD. ①

General confectioner.
5-33-1 Shiba, Minato-ku, Tokyo 108. 03-3456-0116
JR Yamanote Line, Tamachi. No contact

Size	Overseas Branches	Overseas Experience	In Future	Country	Full-Time	Part-Time	Increase	Language	Answer in English	Job-Hunters	Businesses	Researchers
A	3	Y	Y	Asia	0	0				N	N	Y

THE CALPIS FOOD INDUSTRY CO., LTD. ①

Producer of lactic acid drinks.
2-20-3 Ebisu Nishi, Shibuya-ku, Tokyo 150. 03-3780-2131
Tokyu Toyoko Line, Daikanyama. Contact: (Kaigai Jigyo-bu)

Size	Overseas Branches	Overseas Experience	In Future	Country	Full-Time	Part-Time	Increase	Language	Answer in English	Job-Hunters	Businesses	Researchers
B	1	Y	Y	*	1	0			Y	N	N	N

* U.S.A., S.E. Asia

KATOKICHI CO., LTD. ①

Producer of various frozen foods.
Ko-294-1 Kannonji-cho, Kannonji-shi, Kagawa 768. 0875-23-0459
JR Yosan Line, Kannonji. Contact: Mr. Takasu (Kaigai Jigyo-bu)

Size	Overseas Branches	Overseas Experience	In Future	Country	Full-Time	Part-Time	Increase	Language	Answer in English	Job-Hunters	Businesses	Researchers
A		Y	Y	Asia	77	0	Y	P	Y	N	N	N

FUJI FLOUR MILLING CO., LTD. ②

Millers.
3-1-18 Seikai, Shimizu-shi, Shizuoka 424. 0543-34-2311
JR Tokaido Line, Shimizu. No contact

Size	Overseas Branches	Overseas Experience	In Future	Country	Full-Time	Part-Time	Increase	Language	Answer in English	Job-Hunters	Businesses	Researchers
B		Y	Y						N	N	Y	N

MYOJO FOODS CO., LTD. ②

Manufacturer of various types of noodles. Restaurant operator.
3-50-11 Sendagaya, Shibuya-ku, Tokyo 151. 03-3478-2541
JR Yamanote Line, Harajuku. Contact: (Kaigai Jigyo-bu)

Size	Overseas Branches	Overseas Experience	In Future	Country	Full-Time	Part-Time	Increase	Language	Answer in English	Job-Hunters	Businesses	Researchers
B	4	Y	Y	*	1	0	Y	E,Ch	Y	N	N	N

* S.E. Asia, China, U.S.A.

SATO FOODS INDUSTRIES CO., LTD. (OTC)

Manufacturer of natural seasonings.
4-154 Horinouchi, Komaki-shi, Aichi 485. 0568-77-7316
Meitetsu Line, Iwakura. No contact

Size	Overseas Branches	Overseas Experience	In Future	Country	Full-Time	Part-Time	Increase	Language	Answer in English	Job-Hunters	Businesses	Researchers
B	0	Y	Y	*	0	0	N			N	Y	Y

* Europe, U.S.A., Asia

ITO EN, LTD. (OTC)

Manufacturer of various kinds of Japanese tea.
3-47-10 Honcho, Shibuya-ku, Tokyo 151. 03-5371-7111
Marunouchi Line, Nakano Sakaue. Contact: (Jinji-bu) 03-5371-7117

Size	Overseas Branches	Overseas Experience	In Future	Country	Full-Time	Part-Time	Increase	Language	Answer in English	Job-Hunters	Businesses	Researchers
A	0	Y	Y		2	0	Y	*		Y	Y	Y

* English, French, German, Spanish, Chinese

SANYO FOODS CORPORATION

Manufacturer of instant noodles.
3-5-2 Akasaka, Minato-ku, Tokyo 107. 03-3586-9811
Marunouchi or Ginza Line, Akasaka Mitsuke. Contact: Mr. Iwasaki (Somu-bu)

Size	Overseas Branches	Overseas Experience	In Future	Country	Full-Time	Part-Time	Increase	Language	Answer in English	Job-Hunters	Businesses	Researchers
A	4	Y	N						N	N	N	N

HICHIFUKU BREWING CO., LTD.

Manufacturer of natural seasongs.
2-7 Yamagami-cho, Hekinan-shi, Aichi 447. 0566-41-1286
Meitetsu Mikawa Line, Kita Shinkawa. Contact: Mr. Aoki (Kaigai Jigyo-bu)

Size	Overseas Branches	Overseas Experience	In Future	Country	Full-Time	Part-Time	Increase	Language	Answer in English	Job-Hunters	Businesses	Researchers
C	0	N	Y		1	0	Y	E	Y	Y	Y	Y

HÄAGEN-DAZS JAPAN INC.

Manufacturer and retailer of ice-cream. 03-5434-8300
11th Fl. Arco Tower, 1-8-1 Shimo Meguro, Meguro-ku, Tokyo 153.
JR Yamanote Line, Meguro. Contact: Mr. Matsuda (Marketing)

Size	Overseas Branches	Overseas Experience	In Future	Country	Full-Time	Part-Time	Increase	Language	Answer in English	Job-Hunters	Businesses	Researchers
B	0	Y	Y	US	0	0			Y	N	N	Y

CHAPTER 13. WHOLESALERS AND RETAILERS

Our businessmen readers will be wanting to contact companies in this category if they have something to sell. The companies listed here responded to our questionnaire, so may be expected to have an interest in your business. If, however, you need somebody more specialized than those listed, try contacting the relevant trade association from those detailed in Chapter 18. As usual, JETRO or your embassy may also be able to assist.

As regards employment, businesses in this sector were slow to appreciate that a non-Japanese employee could be useful to them. In the last few years, however, some of the more progressive companies have started to see the advantages and employment opportunities have become more common.

The primary need was for people to assist with paperwork in English, but some larger concerns soon started to investigate western business practices, particularly in relation to supermarket operations, and to adopt such elements as they believed advantageous. One hears that, these days, most companies manage to fill positions through introductions which are made, but recently department stores, in particular, have caught on to the idea of having a few foreign faces around, some of them probably just for prestige, but most engaged in positions dealing with English or other foreign language paperwork.

Conditions, remuneration and levels of satisfaction seem to vary considerably. Usually Japanese language ability is regarded as a definite asset in these positions, so, if you do not have that, you should be able to offer something else instead, for example managerial experience in a similar operation in your home country or specialized knowledge of a particular market.

At present, typical positions available are those dealing with correspondence, marketing and guest relations, but in the future there may be more need for buyers. Because of the peculiarities of the Japanese distribution system and the different needs of Japanese consumers, this type of work will require some mental adjustment, but should prove educational.

Recently, the department stores have established branches overseas and this is requiring them to be more interested in recruiting non-Japanese employees and to understand the requirements of overseas consumers. In fact, the department stores are probably the most likely possibility for anybody who is interested in working in this field.

Size | Overseas Branches | Overseas Experience | In Future | Country | ← Non-Japanese →: Full-Time | Part-Time | Increase | Language | Answer in English | ← Answer →: Job-Hunters | Businesses | Researchers

KYOTARU CORP. ①

Chain restaurant operator (sushi kiosks and family restaurants).
1-36-9 Kakigara-cho, Nihonbashi, Chuo-ku, Tokyo 103. 03-3663-4265
Hanzomon Line, Suitengu-mae. Contact: Mr. Okamoto (Kaigai Jigyo-bu)

Size	Overseas Branches	Overseas Experience	In Future	Country	Full-Time	Part-Time	Increase	Language	Answer in English	Job-Hunters	Businesses	Researchers
A	3	Y	Y	US					Y	Y	Y	Y

KASUMI CO., LTD. ①

Supermarket chain operator.
1-3 Higashi Nakanuki-machi, Tsuchiura, Ibaraki 300. 0298-31-0031
JR Joban Line, Kandatsu. No contact

Size	Overseas Branches	Overseas Experience	In Future	Country	Full-Time	Part-Time	Increase	Language	Answer in English	Job-Hunters	Businesses	Researchers
A		Y	N		3	30				N	N	N

UNY CO., LTD. ①

Chain store operator.
3-6-8 Mei-eki, Nakamura-ku, Nagoya 450. 052-585-3111
JR Tokaido Line, Nagoya. No contact

Size	Overseas Branches	Overseas Experience	In Future	Country	Full-Time	Part-Time	Increase	Language	Answer in English	Job-Hunters	Businesses	Researchers
A	1	Y	Y							N	Y	Y

FREX INC. ②

Supermarket chain operator.
185-1 Okuchi-cho, Matsusaka-shi, Mie 515. 0598-51-3125
Kintetsu Line, Matsusaka. Contact: Mr. Mukai (Jinji-bu) 0598-51-3101

Size	Overseas Branches	Overseas Experience	In Future	Country	Full-Time	Part-Time	Increase	Language	Answer in English	Job-Hunters	Businesses	Researchers
B	0	N							Y	Y	Y	

FRIENDLY CORPORATION ②

Family restaurant and pub operator.
3-5-24 Miyahara, Yodogawa-ku, Osaka 532. 06-397-0111
Midosuji or JR Tokaido Line, Shin Osaka. Contact: (Jinji-bu)

Size	Overseas Branches	Overseas Experience	In Future	Country	Full-Time	Part-Time	Increase	Language	Answer in English	Job-Hunters	Businesses	Researchers
B	0	Y	N		0	13				N	N	N

NAKAI CO., LTD. ②

D I Y store operator.
3-62 Okihama Higashi, Tokushima-shi, Tokushima 770. 0886-55-0001
Kotoku Line, Tokushima. Contact: Mr. Okada (Jinji-bu) Ext. 22

Size	Overseas Branches	Overseas Experience	In Future	Country	Full-Time	Part-Time	Increase	Language	Answer in English	Job-Hunters	Businesses	Researchers
B	0	N	N		1	0	Y	E,Ch	N	Y	Y	Y

NISHIMOTO SANGYO CO., LTD. ②

Sales of X-ray films and medical equipment.
1-15 Higashi Koraibashi, Chuo-ku, Osaka 540. 06-942-4901
Sakaisuji Line, Kitahama. Contact: Mr. Komura (Kaigai-bu) 03-3818-1324

Size	Overseas Branches	Overseas Experience	In Future	Country	Full-Time	Part-Time	Increase	Language	Answer in English	Job-Hunters	Businesses	Researchers
B	1	Y	Y	All	1	0	Y	E	Y	Y	Y	Y

GREEN HOUSE CO., LTD. (OTC)

Operator of catering services.
Zen Riren Building, 1-36-4 Yoyogi, Shibuya-ku, Tokyo 151. 03-3379-1211
JR Yamanote or Sobu Line, Yoyogi. Contact: Mr. Kumagai 03-3379-1069

Size	Overseas Branches	Overseas Experience	In Future	Country	Full-Time	Part-Time	Increase	Language	Answer in English	Job-Hunters	Businesses	Researchers
A	2	Y	N		2	0			Y	Y	Y	Y

HÄAGEN-DAZS JAPAN INC.

Manufacturer and retailer of ice-cream. 03-5434-8300
11th Fl. Arco Tower, 1-8-1 Shimo Meguro, Meguro-ku, Tokyo 153.
JR Yamanote Line, Meguro. Contact: Mr. Matsuda (Marketing)

Size	Overseas Branches	Overseas Experience	In Future	Country	Full-Time	Part-Time	Increase	Language	Answer in English	Job-Hunters	Businesses	Researchers
B	0	Y	Y	US	0	0	N		Y	N	N	Y

SEIBU DEPARTMENT STORES, LTD.

Operator of department stores. 03-3989-0111
Sunshine 60, 3-1-1 Higashi Ikebukuro, Toshima-ku, Tokyo 170.
JR Yamanote Line, Ikebukuro. Contact: Ms. Okajima (Jinji-bu)

Size	Overseas Branches	Overseas Experience	In Future	Country	Full-Time	Part-Time	Increase	Language	Answer in English	Job-Hunters	Businesses	Researchers
A	6	Y			72	0	Y		Y	Y	Y	Y

NISHIO RENT ALL CO., LTD. (OTC)

Rental of construction equipment.
3-4-26 Minami Senba, Chuo-ku, Osaka 542. 06-251-7302
Midosuji Line, Shinsaibashi. Contact: (Somu-bu Jinji-ka) 06-251-0070

Size	Overseas Branches	Overseas Experience	In Future	Country	Non-Japanese Full-Time	Non-Japanese Part-Time	Non-Japanese Increase	Non-Japanese Language	Answer in English	Answer Job-Hunters	Answer Businesses	Answer Researchers
B	0	Y	Y	Asia	0	0	Y		N	N	N	N

CHAPTER 14. TRADING COMPANIES

Again this is an area which should interest the businessman with something to sell – or even something to buy. Trading companies in Japan range from huge concerns which are parts of the giant conglomerates to tiny one-man operations founded on the operator's connexions and ability to speak English.

We found it difficult to select from this field, but present here what we hope is a representative sample. Again, if you want somebody who is a specialist in a field not covered here, it would probably be best to contact the relevant trade association from the list in Chapter 18.

Trading companies, by their nature, must possess a certain degree of international awareness, so were among the first to start employing non-Japanese. And yet, at the same time, the larger of such concerns feel a pride in their own language ability and sometimes wish to show that they can manage very well without any help, thank you. So, as is so common in Japanese business circles, they employ non-Japanese and then often do not use them well.

Recently, though, these companies too have started to become aware that doing business in foreign lands can be assisted by having their non-Japanese employees engaged in actual negotiations and in dealing with the inevitable hitches which occur, so opportunities are there for those with business experience, as well as for those just able to check English.

It used to be only the larger concerns which had such opportunities, but, of course, they were also the most conservative in their approach. Now, however, even smaller companies are using non-Japanese members of staff, and work in a smaller company is likely to be much more interesting with more responsibility available and with opportunities for a good person to be involved more in marketing and negotiations.

Size	Overseas Branches	Overseas Experience	In Future	Country	Non-Japanese: Full-Time	Non-Japanese: Part-Time	Non-Japanese: Increase	Non-Japanese: Language	Answer in English	Answer: Job-Hunters	Answer: Businesses	Answer: Researchers

TRADING COMPANIES
(ENGAGED IN BOTH IMPORT AND EXPORT)

CHORI CO., LTD. ①

Specializing in textiles and chemicals.
2-4-7 Kawara-machi, Chuo-ku, Osaka 541. 06-228-5120
Midosuji, Yotsubashi or Chuo Line, Honmachi. Contact: (Jinji-bu, Kaigai Group)

Size	Overseas Branches	Overseas Experience	In Future	Country	Full-Time	Part-Time	Increase	Language	Answer in English	Job-Hunters	Businesses	Researchers
A	42	Y	Y		1	0			Y	N	N	Y

KANEMATSU CORPORATION ①

Specializing in textiles,chemicals and metals.
1-2-1-N Shibaura, Minato-ku, Tokyo 105-05. 03-5440-6739
JR Yamanote Line, Hamamatsucho. Contact: (Personnel Service)

Size	Overseas Branches	Overseas Experience	In Future	Country	Full-Time	Part-Time	Increase	Language	Answer in English	Job-Hunters	Businesses	Researchers
A	100	Y	Y	*	2	10			Y	Y	Y	Y

* China, Vietnam

TSUBAKIMOTO MACHINERY & ENGINEERING CO., LTD. ①

Specializing in vehicle transmissions and materials handling equipment.
2-4 Komatsubara-cho, Kita-ku, Osaka 530. 06-315-5180
JR Tokaido Line, Osaka. Contact: Mr. Yuasa (Kaigai Eigyo-bu)

Size	Overseas Branches	Overseas Experience	In Future	Country	Full-Time	Part-Time	Increase	Language	Answer in English	Job-Hunters	Businesses	Researchers
B	2	Y	Y	*	0	1	Y	E,Ch	Y	Y	Y	Y

* ASEAN Countries

KASHO CO., LTD. ①

Specializing in rubber, chemicals and marine and livestock products.
2-14-9 Nihonbashi, Chuo-ku, Tokyo 103. 03-3276-7705
Ginza, Tozai, Toei Asakusa Line, Nihonbashi. Contact: Mr. Matsui (Gyomu-bu)

Size	Overseas Branches	Overseas Experience	In Future	Country	Full-Time	Part-Time	Increase	Language	Answer in English	Job-Hunters	Businesses	Researchers
B	12	Y	Y				Y	E	Y	Y	Y	Y

KAIGEN CO., LTD. ②

Speciializing in X-ray contrast media.
2-5-14 Dosho-machi, Chuo-ku, Osaka 541. 06-202-8971
Midosuji Line, Yodoyabashi. Contact: Mr. Honda 06-202-8975

Size	Overseas Branches	Overseas Experience	In Future	Country	Full-Time	Part-Time	Increase	Language	Answer in English	Job-Hunters	Businesses	Researchers
B	0	Y	N						N	N	N	N

CORNES & CO., LTD.

General importing and exporting.
Maruzen Bldg., 2-3-10 Nihonbashi, Chuo-ku, Tokyo 103. 03-3272-5771
Ginza, Tozai or Toei Asakusa Line, Nihonbashi. Contact: Mr. Hirano Ext. 523

Size	Overseas Branches	Overseas Experience	In Future	Country	Full-Time	Part-Time	Increase	Language	Answer in English	Job-Hunters	Businesses	Researchers
B	3	Y	Y	US	3	0	Y	E	N	Y	Y	N

DAH CHONG HONG (JAPAN) LTD.

General importing and exporting.
No. 2 Taisho Building, 5-18-2 Roppongi, Minato-ku, Tokyo 106.
Hibiya Line, Roppongi. Contact: Mr. Lui (Somu-bu) 03-3582-0711

Size	Overseas Branches	Overseas Experience	In Future	Country	Full-Time	Part-Time	Increase	Language	Answer in English	Job-Hunters	Businesses	Researchers
B	0	Y	Y	Asia	23	3	Y	E,Ch	Y	Y	N	N

LIAONING CO., LTD.

General importer and exporter. Also concerned with investment in China.
Shin Aoyama Bldg., 1-1-1 Minami Aoyama, Minato-ku, Tokyo 107.
Ginza, Hanzomon Line, Aoyama l-chome. Contact: Mr. Ko 03-3479-5021

Size	Overseas Branches	Overseas Experience	In Future	Country	Full-Time	Part-Time	Increase	Language	Answer in English	Job-Hunters	Businesses	Researchers
C	2	Y	Y	Ch	9	0	Y	Ch	N	Y	Y	N

NIPPON LITON & SILITEK CO., LTD.

Importer and exporter of electrical parts and instruments. 03-3239-6501
Ichigaya K.T. Bldg., 4-7-16 Kudan Minami, Chiyoda-ku, Tokyo 102.
Yurakucho, Toei Shinjuku or JR Sobu Line, Ichigaya. No contact

Size	Overseas Branches	Overseas Experience	In Future	Country	Full-Time	Part-Time	Increase	Language	Answer in English	Job-Hunters	Businesses	Researchers
C	0	Y	Y	Asia	3	0	Y	E,Ch		N	N	N

SOEI TSUSHO CO., LTD.

Importer and exporter of electronics materials, semi-conductors, etc.
4-2-7 Bakuro-machi, Chuo-ku, Osaka 541. 06-241-0900
Midosuji, Yotsubashi, Chuo Line, Honmachi. Contact:Mr.Murakami (Shacho-shitsu)

Size	Overseas Branches	Overseas Experience	In Future	Country	Full-Time (Non-Japanese)	Part-Time (Non-Japanese)	Increase	Language	Answer in English	Job-Hunters (Answer)	Businesses (Answer)	Researchers (Answer)
C	3	Y	Y	Asia	2	0	Y	Ch	Y	Y	Y	Y

IMPORTERS OF SPECIFIC GOODS
(INCLUDING SUBSIDIARY COMPANIES IMPORTING PARENT COMPANY'S PRODUCTS)

BANG & OLUFSEN OF JAPAN LIMITED

Importer of audio products. 03-3261-4431
Kudan New Central Bldg., 1-4-5 Kudan Kita, Chiyoda-ku, Tokyo 102.
Tozai, Hanzomon or Toei Shinjuku Line, Kudanshita. No contact

Size	Overseas Branches	Overseas Experience	In Future	Country	Full-Time	Part-Time	Increase	Language	Answer in English	Job-Hunters	Businesses	Researchers
C		Y								Y	Y	Y

BAUSCH & LOMB INCORPORATED

Importer of contact lenses, sunglasses, frames.
No. 2 Mita Building, 5-5-1 Shiba, Minato-ku, Tokyo 108. 03-3455-5651
JR Yamanote Line, Tamachi. Contact:Mr.Kawabe (Jinji-bu) 03-3455-1238

Size	Overseas Branches	Overseas Experience	In Future	Country	Full-Time	Part-Time	Increase	Language	Answer in English	Job-Hunters	Businesses	Researchers
B					7	0	Y	E		Y	Y	N

BEIERSDORF JAPAN K.K.

Importer of industrial adhesive tapes and medical-related products.
No. 2 Komatsu Building, 2-14-17 Shibuya, Shibuya-ku, Tokyo 150.
JR Yamanote Line, Shibuya. Contact: Ms. Ito 03-3407-5447 Ext. 511

Size	Overseas Branches	Overseas Experience	In Future	Country	Full-Time	Part-Time	Increase	Language	Answer in English	Job-Hunters	Businesses	Researchers
B		Y	N		4	0	Y	E,G	Y	N	N	Y

BRAN & LUEBBE K.K.

Importer of instruments for chemical analysis.
Shoei Bldg., 4-22-8 Sendagaya, Shibuya-ku, Tokyo 151. 03-3423-7501
JR Yamanote or Sobu Line, Yoyogi. No contact

Size	Overseas Branches	Overseas Experience	In Future	Country	Full-Time	Part-Time	Increase	Language	Answer in English	Job-Hunters	Businesses	Researchers
C		Y	N		2	0	Y	E	N	N	N	N

CARRIER TRANSICOLD (JAPAN) LTD.

Importer of freezers for containers, trucks, ships, etc.
Mitsui Bussan Bldg., 14 Nihon Odori, Naka-ku, Yokohama 231.
JR Keihin Tohoku Line, Kannai. Contact: Mr. Yasuda 045-664-6271

Size	Overseas Branches	Overseas Experience	In Future	Country	Full-Time	Part-Time	Increase	Language	Answer in English	Job-Hunters	Businesses	Researchers
D		Y	Y	US	0	0	Y	E	Y	N	N	N

ENI CHEM JAPAN LTD.

Importer of chemicals, foodstuffs and cosmetic products.
Hazama Bldg., 2-5-8 Kita Aoyama, Minato-ku, Tokyo 107. 03-5410-8359
Ginza Line, Gaien-mae. No contact

Size	Overseas Branches	Overseas Experience	In Future	Country	Full-Time	Part-Time	Increase	Language	Answer in English	Job-Hunters	Businesses	Researchers
C		Y	Y	It	1	0	Y	E		N	Y	Y

G E APPLIANCES JAPAN

Importer of home electrical appliances.
3-7-8 Toranomon, Minato-ku, Tokyo 105. 03-3459-8741
Hibiya Line, Kamiyacho. No contact

Size	Overseas Branches	Overseas Experience	In Future	Country	Full-Time	Part-Time	Increase	Language	Answer in English	Job-Hunters	Businesses	Researchers
		Y	Y	UK						N	Y	N

HARRIS K.K.

Importer of semi-conductors. 03-3345-8913
Shinjuku NS Building, 2-4-1 Nishi Shinjuku, Shinjuku-ku, Tokyo 163-08.
JR Yamanote or Chuo Line, Shinjuku. Contact: Mr. Matsumoto (Jinji-bu)

Size	Overseas Branches	Overseas Experience	In Future	Country	Full-Time	Part-Time	Increase	Language	Answer in English	Job-Hunters	Businesses	Researchers
C	1	Y	N		1	0			Y	Y	Y	Y

INTERNATIONAL CONTRACTING CORP.

Importer of electronics components and electro-mechanical products.
Akasaka Q Bldg., 7-9-5 Akasaka, Minato-ku, Tokyo 107. 03-3583-1223
Chiyoda Line, Akasaka. Contact: Mr. Kobayashi (Trade Division)

Size	Overseas Branches	Overseas Experience	In Future	Country	Non-Japanese Full-Time	Non-Japanese Part-Time	Non-Japanese Increase	Non-Japanese Language	Answer in English	Answer Job-Hunters	Answer Businesses	Answer Researchers
D		Y	Y	*	2	1	Y	E,Ch	Y	Y	Y	Y

* U.S.A., S.E. Asia, China

JARDINE WINES AND SPIRITS K.K.

Importer of wines.
Halifax Onarimon Bldg., 3-24-10 Nishi Shinbashi, Minato-ku, Tokyo 105.
Toei Mita Line, Onarimon. Contact: Mr. Ota (Somu Jinji-bu) 03-3434-7370

Size	Overseas Branches	Overseas Experience	In Future	Country	Non-Japanese Full-Time	Non-Japanese Part-Time	Non-Japanese Increase	Non-Japanese Language	Answer in English	Answer Job-Hunters	Answer Businesses	Answer Researchers
B		Y	Y	*	8	0	N		Y	N	Y	Y

* U.K., France, Germany, U.S.A., Italy

JINRO JAPAN INC.

Importer of 'shochu jiro' (distilled spirits).
3-8-21 Toranomon, Minato-ku, Tokyo 105. 03-3432-1320
Hibiya Line, Kamiyacho. Contact: Mr. Chai

Size	Overseas Branches	Overseas Experience	In Future	Country	Non-Japanese Full-Time	Non-Japanese Part-Time	Non-Japanese Increase	Non-Japanese Language	Answer in English	Answer Job-Hunters	Answer Businesses	Answer Researchers
D		Y	Y		6	0	Y	Kor	Y	Y	Y	Y

KOHLER JAPAN K.K.

Importer of bathroom and kitchen ware.
Oak Minami Azabu Bldg., 3-19-23 Minami Azabu, Minato-ku, Tokyo 106.
Hibiya Line, Hiro-o. Contact: (Secretary) 03-3440-4480

Size	Overseas Branches	Overseas Experience	In Future	Country	Non-Japanese Full-Time	Non-Japanese Part-Time	Non-Japanese Increase	Non-Japanese Language	Answer in English	Answer Job-Hunters	Answer Businesses	Answer Researchers
C		Y	Y	US					Y	Y	Y	Y

NORDSON ENGINEERING K.K.

Importer of painting equipment and hot melt applicators.
3-11-13 Kita Shinagawa, Shinagawa-ku, Tokyo 140. 03-5461-8241
Keihin Kyuko Line, Shin Baba. Contact: Mr. To (Kanri-bu)

Size	Overseas Branches	Overseas Experience	In Future	Country	Non-Japanese Full-Time	Non-Japanese Part-Time	Non-Japanese Increase	Non-Japanese Language	Answer in English	Answer Job-Hunters	Answer Businesses	Answer Researchers
C		Y	Y	US					Y	N	Y	N

PORTESCAP JAPAN LTD.

Importer of Swiss-made precision motors.
4-7-10 Nihonbashi Honcho, Chuo-ku, Tokyo 103. 03-3241-0201
JR Sobu (Kaisoku) Line, Shin Nihonbashi. No contact

Size	Overseas Branches	Overseas Experience	In Future	Country	Non-Japanese Full-Time	Non-Japanese Part-Time	Non-Japanese Increase	Non-Japanese Language	Answer in English	Answer Job-Hunters	Answer Businesses	Answer Researchers
D		Y	N		0	0	N			N	N	N

SECO TOOLS JAPAN K.K.

Importer of machine tools. 03-3239-3071
No. 25 Kowa Bldg., 8-7 Sanban-cho, Chiyoda-ku, Tokyo 102.
Yurakucho, Toei Shinjuku or JR Sobu Line, Ichigaya. No contact

Size	Overseas Branches	Overseas Experience	In Future	Country	Non-Japanese Full-Time	Non-Japanese Part-Time	Non-Japanese Increase	Non-Japanese Language	Answer in English	Answer Job-Hunters	Answer Businesses	Answer Researchers
C		Y	Y	*	1	0	Y	E		N	N	N

* Europe, U.S.A.

SHELL JAPAN LTD.

Importer of petro-chemical products, non-ferrous metals and oils.
Kasumigaseki Building, 3-2-5 Kasumigaseki, Chiyoda-ku, Tokyo 100.
Ginza Line, Toranomon. 03-3581-6301 No contact

Size	Overseas Branches	Overseas Experience	In Future	Country	Non-Japanese Full-Time	Non-Japanese Part-Time	Non-Japanese Increase	Non-Japanese Language	Answer in English	Answer Job-Hunters	Answer Businesses	Answer Researchers
B		Y	Y	All	0	0						

TEKELEC LTD.

Importer of computer and communications equipment.
5-28-13 Ogikubo, Suginami-ku, Tokyo 167. 03-3220-0514
Marunouchi or JR Chuo Line, Ogikubo. Contact: Mr. Suzuki

Size	Overseas Branches	Overseas Experience	In Future	Country	Non-Japanese Full-Time	Non-Japanese Part-Time	Non-Japanese Increase	Non-Japanese Language	Answer in English	Answer Job-Hunters	Answer Businesses	Answer Researchers
C		Y	Y	*	2	0	Y		Y	Y	Y	Y

* U.S.A., Europe, Asia

CHAPTER 15. TRAVEL AND TRANSPORTATION

In this chapter we have included all businesses related to the travel industry, including accommodation. We have also included shipping and freighting companies, for want of a more appropriate section in which to place them. In recent years the travel industry has been booming in Japan, both domestically and internationally. A decade ago Narita Airport, serving Tokyo, often seemed almost empty. Now a second terminal has been opened and temporary booths have been set up to cope with the constant flow of travellers. Japan has become a popular holiday destination and millions of Japanese are journeying abroad themselves now. In terms of Japanese currency, tickets become cheaper year by year.

There are certainly opportunities for international co-operation in this area, bearing in mind, of course, that Japanese holidays are usually limited to about a week and that what sells in this country is a complete package with everything pre-arranged for the intrepid overseas adventurer and a comparatively high standard of accommodation and food, in particular, included.

For the job-seeker, there are opportunities in this area too. First class hotels often employ a native speaker of English to deal with any problems which guests from overseas may encounter. It is preferable, of course, for this person also to have a reasonable knowledge of Japanese and since the number of such vacancies is limited, one is unlikely to be successful in this field unless one does have language abilities. It is possible, however, that first languages other than English might be of interest to hotels, if combined with reasonable levels of both Japanese and English.

Some travel and tour agents also employ native English speakers. Tour agents need English-speaking guides for parties from overseas. Although Japanese are usually preferred in such positions, to have one or more native English speakers available for emergencies, as well as dealing with correspondence and other paperwork, is advantageous. Discount travel agents find that non-Japanese account for a sizeable minority of their business, so some of them employ a non-Japanese to deal with such enquiries. Indeed there are some agencies owned and operated by non-Japanese.

Since this is a field which is likely to continue to expand, opportunities for both business and employment are likely to grow still further in the future.

Size	Overseas Branches	Overseas Experience	In Future	Country	←Non-Japanese→ Full-Time	Part-Time	Increase	Language	Answer in English	← Answer → Job-Hunters	Businesses	Researchers

AIRLINES

AIR NEW ZEALAND

Air transportation. 03-3213-0968
Shin Kokusai Building, 3-4-1 Marunouchi, Chiyoda-ku, Tokyo 100.
Yurakucho or JR Yamanote Line, Yurakucho. Contact: (Somu Jinji-bu)

Size	Overseas Branches	Overseas Experience	In Future	Country	Full-Time	Part-Time	Increase	Language	Answer in English	Job-Hunters	Businesses	Researchers
C					0	0	N		Y	Y	Y	Y

AIR NIUGINI

Air ticketing and tours to Papua New Guinea.
3-2-2 Amanuma, Suginami-ku, Tokyo 167. 03-5397-0678
Marunouchi or JR Chuo Line, Ogikubo. No contact

Size	Overseas Branches	Overseas Experience	In Future	Country	Full-Time	Part-Time	Increase	Language	Answer in English	Job-Hunters	Businesses	Researchers
		Y	Y							N	N	N

ALASKA AIRLINES

Air transportation.
3-6-18 Kita Aoyama, Minato-ku, Tokyo 107. 03-3407-8386
Chiyoda, Hanzomon or Ginza Line, Omotesando. No contact

Size	Overseas Branches	Overseas Experience	In Future	Country	Full-Time	Part-Time	Increase	Language	Answer in English	Job-Hunters	Businesses	Researchers
D		Y	Y	*						N	Y	N

* Asia, Oceania

AMERICAN AIRLINES, INC.

Air transportation.
Kokusai Bldg., 3-1-1 Marunouchi, Chiyoda-ku, Tokyo 100. 03-3214-2100
Yurakucho or JR Yamanote Line, Yurakucho. Contact: (Somu-bu) 03-3214-2104

Size	Overseas Branches	Overseas Experience	In Future	Country	Full-Time	Part-Time	Increase	Language	Answer in English	Job-Hunters	Businesses	Researchers
B					4	0			Y	Y	Y	Y

AUSTRALIAN AIRLINES

Airline business. 03-3216-5828
Room 1252 South Wing, 1-7-1 Yurakucho, Chiyoda-ku, Tokyo 100.
Yurakucho or JR Yamanote Line, Yurakucho. Contact: Ms. Miyama

Size	Overseas Branches	Overseas Experience	In Future	Country	Full-Time	Part-Time	Increase	Language	Answer in English	Job-Hunters	Businesses	Researchers
					0	0	N		Y	Y	Y	N

CHINA AIRLINES

Air transportation. 03-3436-1501
Matsuoka Tamuracho Bldg., 5-22-10 Shinbashi, Minato-ku, Tokyo 105.
Toei Mita Line, Onarimon. Contact: Ms. Toshiko Ueda 03-3436-0841

Size	Overseas Branches	Overseas Experience	In Future	Country	Full-Time	Part-Time	Increase	Language	Answer in English	Job-Hunters	Businesses	Researchers
					7	0	Y	E,Ch	Y	Y	Y	N

ETHIOPIAN AIRLINES

Air transportation. 03-3281-1990
Tokyo Daido Seimei Building, 2-7-4 Nihonbashi, Chuo-ku, Tokyo 103.
Ginza, Tozai or Toei Asakusa Line, Nihonbashi. No contact

Size	Overseas Branches	Overseas Experience	In Future	Country	Full-Time	Part-Time	Increase	Language	Answer in English	Job-Hunters	Businesses	Researchers
D		N			0	0						

IBERIA, AIRLINES OF SPAIN

Air transportation.
Ark Mori Bldg., 1-12-32 Akasaka, Minato-ku, Tokyo 107. 03-3582-3889
Hibiya Line, Roppongi. No contact

Size	Overseas Branches	Overseas Experience	In Future	Country	Full-Time	Part-Time	Increase	Language	Answer in English	Job-Hunters	Businesses	Researchers
					0	0					Y	

SINGAPORE AIRLINES LIMITED

Air transportation. 03-3213-1169
Yurakucho Bldg., 1-10-1 Yurakucho, Chiyoda-ku, Tokyo 100.
Yurakucho or JR Yamanote Line, Yurakucho. No contact

Size	Overseas Branches	Overseas Experience	In Future	Country	Full-Time	Part-Time	Increase	Language	Answer in English	Job-Hunters	Businesses	Researchers
		Y	Y		0	0				N	N	N

					Non-Japanese					Answer		
Size	Overseas Branches	Overseas Experience	In Future	Country	Full-Time	Part-Time	Increase	Language	Answer in English	Job-Hunters	Businesses	Researchers

SWISSAIR

Air transportation. 03-3212-1011
Hibiya Park Building, 1-8-1 Yurakucho, Chiyoda-ku, Tokyo 100.
Yurakucho or JR Yamanote Line, Yurakucho. Contact: Mr.Nakamura(Koho-bu)

Size	Overseas Branches	Overseas Experience	In Future	Country	Full-Time	Part-Time	Increase	Language	Answer in English	Job-Hunters	Businesses	Researchers

VARIG BRAZILIAN AIRLINES

Air transportation.
Palace Bldg., 1-1-1 Marunouchi, Chiyoda-ku, Tokyo 100. 03-3211-6761
Tozai, Marunouchi, Chiyoda, Hanzomon or Toei Mita Line, Otemachi. No contact

Size	Overseas Branches	Overseas Experience	In Future	Country	Full-Time	Part-Time	Increase	Language	Answer in English	Job-Hunters	Businesses	Researchers
C					3	0	Y	E,P	Y	Y	Y	Y

VASP BRAZILIAN AIRLINES

Air transportation. 03-3211-2071
Yurakucho Building, 1-10-1 Yurakucho, Chiyoda-ku, Tokyo 100.
Yurakucho or JR Yamanote Line, Yurakucho. Contact: Mr. Watanabe

Size	Overseas Branches	Overseas Experience	In Future	Country	Full-Time	Part-Time	Increase	Language	Answer in English	Job-Hunters	Businesses	Researchers
		N	N				Y	E,P	Y	Y	Y	Y

TRAVEL AGENTS

BEL TOP TRAVEL SERVICE

Travel agent specializing in dealing with non-Japanese.
Nikko Building, 4-2-9 Shiba, Minato-ku, Tokyo 108. 03-3454-6331
JR Yamanote Line, Tamachi. No contact

Size	Overseas Branches	Overseas Experience	In Future	Country	Full-Time	Part-Time	Increase	Language	Answer in English	Job-Hunters	Businesses	Researchers
D	1	Y	N		2	0				N	N	N

H.I.S. CO., LTD.

Travel agent.
SK Bldg., 6-2-18 Nishi Shinjuku, Shinjuku-ku, Tokyo 160. 03-3847-3631
JR Yamanote or Chuo Line, Shinjuku. Contact: Mr. Uchida (Jinji-ka)

Size	Overseas Branches	Overseas Experience	In Future	Country	Full-Time	Part-Time	Increase	Language	Answer in English	Job-Hunters	Businesses	Researchers
B	19	N			30	0	Y	E	N	Y	Y	Y

INDONESIA TOURIST BUREAU CO., LTD.

Travel agent. 03-3597-8842
No. 3 Mori Building, 1-4-10 Nishi Shinbashi, Minato-ku, Tokyo 105.
Ginza, Toei Asakusa or JR Yamanote Line, Shinbashi. Contact: Ms. Burford

Size	Overseas Branches	Overseas Experience	In Future	Country	Full-Time	Part-Time	Increase	Language	Answer in English	Job-Hunters	Businesses	Researchers
C	1	Y	Y	Indo	1				Y	Y	Y	Y

JAPAN TRAVEL BUREAU INC.
(INTERNATIONAL TRAVEL DIV.)

Travel agent.
1-13-1 Nihonbashi, Chuo-ku, Tokyo 103. 03-3276-7803
Ginza, Tozai or Toei Asakusa Line, Nihonbashi. Contact: Mr. Kumabe

Size	Overseas Branches	Overseas Experience	In Future	Country	Full-Time	Part-Time	Increase	Language	Answer in English	Job-Hunters	Businesses	Researchers
A	59			All	0	0			Y	N	Y	Y

JAPAN AMENITY TRAVEL, LTD.

Travel agent.
Ryuwa Bldg., 2-3-5 Yurakucho, Chiyoda-ku, Tokyo 100. 03-3571-4819
Yurakucho or JR Yamanote Line, Yurakucho. Contact: (Gaikokujin Ryoko-bu)

Size	Overseas Branches	Overseas Experience	In Future	Country	Full-Time	Part-Time	Increase	Language	Answer in English	Job-Hunters	Businesses	Researchers
B	4	N							N	N	N	N

JAPAN-SOVIET TOURIST BUREAU, INC.

Travel agent.
5-12-12 Toranomon, Minato-ku, Tokyo 105. 03-3432-6163
Hibiya Line, Kamiyacho. Contact: Mr. Kajiyama (Gaijin Ryoko-ka)

Size	Overseas Branches	Overseas Experience	In Future	Country	Full-Time	Part-Time	Increase	Language	Answer in English	Job-Hunters	Businesses	Researchers
C	0	Y	Y	Rus					Y	N	Y	Y

Size	Overseas Branches	Overseas Experience	In Future	Country	Non-Japanese: Full-Time	Non-Japanese: Part-Time	Non-Japanese: Increase	Non-Japanese: Language	Answer in English	Answer: Job-Hunters	Answer: Businesses	Answer: Researchers

NIPPON TRAVEL AGENCY CO., LTD.

Travel agent. 03-3572-8718
No. 1 Shinbashi Eki-mae Bldg., 2-20-15 Shinbashi, Minato-ku, Tokyo 105
Ginza, Toei Asakusa or JR Yamanote Line, Shinbashi. No contact

Size	Overseas Branches	Overseas Experience	In Future	Country	Full-Time	Part-Time	Increase	Language	Answer in English	Job-Hunters	Businesses	Researchers
A	37	Y	Y	*	1	0	N			N	N	N

* France, Italy, Spain

N T S TRAVEL BOX

Sales of discounted air tickets. 03-3988-9507
1005 Orient Ikebukuro, 1-29-14 Nishi Ikebukuro, Toshima-ku, Tokyo 171.
Marunouchi, Yurakucho or JR Yamanote Line, Ikebukuro. Contact: Mr. Murakami

Size	Overseas Branches	Overseas Experience	In Future	Country	Full-Time	Part-Time	Increase	Language	Answer in English	Job-Hunters	Businesses	Researchers
D	0	N	N		0	0	Y	*	Y	Y	Y	Y

* English, Chinese, Korean

OVER SEAS TRAVEL CENTER CO., LTD.

Travel agent. 03-3367-5322
Shiro Bldg., 7-10-10 Nishi Shinjuku, Shinjuku-ku, Tokyo 160.
Marunouchi, Toei Shinjuku or JR Yamanote Line, Shinjuku. No contact

Size	Overseas Branches	Overseas Experience	In Future	Country	Full-Time	Part-Time	Increase	Language	Answer in English	Job-Hunters	Businesses	Researchers
D	0	Y	N							N	N	Y

TRI PACIFIC LIMITED

Representative travel agent for Australia and New Zealand.
301 Naigai Bldg., 6 Yonban-cho, Chiyoda-ku, Tokyo 102. 03-3234-2668
Yurakucho, Toei Shinjuku or JR Sobu Line, Ichigaya. Contact: Mr. Onoe

Size	Overseas Branches	Overseas Experience	In Future	Country	Full-Time	Part-Time	Increase	Language	Answer in English	Job-Hunters	Businesses	Researchers
D	1	Y	Y	*	0	1	Y		Y	Y	Y	Y

* Oceania

ACADEMY TRAVEL INC.

Travel agent.
Takada 2 Building, 2-6-8 Juso Higashi, Yodogawa-ku, Osaka 532.
Hankyu Line, Juso. 06-303-3538 Contact: Mr. Kruger

Size	Overseas Branches	Overseas Experience	In Future	Country	Full-Time	Part-Time	Increase	Language	Answer in English	Job-Hunters	Businesses	Researchers
C	0	Y	Y	Aust	2	0				Y	Y	Y

TIME TRAVEL CO., LTD.

Travel agent.
No. 2 Zeniya Building, 1-5-9 Azuchi-cho, Chuo-ku, Osaka 541.
Sakaisuji Line, Sakaisuji Honmachi. Contact: Mr. Sugi 06-271-7121

Size	Overseas Branches	Overseas Experience	In Future	Country	Full-Time	Part-Time	Increase	Language	Answer in English	Job-Hunters	Businesses	Researchers
D	0	Y	Y	*			Y	¶	Y	Y	Y	Y

* U.S.A., Hong Kong, Thailand
¶ English, French, German, Spanish

KOBE TOPNOTCH COMPANY

Travel agent.
Green Chapeau Building, 5-3-5 Kotono-o-cho, Chuo-ku, Kobe 651.
JR Tokaido Line, Sannomiya. 078-242-2695 No contact

Size	Overseas Branches	Overseas Experience	In Future	Country	Full-Time	Part-Time	Increase	Language	Answer in English	Job-Hunters	Businesses	Researchers
D	0	Y	N									Y

WORLD EXPRESS CO., LTD.

Travel agent.
Green Chapeau Building, 5-3-5 Kotono-o-cho, Chuo-ku, Kobe 651.
JR Tokaido Line, Sannomiya. Contact: Mr. Fujiwara 078-222-5050

Size	Overseas Branches	Overseas Experience	In Future	Country	Full-Time	Part-Time	Increase	Language	Answer in English	Job-Hunters	Businesses	Researchers
D	1	N					Y	E	Y	Y	Y	Y

ACCOMMODATION

Column key (Non-Japanese: Full-Time, Part-Time, Increase, Language; Answer: Job-Hunters, Businesses, Researchers)

JAPAN YOUTH HOSTELS, INC. (F)

Non-profitable organization supervising 400 Youth Hostels in Japan.
Hoken Kaikan, 1-2 Sadohara-cho, Ichigaya, Shinjuku-ku, Tokyo 162.
Yurakucho, Toei Shinjuku, JR Sobu Line, Ichigaya. Contact: Mr.Imai 03-3269-5831

Size	Overseas Branches	Overseas Experience	In Future	Country	Full-Time	Part-Time	Increase	Language	Answer in English	Job-Hunters	Businesses	Researchers
		Y	Y	Eur					Y	N	N	Y

MINSHUKU CENTER CO., LTD.

Reservations for inexpensive inns or pensions.
Tokyo Kotsu Kaikan, 2-10-1 Yurakucho, Chiyoda-ku, Tokyo 100.
Yurakucho or JR Yamanote Line, Yurakucho. 03-3216-6556 No contact

Size	Overseas Branches	Overseas Experience	In Future	Country	Full-Time	Part-Time	Increase	Language	Answer in English	Job-Hunters	Businesses	Researchers
D		Y	Y	*								

* U.S.A., E.C. Countries

GA-JO-EN KANKO KABUSHIKI KAISHA ①

Hotel.
1-8-1 Shimo Meguro, Meguro-ku, Tokyo 153. 03-3495-9501
JR Yamanote Line, Meguro. Contact: Mr. Miyazaki (Somu-bu) Ext. 21

Size	Overseas Branches	Overseas Experience	In Future	Country	Full-Time	Part-Time	Increase	Language	Answer in English	Job-Hunters	Businesses	Researchers
B	1	N	N						N	N	N	N

GINZA DAI-ICHI HOTEL

Hotel.
8-13-1 Ginza, Chuo-ku, Tokyo 104. 03-3542-5311
Ginza, Toei Asakusa or JR Yamanote Line, Shinbashi. No contact

Size	Overseas Branches	Overseas Experience	In Future	Country	Full-Time	Part-Time	Increase	Language	Answer in English	Job-Hunters	Businesses	Researchers
B	3	N	N							N	N	N

JAPAN NATIONAL TOURIST ORGANIZATION (SG)

Non-profitable organization providing tourist information.
2-10-1 Yurakucho, Chiyoda-ku, Tokyo 100. 03-3216-1901
JR Yamanote Line, Yurakucho. Contact: (Tourist Information Center)

Size	Overseas Branches	Overseas Experience	In Future	Country	Full-Time	Part-Time	Increase	Language	Answer in English	Job-Hunters	Businesses	Researchers
	16	N	N						Y			

SAKURA RYOKAN

Inn.
2-6-2 Iriya, Taito-ku, Tokyo 110. 03-3876-8118
Hibiya Line, Iriya. No contact

Size	Overseas Branches	Overseas Experience	In Future	Country	Full-Time	Part-Time	Increase	Language	Answer in English	Job-Hunters	Businesses	Researchers
		Y					Y	E	N	N	N	N

TRANSPORTATION

					Non-Japanese					Answer		
Size	Overseas Branches	Overseas Experience	In Future	Country	Full-Time	Part-Time	Increase	Language	Answer in English	Job-Hunters	Businesses	Researchers

KOKUSAI KOGYO CO., LTD. ①

Aerial surveying and research. Construction consultation.
Rokuban-cho, Chiyoda-ku, Tokyo 102. 03-3262-6221
JR Sobu Line, Ichigaya. Contact: Mr. Yamamoto (Jinji-bu)

* English, Spanish, Portuguese, Chinese, Korean

Size	Overseas Branches	Overseas Experience	In Future	Country	Full-Time	Part-Time	Increase	Language	Answer in English	Job-Hunters	Businesses	Researchers
A	3	Y	Y		5	0	Y	*	N	N	N	Y

MARUWN TRANSPORT CO., LTD. ①

Transportation of heavy freight.
1-5-11 Akasaka, Minato-ku, Tokyo 107. 03-3587-0111
Ginza Line, Toranomon. Contact: Mr. Yamaguchi 03-3587-0151 Ext. 353

* U.S.A., Asia, Europe

Size	Overseas Branches	Overseas Experience	In Future	Country	Full-Time	Part-Time	Increase	Language	Answer in English	Job-Hunters	Businesses	Researchers
A	0	Y	Y	*	0	0	N		N	N	N	N

TOEI REEFER LINE LTD. (OTC)

Shipping company specializing in frozen tuna and lobsters. 03-3431-0336
Kokusai Hamamatsucho Bldg. 1-9-18 Kaigan, Minato-ku, Tokyo 105.
JR Yamanote Line, Hamamatsucho. Contact: Mr. Nakamura Ext. 261

* S.E. Asia, Europe

Size	Overseas Branches	Overseas Experience	In Future	Country	Full-Time	Part-Time	Increase	Language	Answer in English	Job-Hunters	Businesses	Researchers
C	0	Y	Y	*	1	0	Y	E,Ch	N	Y	Y	Y

KINTETSU WORLD EXPRESS, INC.

International freight forwarding.
Time-Life Bldg., 2-3-6 Otemachi, Chiyoda-ku, Tokyo 100. 03-3270-7258
Various subway lines, Otemachi. Contact:Mr.Tahara (Kokusai Gyomu-bu)

Size	Overseas Branches	Overseas Experience	In Future	Country	Full-Time	Part-Time	Increase	Language	Answer in English	Job-Hunters	Businesses	Researchers
A	55	Y	Y	All	0	0	N		Y	N	N	N

KYOWA TRED, LTD.

Packaging of cargo for export.
5-20-12 Minami Yukigaya, Ota-ku, Tokyo 145. 03-3727-5371
Tokyu Ikegami Line, Ontakeyama. Contact: (Somu-bu)

Size	Overseas Branches	Overseas Experience	In Future	Country	Full-Time	Part-Time	Increase	Language	Answer in English	Job-Hunters	Businesses	Researchers
C		Y	Y	Ch	0	0			N	N	N	Y

OLYMPIC INTERNATIONAL LTD.

Shipping. Ship broking. Shipping information supply.
Sekai Boeki Centre Bldg., 2-4-1 Hamamatsu-cho, Minato-ku, Tokyo 105.
JR Yamanote Line, Hamamatsucho. Contact: Mr. Noguchi 03-3435-5477

Size	Overseas Branches	Overseas Experience	In Future	Country	Full-Time	Part-Time	Increase	Language	Answer in English	Job-Hunters	Businesses	Researchers
D	3	Y	Y		0	0			Y			

SHIKOKU RAILWAY COMPANY (SG)

Rail and other transportation.
1-10 Hamano-cho, Takamatsu-shi, Kagawa 760. 0878-23-0973
JR Yosan Line, Takamatsu. No contact

Size	Overseas Branches	Overseas Experience	In Future	Country	Full-Time	Part-Time	Increase	Language	Answer in English	Job-Hunters	Businesses	Researchers
A	0	N	Y						N	N	N	N

CHAPTER 16. REAL ESTATE

As everybody knows, property in major cities in Japan is extremely expensive. It is also expensive outside the cities, and what is of such great value is the land rather than the buildings.

Both businessman and job-hunter may find it necessary to search for property, the former because he needs an office, the latter because he needs somewhere to live. Both are going to find it expensive. Moreover, the Japanese system requires a great number of down-payments before one can actually have the privilege of moving into one's chosen piece of property. For example, if one rents an apartment in Tokyo, one will typically be expected to produce one month's rent in advance, two month's 'key money' (non-refundable) and two months' deposit (refundable). In addition, the agent will want a commission of one month's rent and it is virtually impossible to find property without going through an agent, since the agent's services cost the seller nothing and provide him with an element of security. That means that if one rents an apartment for, say, ¥70,000 per month, which will be the fee for the average rabbit-hutch within commuting distance of the city, one will be required to lay out ¥420,000, or approximately U.S.$3,500, before moving in. One will also be required to find a guarantor to take responsibility for one's being a good tenant, paying one's rent promptly and doing no damage. If one defaults in any way, the guarantor will be held responsible. In certain areas of Japan additional payments are required before one moves in.

Although a similar system operates for office space, down payments will be even greater and there will probably be a minimum period for renting. It is unusual to find any furnished accommodation or offices available.

This system is, of course, difficult for non-Japanese, because of the enormous outlay involved and the finding of a guarantor. Moreover, some landlords simply refuse to accept foreigners as tenants. This occurs more often with cheaper accommodation than with higher priced property. There are also estate agents who decline to deal with foreigners. Although these problems are on the wane, they have resulted in the establishment of certain agencies which specialize in handling non-Japanese and these appear in our listing. It should be noted that such agents tend to deal with more expensive properties and that anybody who is more interested in the lower end of the market would probably do better to approach an ordinary agent in the locality which interests him most.

Another place to look for higher class property to let is classified advertisements in the English language newspapers. If you want to buy, a thick magazine is published every fortnight (in Japanese) containing lists of properties available — at prices which will astonish you! A similar weekly magazine lists property available to let. There are also a few companies which offer furnished or shared office space. They too advertise in the English language newspapers and some can be found in our listing.

As for employment in this area, it is rarely available, for this is work which can be done by Japanese adequately enough.

One final point of possible interest for the businessman is that the Japanese have been showing interest in investing in property overseas in recent years. This has probably slowed down because of the recent decline in economic prosperity, but property remains so expensive in Japan that the overseas market will always be considered relatively attractive.

Size	Overseas Branches	Overseas Experience	In Future	Country	Non-Japanese: Full-Time	Non-Japanese: Part-Time	Non-Japanese: Increase	Non-Japanese: Language	Answer in English	Answer: Job-Hunters	Answer: Businesses	Answer: Researchers

DIA KENSETSU CO., LTD. ②

Sales of condominiums.
6-28-7 Shinjuku, Shinjuku-ku, Tokyo 160. 03-3205-5565
Marunouchi Line, Shinjuku San-chome. Contact: Mr. Takeuchi (Kaigai Jigyo-bu)

Size	Overseas Branches	Overseas Experience	In Future	Country	Full-Time	Part-Time	Increase	Language	Answer in English	Job-Hunters	Businesses	Researchers
B	1	N	N		0	0	N		Y	N	N	N

MITSUI GREENLAND COMPANY LIMITED (L)

Operation of amusement centre, golf course and hotels.
1616 Shimo Ide, Arao-shi, Kumamoto 864. 0968-66-2111
Nishitetsu Omuta Line, Omuta. Contact: (Somu-bu)

Size	Overseas Branches	Overseas Experience	In Future	Country	Full-Time	Part-Time	Increase	Language	Answer in English	Job-Hunters	Businesses	Researchers
C	0	Y	N									

NIKKEN SEKKEI LTD.

Architectural design.
1-4-27 Koraku, Bunkyo-ku, Tokyo 112. 03-3818-4095
Yurakucho, Tozai, JR Sobu Line, Iidabashi. Contact: Ms. Akatsuka (Kokusai-shitsu)

Size	Overseas Branches	Overseas Experience	In Future	Country	Full-Time	Part-Time	Increase	Language	Answer in English	Job-Hunters	Businesses	Researchers
A	3	Y	Y	Asia	8	5	Y		Y	Y	Y	Y

A B B GADELIUS REAL ESTATE CO.

Estate agent.
5-2-39 Akasaka, Minato-ku, Tokyo 107. 03-3584-2661
Marunouchi or Ginza Line, Akasaka Mitsuke. No contact

Size	Overseas Branches	Overseas Experience	In Future	Country	Full-Time	Part-Time	Increase	Language	Answer in English	Job-Hunters	Businesses	Researchers
C	0	N	N		0	0	N		Y			

FAMILY HOME CO., LTD.

Estate agent specializing in foreign customers.
Kensetsu Kaikan, 2-22 Ota-cho, Naka-ku, Yokohama-shi 231.
JR Keihin Tohoku Line, Kannai. Contact: Mr. Tanaka 045-201-9165

Size	Overseas Branches	Overseas Experience	In Future	Country	Full-Time	Part-Time	Increase	Language	Answer in English	Job-Hunters	Businesses	Researchers
D		N	N		2	0			Y	N	N	N

HOYO TRUST CO., LTD.

Estate agent specializing in foreign customers.
4-19-9 Kita Shinjuku, Shinjuku-ku, Tokyo 169. 03-3532-0658
JR Sobu Line, Higashi Nakano. No contact

Size	Overseas Branches	Overseas Experience	In Future	Country	Full-Time	Part-Time	Increase	Language	Answer in English	Job-Hunters	Businesses	Researchers
		Y							Y			

IKOMA CORPORATION

Estate agent. 03-5251-2571
Asahi Seimei Hibiya Building, 1-5-1 Yurakucho, Chiyoda-ku, Tokyo 100.
Hibiya, Chiyoda or Toei Mita Line, Hibiya. Contact: (Kokusai Jigyo-bu)

Size	Overseas Branches	Overseas Experience	In Future	Country	Full-Time	Part-Time	Increase	Language	Answer in English	Job-Hunters	Businesses	Researchers
B	1	Y	Y	*	1	0	Y	E	Y	Y	Y	Y

* U.S.A., Asia

KDD BUSINESS QUARTERS

Rental office space for overseas-affliated companies.
KDD Otemachi Building, 1-8-1 Otemachi, Chiyoda-ku, Tokyo 100.
Various subway lines, Otemachi. Contact: Ms. Niikura 03-3243-9180

Size	Overseas Branches	Overseas Experience	In Future	Country	Full-Time	Part-Time	Increase	Language	Answer in English	Job-Hunters	Businesses	Researchers
									Y	Y	Y	Y

REGUS / I E O CORPORATION

Rental office space for executives.
I.E.O. Bldg., 4-6-10 Yotsuya, Shinjuku-ku, Tokyo 160. 03-5379-1331
Marunouchi Line, Yotsuya San-chome. Contact: Mr. Kitahara

Size	Overseas Branches	Overseas Experience	In Future	Country	Full-Time	Part-Time	Increase	Language	Answer in English	Job-Hunters	Businesses	Researchers
D		Y							Y	N	Y	N

SANKO ESTATE CO., LTD.

Rental office space.
No. 4 Shuwa Bldg., 8-10-5 Ginza, Chuo-ku, Tokyo 104. 03-3574-6862
JR Yamanote Line, Shinbashi. Contact: Ms. Hanabusa (Kokusai Joho-bu)

Size	Overseas Branches	Overseas Experience	In Future	Country	Full-Time	Part-Time	Increase	Language	Answer in English	Job-Hunters	Businesses	Researchers
B	0	N	N		0	0	N		Y	N	N	N

TOKYO INTERNATIONAL BUSINESS CENTER

Rental office space for overseas companies.
Tobe Bldg., 2-9-17 Shiba Daimon, Minato-ku, Tokyo 105. 03-3578-9002
JR Yamanote Line, Hamamatsucho. Contact: Ms. Kamimoto

Size	Overseas Branches	Overseas Experience	In Future	Country	Non-Japanese Full-Time	Non-Japanese Part-Time	Non-Japanese Increase	Non-Japanese Language	Answer in English	Answer Job-Hunters	Answer Businesses	Answer Researchers
C	4	Y	N	It			Y	It	Y	N	N	N

CHAPTER 17. LAW

Until recently, lawyers from overseas were not permitted to practise in Japan, their only access to clients in this country being as assistants to Japanese lawyers, an inconvenient arrangement for a country which was professedly attempting to 'internationalize'. However, in 1987 amendments were made to the law and now lawyers from overseas can work here, subject to quite a wide range of restrictions.

The most important of the restrictions is that the lawyer must have practised for at least five years in a country or state which permits Japanese lawyers to work there. He must then obtain a licence from the Ministry of Justice in Japan, but, even when that is granted, his work will be limited. For example, he cannot appear in court in Japan, nor can he practise Japanese law, only the legal system in which he is qualified.

At the same time, the old method of engaging non-Japanese assistants to Japanese lawyers continues. Sometimes Japanese legal enterprises recruit newly qualified lawyers from overseas. Sometimes they have arrangements with overseas companies to exchange a member of staff. Sometimes they are just interested in whoever happens to approach them. However, there is a need for such skilled people to augment the expertise of Japanese legal concerns. Japanese knowledge is not regarded as essential, but is usually thought to be an advantage to aid daily communications. In general, those recruited from overseas tend to be specialists while those who are recruited locally tend to be employed for general legal work.

Large companies (other than law businesses) will also recruit their own legal staff and, as international commerce increases, this often includes a legal expert from overseas. In many cases these large companies have offices abroad and ask those offices to find a suitable person to work in the head office in Japan, sometimes with the possibility of being employed later at the branch office in his own country.

Working in a Japanese law office is usually hard. The hours tend to be long and the hierarchy is strict. Pay varies, but tends to be good, even for trainees, because law companies are not usually poor. However, the work required of non-Japanese is often rather below their ability level, as it usually concentrates on the correction of documents in English, rather than utilizing legal skills.

Working for the Japanese office of an overseas lawyer, on the other hand, is likely to be rather similar to working for the same company abroad. Usually conditions, especially pay and allowances, will be attractive. The disadvantages which some people feel are that they are no longer working their way up the conventional ladder to the top and also that they sometimes have to work long or strange hours in order to be able to communicate effectively with the parent company.

For the businessman in need of legal advice concerning Japan, there are certain companies specializing in dealing with the requirements of clients from overseas. Several of these appear in the listing which follows. Their specialities, if any, are mentioned in the first line of the particulars of each. It is worth remembering that litigation is somewhat frowned upon in Japan. Not only is it regarded as an immature way to deal with a problem, but it is also very expensive and painfully slow, so that, in the end, both parties will probably be losers, a rather effective method of deterrence! Even contracts are not taken too seriously, being regarded as evidence that the parties have a definite agreement rather than as evidence of exactly what that agreement was. Therefore, they are often phrased rather loosely to allow for modification as circumstances dictate.

Since this is a society which dislikes litigation, it follows that specialists in such areas as criminal law, civil suits and family law will not be much in demand. Those who are required are those who deal with international law, commercial law, contracts and financial law and, not least, patent attorneys. As international trade and agreements for technology transfer increase, so experts in the laws governing these transactions become more in demand.

There are also difficulties with the different negotiating techniques employed in different parts of the world. Companies are becoming more interested in this area and it is, perhaps, something for the future.

Company	Size	Overseas Branches	Overseas Experience	In Future	Country	Non-Japanese: Full-Time	Non-Japanese: Part-Time	Non-Japanese: Increase	Non-Japanese: Language	Answer in English	Answer: Job-Hunters	Answer: Businesses	Answer: Researchers
CENTURY AUDIT CORPORATION	B	20	N	N		8	0						
HAGIWARA & TATSUNO	D									Y	N		
KASHIWAGI INTERNATIONAL LAW OFFICE						1	0	Y	E,F,G	Y	N	N	N
KAZUKO MUSHIAKE & CO			N	N		0	0	N		Y	N	Y	Y
MISAKO NIIKURA SHIHO-SHOSHI		0	N	N		0	0	N		Y	N	N	Y
MITA LEGAL INTERNATIONAL	D	0	Y	N						Y	N	N	N
OKA LEGAL ASSOCIATES										Y			Y
OSUGA & ASSOCIATES	C	0	Y	Y	*	0	2	Y	E	Y	Y	Y	Y
SHIKANAI & UEDA			Y	Y						Y	Y	Y	Y
SHIMANE & SHIMANE, CPAS	C		Y							Y	N	Y	Y

CENTURY AUDIT CORPORATION

Auditing and certification of treasury reports.
Nihon Sekijujisha Building, 1-1-3 Shiba Daimon, Minato-ku, Tokyo 105.
JR Yamanote Line, Hamamatsucho. 03-3578-1910 No contact

HAGIWARA & TATSUNO

Legal office.
1-20-10 Nishi Shinbashi, Minato-ku, Tokyo 105. 03-3503-2921
Ginza Line, Toranomon. Contact: Mr. Shintaro Hagiwara

KASHIWAGI INTERNATIONAL LAW OFFICE

Legal office.
234-ku Shin Tokyo Bldg., 3-3-1 Marunouchi, Chiyoda-ku, Tokyo 100.
Marunouchi or JR Yamanote Line, Tokyo. 03-32159066 No contact

KAZUKO MUSHIAKE & CO

Financial statements. Tax returns. Management consultation.
2-4-17-1108 Honan, Suginami-ku, Tokyo 168. 03-5378-0481
Marunouchi Line, Honancho. Contact: Ms. Kazuko Mushiake

MISAKO NIIKURA SHIHO-SHOSHI

Legal filing work (real estate, company registration, immigration, etc.).
5-11-23 Yakumo, Meguro-ku, Tokyo 152. 03-3723-3199
Tokyu Toyoko or Oimachi Line, Jiyugaoka. No contact

MITA LEGAL INTERNATIONAL

Company registration. Tax declarations. Visas.
4th Fl. Daiki Building, 4-10-11 Nihonbashi Honcho, Chuo-ku, Tokyo 103.
Ginza or Hanzomon Line, Mitsukoshi-mae. 03-3662-1660 No contact

OKA LEGAL ASSOCIATES

Legal services.
2-16-1-1007 Shinbashi, Minato-ku, Tokyo 105. 03-3580-7400
Ginza, Toei Asakusa or JR Yamanote Line, Shinbashi. Contact: Mr. Hiroshi Oka

OSUGA & ASSOCIATES

Applications for patents.
6-1-18 Koji-machi, Chiyoda-ku, Tokyo 102. 03-3238-0031
Marunouchi or JR Chuo Line, Yotsuya. Contact: Mr. Yoshiaki Osuga

* U.S.A., Canada, Australia, Germany, U.K., France

SHIKANAI & UEDA

Matters related to international law.
Echigoya Building, 2-6-5 Ginza, Chuo-ku, Tokyo 104. 03-3564-5941
Yurakucho Line, Ginza I-chome. Contact: Mr. Shikanai or Mr. Hirata

SHIMANE & SHIMANE, CPAS

Auditing and accounting services and tax advice.
4-27-10 Hokima, Adachi-ku, Tokyo 121. 03-3859-5239
Tobu Isasaki Line, Takenozuka. Contact: Mr. Hidemitsu Shimane

	Size	Overseas Branches	Overseas Experience	In Future	Country	Full-Time (Non-Japanese)	Part-Time (Non-Japanese)	Increase (Non-Japanese)	Language (Non-Japanese)	Answer in English	Job-Hunters (Answer)	Businesses (Answer)	Researchers (Answer)

SHINBASHI INTERNATIONAL LAW OFFICE

International contracts, joint venture product licences, etc.
2-34-7 Nishi Shinbashi, Minato-ku, Tokyo 105. 03-3438-0303
Ginza Line, Toranomon. No contact

Size	Overseas Branches	Overseas Experience	In Future	Country	Full-Time	Part-Time	Increase	Language	Answer in English	Job-Hunters	Businesses	Researchers
		Y	Y	*						Y	Y	Y

* U.S.A., Europe

SUZUYE & SUZUYE

Patent attorney.
UBE Bldg., 3-7-2 Kasumigaseki, Chiyoda-ku, Tokyo 100. 03-3502-3181
Ginza Line, Toranomon. Contact: Mr. Kenji Kobayashi (Gaikoku Kanri-bu)

Size	Overseas Branches	Overseas Experience	In Future	Country	Full-Time	Part-Time	Increase	Language	Answer in English	Job-Hunters	Businesses	Researchers
B		Y	Y	All	2	0			Y	Y	Y	Y

SOMA LAW OFFICE

Civil, criminal and general legal business. Drawing up contracts.
No. 1 Kita Bldg., 4-7-1 Nishi Tenma, Kita-ku, Osaka 530. 06-365-0601
JR Tokaido Line, Osaka. Contact: Mr. Soma or Mr. Nagai

Size	Overseas Branches	Overseas Experience	In Future	Country	Full-Time	Part-Time	Increase	Language	Answer in English	Job-Hunters	Businesses	Researchers
D	0	Y	Y	*	0	1	Y	¶	N	Y	Y	Y

* Asia and U.S.A.
¶ English, Chinese, Korean

KONISHI LAW AND PATENT OFFICE

Legal matters.
Asahi Building, 3-2-4 Nakanoshima, Kita-ku, Osaka 530. 06-231-8041
Yotsubashi Line, Higobashi. Contact: Mr. Toshio Konishi

Size	Overseas Branches	Overseas Experience	In Future	Country	Full-Time	Part-Time	Increase	Language	Answer in English	Job-Hunters	Businesses	Researchers
												Y

KEN IWAHASHI ATTORNEY AT LAW

Civil law cases.
36 Nishi Migiwa-cho, Wakayama 640. 0734-22-2378
JR Nankai Line, Wakayama-shi. No contact

Size	Overseas Branches	Overseas Experience	In Future	Country	Full-Time	Part-Time	Increase	Language	Answer in English	Job-Hunters	Businesses	Researchers
D		N	N							N	N	N

JAPAN FEDERATION OF BAR ASSOCIATIONS (C)

Non-profitable association supervising attorneys.
1-1-1 Kasumigaseki, Chiyoda-ku, Tokyo 100. 03-3580-9841
Yurakucho Line, Sakuradamon. Contact: (Koho-shitsu) Ext. 231

Size	Overseas Branches	Overseas Experience	In Future	Country	Full-Time	Part-Time	Increase	Language	Answer in English	Job-Hunters	Businesses	Researchers
C	0	N	N						Y	N	N	Y

JAPAN COMMERCIAL ARBITRATION ASSOCIATION, NAGOYA BRANCH (C)

Prevention and arbitration of international problems.
Nagoya Chamber of Commerce, 2-10-19 Sakae, Naka-ku, Nagoya 460.
Higashiyama or Tsurumai Line, Fushimi. 052-221-7211 No contact

Size	Overseas Branches	Overseas Experience	In Future	Country	Full-Time	Part-Time	Increase	Language	Answer in English	Job-Hunters	Businesses	Researchers

CHAPTER 18. ASSOCIATIONS

The listing which follows is of all types of associations, but mainly trade organizations. This section is strongly recommended to our businessmen readers. Such associations can usually provide an up-to-date list of members and offer assistance in the introduction of a suitable business partner or a company which might be interested in a particular business proposition.

For those seeking employment, too, these associations may be a useful source of information, for their lists will be more extensive than those which we have published in this book. Note, of course, that it is not to be expected that the associations themselves will have opportunities for employment, nor that they will necessarily know of companies which do have such opportunities.

Also in our listing are economic associations and cultural or educational organizations. The listing finishes with a small selection of hospitals and religious organizations.

Against the names of the various associations, certain notations will be found. (F) indicates a non-profit foundation, (C) a non-profit corporate body and (IM) an association with individual membership. Where (SG) appears, the association is semi-governmental in its nature. We have determined this categorization based mainly on information supplied by the associations themselves.

Size	Overseas Branches	Overseas Experience	In Future	Country	←Non-Japanese→ Full-Time	Part-Time	Increase	Language	Answer in English	← Answer → Job-Hunters	Businesses	Researchers

ECONOMIC ASSOCIATIONS

INSTITUTE OF DEVELOPING ECONOMIES (SG)

Investigation and research of economies of developing countries.
42 Honmura-cho, Ichigaya, Shinjuku-ku, Tokyo 162. 03-3353-4231
Toei Shinjuku Line, Akebonobashi. Contact: (Jinji-ka) Ext. 680

Size	Overseas Branches	Overseas Experience	In Future	Country	Full-Time	Part-Time	Increase	Language	Answer in English	Job-Hunters	Businesses	Researchers
B	0	N	N		0	0	N		Y	N	N	Y

ASSOCIATION FOR PROMOTION OF INTERNATIONAL COOPERATION (F)

Publication of brochures concerning Official Development Assistance.
No. 23 Mori Building, 1-23-7 Toranomon, Minato-ku, Tokyo 105.
Ginza Line, Toranomon. Contact: Mr. Yasuhiro Shigeta 03-3504-2085

Size	Overseas Branches	Overseas Experience	In Future	Country	Full-Time	Part-Time	Increase	Language	Answer in English	Job-Hunters	Businesses	Researchers
C	0	N	N		0	0	N			Y	N	Y

THE ASSOCIATION FOR OVERSEAS TECHNICAL SCHOLARSHIP (F)

Acceptance and training of industrial engineers from overseas.
1-30-1 Senju Higashi, Adachi-ku, Tokyo 120. 03-3888-8211
Chiyoda, Hibiya or JR Joban Line, Kita Senju. No contact

Size	Overseas Branches	Overseas Experience	In Future	Country	Full-Time	Part-Time	Increase	Language	Answer in English	Job-Hunters	Businesses	Researchers
B	5				0	0						

INTERNATIONAL DEVELOPMENT CENTER OF JAPAN (F)

Investigation and research of developing countries and personnel training
Kyofuku Building, 2-9-11 Tomioka, Koto-ku, Tokyo 135. 03-3630-6911
Tozai Line, Monzen Nakacho. Contact: Mr. Yasunobu Kawato

Size	Overseas Branches	Overseas Experience	In Future	Country	Full-Time	Part-Time	Increase	Language	Answer in English	Job-Hunters	Businesses	Researchers
C	0	N			0	0			Y	Y	Y	Y

JAPAN-THAILAND ECONOMIC COOPERATION SOCIETY (C)

Economic and technological co-operation through local organizations.
2-12-13 Hon Komagome, Bunkyo-ku, Tokyo 113. 03-3946-0841
Toei Mita Line, Sengoku. No contact

Size	Overseas Branches	Overseas Experience	In Future	Country	Full-Time	Part-Time	Increase	Language	Answer in English	Job-Hunters	Businesses	Researchers
C	1	N	N		0	0			Y	Y	N	Y

JAPAN TRANSPORT ECONOMICS RESEARCH CENTER (F)

Study and investigation of transport policies. Publications.
1-6-6 Toranomon, Minato-ku, Tokyo 105. 03-3591-8922
Ginza Line, Toranomon. Contact: (Kokusai-bu)

Size	Overseas Branches	Overseas Experience	In Future	Country	Full-Time	Part-Time	Increase	Language	Answer in English	Job-Hunters	Businesses	Researchers
C	1	N	N		3		Y	Eur	Y	N	N	N

NIPPON RIKKO OVERSEAS ASSOCIATION (F)

Japanese language training.
2-43 Kotake-cho, Nerima-ku, Tokyo 176. 03-3972-1171
Seibu Ikebukuro Line, Ekoda. Contact: Mr. Setsuo Ono

Size	Overseas Branches	Overseas Experience	In Future	Country	Full-Time	Part-Time	Increase	Language	Answer in English	Job-Hunters	Businesses	Researchers
C	0	Y	Y	*	0	0	N		Y	Y	N	Y

* Malaysia, Thailand

TOKYO FOREIGN TRADE ASSOCIATION (C)

Management of showroom. Provision of trade information. 03-3434-4241
2nd Fl Toritsu Sangyo Boeki Center, 1-7-8 Kaigan, Minato-ku, Tokyo 105
JR Yamanote Line, Hamamatsucho. Contact: Mr. Aono Ext. 224

Size	Overseas Branches	Overseas Experience	In Future	Country	Full-Time	Part-Time	Increase	Language	Answer in English	Job-Hunters	Businesses	Researchers
C	0		Y		0	0			Y	N	Y	N

JAPAN TRADE AND INVESTMENT INSURANCE ORGANIZATION (F)

Study, investigation, consultation and PR activities. 03-3224-1254
7F Akasaka Twin Tower Hon-kan, 2-17-22 Akasaka, Minato-ku, Tokyo.
Marunouchi or Chiyoda Line, Kokkai Gijido-mae. Contact: Mr. Hironaga

Size	Overseas Branches	Overseas Experience	In Future	Country	Full-Time	Part-Time	Increase	Language	Answer in English	Job-Hunters	Businesses	Researchers
C	0	N	N		0	0			Y	N	N	Y

Size	Overseas Branches	Overseas Experience	In Future	Country	Full-Time (Non-Japanese)	Part-Time (Non-Japanese)	Increase (Non-Japanese)	Language (Non-Japanese)	Answer in English	Job-Hunters (Answer)	Businesses (Answer)	Researchers (Answer)

THE ASSOCIATION FOR INTERNATIONAL TECHNICAL CO-OPERATION (C)

Investigation, study and PR activities for Official Development Assistance
No. 3 Mori Building, 1-4-10 Nishi Shinbashi, Minato-ku, Tokyo 105.
Ginza Line, Toranomon. 03-3591-6461 No contact

Size	Overseas Branches	Overseas Experience	In Future	Country	Full-Time	Part-Time	Increase	Language	Answer in English	Job-Hunters	Businesses	Researchers
	0				0	0						

THE AMERICAN CHAMBER OF COMMERCE IN JAPAN (IM)

Various services to members.
7th Fl. No. 2 Fukide Building, 4-1-21 Toranomon, Minato-ku, Tokyo 105.
Hibiya Line, Kamiyacho. Contact: Ms. Michiko Endo 03-3433-5381

Size	Overseas Branches	Overseas Experience	In Future	Country	Full-Time	Part-Time	Increase	Language	Answer in English	Job-Hunters	Businesses	Researchers
C	0	N	N		4	0			Y	N	N	N

JAPAN ASSOCIATION FOR TRADE WITH RUSSIA AND CENTRAL EASTERN EUROPE (C)

Investigation and study. Provision of information. Lessons and seminars.
Kanayama Building, 1-2-12 Shinkawa, Chuo-ku, Tokyo 104.
Hibiya or Tozai Line, Kayabacho. 03-3551-6215 No contact

Size	Overseas Branches	Overseas Experience	In Future	Country	Full-Time	Part-Time	Increase	Language	Answer in English	Job-Hunters	Businesses	Researchers
C	1				2	0	N					

TRADE ASSOCIATIONS

JAPAN PHARMACEUTICAL ASSOCIATION (C)

Various services to members. 03-3406-1171 Ext. 30
4th Fl. Nagai Kinen-kan, 2-12-15 Shibuya, Shibuya-ku, Tokyo 150.
Ginza, Hanzomon or JR Yamanote Line, Shibuya. Contact:Mr.Wakayama

Size	Overseas Branches	Overseas Experience	In Future	Country	Full-Time	Part-Time	Increase	Language	Answer in English	Job-Hunters	Businesses	Researchers
C	0				0	0			Y			Y

GYPSUM BOARD ASSOCIATION (C)

Public relations related to products.
2-13-12 Nishi Shinbashi, Minato-ku, Tokyo 105. 03-3591-6774
Ginza, Toei Asakusa or JR Yamanote Line, Shinbashi. No contact

Size	Overseas Branches	Overseas Experience	In Future	Country	Full-Time	Part-Time	Increase	Language	Answer in English	Job-Hunters	Businesses	Researchers
D	0	N	N		0	0	N					

CARBON BLACK ASSOCIATION (C)

Various services to members.
1-1-21 Toranomon, Minato-ku, Tokyo 105. 03-3501-3241
Ginza Line, Toranomon. No contact

Size	Overseas Branches	Overseas Experience	In Future	Country	Full-Time	Part-Time	Increase	Language	Answer in English	Job-Hunters	Businesses	Researchers
D	0	N			0	0				N	Y	Y

JAPAN ASBESTOS PRODUCTS INDUSTRIAL ASSOCIATION (C)

Various services to members.
7-12-4 Ginza, Chuo-ku, Tokyo 104. 03-3541-4584
Ginza, Toei Asakusa or JR Yamanote Line, Shinbashi. No contact

Size	Overseas Branches	Overseas Experience	In Future	Country	Full-Time	Part-Time	Increase	Language	Answer in English	Job-Hunters	Businesses	Researchers
D	0	N	N		0	0			N	N	N	N

JAPAN P.V.C. PIPE ASSOCIATION (C)

Promotion of products.
Tobu Bldg., 1-5-26 Moto Akasaka, Minato-ku, Tokyo 107. 03-3470-2251
Ginza or Marunouchi Line, Akasaka Mitsuke. No contact

Size	Overseas Branches	Overseas Experience	In Future	Country	Full-Time	Part-Time	Increase	Language	Answer in English	Job-Hunters	Businesses	Researchers
D	0				0	0						

JAPAN SOAP AND DETERGENT CO-OPERATIVE ASSOCIATION (C)

Various services to members.
Oyu Building, 2-6-8 Kayabacho, Nihonbashi, Chuo-ku, Tokyo 103.
Hibiya or Tozai Line, Kayabacho. 03-3667-6969 No contact

Size	Overseas Branches	Overseas Experience	In Future	Country	Full-Time	Part-Time	Increase	Language	Answer in English	Job-Hunters	Businesses	Researchers
	0				0	0						

JAPAN CALCIUM CYANAMIDE INDUSTRY ASSOCIATION (C)

Promotion of products.
8-11-1 Ginza, Chuo-ku, Tokyo 104. 03-3573-3941
Ginza, Toei Asakusa or JR Yamanote Line, Shinbashi. No contact

Size	Overseas Branches	Overseas Experience	In Future	Country	Non-Japanese: Full-Time	Part-Time	Increase	Language	Answer in English	Answer: Job-Hunters	Businesses	Researchers
D	0	N	N		0	0			N	N	N	N

JAPAN TRANSPARENT-PAPER INDUSTRY ASSOCIATION (C)

Various activities for the development of the industry.
Kami Pulp Kaikan, 5-6 Hisamatsu-cho, Nihonbashi, Chuo-ku, Tokyo 103.
Toei Shinjuku Line, Bakuro Yokoyama. 03-3249-4864 No contact

Size	Overseas Branches	Overseas Experience	In Future	Country	Non-Japanese: Full-Time	Part-Time	Increase	Language	Answer in English	Answer: Job-Hunters	Businesses	Researchers
D	0	Y	Y	*	0	0	N		N	N	N	N

* S.E. Asia

DISSOLVED ACETYLENE ASSOCIATION (C)

Investigation and research into production and distribution.
Kaga Building, 5-30-7 Shinbashi, Minato-ku, Tokyo 105. 03-3433-4643
Ginza, Toei Asakusa or JR Yamanote Line, Shinbashi. No contact

Size	Overseas Branches	Overseas Experience	In Future	Country	Non-Japanese: Full-Time	Part-Time	Increase	Language	Answer in English	Answer: Job-Hunters	Businesses	Researchers
		N	N		0	0				N	N	N

PETROLEUM ASSOCIATION OF JAPAN (C)

Various services to members. 03-3279-3811
Keidanren Kaikan, 1-9-4 Otemachi, Chiyoda-ku, Tokyo 100.
Marunouchi, Tozai, Chiyoda, Hanzomon or Toei Mita Line, Otemachi. No contact

Size	Overseas Branches	Overseas Experience	In Future	Country	Non-Japanese: Full-Time	Part-Time	Increase	Language	Answer in English	Answer: Job-Hunters	Businesses	Researchers
		N	N		0	0						

PLASTIC WASTE MANAGEMENT INSTITUTE (C)

Research into and development of efficient uses of plastic waste.
Fukide Bldg., 4-1-13 Toranomon, Minato-ku, Tokyo 105. 03-3437-2251
Hibiya Line, Kamiyacho. No contact

Size	Overseas Branches	Overseas Experience	In Future	Country	Non-Japanese: Full-Time	Part-Time	Increase	Language	Answer in English	Answer: Job-Hunters	Businesses	Researchers
C	0	N	N		0	0			N			

THE SURFACE FINISHING SOCIETY OF JAPAN (C)

Research into plating, painting and other finishing techniques.
Kyodo Building, 2 Iwamoto-cho, Kanda, Chiyoda-ku, Tokyo 101.
JR Sobu or Yamanote Line, Akihabara. 03-3252-3286 No contact

Size	Overseas Branches	Overseas Experience	In Future	Country	Non-Japanese: Full-Time	Part-Time	Increase	Language	Answer in English	Answer: Job-Hunters	Businesses	Researchers
D	0	N	N		0	0				N	N	Y

JAPAN MACHINERY IMPORTERS' ASSOCIATION (C)

Promotion of imports. Feasibility assessments. Liaison with importers.
1-2-11 Toranomon, Minato-ku, Tokyo 105. 03-3503-9736
Ginza Line, Toranomon. Contact: Mr. Masahito Uno (Shogai-bu)

Size	Overseas Branches	Overseas Experience	In Future	Country	Non-Japanese: Full-Time	Part-Time	Increase	Language	Answer in English	Answer: Job-Hunters	Businesses	Researchers
C	0	N	N		0	0	N		Y	N	Y	N

ELECTRONIC MATERIALS MANUFACTURERS' ASSOCIATION OF JAPAN (C)

Promotion of semi-conducting ceramics, ferrite, magnets, etc.
Kotohira Kaikan Building, 1-2-8 Toranomon, Minato-ku, Tokyo 105.
Ginza Line, Toranomon. Contact: Mr. Takahashi 03-3504-0351

Size	Overseas Branches	Overseas Experience	In Future	Country	Non-Japanese: Full-Time	Part-Time	Increase	Language	Answer in English	Answer: Job-Hunters	Businesses	Researchers
D	0	N	N		0	0			Y	N	N	N

JAPAN BICYCLE MANUFACTURERS' ASSOCIATION (C)

Promotion and public relations activities.
Nihon Jidensha Kaikan No. 3, 1-9-3 Akasaka, Minato-ku, Tokyo 107.
Ginza Line, Toranomon. 03-3582-3311 Ext. 2750 No contact

Size	Overseas Branches	Overseas Experience	In Future	Country	Non-Japanese: Full-Time	Part-Time	Increase	Language	Answer in English	Answer: Job-Hunters	Businesses	Researchers
	0	N			0	0			N	N	N	N

THE JAPAN AUTOMOBILE TIRE MANUFACTURERS' ASSOCIATION, INC. (C)

Various activities for members.
9th Fl. Toranomon Building, 1-1-12 Toranomon, Minato-ku, Tokyo 105.
Ginza Line, Toranomon. Contact: Mr. Mitsumasa Tada 03-3503-0191

Size	Overseas Branches	Overseas Experience	In Future	Country	Non-Japanese: Full-Time	Part-Time	Increase	Language	Answer in English	Answer: Job-Hunters	Businesses	Researchers
C	0	N			0	0			Y	Y	Y	Y

Size	Overseas Branches	Overseas Experience	In Future	Country	Non-Japanese: Full-Time	Non-Japanese: Part-Time	Non-Japanese: Increase	Non-Japanese: Language	Answer in English	Answer: Job-Hunters	Answer: Businesses	Answer: Researchers

JAPAN SOCIETY OF TILE AND BRICK CONSTRUCTION INDUSTRIES (C)

Technical and business guidance. 03-3983-0908
Room 317, 1-48-10 Higashi Ikebukuro, Toshima-ku, Tokyo 170.
Marunouchi, Yurakucho or JR Yamanote Line, Ikebukuro. No contact

Size	Overseas Branches	Overseas Experience	In Future	Country	Full-Time	Part-Time	Increase	Language	Answer in English	Job-Hunters	Businesses	Researchers
D	0	N	N		0	0						

JAPAN OFFICE AND INSTITUTIONAL FURNITURE ASSOCIATION (C)

Improvement of amenities.
Seed Nihonbashi, 2-34-11 Ningyo-cho, Nihonbashi, Chuo-ku, Tokyo 103.
Hibiya Line, Ningyocho. Contact: Mr. Koichi Sakamaki 03-3663-6938

Size	Overseas Branches	Overseas Experience	In Future	Country	Full-Time	Part-Time	Increase	Language	Answer in English	Job-Hunters	Businesses	Researchers
D	0	Y	Y	*	0	0	Y		Y	N	N	Y

* E.C. Countries, U.S.A., Korea

JAPAN ROLLING SHUTTER INDUSTRY ASSOCIATION (C)

Various activities for members. 03-3288-1281
No. 4 NS Building, 1-10-5 Kudan Kita, Chiyoda-ku, Tokyo 102.
Tozai, Hanzomon or Toei Shinjuku Line, Kudanshita. No contact

Size	Overseas Branches	Overseas Experience	In Future	Country	Full-Time	Part-Time	Increase	Language	Answer in English	Job-Hunters	Businesses	Researchers
	0	Y	Y	*	0	0	N		N	N	N	N

* S.E Asia, China

JAPAN COOLING TOWER INSTITUTE (C)

Various activities for members.
Mitsubishi Building, 2-5-2 Marunouchi, Chiyoda-ku, Tokyo 100.
Marunouchi or JR Yamanote Line, Tokyo. 03-3283-4101 No contact

Size	Overseas Branches	Overseas Experience	In Future	Country	Full-Time	Part-Time	Increase	Language	Answer in English	Job-Hunters	Businesses	Researchers
	0				0	0						

JAPAN PAINT MANUFACTURERS ASSOCIATION (C)

Study and research of techniques and business management.
Tobu Bldg., 1-5-26 Moto Akasaka, Minato-ku, Tokyo 107. 03-3478-3451
Ginza or Maruncuchi Line, Akasaka Mitsuke. Contact: (Chosa-bu)

Size	Overseas Branches	Overseas Experience	In Future	Country	Full-Time	Part-Time	Increase	Language	Answer in English	Job-Hunters	Businesses	Researchers
C	0	N	N		0	0				N		

JAPAN LIGHT METAL MERCHANTS' ASSOCIATION (C)

Various activities for dealers.
2-15-8 Ningyo-cho, Nihonbashi, Chuo-ku, Tokyo 103. 03-3668-8653
Hibiya or Toei Asakusa Line, Ningyocho. No contact

Size	Overseas Branches	Overseas Experience	In Future	Country	Full-Time	Part-Time	Increase	Language	Answer in English	Job-Hunters	Businesses	Researchers
	0	N			0	0				N	N	N

ELECTRIC GLASS INDUSTRY ASSOCIATION (C)

Various activities for dealers.
3-1-9 Shinbashi, Minato-ku, Tokyo 105. 03-3501-8905
Ginza, Toei Asakusa or JR Yamanote Line, Shinbashi. No contact

Size	Overseas Branches	Overseas Experience	In Future	Country	Full-Time	Part-Time	Increase	Language	Answer in English	Job-Hunters	Businesses	Researchers
D	0	N	N		0	0				N	N	N

RECORDING INDUSTRY ASSOCIATION OF JAPAN (C)

Collection and distribution of royalties.
2-8-9 Tsukiji, Chuo-ku, Tokyo 104. 03-3541-4411
Hibiya Line, Tsukiji. Contact: Mr. Jiro Imamura (Chosakuken-bu)

Size	Overseas Branches	Overseas Experience	In Future	Country	Full-Time	Part-Time	Increase	Language	Answer in English	Job-Hunters	Businesses	Researchers
C	0	N	N		0	0			Y	N	N	Y

JAPAN SHEEP BREEDERS' ASSOCIATION (C)

Improvement of breeding techniques. Registration, seminars, research.
3-20-9 Yushima, Bunkyo-ku, Tokyo 113. 03-3831-3195
Chiyoda Line, Yushima. No contact

Size	Overseas Branches	Overseas Experience	In Future	Country	Full-Time	Part-Time	Increase	Language	Answer in English	Job-Hunters	Businesses	Researchers
D	0	Y			0	0			N	N	N	N

JAPAN WATER VALVE ASSOCIATION (C)

Various activities for manufacturers. 03-3264-0385
Nihon Suido Kaikan, 4-8-9 Kudan Minami, Chiyoda-ku, Tokyo 102.
Yurakucho, Toei Shinjuku or JR Sobu Line, Ichigaya. No contact

Size	Overseas Branches	Overseas Experience	In Future	Country	Full-Time	Part-Time	Increase	Language	Answer in English	Job-Hunters	Businesses	Researchers
D	0	N	N		0	0						

Size	Overseas Branches	Overseas Experience	In Future	Country	Non-Japanese Full-Time	Non-Japanese Part-Time	Non-Japanese Increase	Non-Japanese Language	Answer in English	Answer Job-Hunters	Answer Businesses	Answer Researchers

JAPAN USED-CAR DEALERS ASSOCIATION (C)

Various activities for members.
3-1-16 Shinjuku, Shinjuku-ku, Tokyo 160. 03-3359-2661
JR Yamanote or Chuo Line, Shinjuku. Contact: Mr. Sei-ichi Chihara

Size	Overseas Branches	Overseas Experience	In Future	Country	Full-Time	Part-Time	Increase	Language	Answer in English	Job-Hunters	Businesses	Researchers
B	0	Y	Y	All	0	0	Y		Y	N	Y	Y

JAPAN MICROSCOPE MANUFACTURERS' ASSOCIATION (C)

Provision of data to members.
2-43-2 Hatagaya, Shibuya-ku, Tokyo 151. 03-3377-2139
Keio New Line, Hatagaya. No contact

Size	Overseas Branches	Overseas Experience	In Future	Country	Full-Time	Part-Time	Increase	Language	Answer in English	Job-Hunters	Businesses	Researchers
	0				0	0				N	N	N

INTERNATIONAL ASSOCIATION OF PORTS AND HARBORS (IM)

Exchange of information and personnel. Improvement of ports. Seminars
4th Fl. Kotohira Kaikan, 1-2-8 Toranomon, Minato-ku, Tokyo 105.
Ginza Line, Toranomon. Contact: Mr. Hiroshi Kusaka 03-3591-4261

Size	Overseas Branches	Overseas Experience	In Future	Country	Full-Time	Part-Time	Increase	Language	Answer in English	Job-Hunters	Businesses	Researchers
D	0	N			0	0			Y	Y	Y	Y

ZENKOKU ELECTRIC WIRE & CABLE INDUSTRIAL CO-OPERATIVE (C)

Analysis of statistical data. Assistance with quality control activities.
Konwa Building, 1-12-22 Tsukiji, Chuo-ku, Tokyo 104. 03-3542-5604
Hibiya or Toei Asakusa Line, Higashi Ginza. No contact

Size	Overseas Branches	Overseas Experience	In Future	Country	Full-Time	Part-Time	Increase	Language	Answer in English	Job-Hunters	Businesses	Researchers
D	0	N	N		0	0				N	N	N

JAPAN SPIRITS & LIQUORS MAKERS ASSOCIATION (C)

Co-operation in collection of taxes.
7F No.I Koura Bldg., 1-1-6 Kayabacho, Nihonbashi, Chuo-ku, Tokyo 103.
Tozai or Hibiya Line, Kayabacho. 03-3668-4621 No contact

Size	Overseas Branches	Overseas Experience	In Future	Country	Full-Time	Part-Time	Increase	Language	Answer in English	Job-Hunters	Businesses	Researchers
D	0	N	N		0	0			N	N	N	N

FOREST CHEMICALS ASSOCIATION OF JAPAN (C)

Research, development and improvement of techniques.
No. 2 Katayama Building, 2-9-3 Iwamoto-cho, Chiyoda-ku, Tokyo 101.
Hibiya Line, Kodenmacho. 03-3851-5331 No contact

Size	Overseas Branches	Overseas Experience	In Future	Country	Full-Time	Part-Time	Increase	Language	Answer in English	Job-Hunters	Businesses	Researchers
D	0	N	N		0	0				N	N	N

JAPAN MARINE PRODUCTS IMPORTERS ASSOCIATION (C)

Information service for members. 03-3214-3407
Yurakucho Building, 1-10-1 Yurakucho, Chiyoda-ku, Tokyo 100.
Yurakucho or JR Yamanote Line, Yurakucho. No contact

Size	Overseas Branches	Overseas Experience	In Future	Country	Full-Time	Part-Time	Increase	Language	Answer in English	Job-Hunters	Businesses	Researchers
D	0				0	0				N		

JAPAN GOLF GOODS ASSOCIATION (C)

Various activities for members.
4th Fl. Kobayashi Building, 6-11-11 Soto Kanda, Chiyoda-ku, Tokyo 101.
Ginza Line, Suehirocho. Contact: Mr. Akira Kida 03-3832-8589

Size	Overseas Branches	Overseas Experience	In Future	Country	Full-Time	Part-Time	Increase	Language	Answer in English	Job-Hunters	Businesses	Researchers
D	0	Y			0	0	N		N	N	Y	N

JAPAN FROZEN FOOD ASSOCIATION (C)

Various activities for members.
6-10 Kofune-cho, Nihonbashi, Chuo-ku, Tokyo 103. 03-3667-6671
Hibiya or Toei Asakusa Line, Ningyocho. No contact

Size	Overseas Branches	Overseas Experience	In Future	Country	Full-Time	Part-Time	Increase	Language	Answer in English	Job-Hunters	Businesses	Researchers
D	0	N	N		0	0				N	N	N

JAPAN CONVENIENCE FOODS INDUSTRY ASSOCIATION (C)

Quality control and promotion of demand for instant Chinese noodles.
3rd Fl. Kimura Building, 5-5-5 Asakusabashi, Taito-ku, Tokyo 111.
JR Yamanote Line, Akihabarara. Contact: Mr. Fukushima 03-3856-0811

Size	Overseas Branches	Overseas Experience	In Future	Country	Full-Time	Part-Time	Increase	Language	Answer in English	Job-Hunters	Businesses	Researchers
D	0	N	N		0	0	N		N	N	Y	Y

JAPAN FRUIT GROWERS CO-OPERATIVE ASSOCIATION (C)

Export of various fruits.
3-2-1 Tokai, Ota-ku, Tokyo 143. 03-5492-5420
Tokyo Monorail, Ryutsu Centre. No contact

Size	Overseas Branches	Overseas Experience	In Future	Country	Non-Japanese Full-Time	Non-Japanese Part-Time	Non-Japanese Increase	Non-Japanese Language	Answer in English	Answer Job-Hunters	Answer Businesses	Answer Researchers
C	0	Y	N		0	0				N	Y	N

SHOP SYSTEM STUDY SOCIETY (F)

Research into complex or large-scale shops. Competitions. Seminars.
301 Horaiya Bldg., 5-2-1 Roppongi, Minato-ku, Tokyo 106. 03-3401-4021
Hibiya Line, Roppongi. Contact: Ms. Akiko Izumi (Kaigai Jigyo-bu)

Size	Overseas Branches	Overseas Experience	In Future	Country	Non-Japanese Full-Time	Non-Japanese Part-Time	Non-Japanese Increase	Non-Japanese Language	Answer in English	Answer Job-Hunters	Answer Businesses	Answer Researchers
D	0	N			0	0	Y	E	N	N	N	Y

JAPAN LONG COURSE FERRY SERVICE ASSOCIATION (C)

Information and PR activities for members. 03-3501-0889
920 Iino Building, 2-1-1 Uchi Saiwai-cho, Chiyoda-ku, Tokyo 100.
Marunouchi, Hibiya or Chiyoda Line, Kasumigaseki. No contact

Size	Overseas Branches	Overseas Experience	In Future	Country	Non-Japanese Full-Time	Non-Japanese Part-Time	Non-Japanese Increase	Non-Japanese Language	Answer in English	Answer Job-Hunters	Answer Businesses	Answer Researchers
	0	N	N		0	0	Y		Y			

THE JAPAN SMOKING ARTICLES CORPORATE ASSOCIATION (C)

Various activities for members.
3-19-5 Kotobuki, Taito-ku, Tokyo 111. 03-3845-6121
Ginza Line, Tawaramachi. Contact: (Ryutsu Shinko-bu)

Size	Overseas Branches	Overseas Experience	In Future	Country	Non-Japanese Full-Time	Non-Japanese Part-Time	Non-Japanese Increase	Non-Japanese Language	Answer in English	Answer Job-Hunters	Answer Businesses	Answer Researchers
C	1				0	0			Y	N	Y	Y

JAPAN MARKETING ASSOCIATION (C)

Marketing education, seminars and publications.
Wako Building, 4-8-5 Roppongi, Minato-ku, Tokyo 106. 03-3403-5101
Hibiya Line, Roppongi. Contact: (Kokusai-bu)

Size	Overseas Branches	Overseas Experience	In Future	Country	Non-Japanese Full-Time	Non-Japanese Part-Time	Non-Japanese Increase	Non-Japanese Language	Answer in English	Answer Job-Hunters	Answer Businesses	Answer Researchers
C		N	N		0	0			Y	N	N	Y

JAPAN FRANCHISE ASSOCIATION (C)

Promotion of franchise system.
602 Elsa Bldg., 3-13-12 Roppongi, Minato-ku, Tokyo 106. 03-3401-0421
Hibiya Line, Roppongi. No contact

Size	Overseas Branches	Overseas Experience	In Future	Country	Non-Japanese Full-Time	Non-Japanese Part-Time	Non-Japanese Increase	Non-Japanese Language	Answer in English	Answer Job-Hunters	Answer Businesses	Answer Researchers
D	0	N			0	0	N		N			

JAPAN BLOODHORSE BREEDERS' ASSOCIATION (C)

Various activities for members. 03-5473-7091
Shinbashi Bunkan, 4-5-4 Shinbashi, Minato-ku, Tokyo 158.
Ginza, Toei Asakusa or JR Yamanote Line, Shinbashi. No contact

Size	Overseas Branches	Overseas Experience	In Future	Country	Non-Japanese Full-Time	Non-Japanese Part-Time	Non-Japanese Increase	Non-Japanese Language	Answer in English	Answer Job-Hunters	Answer Businesses	Answer Researchers
C	0	N			0	0				N	Y	N

JAPAN FEDERATION OF BAR ASSOCIATIONS (C)

Guidance and supervision of lawyers and lawyers' associations.
1-1-1 Kasumigaseki, Chiyoda-ku, Tokyo 100. 03-3580-9841
Marunouchi, Hibiya or Chiyoda Line, Kasumigaseki. Contact: Ext. 231

Size	Overseas Branches	Overseas Experience	In Future	Country	Non-Japanese Full-Time	Non-Japanese Part-Time	Non-Japanese Increase	Non-Japanese Language	Answer in English	Answer Job-Hunters	Answer Businesses	Answer Researchers
C	0	N	N		0	0			Y	N	N	Y

JAPAN CONSUMERS' ASSOCIATION (F)

Provision of information. Examination of merchandise.
Eight Building, 4-5-9 Hatchobori, Chuo-ku, Tokyo 104. 03-3553-8601
Hibiya or JR Keiyo Line, Hatchobori. No contact

Size	Overseas Branches	Overseas Experience	In Future	Country	Non-Japanese Full-Time	Non-Japanese Part-Time	Non-Japanese Increase	Non-Japanese Language	Answer in English	Answer Job-Hunters	Answer Businesses	Answer Researchers
C	0	N	N		0	0			N	N	N	N

JAPAN CONSUMER INFORMATION CENTER (C)

Research, study and provision of information.
3-13-22 Takanawa, Minato-ku, Tokyo 108. 03-3443-9061
JR Yamanote Line, Shinagawa. No contact

Size	Overseas Branches	Overseas Experience	In Future	Country	Non-Japanese Full-Time	Non-Japanese Part-Time	Non-Japanese Increase	Non-Japanese Language	Answer in English	Answer Job-Hunters	Answer Businesses	Answer Researchers
B	0	N	N		0	0	N		N	N	N	N

CULTURAL AND ACADEMIC ASSOCIATIONS

Column headings: Size; Overseas Branches; Overseas Experience; In Future; Country; Non-Japanese: Full-Time, Part-Time, Increase, Language; Answer in English; Answer: Job-Hunters, Businesses, Researchers

INTERNATIONAL EDUCATION CENTER (F)

Promotion of inter-cultural understanding. Language school.
1-21 Yotsuya, Shinjuku-ku, Tokyo 160. 03-3359-9621
Marunouchi or JR Chuo Line, Yotsuya.Contact: Mr. Masato Mori Ext. 222

Size	Overseas Branches	Overseas Experience	In Future	Country	Full-Time	Part-Time	Increase	Language	Answer in English	Job-Hunters	Businesses	Researchers
B		N	N		55	50	Y	E	Y	Y	N	N

ASSOCIATION OF INTERNATIONAL EDUCATION, JAPAN (F)

Provision of assistance to students from overseas, including scholarships
4-5-29 Komaba, Meguro-ku, Tokyo 157. 03-3467-3521
Inokashira Line, Komaba Todai-mae. No contact

Size	Overseas Branches	Overseas Experience	In Future	Country	Full-Time	Part-Time	Increase	Language	Answer in English	Job-Hunters	Businesses	Researchers
	0									N	N	N

THE INTERNATIONAL STUDENTS INSTITUTE (F)

Cultural exchange. Operation of boarding house. Language school.
3-22-7 Kita Shinjuku, Shinjuku-ku, Tokyo 169. 03-3371-7265
JR Sobu Line, Okubo. Contact: Mr. Hayao Muguruma Ext. 13

Size	Overseas Branches	Overseas Experience	In Future	Country	Full-Time	Part-Time	Increase	Language	Answer in English	Job-Hunters	Businesses	Researchers
C	0	Y	Y	*					Y	N	N	N

* ASEAN Countries

ASSOCIATION FOR JAPANESE-LANGUAGE TEACHING (C)

Development of teaching methods and materials.
6th Fl. Kowa International, 4-12-24 Nishi Azabu, Minato-ku, Tokyo 106.
Hibiya Line, Roppongi. Contact: Ms. Sachiko Adachi 03-3400-9031

Size	Overseas Branches	Overseas Experience	In Future	Country	Full-Time	Part-Time	Increase	Language	Answer in English	Job-Hunters	Businesses	Researchers
C	0	Y	Y	Aust					Y			Y

ASIAN CULTURAL CENTRE FOR UNESCO (F)

Preservation of Asian cultural assets. Educational publications.
Nihon Shuppan Kaikan, 6 Fukuro-cho, Shinjuku-ku, Tokyo 162.
Tozai Line, Kagurazaka. 03-3269-4435 No contact

Size	Overseas Branches	Overseas Experience	In Future	Country	Full-Time	Part-Time	Increase	Language	Answer in English	Job-Hunters	Businesses	Researchers
										N	N	Y

THE ASIAN STUDENTS CULTURAL ASSOCIATION (F)

Operation of boarding house. Japanese language school.
Asia Bunka Kaikan, 2-12-13 Hon Komagome, Bunkyo-ku, Tokyo 113.
Toei Mita Line, Sengoku. Contact: (Any section) 03-3946-4121

Size	Overseas Branches	Overseas Experience	In Future	Country	Full-Time	Part-Time	Increase	Language	Answer in English	Job-Hunters	Businesses	Researchers
C	0	N	N		0	0	N		Y	N	N	Y

JAPAN NATIONAL TOURIST ORGANIZATION (SG)

Tourist promotion and tourist information services.
2-10-1 Yurakucho, Chiyoda-ku, Tokyo 100. 03-3216-1901
JR Yamanote Line, Yurakucho. Contact: Tourist Information Center

Size	Overseas Branches	Overseas Experience	In Future	Country	Full-Time	Part-Time	Increase	Language	Answer in English	Job-Hunters	Businesses	Researchers
	20	N	N						Y			

THE INSTITUTE OF EASTERN CULTURE (F)

Inernational academic exchange. Publications. International conferences.
2-4-1 Nishi Kanda, Chiyoda-ku, Tokyo 101. 03-3262-7221
Toei Mita or JR Sobu Line, Suidobashi. Contact: Mr. Hiroshi Yanase

Size	Overseas Branches	Overseas Experience	In Future	Country	Full-Time	Part-Time	Increase	Language	Answer in English	Job-Hunters	Businesses	Researchers
D		Y							Y	N	N	Y

JAPAN POLAR RESEARCH ASSOCIATION (F)

Assistance to researchers and organizations.
2-3-4 Hirakawa-cho, Chiyoda-ku, Tokyo 102. 03-3239-7615
Hanzomon Line, Hanzomon. No contact

Size	Overseas Branches	Overseas Experience	In Future	Country	Full-Time	Part-Time	Increase	Language	Answer in English	Job-Hunters	Businesses	Researchers
D	0	N	N		0	0						Y

NANYO GUNTO KYOKAI (F)

Introduction of history of Micronesia.
2-23-14 Koishikawa, Bunkyo-ku, Tokyo 112. 03-3818-3967
Marunouchi Line, Korakuen. Contact: Mr. Teruo Kosuge

Size	Overseas Branches	Overseas Experience	In Future	Country	Non-Japanese Full-Time	Non-Japanese Part-Time	Non-Japanese Increase	Language	Answer in English	Answer Job-Hunters	Answer Businesses	Answer Researchers
D	0	N	N		0	0	N			N	N	N

THE INSTITUTE OF STATISTICAL RESEARCH (F)

Academic research organization. 03-3591-8496
8th Fl. Nissei Building, 1-18-16 Shinbashi, Minato-ku, Tokyo 105.
Ginza, Toei Asakusa or JR Yamanote Line, Shinbashi. No contact

Size	Overseas Branches	Overseas Experience	In Future	Country	Non-Japanese Full-Time	Non-Japanese Part-Time	Non-Japanese Increase	Language	Answer in English	Answer Job-Hunters	Answer Businesses	Answer Researchers
C	0	Y	N		0	0	N		N			Y

THE PHOTOGRAPHIC SOCIETY OF JAPAN (C)

Promotion of international friendship through photography.
1st Fl. JCII Bldg., 25 Ichiban-cho, Chiyoda-ku, Tokyo 102. 03-5276-3585
Hanzomon Line, Hanzomon. No contact

Size	Overseas Branches	Overseas Experience	In Future	Country	Non-Japanese Full-Time	Non-Japanese Part-Time	Non-Japanese Increase	Language	Answer in English	Answer Job-Hunters	Answer Businesses	Answer Researchers
D	0	N	N		0	0				N	N	N

IKEBANA INTERNATIONAL (C)

Promotion of traditional Japanese art and culture.
8F B-kan Ochanomizu Square, 1-6 Kanda Surugadai, Chiyoda-ku, Tokyo
JR Chuo Line, Ochanomizu. Contact: Ms. Kurosawa 03-3293-8188

Size	Overseas Branches	Overseas Experience	In Future	Country	Non-Japanese Full-Time	Non-Japanese Part-Time	Non-Japanese Increase	Language	Answer in English	Answer Job-Hunters	Answer Businesses	Answer Researchers
C	94	N	N		0	2			Y	N	N	Y

THE SATOH ARTCRAFT RESEARCH AND SCHOLARSHIP FOUNDATION (F)

Study of and research into arts and crafts. Scholarships.
5-9-39 Jyomyoji, Kamakura-shi, Kanagawa 248. 0467-23-0118
JR Yokosuka Line, Kamakura. No contact

Size	Overseas Branches	Overseas Experience	In Future	Country	Non-Japanese Full-Time	Non-Japanese Part-Time	Non-Japanese Increase	Language	Answer in English	Answer Job-Hunters	Answer Businesses	Answer Researchers

TOKYU FOUNDATION FOR INBOUND STUDENTS (F)

International exchange and scholarships.
1-21-2 Dogenzaka, Shibuya-ku, Tokyo 150. 03-3461-0844
Ginza, Hanzomon or JR Yamanote Line, Shibuya. Contact: (Any officer)

Size	Overseas Branches	Overseas Experience	In Future	Country	Non-Japanese Full-Time	Non-Japanese Part-Time	Non-Japanese Increase	Language	Answer in English	Answer Job-Hunters	Answer Businesses	Answer Researchers
D	0	N	N		0	0			Y	N	N	Y

HONDA FOUNDATION (F)

Symposia and awards.
2-6-20 Yaesu, Chuo-ku, Tokyo 104. 03-3274-5125
Marunouchi or JR Yamanote Line, Tokyo. No contact

Size	Overseas Branches	Overseas Experience	In Future	Country	Non-Japanese Full-Time	Non-Japanese Part-Time	Non-Japanese Increase	Language	Answer in English	Answer Job-Hunters	Answer Businesses	Answer Researchers
D		N										

PUBLISHERS ASSOCIATION FOR CULTURAL EXCHANGE (C)

Promotion of Japanese publishing industry. Introductory publications.
1-2-1 Sarugaku-cho, Chiyoda-ku, Tokyo 101. 03-3291-5685
JR Chuo Line, Ochanomizu. No contact

Size	Overseas Branches	Overseas Experience	In Future	Country	Non-Japanese Full-Time	Non-Japanese Part-Time	Non-Japanese Increase	Language	Answer in English	Answer Job-Hunters	Answer Businesses	Answer Researchers
D	0	N	N							N	N	Y

JAPAN INTERPRETERS' ASSOCIATION (C)

Administration of official interpreters' examinations.
Chiyoda Seimei Building, 1-5-20 Takadanobaba, Shinjuku-ku, Tokyo 169
Tozai or JR Yamanote Line, Takadanobaba. 03-3209-4741 No contact

Size	Overseas Branches	Overseas Experience	In Future	Country	Non-Japanese Full-Time	Non-Japanese Part-Time	Non-Japanese Increase	Language	Answer in English	Answer Job-Hunters	Answer Businesses	Answer Researchers
		N	N							N	N	N

JAPAN LIBRARY ASSOCIATION (C)

National co-ordination of libraries.
1-1-10 Taishido, Setagaya-ku, Tokyo 154. 03-3410-6411
Ginza, Hanzomon or JR Yamanote Line, Shibuya. Contact: (Somu-bu)

Size	Overseas Branches	Overseas Experience	In Future	Country	Non-Japanese Full-Time	Non-Japanese Part-Time	Non-Japanese Increase	Language	Answer in English	Answer Job-Hunters	Answer Businesses	Answer Researchers
C	0	N	N						Y	N	N	Y

JAPAN-AMERICAN CULTURAL SOCIETY (C)

International cultural exchange. 03-3239-7231
4th Fl. Kudan Best Building, 1-10-3 Kudan Kita, Chiyoda-ku, Tokyo 102.
Tozai, Hanzomon or Toei Shinjuku Line, Kudanshita. Contact: Ms. Ohashi

Size	Overseas Branches	Overseas Experience	In Future	Country	Full-Time (Non-Japanese)	Part-Time (Non-Japanese)	Increase (Non-Japanese)	Language (Non-Japanese)	Answer in English	Job-Hunters (Answer)	Businesses (Answer)	Researchers (Answer)
D	3	N	N		0	0			Y	Y	N	Y

AMERICA-JAPAN SOCIETY OF HOKKAIDO (IM)

Promotion of international understanding. Cultural exchange.
American Center, Odori Nishi 28-chome, Chuo-ku, Sapporo 064.
Tozai Line, Maruyama Koen. Contact: Mr. Asanobu Hasei 011-641-0211

Size	Overseas Branches	Overseas Experience	In Future	Country	Full-Time (Non-Japanese)	Part-Time (Non-Japanese)	Increase (Non-Japanese)	Language (Non-Japanese)	Answer in English	Job-Hunters (Answer)	Businesses (Answer)	Researchers (Answer)
	0	N			0	0			Y	Y	N	Y

JAPAN PANAMA FRIENDSHIP ASSOCIATION (C)

International friendship.
No. 38 Kowa Building, 4-12-24 Nishi Azabu, Minato-ku, Tokyo 106.
Hibiya Line, Roppongi. Contact: Ms. Mayumi Kishiro 03-3407-9117

Size	Overseas Branches	Overseas Experience	In Future	Country	Full-Time (Non-Japanese)	Part-Time (Non-Japanese)	Increase (Non-Japanese)	Language (Non-Japanese)	Answer in English	Job-Hunters (Answer)	Businesses (Answer)	Researchers (Answer)
D	0	N	N		0	0	N		Y	Y	Y	Y

THE JAPAN-FINLAND SOCIETY (C)

International exchange.
30-4-306 Sakuragaoka-cho, Shibuya-ku, Tokyo 150. 03-3464-6093
Ginza, Hanzomon or JR Yamanote Line, Shibuya. No contact

Size	Overseas Branches	Overseas Experience	In Future	Country	Full-Time (Non-Japanese)	Part-Time (Non-Japanese)	Increase (Non-Japanese)	Language (Non-Japanese)	Answer in English	Job-Hunters (Answer)	Businesses (Answer)	Researchers (Answer)
	0	N	N		0	0	N			N	N	Y

THE AMERICA-JAPAN SOCIETY, INC. (C)

International cultural exchange.
370 Maru Building, 2-4-1 Marunouchi, Chiyoda-ku, Tokyo 100.
Marunouchi or JR Yamanote Line, Tokyo. 03-3201-0780 No contact

Size	Overseas Branches	Overseas Experience	In Future	Country	Full-Time (Non-Japanese)	Part-Time (Non-Japanese)	Increase (Non-Japanese)	Language (Non-Japanese)	Answer in English	Job-Hunters (Answer)	Businesses (Answer)	Researchers (Answer)
	23	N	N							N	N	N

THE CANADA-JAPAN SOCIETY (C)

Cultural organization aiming to deepen friendship with Canada.
302 Laurel Nagatacho, 2-17-5 Nagata-cho, Chiyoda-ku, Tokyo 100.
Marunouchi or Ginza Line, Akasaka Mitsuke. 03-3581-0925 No contact

Size	Overseas Branches	Overseas Experience	In Future	Country	Full-Time (Non-Japanese)	Part-Time (Non-Japanese)	Increase (Non-Japanese)	Language (Non-Japanese)	Answer in English	Job-Hunters (Answer)	Businesses (Answer)	Researchers (Answer)
										N	N	N

THE JAPAN-BRAZIL CENTRAL ASSOCIATION (C)

International exchange. 03-3504-3866
Shin Saiwai Building, 1-17-1 Shinbashi, Minato-ku, Tokyo 214.
Ginza, Toei Asakusa, JR Yamanote Line, Shinbashi. Contact: Mr. Nagata

Size	Overseas Branches	Overseas Experience	In Future	Country	Full-Time (Non-Japanese)	Part-Time (Non-Japanese)	Increase (Non-Japanese)	Language (Non-Japanese)	Answer in English	Job-Hunters (Answer)	Businesses (Answer)	Researchers (Answer)
D	0								Y	N	N	Y

THE JAPAN SINGAPORE ASSOCIATION (C)

Provision of various kinds of information. 03-3403-3719
Asian Center of Japan, 8-10-32 Akasaka, Minato-ku, Tokyo 107.
Ginza or Hanzomon Line, Aoyama I-chome. Contact: Mr. Tanaka

Size	Overseas Branches	Overseas Experience	In Future	Country	Full-Time (Non-Japanese)	Part-Time (Non-Japanese)	Increase (Non-Japanese)	Language (Non-Japanese)	Answer in English	Job-Hunters (Answer)	Businesses (Answer)	Researchers (Answer)
D	0	N	N		1	0	N		Y	N	Y	Y

THAI CULTURE STUDY ASSOCIATION (IM)

Cultural exchange, language lessons and seminars.
C/o Unno, 1-12-12-401 Sakura Shin-machi, Setagaya-ku, Tokyo 154.
Shin Tamagawa Line, Sakura Shinmachi. 03-3420-0229 No contact

Size	Overseas Branches	Overseas Experience	In Future	Country	Full-Time (Non-Japanese)	Part-Time (Non-Japanese)	Increase (Non-Japanese)	Language (Non-Japanese)	Answer in English	Job-Hunters (Answer)	Businesses (Answer)	Researchers (Answer)
	1											

ASSOCIATION JAPAN-CAMBODIA (IM)

International exchange.
2-11-2 Hirakawa-cho, Chiyoda-ku, Tokyo 102. 03-3230-0526
Yurakucho Line, Hirakawacho. No contact

Size	Overseas Branches	Overseas Experience	In Future	Country	Full-Time (Non-Japanese)	Part-Time (Non-Japanese)	Increase (Non-Japanese)	Language (Non-Japanese)	Answer in English	Job-Hunters (Answer)	Businesses (Answer)	Researchers (Answer)
D	0	N	N		0	0	N			N	Y	Y

Column headings: Size | Overseas Branches | Overseas Experience | In Future | Country | ←Non-Japanese→ (Full-Time | Part-Time | Increase | Language) | Answer in English | ←Answer→ (Job-Hunters | Businesses | Researchers)

KOREAN CULTURAL SERVICE (SG)

Introduction of Korean culture. 03-3983-9271
5th Fl. Sunshine 60, 3-1-1 Higashi Ikebukuro, Toshima-ku, Tokyo 170.
JR Yamanote Line, Ikebukuro or Yurakucho Line, Higashi Ikebukuro. No contact

Size	Overseas Branches	Overseas Experience	In Future	Country	Full-Time	Part-Time	Increase	Language	Answer in English	Job-Hunters	Businesses	Researchers
		N	N							N	N	Y

ASSOCIAZIONE ITALO-GIAPPONESE (F)

Cultural exchange.
207 Akasaka Chuo Mansion, 7-2-17 Akasaka, Minato-ku, Tokyo 107.
Ginza or Hanzomon Line, Aoyama I-chome. 03-3402-1632 No contact

Size	Overseas Branches	Overseas Experience	In Future	Country	Full-Time	Part-Time	Increase	Language	Answer in English	Job-Hunters	Businesses	Researchers
D					0	0						

JAPAN SPANISH SOCIETY (F)

Cultural exchange, language lessons and seminars.
6th Fl. Shinsei Kaikan, 33 Shinano-machi, Shinjuku-ku, Tokyo 160.
JR Sobu Line, Shinanomachi. Contact: Casa de España 03-3353-0428

Size	Overseas Branches	Overseas Experience	In Future	Country	Full-Time	Part-Time	Increase	Language	Answer in English	Job-Hunters	Businesses	Researchers
D		Y	Y	*	0	20	Y	S	Y	Y	Y	Y

* Spain, Central and South America

THE JAPAN-SCOTLAND SOCIETY (IM)

Cultural exchange.
1st Fl. Nakai Bldg., 5-25-6 Hiro-o, Shibuya-ku, Tokyo 150. 03-3473-1891
Hibiya Line, Hiro-o. Contact: Ms. Mimura (Wed.) or Ms. Yamazaki (Fri.)

Size	Overseas Branches	Overseas Experience	In Future	Country	Full-Time	Part-Time	Increase	Language	Answer in English	Job-Hunters	Businesses	Researchers
												Y

JAPAN-ARAB ASSOCIATION (IM)

Promotion of friendship.
4th Fl. Toshiba Building, 1-1-1 Shibaura, Minato-ku, Tokyo 105.
JR Yamanote Line, Hamamatsucho. Contact: Mr. Minamii 03-3798-3515

Size	Overseas Branches	Overseas Experience	In Future	Country	Full-Time	Part-Time	Increase	Language	Answer in English	Job-Hunters	Businesses	Researchers
		N	N						Y	N	N	Y

JAPAN-LIBYA FRIENDSHIP ASSOCIATION (IM)

Promotion of cultural exchange.
No. 3 Mori Building, 1-4-10 Nishi Shinbashi, Minato-ku, Tokyo 105.
Ginza Line, Toranomon. 03-3591-6525 No contact

Size	Overseas Branches	Overseas Experience	In Future	Country	Full-Time	Part-Time	Increase	Language	Answer in English	Job-Hunters	Businesses	Researchers

JAPAN EURASIA ASSOCIATION OF OSAKA (IM)

Cultural exchange, language lessons and publications.
7-3-4-373 Tani-machi, Chuo-ku, Osaka 542. 06-763-0877
Tanimachi Line, Tanimachi Roku-chome. Contact: Mr. Masaaki Sakaki

Size	Overseas Branches	Overseas Experience	In Future	Country	Full-Time	Part-Time	Increase	Language	Answer in English	Job-Hunters	Businesses	Researchers
					1	0			Y	Y	N	Y

JAPAN INTERNATIONAL PEACE RESEARCH ASSOCIATION (F)

Study of international peace. Information exchange. Publications.
1-1-7-1103 Moto Akasaka, Minato-ku, Tokyo 107. 03-3470-5013
Marunouchi or Ginza Line, Akasaka Mitsuke. No contact

Size	Overseas Branches	Overseas Experience	In Future	Country	Full-Time	Part-Time	Increase	Language	Answer in English	Job-Hunters	Businesses	Researchers
	0	N			0	0	N			N	N	Y

ESPERANTO-SOCIETO DE KAWASAKI (IM)

Promotion of Esperanto and cultural exchange.
C/o Ms. Kitagawa, 2-93 Furuichiba, Saiwai-ku, Kawasaki 211.
Tokyu Toyoko Line, Musashi Kosugi. Contact:Ms.Kitagawa 044-533-1906

Size	Overseas Branches	Overseas Experience	In Future	Country	Full-Time	Part-Time	Increase	Language	Answer in English	Job-Hunters	Businesses	Researchers
		N	N						Y	N	N	Y

YOKOHAMA ASSOCIATION FOR INTERNATIONAL COMMUNICATIONS AND EXCHANGES (F)

Cultural exchange with sister city. Provision of information. 045-671-7128
3rd Fl. Sanbo Center Building, 2 Yamashita-cho, Naka-ku, Yokohama.
Keihin Tohoku Line, Kannai. Contact: Information Corner 045-671-7209

Size	Overseas Branches	Overseas Experience	In Future	Country	Full-Time	Part-Time	Increase	Language	Answer in English	Job-Hunters	Businesses	Researchers
C	0	N	N		1	0			Y	Y	N	Y

Size	Overseas Branches	Overseas Experience	In Future	Country	←Non-Japanese Full-Time	Part-Time	Increase	Language→	Answer in English	←Answer Job-Hunters	Businesses	Researchers→

AMNESTY INTERNATIONAL JAPANESE SECTION (IM)

Various activities to protect human rights.
No. 3 Yamatake Building, 2-3-22 Nishi Waseda, Shinjuku-ku, Tokyo 169.
Tozai Line, Waseda. 03-3203-1050 No contact

Size	Overseas Branches	Overseas Experience	In Future	Country	Full-Time	Part-Time	Increase	Language	Answer in English	Job-Hunters	Businesses	Researchers
C		N	N		0	0			Y	Y	N	Y

THE BRITISH COUNCIL

Cultural exchange. Library and information services. Seminars.
1-2 Kagurazaka, Shinjuku-ku, Tokyo 162. 03-3235-8031
Yurakucho, Tozai or JR Sobu Line, Iidabashi. No contact

Size	Overseas Branches	Overseas Experience	In Future	Country	Full-Time	Part-Time	Increase	Language	Answer in English	Job-Hunters	Businesses	Researchers
										N	N	Y

YOKOSUKA CITY OFFICE (SG)

International cultural exchange.
11 Ogawa-machi, Yokosuka-shi, Kanagawa 238. 0468-22-4000
Keihin Kyuko Line, Yokosuka Chuo. Contact: Ms. T. Yamada Ext. 1412

Size	Overseas Branches	Overseas Experience	In Future	Country	Full-Time	Part-Time	Increase	Language	Answer in English	Job-Hunters	Businesses	Researchers
A	0				0	1	Y	P	Y	N	N	N

HIGASHI OSAKA SISTER CITY ASSOCIATION (SG)

Promotion of understanding and friendship with sister cities.
Higashi Osaka-shi Yaku-sho, 1-1-1 Inaba, Higashi Osaka-shi 578.
Kintetsu Nara Line, Wakae Iwata. 0729-62-1331 No contact

Size	Overseas Branches	Overseas Experience	In Future	Country	Full-Time	Part-Time	Increase	Language	Answer in English	Job-Hunters	Businesses	Researchers

KARIYA INTERNATIONAL FRIENDSHIP ASSOCIATION (SG)

Exchange of students and citizens.
1-1 Toyo-cho, Kariya-shi, Aichi 448. 0566-23-1111
Meitetsu or JR Tokaido Line, Kariya. Contact: (Yuko Kyokai) Ext. 2213

Size	Overseas Branches	Overseas Experience	In Future	Country	Full-Time	Part-Time	Increase	Language	Answer in English	Job-Hunters	Businesses	Researchers
D	0	N	N						Y	N	N	Y

HOSPITALS

IMPERIAL GIFT FOUNDATION AIIKU ASSOCIATION FOR MATERNAL CHILD HEALTH & WELFARE (F)

Operation of Aiiku Hospitals.
5-6-8 Minami Azabu, Minato-ku, Tokyo 106. 03-3473-8311
Hibiya Line, Hiro-o. Contact: Mr. Iino (Koho Shido-ka) Ext. 116

Size	Overseas Branches	Overseas Experience	In Future	Country	Full-Time	Part-Time	Increase	Language	Answer in English	Job-Hunters	Businesses	Researchers
B	0	N			0	0	Y	E	N	N	N	Y

INTERNATIONAL CATHOLIC HOSPITAL

General hospital.
2-5-1 Naka Ochiai, Shinjuku-ku, Tokyo 161. 03-3951-1111
Seibu Shinjuku Line, Shimo Ochiai. Contact: Ms.Mano (Somu-ka) Ext.132

Size	Overseas Branches	Overseas Experience	In Future	Country	Full-Time	Part-Time	Increase	Language	Answer in English	Job-Hunters	Businesses	Researchers
B	0				1	2	N		Y	N		

NOZAKI EYE CLINIC

Ophthalmologist. 03-3461-1671
Kasuya Building, 2-9 Sakuragaoka-machi, Shibuya-ku, Tokyo 150.
Ginza, Hanzomon or JR Yamanote Line, Shibuya. No contact

Size	Overseas Branches	Overseas Experience	In Future	Country	Full-Time	Part-Time	Increase	Language	Answer in English	Job-Hunters	Businesses	Researchers

SAIANDO MEDICAL CORPORATION SHADAN, INOUE EYE HOSPITAL (C)

Ophthalmologist.
4-3 Kanda Surugadai, Chiyoda-ku, Tokyo 101. 03-3295-0911
JR Chuo Line, Ochanomizu. No contact

Size	Overseas Branches	Overseas Experience	In Future	Country	Full-Time	Part-Time	Increase	Language	Answer in English	Job-Hunters	Businesses	Researchers
B	0	N	N				Y		Y			

TOKYO ADVENTIST HOSPITAL

General hospital.
3-17-3 Amanuma, Suginami-ku, Tokyo 167. 03-3392-6151
Marunouchi or JR Chuo Line, Ogikubo. Contact: Mr. Nishiura (Jinji-ka) Ext. 4650

					Non-Japanese					Answer		
Size	Overseas Branches	Overseas Experience	In Future	Country	Full-Time	Part-Time	Increase	Language	Answer in English	Job-Hunters	Businesses	Researchers
B	166	N	N		2	1	Y		Y	Y	N	N

TOKYO CLINIC DENTAL OFFICE

Dentist.
No. 32 Mori Building, 3-4-30 Shiba Koen, Minato-ku, Tokyo 105.
Hibiya Line, Kamiyacho. Contact: Ms. Fukasawa 03-3431-4225

Size	Overseas Branches	Overseas Experience	In Future	Country	Full-Time	Part-Time	Increase	Language	Answer in English	Job-Hunters	Businesses	Researchers
					0	1			Y	Y	Y	Y

RELIGIOUS ORGANIZATIONS

FRANCISCAN CHAPEL CENTER

Catholic church.
4-2-37 Roppongi, Minato-ku, Tokyo 106. 03-3401-2141
Hibiya Line, Roppongi. No contact

Size	Overseas Branches	Overseas Experience	In Future	Country	Full-Time	Part-Time	Increase	Language	Answer in English	Job-Hunters	Businesses	Researchers

ISLAMIC CENTER – JAPAN

Islamic religious centre.
1-16-11 Ohara, Setagaya-ku, Tokyo 156. 03-3460-6169
Keio Line, Sasazuka. No contact

Size	Overseas Branches	Overseas Experience	In Future	Country	Full-Time	Part-Time	Increase	Language	Answer in English	Job-Hunters	Businesses	Researchers

TOKYO UNION CHURCH

Church.
5-7-7 Jingu-mae, Shibuya-ku, Tokyo 150. 03-3400-0047
JR Yamanote Line, Harajuku. No contact

Size	Overseas Branches	Overseas Experience	In Future	Country	Full-Time	Part-Time	Increase	Language	Answer in English	Job-Hunters	Businesses	Researchers
D							Y	E	Y		Y	Y

CHAPTER 19. UNIVERSITIES AND COLLEGES

This chapter is likely to be of interest mainly, of course, to those who wish to study in Japan. However, it should be borne in mind that opportunities to study Japanese, for example, are more plentiful at private language schools than at recognized universities and colleges. These can be found in Chapter 4 – 'Language and Other Schools'.

Over a third of Japanese continue to universities or colleges, so it will be no surprise that there are very many such institutions in the country. They are divided into government and private sectors. The government universities tend to have the higher reputations, with the top two generally regarded as The University of Tokyo and Kyoto University. The best of the private universities are usually thought to be Waseda University and Keio University, both in Tokyo. Students must pay for their education and government institutions are considerably cheaper than private ones, so the competition for those is particularly fierce.

As explained elsewhere in this book, although the pressure to get into a highly-regarded university is particularly severe on students and leads to a high standard of high-school education, once the student is safely accepted into the realms of higher education, he is able to relax and enjoy four years of leisure, for there is little chance of his failing to graduate at the end of that period. This means that, in many cases, the standard of university education is not particularly high and the further one gets from the top-ranking universities the more this is likely to be so.

There are courses at universities and colleges which are open to non-Japanese, but most of these require knowledge of the Japanese language. Some universities also offer courses in studying Japanese. When examining the listing on the succeeding pages, it is necessary to bear in mind that most of the non-Japanese students mentioned are from various parts of Asia. Comparatively few are westerners. It is also worth remembering that fees at universities and colleges are high and that any student will probably have to work part-time to support his education. This is permitted to those with cultural visas, for a maximum of twenty hours per week, provided permission is obtained from the immigration authorities.

Research possibilities for non-Japanese are very limited because there is fierce competition among Japanese for such opportunities. However, if one has some very special background to offer, there might be some chance. Large companies have their own research facilities, of course, and that might be another possibility, although, again, there will be a great deal of competition from well-qualified Japanese.

As for teaching positions at institutions of higher education, non-Japanese are employed, particularly in foreign language faculties, but most universities have their own channels of recruitment, often having arrangements with certain American universities, for instance, to accept one or two graduates each year. Outside such avenues, as so often in Japan, connexions are most useful. The chances of writing or telephoning a university on speculation and obtaining a position are somewhat limited, but, of course, one can always try.

In any case, it should be borne in mind that, with the educational background mentioned above, the intellectual stimulation reaped from a language teaching position at a university or college will be somewhat limited. On the other hand, the pay will be very good, the hours undemanding and the holidays long, so the prospects are not totally unappealing, particularly in a nation where free time is at such a premium.

In the listing which follows, the box headings are changed from those used in previous chapters, it should be noted. As for the type of institution, we have distinguished national universities, public universities (i.e. established by local governments), private universities and colleges. Then we have listed the total number of students and the number of overseas students. Where the institution offers scholarships, this is indicated by a 'Y' (yes) in the fourth box. A 'Y' in the fifth box shows that scholarships, although not offered by the institution itself, are available for certain students wishing to attend.

The final box shows whether the institution makes some provision of special assistance to overseas students. This may be in the form of special lectures, especially in learning the Japanese language or culture, a course designed specifically for overseas students, assistance with accommodation, financial assistance or loans, or any other consideration whatever.

As usual, this is not a comprehensive listing. It contains only those institutions which responded to our questionnaire.

Institution	Address / Contact	Type	Students	Overseas Students	Own Scholarships	Other Scholarships	Assistance
TOKYO UNIVERSITY OF FOREIGN STUDIES	4-51-21 Nishigahara, Kita-ku, Tokyo 114. 03-3917-6111 Toei Mita or JR Yamanote Line, Sugamo. Contact: Ms. Inoue (Ryugakuse-tanto)	National	3,420	231	N	N	N
TOKYO METROPOLITAN UNIVERSITY	1-1 Minami Osawa, Hachioji-shi, Tokyo 192-03. 0426-77-1111 Keio Line, Minami Osawa. Contact: (Ryugakusei-tanto) Ext. 2223	Public	5,122	200	N	Y	Y
AOYAMA GAKUIN UNIVERSITY	4-4-25 Shibuya, Shibuya-ku, Tokyo 150. 03-3409-8111 JR Yamanote Line, Shibuya. Contact: (Kokusai Koryu Centre) Ext. 2041	Private	20,000	100	N	Y	Y
ASIA UNIVERSITY	5-24-10 Sakai, Musashino-shi, Tokyo 180. 0422-54-3111 JR Chuo Line, Musashi Sakai. Contact: Mr. Kakiuchi (Kokusai Koryu-bu)	Private	8,000	490	Y	Y	Y
CHUO UNIVERSITY	742-1 Higashi Nakano, Hachioji-shi, Tokyo 192-03. 0426-74-2211 Keio Line, Tama Dobutsuen. Contact: Mr.Takase (Kokusai Koryu Centre)	Private	37,795	271	Y	Y	N
DOKKYO UNIVERSITY	1-1 Gakuen-cho, Soka-shi, Saitama 340. 0489-42-1111 Ext. 2007 Tobu Isesaki Line, Matsubara Danchi. Contact: Mr. Okoshi (Kokusai Koryu)	Private	8,600	116	Y	Y	Y
HOSEI UNIVERSITY	2-17-1 Fujimi, Chiyoda-ku, Tokyo 102. 03-3264-9516 JR Sobu Line, Iidabashi. Contact: (Kokusai Koryu Centre) 03-3264-9315	Private	45,845	381	Y	Y	N
INTERNATIONAL CHRISTIAN UNIVERSITY	3-10-2 Osawa, Mitaka-shi, Tokyo 181. 0422-33-3071 JR Chuo Line, Mitaka. Contact: Mr. Yamaguchi (Gakusei-ka)	Private	2,596	200	Y	Y	N
KEIO UNIVERSITY	2-15-45 Mita, Minato-ku, Tokyo 108. 03-3453-4511 Toei Mita or Asakusa Line, Mita. Contact: Mr. Kato (Kokusai Centre)	Private	28,956	773	Y	Y	Y
KEISEN JOGAUEN COLLEGE	2-10-1 Minamino, Tama-shi, Tokyo 206. 0423-76-8215 Odakyu or Keio Line, Tama Centre. Contact: Ms. Kubota (Gakusei-ka)	Private	850	0	Y	N	Y

University	Address / Access / Contact	Telephone	Type	Students	Overseas Students	Own Scholarships	Other Scholarships	Assistance
KOGAKUIN UNIVERSITY	1-24-2 Nishi Shinjuku, Shinjuku-ku, Tokyo 163-91. JR Yamanote or Chuo Line, Shinjuku. Contact: Mr. Shimizu (Gakusei-bu)	03-3342-1211	Private	5,600	19	N	Y	N
MEIJI GAKUIN UNIVERSITY	1-2-37 Shirogane-dai, Minato-ku, Tokyo 108. JR Yamanote Line, Shinagawa. Contact: Ms. Kikuchi (Kokusai Koryu Centre)	03-3448-5111	Private	12,683	37	Y	Y	Y
MUSASHI UNIVERSITY	1-26-1 Toyotama Kami, Nerima-ku, Tokyo 181. Seibu Ikebukuro Line, Ekoda. Contact: Mr. Ogura (Gakusei-bu)	03-3991-1191	Private	3,759	6	N	N	N
NIHON UNIVERSITY	4-8-24 Kudan Minami, Chiyoda-ku, Tokyo 102. Yurakucho, Toei Shinjuku, JR Sobu Line, Ichigaya. Contact: (Kokusai-ka)	03-5275-8116	Private	68,138	969	Y	Y	N
OBIRIN UNIVERSITY	3758 Tokiwa-cho, Machida-shi, Tokyo 194-02. Odakyu Line, Machida. Contact: Mr. Haneda (Kokusai Koryu Centre)	0427-97-2661 Ext. 376	Private	4,128	50	N	Y	Y
REITAKU UNIVERSITY	2-1-1 Hikarigaoka, Kashiwa-shi, Chiba 277. JR Joban Line, Minami Kashiwa. Contact: Mr. Mizuno (Kokusai Koryu-ka)	0471-73-3691	Private	1,500	200	Y	Y	Y
RIKKYO UNIVERSITY	Nishi Ikebukuro 3-chome, Toshima-ku, Tokyo 171. JR Yamanote Line, Ikebukuro. Contact: Ms. Hirano (Kokusai Centre)	03-3985-2231	Private	12,669	150	Y	Y	Y
SOKA UNIVERSITY	1-236 Tangi-cho, Hachioji-shi, Tokyo 192. Keio or JR Chuo Line, Hachioji. Contact: Ms. Yamamori (Kokusai-ka)	0426-91-2211	Private	6,812	124	N	Y	N
SCIENCE UNIVERSITY OF TOKYO	1-3 Kagurazaka, Shinjuku-ku, Tokyo 162. Tozai, Yurakucho or JR Sobu Line, Iidabashi. Contact: Mr. Toho (Gakusei-ka)	03-3260-4271 Ext. 1642	Private	5,000	46	N	N	Y
TOKYO DENKI UNIVERSITY	2-2 Kanda Nishiki-cho, Chiyoda-ku, Tokyo 101. JR Chuo Line, Ochanomizu. Contact: Mr. Inage (Gakusei-ka)	03-5280-3466	Private	9,750	24	Y	Y	N

TOKYO KEIZAI UNIVERSITY

1-7 Minami-cho, Kokubunji-shi, Tokyo 185. 0423-21-1941
JR Chuo Line, Kokubunji. Contact: Ms. Kimura or Mr. Sasaki (Kikaku Koho-ka)

Type	Students	Overseas Students	Own Scholarships	Other Scholarships	Assistance
Private	8,018	18	Y	N	N

TSUDA COLLEGE

2-1-1 Tsuda-machi, Kodaira-shi, Tokyo 187. 0423-42-5132
Seibu Kokubunji Line, Takanodai. Contact: Ms. Yamazaki or Ms. Machida

Type	Students	Overseas Students	Own Scholarships	Other Scholarships	Assistance
Private	2,594	14	Y	Y	Y

WASEDA UNIVERSITY

1-6-1 Nishi Waseda, Shinjuku-ku, Tokyo 169-50. 03-3203-4141
Tozai Line, Waseda.Contact: Mr.Sasaki (Kokusai Koryu Centre)Ext. 2133

Type	Students	Overseas Students	Own Scholarships	Other Scholarships	Assistance
Private	59,510	1,026	Y	Y	Y

CHIBA UNIVERSITY

1-33 Yayoi-cho, Inage-ku, Chiba 263. 043-251-1111
JR Sobu Line, Nishi Chiba. Contact: (Ryugakusei-ka) Ext. 2139

Type	Students	Overseas Students	Own Scholarships	Other Scholarships	Assistance
National	13,158	495	N	N	N

TOKYO INTERNATIONAL UNIVERSITY

1-13-1 Matoba Kita, Kawagoe-shi, Saitama 350. 0492-32-1111
Tobu Tojo Line, Kasumigaseki. Contact: Ms. Inoue (Kokusai Centre) Ext. 253

Type	Students	Overseas Students	Own Scholarships	Other Scholarships	Assistance
Private	6,700	240	N	N	N

KINKI UNIVERSITY

3-4-1 Kowakae, Higashi Osaka-shi, Osaka 577. 06-721-2332 Ext. 2864
Kintetsu Osaka Line, Nagase. Contact: Mr. Watabe (Ryugaku Centre)

Type	Students	Overseas Students	Own Scholarships	Other Scholarships	Assistance
Private	29,845	352	Y	Y	Y

OSAKA UNIVERSITY OF FOREIGN STUDIES

8-1-1 Aomadani, Mino-o-shi, Osaka 562. 0727-28-4514
Hankyu Senri Line, Kita Senri. Contact: Mr. Murase (Ryugakuse-ka)

Type	Students	Overseas Students	Own Scholarships	Other Scholarships	Assistance
National	4,600	200	N	Y	Y

KANSAI GAIDAI UNIVERSITY

16-1 Kita Katahoko-cho, Hirakata-shi, Osaka 573. 0720-51-6751
Keihan Line, Hirakata-shi. Contact: Mr. Yamamoto (Kokusai Koryu-ka)

Type	Students	Overseas Students	Own Scholarships	Other Scholarships	Assistance
Private	5,196	241	Y	N	Y

KYOTO UNIVERSITY

Yoshida Hon-machi, Sakyo-ku, Kyoto 606-01. 075-753-2543
Keihan Line, Idemachi Yanagi. Contact: Ms. Otsuka (Ryugakusei-ka)

Type	Students	Overseas Students	Own Scholarships	Other Scholarships	Assistance
National	17,747	808	N	Y	N

KYOTO SEIKA UNIVERSITY

137 Iwakura Kino-machi, Sakyo-ku, Kyoto 606. 075-702-5707
Eizan Line, Kyoto Seikadai-mae. Contact: Mr. Maeda (Kokusai Koryu-ka)

Type	Students	Overseas Students	Own Scholarships	Other Scholarships	Assistance
Private	2,500	60	Y	Y	

	Type	Students	Overseas Students	Own Scholarships	Other Scholarships	Assistance

KYOTO UNIVERSITY OF FOREIGN STUDIES

6 Nishi-in Kasame-machi, Ukyo-ku, Kyoto 615. 075-322-6043
Hankyu Line, Nishiin. Contact: Mr. Tsujimoto (Kokusai Koryu-bu)

Private	3,761	54	N	N	N

RYUKOKU UNIVERSITY

67 Tsukamoto-cho, Fukakusa, Fushimi-ku, Kyoto 612. 075-642-1111
Keihan Line, Fukakusa. Contact: (Kokusai-ka) Ext. 719 or 720

Private	13,000	213	Y	Y	Y

KWANSEI GAKUIN UNIVERSITY

0798-53-6111
1-155 Ichiban-cho, Uegahara, Nishinomiya-shi, Hyogo 662.
Hankyu Imazu Line, Kotoen. Contact: (Kokusai Koryu-ka) Ext. 3183

Private	14,874	258	Y	N	Y

NANZAN UNIVERSITY

18 Yamazato-cho, Showa-ku, Nagoya 466. 052-832-3123
Tsurumai Line, Irinaka. Contact: (Kyomu-ka, Gakusei-ka or Kokusai-ka)

Private	5,500	200	Y	N	Y

AICHI UNIVERSITY

1-1 Machihata-machi, Toyohashi-shi, Aichi 441. 0532-47-4131
Atsumi Line, Daigaku-mae. Contact: Mr. Sakagami (Kokusai Koryu-ka)

Private	10,193	123	Y	Y	Y

NAGOYA GAKUIN UNIVERSITY

1350 Kami Shinano-cho, Seto-shi, Aichi 480-12. 0561-42-0737
Meitetsu Seto Line, Owari Seto. Contact: (Ryugakusei-ka)

Private	4,500	37	Y	N	Y

AICHI GAKUIN UNIVERSITY

05617-3-1111
12 Aza Araike, Oaza Iwasaki, Nishin-cho, Aichi-gun, Aichi 470-01.
Higashiyama Line, Fujigaoka. Contact: Mr. Fujimura (Shomu-ka)

Private	11,602	137	Y	Y	N

HOKKAIDO UNIVERSITY

Kita 8-jo Nishi 5-chome, Kita-ku, Sapporo 060. 011-716-2111
JR Lines, Sapporo. Contact: (Ryugakusei-ka) 011-736-1408

National	15,000	400	N	N	Y

TOHOKU UNIVERSITY

2-1-1 Katahira, Aoba-ku, Sendai-shi, Miyagi 980. 022-227-6200
JR Tohoku Line, Sendai. Contact: (Kokusai Koryu-bu)

National	16,035	624	N	N	Y

KYUSHU UNIVERSITY

6-10-1 Hakozaki, Higashi-ku, Fukuoka-shi, Fukuoka 812. 092-641-1101
Subway Line No. 2, Hakozaki Kyudai-mae. Contact: (Ryugakusei-ka)

National	14,100	570	N	Y	

NIPPON BUNRI UNIVERSITY

1727 Oaza Ichiki, Oita-shi, Oita 870-03. 0975-92-1600
JR Nippo Line, Ozai. Contact: Mr. Otsuka (Gakusei-ka) Ext. 222

Type	Students	Overseas Students	Own Scholarships	Other Scholarships	Assistance
Private	5,500	90	Y	Y	N

MUSASHINO INSTITUTE OF FOREIGN LANGUAGES

1-27-2 Naka-machi, Musashino-shi, Tokyo 180. 0422-51-7803
JR Chuo Line, Mitaka. Contact: Ms. Naganuma (Jimu-kyoku)

Type	Students	Overseas Students	Own Scholarships	Other Scholarships	Assistance
College					

TOKYO FOREIGN LANGUAGE COLLEGE

7-3-8 Nishi Shinjuku, Shinjuku-ku, Tokyo 160. 03-3367-1101
JR Yamanote Line, Shinjuku. Contact: Mr. Binder (Kyomu-bu) Ext. 110

Type	Students	Overseas Students	Own Scholarships	Other Scholarships	Assistance
College					

COLLEGE OF BUSINESS AND COMMUNICATION

22-9 Eki-mae Honcho, Kawasaki-ku, Kawasaki-shi, Kanagawa 210.
JR Keihin Tohoku Line, Kawasaki. Contact: Mr. Koshiro 044-244-1959

Type	Students	Overseas Students	Own Scholarships	Other Scholarships	Assistance
College					

ANABUKI COLLEGE

7-12 Kajiya-machi, Takamatsu-shi, Kagawa 760. 0878-23-2266
JR Yosan Line, Takamatsu. No contact

Type	Students	Overseas Students	Own Scholarships	Other Scholarships	Assistance
College					

CHAPTER 20. VISITING JAPAN

This section is designed to give some guidance to those who find a visit to Japan to be inevitable, as we hope that most of our readers will.

TRANSPORTATION

(a) From Narita Airport

For most visitors, the arrival point in Japan is Narita Airport, outside Tokyo. So the most valuable piece of information for them is how to get to the city.

Note that Narita Airport is a long way from Tokyo. The journey of some 70 kilometres takes an hour by the fastest possible routes, which are the JR 'Narita Express' and the Keisei 'Skyliner'. From the airport to the city, there are, in fact, three choices: the 'limousine bus', a Japan Railways line or the Keisei private railway line.

The 'bus is expensive and susceptible to the vagaries of traffic conditions. Most journeys go to the Tokyo City Air Terminal, which is itself not in a particularly convenient location, although it has recently been connected to the subway system (Suitengu-mae station on the Hanzomon Line), which makes it much more accessible. Certain journeys go to a selection of the most expensive hotels, which is convenient if you wish to stay in one of those. There are also occasional trips to Tokyo Station, to Yokohama and to Haneda (domestic) Airport. At present the 'bus costs approximately ¥3000.

The Japan Railways line departs from the basement of each of the two terminal buildings and has two types of train, the 'Narita Express' and a *kaisoku* (rapid) train. Departures for the express are every half-hour during the early morning, afternoon and early evening and every hour in the middle of the day and during the late evening. Departures are at 13 and 43 minutes past the hour. The *kaisoku* train runs every hour on the hour. There is a very great difference in price between the two, with the express costing more than twice as much as the *kaisoku* train. However, if your budget is not limited, the express is quick and comfortable and you have a reserved seat. If you want to economize, however, the *kaisoku* train is not so slow, taking about 90 minutes to Tokyo, and it will not be crowded on leaving Narita Airport, although it may become so later in the journey at some times of the day. The express runs to Tokyo station, where most trains are divided, one half of the train continuing to Yokohama, with occasional journeys extended to Ofuna, and the other half going round Tokyo's Yamanote loop line to the major centre of Shinjuku. A few runs continue on to Ikebukuro, further round the Yamanote Line. The *kaisoku* train follows the same route, but with stops on the way, to Tokyo. Then most journeys go on also to Yokohama, Ofuna, Kamakura and beyond. At the time of writing, the 'Narita Express' costs ¥2,890 to Tokyo and the *kaisoku* train costs ¥1,260.

The Keisei Line is cheapest of all. It also departs from the basements of the terminal buildings, sharing the stations there with the Japan Railways line. The Keisei Line also offers an express, named the 'Skyliner'. It runs every forty minutes until 10.00p.m. It is not as expensive as the JR train. The supplementary charge amounts to about 85% of the basic fare, which is itself about a quarter cheaper than the JR fare. Overall the Keisei 'Skyliner' is about a third cheaper than the JR Narita Express. Keisei offers a selection of trains in addition to the 'Skyliner'. There are *tsukin tokkyu* (commuter express), *tokkyu* (limited express), *kyuko* (express) and *futsu* (ordinary) trains. There are no supplementary charges for any of these four types and the *tokkyu*, which runs with approximately the same frequency as the 'Skyliner', is almost as quick as it, although less comfortable. The Keisei Line runs to Ueno, another main station on the Yamanote loop line. However, the station is separate from the JR station, so, if you wish to change to the JR system, it is preferable to do so at Nippori, reached three minutes before Ueno and a station at which all trains, including the 'Skyliner', stop. At present, the 'Skyliner' costs ¥1,740 and other trains cost ¥940.

The Keisei Line is also connected to the subway system. From Aoto, a branch line runs to Oshiage, from where the Toei Asakusa Line commences. Some Keisei trains from Narita Airport run right through onto the Toei Asakusa Line, without any change of train. These trains will be marked Nishi Magome on the destination board, that being the final station on the Toei Asakusa Line. If you wish to get onto the subway, but no Nishi Magome train is available, take any train except the 'Skyliner' (which does not stop) to Aoto, about an hour's journey from Narita Airport, and change to any train leaving from platform 1.

(b) Tokyo

Japan is a country where one rarely considers any mode of transport other than railway, except for very short journeys. Tokyo is no exception. It is a maze of railway lines. Let us start by distinguishing the various rail systems.

First of all, there are the lines operated by Japan Railways (JR). There is the circular Yamanote Line (green striped trains) running round Tokyo and passing through many of the main centres. This is bisected by another line which carries both Chuo Line (orange) trains and Sobu Line (yellow) trains. Paralleling the Yamanote Line for about half of its route is the Keihin Tohoku Line (blue trains). This is the central area. The Chuo, Sobu and Keihin Tohoku Lines all extend further, while from the main centres of Shinjuku, Tokyo and Ueno various other suburban and long-distance trains start. *Shinkansen* (bullet train) services start from Tokyo station and run west (blue trains) to Nagoya, Kyoto, Osaka, Kobe, Hiroshima and Hakata (Fukuoka). They run north (green trains) to Niigata, Fukushima, Yamagata, Sendai and Morioka.

Next there is the subway system. Now the subway is operated not by a single company, as one might expect, but by two separate companies, known as Toei and Eidan. Toei, the municipal authority, also operates 'buses in the central area of Tokyo and the single remaining tram route. The names of its subway lines are usually prefixed by the word 'Toei'. There are four such lines. Eidan operates eight subway lines. There is no free interchange between Toei and Eidan lines. However, if one buys a ticket for a journey which involves the use of both systems, a discount of ¥40 is given on the addition of the two fares. One must, however, purchase the correct type of ticket for this journey. The Eidan lines are generally a little cheaper than the Toei lines, if one has a choice.

Then there is the private railway network. There are several private companies operating in the Tokyo area. Many of the lines start at stations on the Yamanote loop line and run to destinations not served by JR, although some of them run in direct competition with JR. We have already met the Keisei Line from Narita Airport and there are, for example, two companies running to Yokohama in competition with the JR service. In general, the private railways are cheaper than JR.

With one of the railway systems, one can reach almost anywhere in the Tokyo area. Consult the subway map which we have provided and decide which route to follow, remembering that it will usually be more simple and cheaper to keep to one system as far as possible.

'Buses are generally used in Tokyo only to supplement the rail system, that is to say to get from the nearest station to one's precise destination. Because of the clogged condition of Tokyo's roads, they are generally too slow for anything else. Considering the short distances for which most people use 'buses, they are surprisingly expensive, most now having a flat fare of ¥200 within the city area. There is no transfer system.

Taxis are also expensive. At the time of writing, they start at ¥600, including the first two kilometres or waiting time in lieu thereof. Even though they are so costly, they are well patronized and, indeed, if there are four or five people, it may be cheaper to take a taxi than a 'bus, as well as being more convenient. Tipping is not expected.

For the rail system, tickets are nearly always purchased from machines. These machines are very clever. They can give change and issue quite a variety of different tickets. Many of them will accept ¥1,000 notes as well as coins. Just put your money in and press the appropriate button for the value of ticket which you require. Out will come your ticket and your change. Somewhere around most subway stations, there is usually a notice in English showing fares, but if you cannot find it do not worry. Just buy a minimum price ticket and pay the difference at the other end. It is always acceptable to do this. If a conductor happens to come through your train, you can pay him instead. If you should be unlucky enough to have a problem with a ticket machine, you will find two buttons, usually at the top left. Press the bottom one to have your money refunded. Press the top one to report some malfunction. Many stations now have automatic gates into which you insert your ticket to enter and exit. If you do not have the correct ticket for exiting, you should put it into the excess fare machine which will then tell you how much more you have to pay. Put in the extra money and you will be issued with a new ticket which will open the automatic gates for you to leave the station. At stations where there are no automatic gates, present your ticket at the window by the exit to be told how much excess fare is owing.

For 'buses, there are two different fare systems. If you enter at the front of the 'bus, as in central Tokyo, you pay the fare to the driver as you go in. There is a plastic box into which you drop the correct money and a notice below the box telling you how much to pay. If you do not have the correct money, there is a machine which will change coins or ¥1,000 notes. Put your coin or note into the slot and the change will come out below. In central Tokyo, you put in enough money for the full fare and the change is returned. However, where the flat fare system is not in operation, the machine will just give you small change for the coin or note which you inserted and you then have to put the fare into the fare box. If you entered at the front of the 'bus, you exit towards the rear. However, if you enter towards the rear of the 'bus, as in Tokyo suburbs or more rural locations, you will find a different system in operation. From a machine by the door you accept the proffered slip of paper. On the slip is a number. Keep this piece of paper carefully. On a display at the front of the 'bus a series of fares is shown. Your fare is the one under the number on your slip of paper. You can watch it increase frighteningly minute by minute! When you get off, drop into the box the appropriate fare and your numbered ticket. If you get on at the start of the route, sometimes the machine does not offer you a ticket. In that case your fare will be displayed beneath the number 0. If you lose your ticket, you are supposed to pay the highest fare on the board, so try not to!

How about saving money? Yes, there are ways — legal ways, that is. First of all, if you are going to be travelling the same route regularly you can buy a season ticket. These are available for one, three or six months and can be purchased for any rail or 'bus journey. They are sold at most railway stations and at 'bus company offices. For Toei 'buses in central Tokyo, the season ticket does not specify a route, but permits free travel on any Toei 'bus within the period of validity. If a month is too long, there are other possibilities. You can buy a strip of eleven tickets for the price of ten for any rail journey involving only a single company. These tickets are valid for two months, or three months in the case of JR. Slightly different rules apply depending on the company. Usually, you must present what remains of the whole strip when entering, after which you tear off the end ticket and surrender it when you exit at your destination. You cannot present a single torn-off ticket when entering, because the expiry date is marked only on the last ticket. JR, however, marks the expiry date on all tickets and allows their use individually. With all systems, it is permitted for two or more people to use tickets on the same strip, including when travelling together. Tickets are valid for travel in either direction between the two points marked on them, including intermediate stops, but one cannot break one's journey. The ticket must be surrendered when one leaves the

MAP OF TOKYO SUBWAY SYSTEM

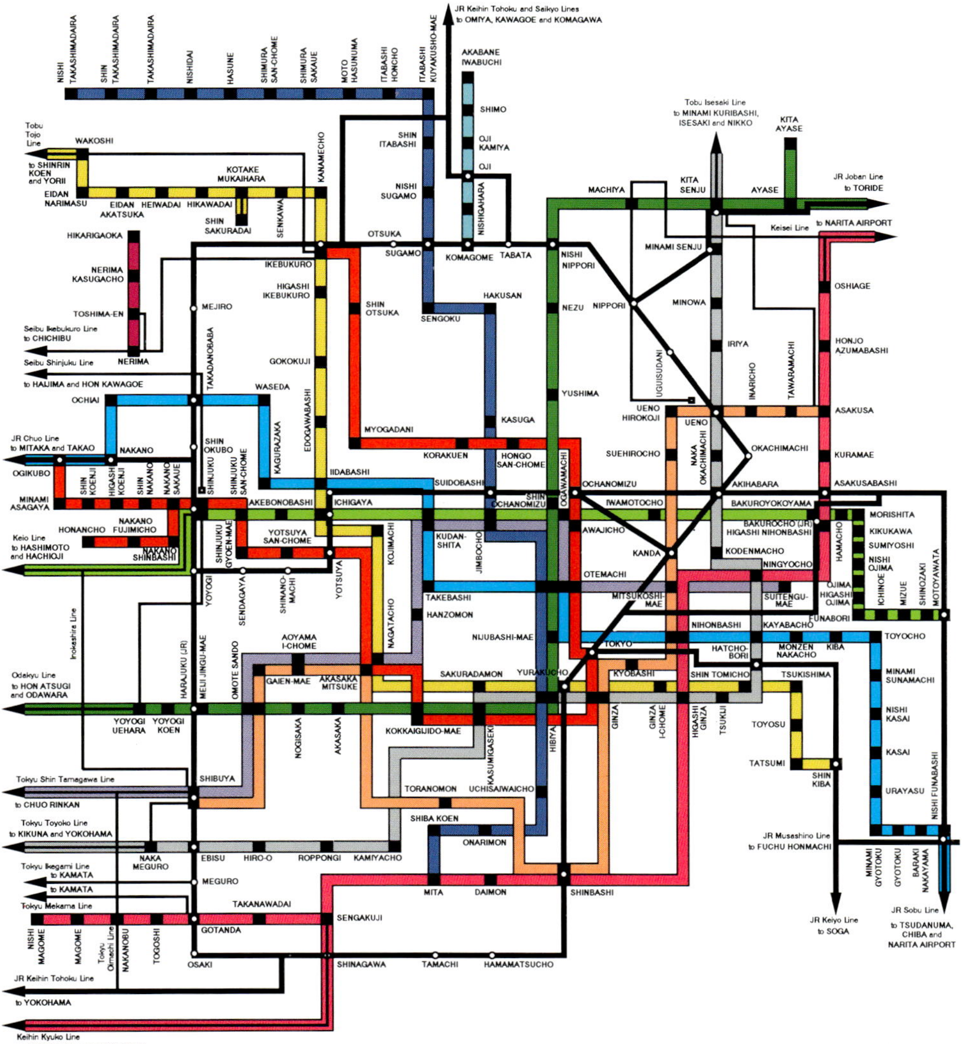

KEY:

	MARUNOUCHI LINE		HANZOMON LINE		JR LINES
	GINZA LINE		NANBOKU LINE		PRIVATE LINES
	HIBIYA LINE		TOEI ASAKUSA LINE		SUBWAY STATIONS (stations which touch, even diagonally, are connected)
	TOZAI LINE		TOEI MITA LINE		JR STATIONS (outside Yamanote Line shown only when offering interchange with subway)
	CHIYODA LINE		TOEI SHINJUKU LINE		
	YURAKUCHO LINE		TOEI LINE NO. 12		SOME SUBWAY TRAINS CONTINUE onto JR or private lines

MAP OF OSAKA SUBWAY SYSTEM

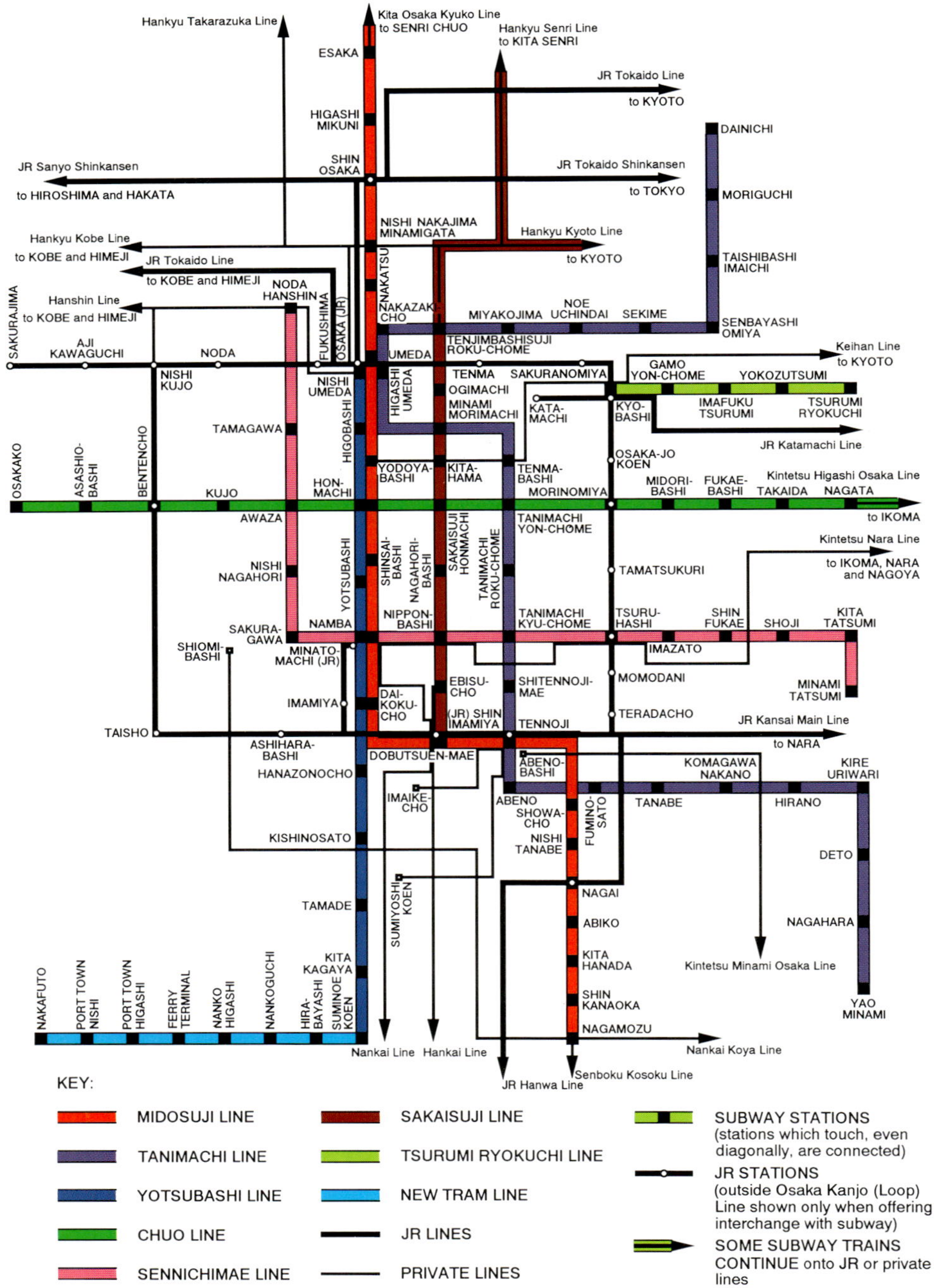

station. It should also be noted carefully that one cannot use such tickets for a longer journey than the one specified by paying the difference in fares. If one goes beyond the station marked on the ticket, one must pay the *full* fare for the additional journey (with the exception of the subway system — see after). These tickets are called *kai-su-ken* and they are usually bought from the ticket window, although some major stations now have machines which can issue them.

There are two special types of *kai-su-ken* offered by JR. One is called *Yamanote kai-su-ken*. These tickets allow one to enter and exit at any JR station on or within the Tokyo Yamanote line. At the time of writing they cost ¥1,600 for eleven tickets, making them economical for any but the shortest journeys. They are also convenient, of course, since one does not have to queue for a ticket every time one travels. The other type is called *Tokyo-to ku-nai kai-su-ken*. These tickets are valid for any JR journey within Greater Tokyo, that is within the 23 wards (*ku*) of Tokyo. The exact area is marked on the tickets. They currently cost ¥2,900 for eleven tickets.

The subway *kai-su-ken* system is a little different. One purchases eleven tickets at a certain value for the price of ten. Then, as one enters the station, a machine or automatic gate marks on the ticket your starting point. If you go beyond the limits of the area for which your ticket is valid, in this case, unlike with other railway systems, you can just pay the excess. So these tickets are particularly useful, since, if you purchase minimum price tickets, they can be used for any subway journey, as long as you pay any excess charge on leaving the station at your destination. Toei and Eidan both have this system, although, of course, you cannot use Toei tickets on Eidan lines or *vice versa*. For subways, *kai-su-ken* can be purchased from a machine at most stations.

There are *kai-su-ken* for 'buses too. In this case they consist of books or strips of tickets marked with certain values. They can be used on any 'bus services operated by the issuing company. In central Tokyo, there are books of tickets currently priced at ¥1,000 and ¥3,000 which can be used on the services of any of the variety of companies which operate in the area. Most of the tickets are priced at the current 'bus fare. Alternatively, one can buy books of tickets, currently priced at ¥1,000 and ¥4,000, for a particular company. In general, the higher the cost of the book of tickets, the greater the discount, but the least that you can expect is eleven tickets for the price of ten. As one moves from central

Tokyo into the suburbs, where there is no flat fare, one finds that the various companies have different types of *kai-su-ken*, but usually they offer a book of mixed tickets or a strip of eleven tickets at a particular value for the price of ten, or both. 'Bus *kai-su-ken* do not have a time limit and they can be used in combination with coins or other *kai-su-ken.* They can be bought from the offices of the 'bus company, and usually from 'bus drivers also, although the choice carried by drivers is necessarily limited.

There are also four types of one-day ticket available in central Tokyo. The one which is likely to be most useful to readers is that sold by the Eidan company. It permits use of all that company's eight subway lines for the price of ¥650, at the time of writing. Since the minimum fare at present is ¥140, one has only to make five journeys in a day to benefit from this ticket. Called an *ichi-nichi jo-sha-ken* (one day ticket), it can be purchased from a machine at many stations now, for use on the same day. Otherwise, it can be bought at one of the company's offices. Tickets sold at the office do not have to be used on the date of sale. If there is no suitable machine at your station and no office, you are entitled to purchase a ticket to the nearest station with an office, getting your ticket stamped with a special rubber stamp as you enter the station, then retain the ticket on exiting at the other end and get a refund when you purchase your one-day ticket. The same rule applies to season tickets and *kai-su-ken* if they cannot be issued at your station, and in these cases you can also ask for a ticket home if necessary.

The Toei company also has an *ichi-nichi jo-sha-ken* (one-day ticket). For the same price of ¥650, this permits use of the four Toei subway lines, as well as the Toei 'buses (green and cream) which run in the central area and the single tram route, known as the Arakawa Line, which runs between Waseda and Minowa. It can be purchased from machines and at Toei offices.

JR also offers a one-day ticket for use on its services within the area of Greater Tokyo, the 23 wards (*ku*) mentioned previously. This ticket is called a *to-ku-nai free kippu* and it costs ¥720 and is available at any station within the area.

The last ticket offers a combination of all the above three tickets. It is called a *Tokyo free kippu*. Although this sounds appealing, the ticket costs ¥1,480 for a day and the fact is that you can reach most places with just one of the tickets. However, if this ticket is your choice, it is available from any JR station in the area and from subway offices.

One more way of saving money and time is to purchase a pre-paid card to use instead of cash for the purchase of tickets. Such cards are offered by JR, the Eidan subway company and some of the private railway companies. The JR card is called an 'Orange Card' (this is the name in Japanese, not a translation) and it is available in denominations of ¥1,000, ¥5,000 and ¥10,000. Perhaps you will not be surprised to hear that it is not usually orange! The ¥1,000 card offers no discount, but with the ¥5,000 card you can purchase tickets to the value of ¥5,300 and with the ¥10,000 card, you get ¥10,700 of purchasing power. It used to be the case that only one machine at a station would accept cards — and in front of that machine there always seemed to be a little old lady searching her handbag for the last ¥10 necessary to make up her fare. Now, however, more machines have been installed which accept cards, including some which accept only cards. Since relatively few people use the card system, one can usually purchase one's ticket rapidly, in addition to having the opportunity to save a little money. Where there are excess fare machines near the exits to stations, you can also use your card to pay any excess owing.

The Eidan subway company offers cards called 'Metrocards' in denominations of ¥1,000, ¥2,000 and ¥3,000. There is, however, no discount, only convenience. The private railways vary, but a typical offering is ¥1,000, ¥3,000 and ¥5,000 cards, with the last providing ¥5,300 of tickets. The pre-paid cards offered by the various companies are usually quite colourful and there are now collectors of such cards. If one goes somewhere in Japan, an Orange Card showing local scenery makes a good souvenir for Japanese friends. It can be used anywhere on the JR system.

(c) Other Cities

If one reckons that Yokohama is part of the Tokyo complex — and, in practice, one will not notice when one passes from Tokyo to Kawasaki to Yokohama — then Japan's second city complex is Osaka-Kobe-Kyoto. These cities have more distinct boundaries, but are within commuting distance of each other. Osaka is the business city, Kobe the port and Kyoto the historical city. Osaka also has a subway system, although it is smaller than Tokyo's and, fortunately, operated by a single company. Kyoto can boast a single line, running north and south under one of the main thoroughfares. There is also a spaghetti of private railways in the area. Osaka and Kyoto, for instance, are connected by a JR line, by two private companies offering fast, frequent and comfortable services at half of the price charged by JR and by a third private company offering a less direct service. Where the trains do not run, there are 'bus services. In Kyoto, since it is a tourist city, many of the 'buses even have their destinations marked in Roman script.

Rules for trains and 'buses are similar to those in Tokyo, as indeed, they are throughout Japan. A one-day ticket is available in Kyoto for the subway and city 'buses. At ¥1,050, however, it is not cheap, being designed mainly for single-day tourists. As everywhere, season tickets and *kai-su-ken* can be purchased. Kyoto also offers a 'bus plus subway ticket, for those who need to change from one to the other. It gives a discount on the combination of the two fares. At subway stations, it can be purchased from a machine (but remember to take the ticket from the automatic gate when you leave the station). On the 'bus, it can be purchased by telling the driver what you want (*bus plus chika-tetsu kippu*), although, of course, you can buy such a ticket only when getting off at a subway station. You will be given a voucher which you then insert into the ticket machine in the subway station. The voucher is for the minimum subway fare, so, if you want to go further, you add coins for the extra amount. Then press the appropriate fare button and out pops your ticket. There is a similar system in some parts of Osaka. Osaka also has a one-day subway ticket available for ¥810.

Other cities in Japan with subway systems are Yokohama (one line), Nagoya, Sapporo, Sendai (one line) and Fukuoka. Cities with tram systems are Sapporo (one line), Hakodate, Tokyo (one line), Toyama (one line), Hiroshima, Matsuyama, Kochi, Nagasaki, Kumamoto and Kagoshima. There are also several places where small private railways operate vehicles which do not seem to be quite sure whether they are trains or trams.

Cities offering one-day tickets for public transport include Sapporo (subway or subway, 'buses and trams), Hakodate ('buses and trams, one or two days), Hiroshima (trams or trams plus ferry to Miyajima), Matsuyama ('buses or trams), Kochi (trams within city limits), Nagasaki (trams) and Kagoshima (trams).

(d) Long-Distance Travel

It will be no surprise to discover that trains are also the best choice for long-distance travel. Despite recent pruning, the JR network covers the whole of Japan. It offers a fast and highly efficient service. Moreover, although it is not exactly cheap, there is not really anything cheaper. In fact, JR is not a single company, but a group of regional companies made from the old Japan National Railways (JNR). However, since the regional companies co-operate closely with each other, it is hardly apparent that JR is not a single organization. The JR service is supplemented by private lines, in the countryside as well as in the cities, so that if a place does not have a railway station, it must be very small indeed. Let us first, though, look at the other possibilities, which do exist.

Japan's roads are frequently congested, the 'expressways', for which huge tolls are exacted, as well as the ordinary highways, so driving is not only expensive but also not much fun. However, if that is what you decide to do, cars are available for hire at moderate rates. Since charges vary considerably, however, you should shop around before making a decision.

Long-distance 'buses have started operations in the last few years on a limited number of routes. Many of these run only at night. Prices are similar to, or just a little lower than, those for express trains. However, if you travel by night, you will save the cost of accommodation. The most popular route is between Tokyo and Kyoto or Osaka. In the daytime, you must change 'buses at Nagoya, but services are frequent. JR operates the 'buses between Tokyo and Nagoya, in competition with its own trains! Between Nagoya and Kyoto, again JR runs 'buses, but there are other operators too, while between Nagoya and Osaka there is a slightly less frequent service, again shared by JR and other operators. At night JR runs 'buses right through between Tokyo and Kyoto and between Tokyo and Osaka. On these night services, however, there is a seat reservation charge of ¥1,500 and you cannot travel without a reservation.

The air service offered is comprehensive and efficient. There are three major domestic airlines: Japan Air Lines (JAL), All Nippon Airways (ANA) and Japan Air System (JAS). Some smaller airlines offer supplementary services in more remote areas and to places which can accommodate only small aircraft. Note that in Tokyo nearly all domestic services use Haneda Airport, not Narita International Airport. Haneda is much more conveniently located, within the Tokyo city limits, and is reached by a monorail from Hamamatsucho on the

Yamanote Line or by a branch line of the Keihin Kyuko private railway which is joined to the Toei Asakusa subway line. The monorail is more convenient. Air travel is, of course, comparatively expensive. The airlines do not generally offer cheap tickets, but there are agents, usually operating from miniscule shops, or even, occasionally, just on the street, who will sell tickets at discount prices. These agents, it should be said, are more reliable than they appear!

For those who are really short of money (not, we hope, our businessmen readers), hitch-hiking is very easy and pleasurable in Japan. That is because Japanese never do it. If you should try this method of transportation, you are likely to experience the overwhelming hospitality of the Japanese at its very best.

Then there are ferries. Perhaps surprisingly, Japan retains an extensive ferry service, not merely for short crossings between islands, but for long-distance travel too, in competition with land transport. The problem with ferries is that they are slow. However, prices compare favourably with land transportation in many cases and, of course, accommodation, albeit of a rather basic kind, on carpeted or *tatami*-mat floors in the lowest classes, is included. Since seas are rarely rough in Japan, it is a pleasant way to travel if you have enough time and if there is a service going to your destination. There are also regular international ferry services to Korea (from Fukuoka, Shimonoseki, Kobe and Osaka), to Taiwan (from Naha in Okinawa) and to China (from Yokohama, Osaka and Kobe) as well as an occasional service from Yokohama to Russia.

Which brings us back to trains. To plan your journey, the best thing to do is to purchase a railway timetable. Various versions are published in Japanese and JR gives away a rudimentary timetable in English. This version lists only express trains in most cases and only for main or tourist-oriented services. Also, it is sometimes out of date. If you need to go only to main centres and only by express trains, it will prove helpful, but often those who have this timetable do not appreciate that there are cheaper alternative services available. If you buy the Japanese version, you may not be able to read the names of the stations, but, by looking at the maps at the start of the book and comparing with a map in Japanese and Roman script, you will easily find your destination. The number of the page which you should consult is written on the railway line. Turn to that page and you will find all the trains available. The timetable is published by two different companies (JR and the Japan Travel Bureau — JTB) in three different sizes. The larger versions are easier to read. The timetable lists every rail service in Japan, all major long-distance and local 'bus routes, ferries, pleasure-boat trips, air services including international flights, funicular railways, monorails, ropeways and just about any other form of public transport you could imagine, except taxis. And it is very rare indeed to find a mistake in the thousand or so pages which make up this monthly publication. It is a remarkable book.

If all of this seems too complicated, in Tokyo JR operates an information service by telephone in English. The telephone number is 03-3423-0111 and the service is available from 10.00 until 6.00 on Monday to Friday. This is very convenient, of course, but you should not forget that, by using such a service, you get somebody else's opinion of what you should do, rather than what you yourself might have chosen had you known all the facts and possibilities. For the businessman, this service may well be perfect. If your finances are limited, however, it might be better to investigate the choices by yourself — or read on in this book! If you prefer to consult personally with somebody in English, you will find an English-speaker (usually overworked) in a marked section of the main booking office ('Travel Service Centre') on the Yaesu side of Tokyo station.

The system with JR trains is that first you buy a basic fare ticket to wherever you want to go. That ticket is enough to get you there, but if you want to use any express trains, you will need a supplementary ticket, of course at supplementary charge. If you want a reserved seat, there will be an additional charge for that. If you want to travel in the 'green car' (first class — 'green car' are the actual words used in Japanese; they are not a translation), that will cost still more. Most people buy their supplementary tickets before they start their journeys, but it is usually possible to get on the train and then pay the conductor.

Let us now look at the various trains available and the costs which will be involved in taking them. First, as a rough guide, you can reckon that travel in Japan using an ordinary ticket will cost about ¥15 per kilometre. It does not get appreciably cheaper with distance. The train which everybody associates with Japan, of course, is the *shinkansen* (bullet train). These magnificent monsters whizz along at up to 270 kilometres per hour and, in the nearly thirty years for which they have been operating, there has never been a fatal accident involving a passenger on a train (over 200 suicides in front of trains, though, and a fair sprinkling of inattentive railway workers dispatched). They operate on a totally separate system from the rest of the trains, and there is a good reason for that, for they use a standard 4 feet 8½ inches track, while all the other JR services use a 3 feet 6 inches gauge. Even the west Japan (blue) trains and the north Japan (green) trains cannot use the same tracks, because the frequency of the electric current is different. This separation extends to there being barriers within the stations to prevent passengers without *shinkansen* tickets from entering the *shinkansen* section (although you can get in with just a platform ticket). If you want to travel by *shinkansen,* you will have to pay a very sizeable surcharge. As a rough guide, reckon that the supplement will add about two-thirds of the basic fare. The train is divided into reserved and unreserved sections, with the reserved section being the larger. If you want a reserved seat, it will add another ¥300, ¥500 or ¥700, depending on the season. On the platform the places to queue for unreserved seats will be marked.

The next fastest type of train is known as a *tokkyu* (limited express). It can usually be recognized by its high-level driver's cab. In general, *tokkyu* trains do not run where there are *shinkansen* routes. This type of train too attracts a sizeable surcharge, which may add something like 50% to the basic fare. However, if you change from the *shinkansen* to a *tokkyu* or *vice versa* on the same day, the lower supplement, usually the *tokkyu* charge, will be reduced by half. There are also night *tokkyu* trains which offer sleeping accommodation for another extra charge of ¥5,150 for the lowest class of accommodation, a class which is not necessarily available on all trains. These trains are quite comfortable and they travel at speeds of up to 130 kilometres per hour.

Next is the *kyuko* (express). These are fairly ordinary types of trains which stop at only a limited number of stations and usually offer some reserved seating. The number of such trains has been reduced considerably in recent years, so that they now run mainly on lines where conditions do not permit the operation of trains fast enough to be deemed *tokkyu*. There are supplements for travelling on *kyuko* trains too. As a general guide, add a third to the basic fare for using a *kyuko*.

Next down the list are *kaisoku* (rapid) trains. These are trains which simply skip some stations and may or may not be a little more comfortable than ordinary trains. There is no supplement for using a *kaisoku*.

And, finally, there are *futsu* (ordinary) trains which stop at every station and for which there are, of course, no supplements.

It should be noted that the above categories apply to JR, not necessarily to private railways, which may use some different terms for their trains, commonly, for example, inserting a *jun-kyu* (semi-express) below the *kyuko*. Also, the express categories of private railways do not necessarily require supplementary charges. Usually, if a private railway train requires a supplement, it looks as though it does — and, indeed, this is generally true with JR too.

Well, now, how do we save money on long-distance trains? There is one way which is well known to almost every person who comes to Japan, and that is the 'Japan Rail Pass'. This pass offers unlimited rail travel on JR for a period of one, two or three weeks. It must be purchased abroad and is not available in Japan. Ordinary and 'Green' (first class) passes are available. The price is quoted in yen and then converted to the local currency, usually at a rate slightly favourable for the sales agent. The one week ordinary pass, for example, currently costs ¥27,800, and the three weeks ordinary pass ¥56,600. Since the cost of a one week pass is only a little more than the return fare from Tokyo to Osaka by *shinkansen*, the pass is really rather good value, expensive though it may seem when prices are converted into your local currency. Although it is designed for the tourist, of course, especially the one with only a limited time to spend in Japan, it could also prove a very useful bargain for the businessman who has to do some travelling around. It is important to note, though, in relation to this pass, that it can be used only by those with entry permits as temporary visitors. It cannot be used, for instance, by those with working visas. When you purchase the pass overseas, you will be issued with a voucher which is exchangeable at certain JR offices for the pass itself. The offices most commonly used for this purpose are at Tokyo station (Yaesu side) and at Narita Airport. There your passport will be checked to ensure that you are a temporary visitor. If you use one of the other JR offices which are authorized to make the exchange you *might* not get checked as strictly, but, there again, you might. Once you have exchanged your voucher for the actual pass, you can change your reservations as many times as you wish, but you cannot change the dates of validity on the pass, even, it seems, if you have not started using it.

The Japan Rail Pass includes all express supplements and reservation charges. What it does not include is sleeping accommodation. Note carefully, then, that if you want to use a sleeper you must pay not only the sleeper charge, but also the express charge, which makes it very expensive — usually around

¥10,000. The pass itself is sufficient authority to travel. You can just go into any station, get onto any train and travel in unreserved accommodation. However, if you reserve, which costs nothing, you will be spared the necessity of being on the platform early enough to ensure a good seat. You will be issued with a ticket allocating you a specific seat. A and D seats are window seats or, in the *shinkansen*, A and E in most ordinary carriages. If you want to travel in non-smoking accommodation, you should say so. The booking office clerk will probably understand the words 'no smoking', but, in case not, the Japanese is *kin-en*. The Japanese for 'smoking' is *kitsu-en.* If you choose a 'Green' pass, it is worth noting that on some trains there is no non-smoking green car accommodation available.

But, of course, the Japan Rail Pass does not suit everybody and there are other bargains, available to Japanese as well, which might prove better value. One of these is what might reasonably be translated as an excursion ticket. Suppose that you arrive in Tokyo and want to go to the Osaka area to investigate several business opportunities. You can buy a ticket, for about the same price as the ordinary return fare, which will permit you to go to Osaka and come back and also travel freely within a fixed area for a certain period of time. In this particular case, the free area would include all JR lines in and around Osaka, Kyoto and Kobe. The time allowed depends on the distance from the point of origin. In this case, it would be a week. Travel to and from the area is by ordinary train, or by *kyuko*, but if you want to take a faster train, you may do so by paying just the supplement. If the free area chosen is a large one, such as Hokkaido or Kyushu, then travel within the area by *tokkyu* is permitted, as long as unreserved accommodation is used. If it is a smaller area, only ordinary trains are allowed, unless appropriate supplements are paid. JR 'buses within the area can also be used. These tickets are called *shu-yu-ken* and are available for almost any area of Japan from any major starting point, as long as it is far enough away from your destination for the journey to be considered an excursion. It is permissible to stop off on the way there or back or both, as long as you stay within the validity of the ticket. It is also permissible to start back at the very end of the period of validity and to arrive on the next day, as long as you do not take any stops.

If you just want to go somewhere and come back, you will get a 10% reduction by buying a return ticket if the single journey is over 600 kilometres.

The validity of the ticket will depend on the length of the journey. You get two days for the first 200 kilometres and one day for each 200 kilometres or part thereof after that. This applies to single tickets as well as to returns. Stopovers are permitted, except within the actual cities of departure and destination.

If you want to take the *shinkansen* on a popular route, such as Tokyo to Osaka, you can go to one of those miniscule travel agents mentioned in connexion with cheap air tickets. They have cheap rail tickets too. If one buys tickets in bulk, one can get a discount, so these agents purchase fifty and retail them cheaply, sharing the savings with their customers. You can usually obtain a reserved *shinkansen* ticket rather more cheaply than you would be able to buy an unreserved one from the station. You then have to take the ticket to the booking office to make the reservation (no charge), otherwise you would still have to travel in the unreserved accommodation. All this is quite legal, in case you worry. You have until the date marked on the ticket to use it, usually quite a generous allowance, although the exact time will depend on when the agent bought his tickets. It should be noted that these bulk tickets cannot be used for about ten days in each of the three peak travelling seasons, that is at New Year, in 'Golden Week' (at the end of April and beginning of May) and at *o-bon*, in the middle of August. If you want to find an agent selling such tickets, go to the Yaesu side of Tokyo station and ask to be directed to Maruzen book store. On the way, along the small street which you will follow, you will find two or three such tiny agencies. There are plenty of others in different parts of Tokyo, of course, and no doubt in other big cities too, but, with such minute premises, they are sometimes difficult to locate.

For those who really want to economize, there is a JR ticket called the *sei-shun ju-hachi kippu*. This writer refers to it as the Blue Spring ticket, because *sei-shun* literally translated means just that. In fact, though, the real meaning is 'youth' and *ju-hachi* means eighteen. (*Kippu* means ticket.) However, there is no age limit for this ticket; it is just a name. For ¥11,300, Blue Spring gives you five one-day tickets. You can go wherever you like in Japan from midnight until midnight. This is really excellent value for ¥2,260 per day. The catch is that you can use only ordinary and *kaisoku* trains. If you want to take any sort of express, you must pay the full fare, including the supplement, for that journey (not just the supplement). However, unlike with the Japan Rail Pass, time is not ticking away on your ticket while you are stationary. You do not have to use your five tickets on consecutive days, nor do they all have to be used by the same person. They can be used by anybody at any time within the period of validity. Blue Spring tickets are available only around school holiday times, however, and can be used during the periods 20th February until 10th April, 20th July until 10th September and 10th December until 20th January. Sales of the tickets cease ten days before the end of each period and tickets cannot be carried over into the next Blue Spring season.

This is not an exhaustive list of cheap rail tickets available, but it covers most types likely to be of interest to our readers. If none of them suits your own requirements, try telephoning the JR information service, but the chances are that there is nothing quite designed for you. For most people, the most useful tickets are the Japan Rail Pass and the *shu-yu-ken.*

ACCOMMODATION

Accommodation is likely to be a problem for all types of visitor to Japan. Land prices are so high, particularly within the city areas, that hotel rates are also exorbitant. If you want a first-class hotel, at a first-class price, you will have no problems at all, but if you want to limit your expenditure, you will need a little assistance.

Two lists follow. The first is a list of medium-priced hotels, suitable for the businessman. These are hotels where somebody should speak some English and which have indicated a willingness to cater for guests from overseas. The second is a list of low-priced accommodation, usually of the hostel type, suitable for the job-hunter who is still hunting and who must manage on a very limited budget in the meantime.

For the businessman first. These are moderate hotels where a reasonable standard of accommodation and service can be expected. Note that in Japan there are two types of hotel, western and Japanese-style. The western hotels are like hotels anywhere else, although usually with rather small rooms, but the Japanese-style hotels (often known as *ryokan*) have their own conventions, about which just a few words. First of all, do not forget to take off your shoes at the entrance and to put on the slippers which will be waiting. Your room will usually be a *tatami* mat room, with little furnishing. You should take off your slippers before stepping onto the *tatami* mats. (Remember to wear socks without holes!) You will sleep on the floor on top of mattresses (*futon*) which will be laid out at night and folded away in a cupboard during the day. If you take dinner in the hotel, it will often be served in your room, but breakfast is more likely to be in a dining room. You will find a *yukata* (robe) provided, for use within the hotel and nearby in the evenings. Probably there will be only communal baths, usually one for males and one for females, although sometimes the same bath is used by both sexes at different times.

The procedure for the bath is this. Go into the outer room and take off everything. (It is a good idea to leave valuables at the front desk or locked in your room, if it has a lock.) Put your clothes into one of the baskets provided. Now, taking only essentials, such as soap, shampoo and a flannel, proceed to the main bathroom. Take one of the plastic stools and a plastic bowl and go to one of the pairs of taps sticking out of the wall. Often there are showers too for washing hair whilst seated. Have at least a perfunctory wash, ensuring that all soap is completely rinsed from your body. At this stage you may enter the bath. Be careful! If there are two baths, one will be extremely hot and the other unbearable. If there is only one, it may just be extremely hot. You may soak in the bath for as long as you can bear it. Then you can get out and have a more thorough wash or wash your hair or shave or any other business before having another dip — or, indeed, as many dips as you can stand. It is also quite permissible to sit around chatting if you wish. When you are thoroughly boiled or steamed, retreat to the ante-room and dry yourself on the towel which you should have remembered to take with you and leave there. Then return to your room. Remember never to allow any soap to get into the bath! Some Japanese-style hotels also have western rooms, but the bathing facilities may still be communal. Also, they will usually be available only in the evening. Most businessmen will probably feel more comfortable in a western-style hotel, but why not try a Japanese-style one at least once? This is Japan, after all, and you may well find that you like it.

In the following list, 'W' indicates a western-style hotel, 'J' a Japanese-style one, 'J/W' a Japanese-style hotel with some western rooms available and 'W/J' a western-style hotel with some Japanese rooms. Meals are usually available in the hotel, but prices quoted do not include such meals. In addition to prices quoted, almost all establishments will add a government tax of 3% and the higher class hotels are likely to add a service charge of 10% as well. More serious yet, prices keep going up in this area, so those listed below are likely to be out of date even before you get them. Therefore, regarding 1992 as a base, you would be wise to add 5% per year to the rates which we give.

Prices mentioned below are for the cheapest rooms, and, in the case of some of the western-style hotels, as well as in most Japanese-style hotels, this may mean for rooms without private bathing facilities.

We have listed establishments by area, although the last two Tokyo categories are wide-ranging. Please consult our rail maps to gain a better idea of location. If you reach Tokyo by JR lines from Narita Airport, you are likely to find hotels in the Shinjuku or Ikebukuro area convenient, but those in the proximity of other Yamanote Line stations or of Koiwa, Ryogoku or Oimachi stations would also be reasonably situated, Koiwa and Ryogoku being more easily reached by the *kaisoku* train than by the 'Narita Express'. If you travel by Keisei Line, hotels around Ueno or Asakusa would be easiest to reach, but

Keisei Koiwa is also on your route, if you do not use the 'Skyliner', while Asakusabashi, Ningyocho and Gotanda are all on the Toei Asakusa Line, onto which some Keisei trains from Narita Airport run directly.

We have listed accommodation only in Tokyo and the Osaka-Kyoto-Kobe area in this book, firstly because those are the areas which our readers are most likely to visit and secondly because, having arrived in one of these two areas, it is relatively easy to obtain information regarding the smaller cities. The Tourist Information Centers which can be found in these cities operate a free booking service for hotels throughout Japan. There is an office in the central part of No. 1 Terminal Building at Narita Airport. It is open until 8.00p.m. on weekdays. There is another office outside Yurakucho station on the Tokyo Yamanote Line (address: 1-6-6 Yurakucho). A third office is in Kyoto, not far from Kyoto Station (address: Kyoto Tower Building, Higashi Shiokoji-cho. Go out of the main exit of the station, pass to the right of the 'bus terminal area and take the main street running straight ahead. The Tourist Information Center is a short distance on the left). You may also telephone these offices for assistance on any matters, including, but not limited to, accommodation, during normal office hours. The telephone numbers are: in Tokyo 3503-4400, in Kyoto 371-5649, outside those two cities 0088-22-2800 for information on eastern Japan or 0088-22-4800 for information on western Japan. The 0088 calls are free, but, if a public telephone is used, it is necessary to insert a coin or card which will be refunded at the end of the call. Red or pink public telephones cannot be used for such calls.

And if you should arrive in any place without accommodation booked, at the railway station there is often an accommodation office and, although you cannot expect too much English to be spoken, the staff will usually be able to find accommodation for you if you specify the sort of price which you wish to pay. If there is no office, there are likely to be advertisements for accommodation around the station or, if you are really stuck, the station staff may well be able to suggest somewhere. In any case, in smaller places the accommodation available tends to congregate around the stations, of course.

Here, then, are our listings of the cheaper hotel accommodation available in the two main centres of Japan. Note that, if writing, you should, of course, add the name of the city — Tokyo, Osaka, Kyoto or Kobe — which we have omitted to save space and, if telephoning, you should add the city prefix if you are outside the local area. Narita Airport is far outside the Tokyo area. The prefixes are at the top of the telephone column — 03 for Tokyo, 06 for Osaka, 075 for Kyoto and 078 for Kobe. Omit the initial 0 if telephoning from overseas. Also do not forget our warning about allowing for price increases since the list was compiled.

MODERATELY-PRICED HOTELS — TOKYO AREA

Name	*Address*	*Station*	*Tel.*	*Rooms*	*Style*	*Sing.*	*Twin*
Asakusa Area			*(prefix 03)*			*(¥)*	*(¥)*
Kikuya Ryokan	2-18-9 Nishi Asakusa.	Tawaramachi	3481-4051	10	J/W	5500	8800
Ryokan Mikawaya Bekkan	1-31-11 Asakusa.	Asakusa	3843-2345	12	J	5700	10400
Hotel Asakusa Mikawaya	2-7-11 Hanakawado.	Asakusa	3844-7757	22	J/W	6000	10000
Asakusa Plaza Hotel	1-2-1 Asakusa.	Asakusa	3845-2621	59	W	6700	12500
Asakusa Vista Hotel	2-2-9 Kotobuki.	Tawaramachi	3842-8421	129	W	8500	15000
Ueno Area							
Suzuki Ryokan	7-15-23 Yanaka.	Nippori	3821-4944	15	J	4000	8000
Ryokan Katsutaro	4-16-8 Ikenohata.	Nezu or Ueno	3821-9808	7	J	4200	8400
Sawanoya Ryokan	2-3-11 Yanaka.	Nezu	3822-2251	12	J	4500	8400
Business Hotel Koshin	2-19-24 Negishi.	JR Uguisudani	3876-2601	52	W	5900	9500
Tsukuba Hotel	2-7-8 Moto Asakusa.	Inaricho	3834-2556	111	W/J	6000	10000
Sakura Ryokan	2-6-2 Iriya.	Iriya	3876-8118	20	J/W	6500	10000
Suigetsu Hotel	3-3-21 Ikenohata.	Nezu or Ueno	3822-4611	129	W/J	6500	11500
Hotel San Targas	2-19-3 Higashi Ueno.	Ueno	3833-8686	67	W	7000	12400
Hotel New Ueno	7-2-5 Ueno.	Ueno	3841-3221	65	W	8000	15000
Ueno Terminal Hotel	2-21-10 Higashi Ueno.	Ueno	3831-1110	61	W	8500	16000
Central Tokyo							
Asia Kaikan	8-10-32 Akasaka.	Aoyama I-chome	3402-6111	172	W	5100	9600
Central Hotel	3-17-9 Uchi Kanda.	JR Kanda	3256-6251	110	W	6000	8900
Hotel Mita Kaikan	2-20-12 Shiba.	Shiba Koen	3453-6601	88	W	6400	10300
New Surugadai Hotel	3-14 Kanda Ogawa-machi.	Ochanomizu	3291-0841	53	W	6500	9000
New Central Hotel	2-7-2 Kanda Tamachi.	JR Kanda	3256-2171	310	W	6700	9500
Tokyo Green Hotel	2-6 Kanda Awaji-cho.	JR Ochanomizu	3255-4161	206	W	7500	13600
Hotel Nihonbashi Saibo	3-3-16 Ningyo-cho.	Ningyocho	3668-2323	119	W	7500	14000
Tokyo City Hotel	1-5-4 Nihonbashi Honcho.	Mitsukoshi-mae	3270-7671	255	W	7800	12600
Ginza Capital Hotel	2-1 Tsukiji.	Tsukiji	3543-8211	500	W	8000	13800

Hotel Gimmond Tokyo	1-6 Odenma-cho.	Kodenmacho	3666-4111	217	W	8500	15000

Shibuya Area

Hotel Sunroute Shibuya	1-1-11 Nanpei-dai.	JR Shibuya	3464-6411	180	W	6300	15500
Shinjuku Park Hotel	5-27-9 Sendagaya.	JR Yoyogi	3356-0241	200	W	7500	11800

Shinjuku Area

Tokyo Business Hotel	6-3-2 Shinjuku.	Shinjuku Gyoen-mae	3356-4605	200	W	5000	10550
Kadoya Hotel	1-23-1 Nishi Shinjuku.	JR Shinjuku	3346-2561	70	W	6500	10000
Business Hotel Sekitei	2-31-16 Kabuki-cho.	JR Shinjuku	3205-3151	28	W	6500	10000
Shinjuku Town Hotel	7-16-15 Nishi Shinjuku.	JR Shinjuku	3365-2211	50	W	6800	12000
Hotel Tateshina	5-8-6 Shinjuku.	Shinjuku San-chome	3350-5271	26	W	7000	12000
Taisho Central Hotel	1-27-7 Takadanobaba.	JR Takadanobaba	3232-0101	196	W	7800	13000

Ikebukuro Area

Hotel San Targas Otsuka	2-17-15 Kita Otsuka.	JR Otsuka	3940-6700	112	W	5500	7200
Otsuka Sun First Hotel	2-40-8 Minami Otsuka.	JR Otsuka	3944-4141	48	W	6000	10500
Business Hotel Three Star	1-17-7 Ikebukuro Honcho.	JR Ikebukuro	3982-3331	40	W	7000	13000
Hotel Grand Business	1-30-7 Higashi Ikebukuro.	JR Ikebukuro	3984-5121	294	W	7200	11400
Plaza Inn Ikebukuro	1-20-6 Higashi Ikebukuro.	JR Ikebukuro	3985-0121	86	W	7500	12500
Dai-Ichi Inn Ikebukuro	1-42-8 Higashi Ikebukuro.	JR Ikebukuro	3986-1221	155	W	8000	13000
Ikebukuro Centre City Hotel	2-62-14 Ikebukuro.	JR Ikebukuro	3985-1311	201	W	8500	16000

Other Locations on or near Yamanote Line

Ours Inn Hankyu	1-50-5 Oi.	JR Oimachi	3775-6121	800	W	5000	None
Ryokan Sansuiso	2-9-5 Higashi Gotanda.	JR Gotanda	3441-7475	9	J	5000	8400
Shiba Yayoi Convention Hall	1-10-27 Kaigan.	JR Hamamatsucho	3434-6841	155	W	6000	10000
Ryogoku River Hotel	2-13-8 Ryogoku.	JR Ryogoku	3634-1711	80	W	6400	12300
Ryogoku Pearl Hotel	1-2-24 Yokoami.	JR Ryogoku	3625-8080	283	W	7500	13000
Hotel Mercury	2-1-9 Asakusabashi.	Asakusabashi	3866-1211	50	W	7500	12800

A Little Further out of Central Tokyo

Maruko Inn Tokyo	2-17-9 Taishido.	Sangenjaya	3795-0505	112	W	6000	12000
Ryokan Kangetsu	1-2-20 Chidori.	Chidoricho	3751-0007	58	J/W	6000	10000
Ryokan Kaneda	5-21-1 Minami Koiwa.	JR Koiwa	3657-1747	17	J/W	6500	9000
Eastern Hotel	1-39-13 Nakano Chuo.	Nakano Sakaue	3371-1751	39	W	6500	10000
Business Hotel New Hideoka	2-9-17 Sangenjaya.	Sangenjaya	3412-7871	23	W	7000	12000
Hotel Toyo	1-16-16 Toyo.	Kiba	3615-1041	124	W	7200	11000
Hotel Sun Patio	3-15-5 Nishi Kasai.	Nishi Kasai	3877-3810	68	W	7500	13000
Sky Court Koiwa	6-11-4 Kita Koiwa.	Keisei Koiwa	3672-4411	100	W	7500	15000

MODERATELY -PRICED HOTELS — OSAKA AREA

Name	*Address*	*Station*	*Tel.*	*Rooms*	*Style*	*Sing.*	*Twin*
Osaka			*(prefix 06)*			*(¥)*	*(¥)*
Ebisu-so Ryokan	1-7-33 Nipponbashi Nishi.	Ebisucho	643-4861	15	J	4200	7400
Osaka Corona Hotel	1-3-21 Nishi Awaji.	JR Shin Osaka	323-3151	108	W	5700	10500
Hotel Kansai	9-15 Togano-cho.	JR Osaka	312-7971	633	W	6000	7800
Business Hotel Nissei	4-31 Namba Sennichi-mae.	Namba	632-8111	132	W	6300	11000
Namba Plaza Hotel	1-20 Sennichi-mae.	Namba	641-3000	177	W	6400	10000
Hotel Osaka World	1-5-23 Sonezaki.	JR Osaka	361-1100	182	W	6400	10700
Hokke Club Osaka	12-19 Togano-cho.	JR Osaka	313-3171	149	W	6400	11600
Hotel Mitsufu	4-8-22 Nishi Nakajima.	Nishi Nakajima Minamigata	304-5171	157	W	6500	10000
Shin Osaka Sunny Stone Hotel	4-12-2 Nishi Nakajima.	Nishi Nakajima Minamigata	390-0001	208	W	6600	10800
Hotel Consult	1-12-7 Nishi Nakajima.	Nishi Nakajima Minamigata	304-1511	322	W	6600	12000
Hotel Kurebe Umeda	3-5-23 Nishi Tenma.	Minami Morimachi	361-7201	272	W	6600	12100
Hotel NCB	6-2-27 Nakanoshima.	JR Osaka	443-2255	156	W	6700	11000
Hotel Sun White	3-7-6 Tani-machi.	Tanimachi Yon-chome	942-3711	157	W	6900	12600
Hotel Oaks Shin Osaka	1-11-34 Nishi Nakajima.	Nishi Nakajima Minamigata	302-5141	232	W	7000	13000
Hotel Clayton Ritz	2-13-32 Nishi Nakajima.	Nishi Nakajima Minamigata	885-1211	111	W	7100	8700
Hotel Keihan Osaka	1-2-10 Tani-machi.	Tenmabashi	945-0321	310	W	7200	11600
Hotel Nankai Namba	1-17-11 Namba Naka.	Namba	649-1521	205	W	7300	12000
Mitsui Garden Hotel Osaka	2-5-7 Koraibashi.	Yodoyabashi	223-1131	343	W	7300	13000
Hotel Amenity Shinsaibashi	2-17-3 Nishi Shinsaibashi.	Shinsaibashi	212-5111	124	W	7300	13000
Tennoji Toei Hotel	81-3 Hiden-in-cho.	JR Tennoji	775-2121	146	W	7300	14000
Chisan Hotel Shinsaibashi	2-4-10 Minami Senba.	Nagahoribashi	263-1511	292	W	7500	14000
Toko Hotel	1-3-19 Minami Mori-machi.	Minami Morimachi	363-1201	292	W	7700	13400
Umeda O S Hotel	2-11-5 Sonezaki.	JR Osaka	312-1271	283	W	7800	14000
Ark Hotel Osaka	1-19-18 Shimanouchi.	Nagahoribashi	252-5111	364	W	7900	12000
Osaka Shanpia Hotel	6-23 Minami Ogi-machi.	JR Osaka	312-5151	289	W	7980	13600
Chisan Hotel Shin Osaka	6-2-19 Nishi Nakajima.	JR Shin Osaka	302-5571	377	W	8000	12000
Hotel Green Plaza Osaka	2-5-12 Nakazaki Nishi.	JR Osaka	374-1515	118	W	8000	12500
Lions Hotel Osaka	2-2-10 Koraibashi.	Kitahama	201-1511	194	W	8000	14000
New Osaka Hotel	5-14-10 Nishi Nakajima.	JR Shin Osaka	305-2345	268	W	8000	15500
International Hotel, Osaka	2-23 Honmachi-bashi.	Honmachi	941-2661	392	W	8000	16500

Name	Address	Station	Tel.	Rooms	Style	Sing.	Twin
Kyoto			(prefix 075)			(¥)	(¥)
Riverside Takase	Higashino-toin Nishiiru.	JR Kyoto	351-7920	5	J	3700	6400
Ryokan Mishima	Higashi Oji Higashiiru Umamachi-dori.	JR Kyoto	551-0033	7	J	4000	7000
Ryokan Murakamiya	Shichijo Agaru Sasaya-cho 270.	JR Kyoto	371-1260	8	J	4000	8000
Ryokan Hinomoto	Matsubara Agaru Kotake-cho 375.	JR Kyoto	351-4563	6	J	4000	8000
Pension Arashiyama	67 Miyanomoto-cho.	Arashiyama	881-2294	11	J/W	4000	9500
Pension Higashiyama	Shirakawa-suji Sanjo Sagaru.	JR Kyoto	882-1181	13	J/W	4000	9500
Pension Station Kyoto	Shichijo Agaru Shin-machi.	JR Kyoto	882-6200	13	J/W	4000	9500
Ryokan Kyoka	Higashino-toin Higashiiru.	JR Kyoto	371-2709	10	J	4200	8400
Ryokan Rakucho	67 Higashi Hangi-cho.	Kita Oji	721-2174	8	J	4300	7600
Matsubaya Ryokan	Higashino-toin Nishiiru.	JR Kyoto	351-4268	11	J	4300	8600
Ryokan Hiraiwa	Kaminokuchi Agaru Hayao-cho 314.	JR Kyoto	351-6748	21	J	4500	8000
Ryokan Seiki	Yamato Oji Kadowaki-cho 188-1.	JR Kyoto	551-4911	9	J	4500	8000
Ryokan Ohto	Hitosujime Minami Sagaru.	JR Kyoto	541-7803	10	J	5500	9000
Kyoto Palaceside Hotel	Karasuma-dori Shimo Dachiuri Agaru.	Marutamachi	431-8171	120	W	6000	10000
Maruko Inn Kyoto	Nishino-toin-dori Shijo Minamiiru.	Shijo	361-0505	80	W	6800	12000
Ark Hotel Kyoto	Mibu Kayogosho-cho 1.	Omiya	812-1111	144	W	7500	15000
Kyoto Garden Hotel	Muromachi-dori Oike Minamiiru.	Oike	255-2000	100	W	7600	13600
Sun Hotel Kyoto	Kawaramachi-dori Sanjo Sagaru.	Kawaramachi	241-3351	141	W	7800	13000
Kyoto Tokyu Inn	Horikawa-dori Gojo Sagaru.	JR Kyoto	593-0109	395	W	7900	12400
Kyoto Central Inn	Shijo Kawara-machi Nishiiru.	Kawaramachi	211-1666	128	W	8000	12000
Sanjo Karasuma Hotel	Karasuma Nishiiru Mikura-cho 80.	Oike	256-3331	154	W	8000	13000
Hotel Keihan Kyoto	Higashi Kujo Nishi Sanno-cho 31.	JR Kyoto	661-0321	275	W	8000	16000
Kobe			(prefix 078)				
Kobe Towerside Hotel	6-1 Hatoba-machi.	JR Motomachi	351-2151	136	W	5600	9500
Kobe Union Hotel	2-1-9 Nunobiki-cho.	JR Sannomiya	222-6500	149	W	6300	11000
Quality Inn Kobe	4-1-12 Isogami-dori.	JR Sannomiya	241-2233	96	W	6500	11000
Sunside Hotel	4-1-3 Kumoi-dori.	JR Sannomiya	232-3331	98	W	6600	12400
Green Hill Hotel Dai-Ichi	2-5-16 Kano-machi.	JR Sannomiya	222-1221	97	W	6600	13000
Chisan Hotel Kobe	2-3-1 Nakamachi-dori.	JR Kobe	341-8111	241	W	7200	15000
Casa Bella Inn Kobe	Nishi Kami Tachibana-dori.	Okurayama	578-0001	152	W	7300	14500
Dai-Ichi Grand Hotel	2-1-23 Naka Yamate-dori.	JR Sannomiya	331-5550	100	W	7400	12000
Kobe Plaza Hotel	1-13-12 Motomachi-dori.	JR Motomachi	332-1141	144	W	8000	16000

For the job-hunter, however, most of the accommodation on the lists given in the previous pages will be just too costly. For him it will have to be hostel accommodation if he wishes to economize. There are two Youth Hostels in Tokyo, but usually there is a time limit of a few days for staying there. There are also various private hostels, and recently '*Gaijin* Houses' have sprung up, offering longer-term accommodation. In the Osaka area, there are more Youth Hostels, supplemented by private hostels. Here is a list of just a few. Average prices are ¥2,000 to ¥2500 per person per night.

TOKYO AREA

Name	*Station*	*Line*	*Tel.*
Tokyo Kokusai Youth Hostel	Iidabashi	JR Sobu, Yurakucho,Tozai	03-3235-1107
Tokyo Yoyogi Youth Hostel	Sangubashi	Odakyu	03-3467-9163
Okubo House	Shin Okubo	JR Yamanote	03-3361-2348
Kimi Ryokan	Ikebukuro	JR Yamanote, Marunouchi, Yurakucho	03-3971-3766
Yoshida House	Toshima-en	Seibu Shinjuku	03-3926-4563
English House	Mejiro	JR Yamanote	03-3988-1743
Takao Youth Hostel	Takaosan-guchi	Keio	0426-61-0437

OSAKA

Osaka Shiritsu Nagai Youth Hostel	Nagai	JR Hanwa, Midosuji	06-699-5631
Osaka Hattori Ryokuchi Youth Hostel	Ryokuchi Koen	Kita Osaka Kyuko	06-862-0600

KYOTO

Higashiyama Youth Hostel	Higashiyama Sanjo	Keihan	075-761-8135
Kyoto Ohara Youth Hostel	Kita Oji	Subway	075-744-2528
Kitayama Youth Hostel	Kita Oji	Subway	075-492-5345
Tani House	Kita Oji	Subway	075-492-5489
Uno House	Kyoto	JR Tokaido	075-231-7763
Ise Dorm	Kyoto	JR Tokaido	075-771-0566
Tani Guest House	Kyoto	JR Tokaido	075-681-7437

KOBE

Kobe Tarumi Youth Hostel	Tarumi	JR Tokaido, Sanyo Dentetsu	078-707-2133

FINDING AN ADDRESS

Newcomers to Japan are usually confused by the address system and claim that they can never find any place. Those who have been here for a while, however, usually decide that the system, while different, is quite manageable. The first thing to remember is that in Japanese the address is written in exactly the reverse order of that used in English. That is to say that the prefecture or city comes first and the addressee's name comes last. Although the Japanese are kind enough to use the English order when writing in Roman script, some confusion sometimes arises.

Let us suppose that you have an address which you want to find, for example 'Dai-san Taihei Building, 1-25-3 Higashi Ikebukuro, Toshima-ku, Tokyo 170.' The number 170 is just a postcode. Tokyo is divided into 23 *ku* or wards, of which Toshima is one. If you manage to reach the nearest railway station, in this case the Higashi Ikebukuro subway station, you will almost inevitably find a large map of the immediate area on the wall. Of course, it will be in Japanese, but it is the numbers which are most important and if in doubt you can always ask assistance. Higashi Ikebukuro, like most other towns, is divided into *chome*. The *chome* is the first number in the Romanized form of the address, 1 in this case. There are usually about six to eight *chome* in each town. Once you ascertain that you are in the correct *chome*, by using the map on the wall to direct you, things become easier. The second number in the address, 25 in this case, represents the block. In Japan, only main streets have names and addressing is done by block, not by street. This means that people living on opposite sides of the same road will have only the *chome* number in common. They will be in different blocks. Even if you do not know the relationship of one block number to another, with a little walking around, you will soon discover the pattern. Look on the telegraph poles and you will find signs with white lettering on a green or blue background showing the number of the *chome* and block. If you see 1-3, for example, you will know that you are still quite a long way from 1-25. When you see 1-24, you will expect it to be in the next block one way or another. Once you have located the correct block, you will find that the buildings are numbered in consecutive order around the block. Walk round until you come to the number which you want. Little signs with white lettering usually on a blue background are attached to most buildings showing the block and number. In addition, in this case you have the name of the building, which may well be displayed in Roman characters, since that method has become fashionable. If there is a fourth number in the address, it will indicate that it is an apartment. The first digit in an apartment number almost always represents the floor on which it is situated.

So, you see, addresses are not so difficult after all. You just have to get used to the system!

USING THE TELEPHONE

The telephone system is remarkably efficient in Japan and there are public telephones available everywhere. Local calls are very cheap, at ¥10 for three minutes. Long distance calls, however, can be surprisingly expensive, although a discount is given for calls made after 7.00p.m.

There are various types of public telephone, but the most common ones now are those which are green in colour. Most will accept either coins or cards, but some take only one or the other. The coins which can be used are the ¥10 and the ¥100. A few of the older pink or blue public telephones will accept only ¥10 coins.

In recent years, the monopoly of a single domestic telephone company (Nippon Telegraph and Telephone Corporation — NTT) has been broken and competitors have been permitted. If you stay in Japan for a long time, this is something to bear in mind, but for the visitor the only relevance will be in relation to the purple or white public telephones which you will find at main railway stations. These are operated by the JR group of companies, using spare lines on the railways' own communications system. At the destination, the call is plugged into the NTT network and the railways pay NTT the cost of a local call. For long distance calls, these telephones are much cheaper than the NTT telephones and are worth taking advantage of. Do not use them for local calls, however, as they are considerably more expensive if used in that way.

International calls can be made from those green public telephones which have a gold panel on the front. They are usually housed in boxes which display the words 'International Telephone'. It is not generally realized, though, that international calls can also be made from any card-only green telephone. These are the small squat green telephones which you will see around. To make an international call first dial 001 or 0041 or 0061, followed by the country code and the number, usually minus the initial 0. The three different initial numbers represent three different companies. There used to be only 001 (Kokusai Denshin Denwa – KDD), but this market too was opened up recently and the two competitors offered so much lower rates that KDD was forced to reduce its prices to compete, which is worth remembering if you are in doubt as to which company to use. 0041 (International Telecom Japan – ITJ) and 0061 (International Digital Communications – IDC) still offer cheaper services, in most cases, than 001, but they do not have lines to all countries. It is cheaper to make international calls after 7.00p.m. and cheaper still between 11.00p.m. and 8.00a.m. To make international calls from a public telephone, you need ¥100 coins or a telephone card. ¥10 coins cannot be used and in the case of the card the cost will be charged in ten-unit blocks, so cards with less than ten units remaining cannot be used.

Telephone cards are available in denominations of ¥500 and ¥1,000. The ¥500 card gives 50 ¥10 units, but the ¥1,000 card gives 105 ¥10 units, so offers a slight advantage. The cards are often attractively decorated and are collected by certain people. They are available from tobacconists, souvenir shops, machines in or near some telephone boxes, and a wide variety of stores. It is almost always possible to buy a telephone card at a railway station. The Japanese for telephone card is 'telephone card' (pronounced *terehon cardo*) and, although the word for telephone is *denwa*, telephone would be understood.

There are, of course, telephone directories in Japan, but it is an odd feature of the country that nobody seems to use them. Asked why, most people reply that they can never find what they want because of the difficulties associated with the Japanese writing system. Whenever anybody wants to find out a number, he telephones directory enquiries. This service used to be free, but it became so costly for the telephone company to operate that now there is a charge of ¥30 per number. There is a directory enquiries service in English too. The number is 03-3586-0110. The cost is as for an ordinary telephone call.

EATING

One of the excellent features of Japan is its eating establishments. One can find all types of cuisine and at all prices. If one wants a lavish high-class meal, one can have it, but the great thing is that one does not have to spend a lot on food if one does not want to. In fact, considering the country's reputation for high prices, food is really rather reasonably priced.

One type of establishment which always does give a shock with its prices is the coffee shop. Such businesses are everywhere throughout Japan and a cup of coffee or similar usually costs at least ¥300, sometimes considerably more. What one is paying for is not the coffee, but the space to chat and stay as long as one wishes, and space is expensive in Japan, especially in the big cities. Go into a coffee shop in the morning, however, and you will usually find a bargain available known as 'morning service' (this is the Japanese name, not a translation). For only slightly more than you would pay for your cup of coffee you can have a light breakfast, typically a boiled egg with toast and maybe a small salad, and, of course, the cup of coffee.

When lunch-time comes, there are numerous small restaurants offering a special lunch menu. Since this is known, in Japanese, as *lunchi*, your linguistic powers will not be overstrained by ordering. Sometimes such exotic choices are offered as *Lunchi A* and *Lunchi B*. Restaurants almost always have their delicacies on display in the window in the form of very skilfully made wax models. However, since the lunch menu changes every day, it is not usually so displayed. Some restaurants put a real meal on display outside under a plastic cover. Others just write the day's dishes on a blackboard, or even just on a special lunch menu on the table. What you can expect, however, is soup, a main course with rice, perhaps a small salad and coffee or tea. If you find that you are being asked a question after ordering your *lunchi*, it is most likely to be whether you want tea or coffee and whether you want it hot or iced. The Japanese for coffee is 'coffee' (pronounced *kohi*) and the Japanese for tea is *ko-cha*, but 'tea' will be understood by everybody. The Japanese for hot is 'hot' (pronounced *hotto*) and the Japanese for iced is 'ice'. You will be beginning to think that this is not such a difficult language after all! *Lunchi* can be had for about ¥600 in an ordinary class of establishment. Better class restaurants also offer a lunch menu at around ¥1,000 to ¥1,200. Whichever you go for, *lunchi* is a bargain by Japanese standards.

For the impoverished job-hunter, there is the famous Shakey's Pizza Parlor. Branches can be found throughout Japan and all offer an eat-all-you-can lunch of pizza, fried potatoes and spaghetti for ¥600. You can do this for a couple of days, after which you will not want anybody even to mention pizza for the next month! One catch is that eating a lot of pizza makes you very thirsty and, of course, drinks are not included and there is no water around. Even so, it is a real bargain for a starving foreigner.

Dinner is a little more difficult, for there are fewer special offers at this time. If you want to eat a reasonable meal at a moderate price, however, try the top floors of department stores. There you will often find such a range of eating establishments that you will not know which to choose. If you are hungry, you will probably get best value from one of the 'set' menus, that is one which offers a combination of two or three smaller dishes with rice and maybe with coffee or similar to follow. A reasonable meal is likely to cost ¥1,000 to ¥1,500 in such a restaurant.

If you want to go out for a drink, there are many cheap drinking places in certain areas. The cheaper it looks, the better it will usually be (and the cheaper!). If you drink in such an establishment, the rule usually is that you must eat something as well, but you are likely to find it difficult to read the menu, which will be on pieces of paper stuck on the wall. If in doubt, try *yakitori*, grilled chicken on skewers. All such places will serve beer, which is 'beer' in Japanese. However, in Japan people do not generally go drinking by themselves, and you are likely to enjoy this experience more if you go with an experienced guide. Places to avoid are those with hostesses or with touts outside. They are likely to be very expensive indeed, so be careful.

If you need a quick and cheap snack at any time, a noodles shop is usually the solution. These can be found in many places, including, quite often, the platforms of railway stations. There is usually a variety of dishes and a choice of *soba* (thin noodles) or *udon* (thick noodles). A fairly standard choice is *tempura soba* or *tempura udon*. A bowl of noodles is likely to cost about ¥350.

Another relatively cheap way to eat, especially when travelling, is to indulge in *o-bento*, a type of lunch-box which can be purchased at small shops which usually display an illustrated menu outside or above the counter. It can also be bought at railway stations, either from kiosks or from vendors on the platforms. *O-bento* bought at stations is often known as *eki-ben* (station lunch-box). Unfortunately, this type of *o-bento* has become rather expensive in recent years, as has that sold actually on the train. It is usually better to purchase outside the station and get better value. Supermarkets and 'convenience stores' usually sell *o-bento* also.

There are plenty of pseudo-European bakeries around in Japan too. There is almost always one in or just outside a main railway station, for example. If one purchases a few items at such an establishment, the cost will not be outrageous. Since this is Japan, however, not Europe, there will be a few surprises. One to watch out for is that something which is heavy and looks as though it might contain a chocolatey substance may well have *anko* (sweet bean paste) in it. You might immediately fall in love with *anko* — and, there again, you might not!

If you have occasion to shop and cook for yourself, you may be surprised to find that, as long as you are willing to adapt your diet to the local conditions, you can eat quite cheaply. This adaptation principally means cutting out expensive meat, especially beef, but you can still eat chicken. If you look around supermarkets at closing time, you can find a lot of bargains in the form of ¥100 off stickers on items that will not be at their best the next day. You can also find bargain plates outside greengrocers' shops, usually a little assortment of items which will not remain fresh for much longer, for ¥100 or so. However, these goods need eating quickly, of course, because shopkeepers know when things will last and when they will not. Bakeries sell the crusts of bread very cheaply, or even sometimes give them away, because nobody in Japan wants to lower himself to eat crusts. These are called *pan no mimi*. *Pan* is the French word *pain* and *mimi* means ears. A large bag of crusts typically costs about ¥50.

MONEY AND BANKS

At the time of writing the Japanese currency has a value of about ¥120 to the U.S. dollar. That means that it has approximately doubled in value against the dollar in the last decade. By the time that this book is read maybe one yen will be equal to one cent.

Notes are issued in denominations of ¥10,000, ¥5,000 and ¥1,000. There are coins for ¥500, ¥100, ¥50, ¥10, ¥5 and ¥1.

When arriving in Japan, it is not a bad idea to change quite a lot of money at the airport. You are sure to need quite a lot, rates do not vary much among the banks, including those at the airport, and you will be able to make the change much more quickly there than at any other bank.

Most banking in Japan, for the ordinary citizen, is done by machine. Machines are quick, efficient and even polite, for they often boast little recorded messages. If you have to do business inside the bank, however, it will be quite different. The most simple transaction will take twenty minutes, because, while machines can be trusted, the actions of humans must be checked and rechecked to ensure that no mistakes have been made. If possible, therefore, try to avoid Japanese banks or do everything possible in a single visit. It should also be noted that the fees charged by banks for their services are sometimes quite a shock. It is best to ask first. There are several overseas banks in the area of Otemachi in Tokyo and, where it is permitted by government regulations, their charges are often somewhat lower.

POSTAL SERVICES

Postal services are very reliable and safe, but not particularly quick. Postage rates within Japan are ¥62 for a letter and ¥41 for a postcard. Except for the imposition of a 3% tax, these rates have not changed for more than twelve years. It is common to use express mail to ensure rapid delivery, but this costs ¥210 extra. Express mail is delivered even on Sundays and holidays and reaches all reasonable destinations the next day if posted by a stated time, usually about 5.00p.m. It can be posted in a postbox, if it is clearly marked, in red, as express mail.

International letters cost ¥120 to Europe, South America and Africa, ¥100 to North America, Australasia and the Middle East and ¥80 to most Asian countries. Rates are for 10 grams. Postcards cost ¥80. Air letter forms (aerogrammes) are also available for ¥80 and can be sent for that price to anywhere in the world. Moreover, if you spoil an air letter form or a pre-paid postcard or anything else with pre-paid postage, you can take it back to the Post Office and obtain a refund, minus a small handling charge.

When international mail is posted in a postbox, and there are two slots, it should be put into the slot marked 'Other Mail', or something similar, not into the one for letters and postcards. The same applies to all express mail. Rates for international mail have actually decreased twice in the last decade. Is there any other country in the world where such a phenomenon has occurred?

The Post Office also operates a money transfer service internationally which is far cheaper than anything provided by the banks, although it takes time.

The Central Post Office for Tokyo is just outside the Marunouchi South Exit of Tokyo Station.

BUSINESS HOURS

Business hours in Japan are mostly similar to those in western countries. Offices usually work from 9.00 until 5.30 or 6.00. Sunday is a holiday. For larger companies Saturday is also a holiday, but for smaller companies Saturday may be a half day, or two Saturdays in a month may be worked. Outside these hours, there will probably be somebody in the office, but there may be nobody to answer the switchboard. If you know a person's direct number, however, you are likely to be able to get a response until quite late at night.

Shops tend to open late and stay open late. Fairly typical hours for a large store would be 10.00 until 7.00 or 8.00. Smaller shops will be open later, maybe until 10.00. In larger towns now, it is usually possible to find 'convenience stores' which are open 24 hours a day, 365 days a year, so nobody is likely to starve in Japan!

ENTERTAINMENT

Entertainment tends to be terribly expensive in Japan. It costs about ¥1,800 for a cinema seat, for instance, and for live entertainment the cheapest seats are often as expensive as ¥5,000.

There is plenty of low-class television entertainment. In Tokyo there are six channels, but only Channels 1 and 3, operated by the non-commercial NHK, profess to offer any intellectual stimulation. When films are broadcast, often late at night at weekends, the original soundtrack may be broadcast on a second frequency. As mentioned previously, most channels also offer a news programme with an English version, but it could hardly be said to be a professional-sounding presentation. In any case, much of the Japanese news seems to consist of politics and, since there is virtually only one political party, such reports are somewhat less than thrilling.

The only local radio in English is the Far East Network (FEN) operated by the American armed forces for those of their number who are stationed here. Its intellectual level is about what one might expect, considering its audience. If you have a short-wave radio, you can listen to Voice of America at certain hours. It is also possible to tune in to the BBC, Radio Australia and Radio Moscow, but reception is often a problem with these stations.

NEWSPAPERS

There are four English language newspapers. The 'Japan Times', the 'Daily Yomiuri' and the 'Mainichi Daily News' are morning papers and the 'Asahi Evening News' is, naturally, an evening paper. All maintain a relatively high standard. In fact, when compared with the general standard of English in Japan, they are quite amazingly good. The most popular is the 'Japan Times', but it costs ¥160, whereas the 'Daily Yomiuri' is available for ¥100 and so seems to this writer, at least, to be better value.

All of the English language papers are produced in Tokyo, so the further one goes from that city, the more difficult they are to procure. In more remote places, they may be a day old, if obtainable at all.

JAPANESE LANGUAGE

One sometimes hears that Japanese is considered one of the world's most difficult languages. In fact, though, it is not particularly difficult to struggle along in speaking a few words or to understand when spoken to. What is so hard is to learn to read and write. So difficult is it that the Japanese themselves, when presented with the name of an unknown town, for example, cannot necessarily read it!

This is not intended to be the start of a course in practical Japanese, particularly as the writer himself cannot claim any great proficiency in the language, but a little explanation of the system may at least help the reader to understand the problems. First of all, there are three ways of writing things in Japanese. There are two phonetic alphabets and there is the Chinese character system. Any Japanese word can be written phonetically using the *hiragana* alphabet of 52 characters. In fact, this is how children do first learn to read and write. Any JR station, and most private ones, will have its name written in *hiragana*, so, if you learn this alphabet, you will always know where you are, at least. However, since all JR stations also have the name in Roman script, it is hardly worth learning *hiragana* for this purpose alone. The first five characters in the alphabet represent vowel sounds. The remainder, with one exception, represent a combination of a consonant plus a vowel, for example *ka, ki, ku, ke, ko*. The only consonant which can exist independently is that single exception *n*. This system means, of course, that not only is the number of vowels used in Japanese limited to five, but also the number of consonants recognized as distinct is limited too. This is the cause of much mispronunciation of English and other languages, as we shall see in the next paragraph.

The second phonetic alphabet is called *katakana* and it is used to distinguish nasty foreign words which have crept into Japanese, of which there are very many. The *hiragana* characters tend to be rounded and the *katakana* characters angular. *Katakana* represents exactly the same sounds as *hiragana*. Because of the limited number of consonants, and because of the necessity of placing a vowel between any two consonants, n excepted, *katakana* leads to mutilation of the English language, from which most words are stolen, and of other languages too. It is well-known that Japanese cannot distinguish l and r. It is less well-known that they cannot distinguish b and v, or f and h, or s and th. They are also unable to distinguish the vowels a and u. Thus, when expressed in *katakana*, the words ''bus' and 'bath' are identical. Moreover, when loan-words are too long, the Japanese shorten them, without regard, of course, to the etymology. So 'television' is, in Japanese, *terebi* and 'mass communications' is *masukomi*. One detestable favourite of this writer is *remicon*, which is, believe it or not, 'ready-mixed concrete'. This butchering of one's language is sometimes hard to forgive, especially as it is often carried over when people are actually speaking English. It can also mean that even though an English word is being used, a native speaker of the language may not readily comprehend it. Moreover, if you say something in English, even though the person to whom you are speaking knows the word, he may not understand it because of your strange pronunciation (!), principally your failure to insert a few extra vowels. They are perhaps unusual cases, because the vowels have actually been changed, but a Japanese person will not easily comprehend the word 'button', because in Japanese it is *botan* and he will not know what a 'tunnel' is, because in Japanese it is *tonneru.* However, if you want to learn something Japanese, the *katakana* alphabet is a good place to start, because, as soon as you have mastered it, you will be able to read and understand what you have read. You will, for example, be able to read the names of the western dishes on a menu, because they are usually written in *katakana*, and that is a very useful ability! You will probably find yourself mouthing the words to try to imagine what they might have been before they underwent the *katakana* metamorphosis, but in most cases you will get there in the end.

The third way of writing is to use Chinese characters. This is regarded as being much more sophisticated than using *hiragana*, but it is also much more difficult. The characters themselves take a good deal of memorizing. About 2,000 are taught at school and about 3,000 are in common use. They are often used in combination with *hiragana*, with the Chinese characters, or *kanji* as they are usually called, expressing the root meaning and *hiragana* showing the verb endings, particles and prepositions. The real problem with *kanji*, though, is an historical one. Japanese already existed in spoken form when *kanji* were imported from China in order to write it down. Of course, the Japanese words were different from the Chinese words for the same things, but when the *kanji* arrived, they brought with them both the meaning and the Chinese sound. For example, the Japanese word for 'east' is *higashi*, but the character meaning east (東) can also be read, in compounds, *to*. If you show that character to a Chinese, even now, he will read *ton*, almost like the Japanese alternative pronunciation. Virtually all Japanese *kanji* have at least two possible readings, therefore, and sometimes more. For example, that *kanji* for 'east' can also be read *azuma*. Thus, when dealing with compounds, which most words are, Japanese are not necessarily sure how to read their own language, if the compound is not one with which they are familiar. You will often see *kanji* with small *hiragana* characters over the top to tell the reader how to pronounce them, especially in the case of place or personal names. Well, you may be thinking, if the Japanese cannot read their own language, what hope have I, a mere foreigner? But do not despair! This book will only suggest that you manage to recognize a very few of the most useful characters. *Kanji* are really quite fun — and a sort of detective game into the bargain!

There are just a few more things to mention. Now Japanese is, luckily, not a tonal language, like Chinese or Thai, for instance. In fact, it is somewhat like English in terms of speech. If you pronounce words in an absolutely flat way without any stress or accent, that may not be ideal, but you will generally be understood. The same would apply in English. If, however, you put stress or accent in the wrong place, you probably will not be understood, again as in English. English-speakers, particularly certain nationalities, sometimes feel an overwhelming temptation to stress the penultimate syllable. This is nearly always wrong in Japanese and is apt to lead to total incomprehension, when the same pronunciation, even if not quite correct, would probably be understood if rendered without any stress at all. So, unless you really know where the stress goes, make a conscious effort not to put any.

Also note that, when Japanese is written in Roman script, a final u is nearly always weak, just as a final e is in English. Sometimes it is weak even in the middle of the word, particularly if it is at the end of one of the *kanji* which make up the word. Thus, when you are looking for the Tourist Information Center at Yurakucho, you will want to ask, not for 'Yura*ku*cho', as many people do, but for 'Yurakcho'. A final e in the Romanized form of Japanese, however, is pronounced.

People learning a few words of a foreign language often seem to study rather unnecessary formalities or politenesses, asking, for example, "What is the Japanese for 'Thank you'?" In fact, Japanese often use the English term 'Thank you' themselves (or, more phonetically, *san-kyu*), but would, in any case, understand an expression of gratitude without any Japanese words. When people ask what is most important in a foreign language, this writer always advises, "Learn to ask 'How much?' and learn to count. They are the most important words in any language." Therefore this little section tries to give just a few practical words. Counting is a little difficult in Japanese. The words given are for ordinary numbers, for money or for time, but they cannot be used for counting objects. That is to say that they cannot be used for saying, "I want *two* of those." A different set of words is used for that purpose, and they are more difficult. If you want two, try holding up two fingers, or even saying 'two' in English. Note that there are two words for 'four' and two words for 'seven'.

Questions are made in Japanese by putting *-ka* at the end of the sentence, so when you hear *-ka*, panic, because an answer is required!

Hai means 'yes', but it is a deceiving word, because it is also quite likely to mean 'I understand', or even 'I beg your pardon', when asking for a repetition. It is not safe to assume that somebody means 'yes' just because he says *hai*. Much safer is *so desu* (it is so). That is usually a definite statement of agreement. Japanese people do not like to say 'no', so it is difficult to give a translation for this apparently simple word. *Iie* is used in the sense of 'not at all'. Thus, "You are very kind." "*Iie* (not at all)." *Chigai masu* is used to disagree politely. Thus, "Is this the train for Kyoto?" "*Chigai masu* (no, it is not)." *Kekko desu* (literally, 'it's all right' and also used to mean that, so again confusing) is for 'no, thank you', to decline an offer, but it needs to be said with a negative tone of voice, or some negative gesture. Thus, "Do you want to subscribe to a newspaper?" "*Kekko desu* (no, thank you)." And close the door firmly!

Two short lists follow. The first is of spoken Japanese which might be useful. The second gives Japanese readings and translations of *kanji* which might be encountered in everyday life.

(a) Useful Spoken Phrases

English	*Japanese*
How much (is it)?	*Ikura (desu-ka)?*
At what time?	*Nan ji-ni?*
train	*densha*
'bus	*basu*
taxi	*takushi*
hotel	*hoteru*
Excuse me. / I am sorry. / Thank you.	*Sumi masen.*
yes	*hai / so desu*
no	*iie / chigai masu / kekko desu*
I understand.	*Wakari mashita.*
I do not understand.	*Wakari masen.*
Where is . . . . . . ?	. . . . . . *doko desu-ka?*
ticket	*kippu*
no smoking	*kin-en*
single (room)	*shinguru (rumu)*
double	*daburu*
twin	*tsuin*
bath	*o-furo* or *basu*
dining-room	*shoku-do*
(I made a) reservation.	*Yoyaku (shi-mashita).*
name (one's own)	*namae*
name (somebody else's)	*o-namae*
address	*jusho*
English (language)	*eigo*
Japanese (language)	*nihon-go*
Japan	*nihon*
this	*kore*
that	*sore*
expensive	*takai*
cheap	*yasui*
map	*chizu*
police	*keisatsu*
please / yes, please	*o-negai shimasu*

(b) Useful kanji

Kanji	*Japanese*	*English*
一	*ichi*	one
二	*ni*	two
三	*san*	three
四	*shi* or *yon*	four
五	*go*	five
六	*roku*	six
七	*shichi* or *nana*	seven
八	*hachi*	eight
九	*ku* or *kyu*	nine
十	*ju*	ten
十一	*ju-ichi*	eleven
二十	*ni-ju*	twenty
百	*hyaku*	one hundred
二百	*ni-hyaku*	two hundred
千	*sen* (or *i-sen*)	one thousand
二千	*ni-sen*	two thousand
一万	*ichi-man*	ten thousand
一万一千	*ichi-man i-sen*	eleven thousand
十万	*ju-man*	one hundred thousand
百万	*hyaku-man*	one million
円	*en*	yen
年	*nen*	year
月	*gatsu*	month
日	*nichi*	day or date
時	*ji*	hour or o'clock
分	*hun* or *pun*	minute(s)
駅	*eki*	station
入口	*iri-guchi*	entrance
出口	*de-guchi*	exit
男	*otoko*	men
女	*ona*	ladies
指定席	*shitei seki*	reserved seat
自由席	*jiyu seki*	unreserved seat

ADVICE AND INFORMATION

Here is a list of telephone numbers where English (or another language, as indicated) should be spoken and which can be used to obtain advice and information, or in case of emergency. Several of these numbers have been mentioned in earlier pages.

Service	*Number*
Japan Helpline — emergencies, counselling, 24 hours, free	0120-46-1997
Tokyo English Lifeline — emergencies, counselling, 9-1, 7-11	03-3264-4347
Police (Japanese) — free	110
Fire, ambulance (Japanese) — free	119
Tourist Information Center — assistance, 9-5, in Tokyo	03-3502-1461
Tourist Information Center — assistance, 9-8, Narita Airport	0476-32-8711
Tourist Information Center — assistance, 9-5, in Kyoto	075-371-5649
Tourist Information Center — assistance, 9-5, East Japan, free	0088-22-2800
Tourist Information Center — assistance, 9-5, West Japan, free	0088-22-4800
Teletourist Service — forthcoming events, Tokyo	03-3503-2911
Teletourist Service (French) — forthcoming events, Tokyo	03-3503-2926
Teletourist Service — forthcoming events, Kyoto	075-361-2911
JR East Infoline — railway services	03-3423-0111
Tokyo Subway Information	03-3502-1461
Postal Services Information — 9.30-4.30	03-5472-5851
Japan Hotline — directory enquiries, general information	03-3586-0110
NTT Telephone Information, Tokyo	03-3277-1010
NTT Telephone Information, Narita	0476-28-1010
NTT Telephone Information, Yokohama	045-322-1010
NTT Telephone Information, Osaka	06-313-1010
NTT Telephone Information, Nagoya	052-541-1010
NTT Telephone Information, Hiroshima	082-262-1010
NTT Telephone Information, Sapporo	011-219-1010
NTT Telephone Information, Sendai	022-232-1010
NTT Telephone Information, Fukuoka	092-632-1010
Tokyo City Air Terminal — flight information	03-3665-7111
Foreign Residents' Advisory Center — 9.30-12, 1-4	03-5320-7744
Foreign Residents' Advisory Center (French)	03-5320-7755

Foreign Residents' Advisory Center (Chinese)	03-5320-7766
Foreign Residents' Advisory Center (Korean)	03-5320-7700
Tokyo Regional Immigration Bureau — information, 9.30-12, 1-4	03-3213-8527
Immigration Office — computerized information	03-3213-8141
Central Immigration Office	03-3580-4111
Tokyo Regional Immigration Bureau	03-3213-8111
Narita District Immigration Office	0476-32-6812
Osaka Regional Immigration Bureau	06-941-0771
Osaka Immigration Information (Eng., Ch., Sp., Port.)	06-774-3409
Tokyo City Air Terminal Immigration Office — re-entry permits	03-3664-3046
Tokyo Bar Association (English and Chinese) — legal advice	03-3581-2302
Ministry of Justice (English, German, Chinese) — legal advice	03-3214-0424
Labor for Foreign Laborers Rights (Eng., Ch., Kor., Span., Port.)	03-3357-5506
Legal Assistance — 11-8	03-3591-1301
HELP — for Asian women with problems	03-3368-8855
Kaigai Nikkei Koryu Center (Eng., Sp., Port.) — for workers, 4-5	03-5256-5301
Yokohama International Tourist Association — information, 9-5	045-641-4759
YOKE (multilingual) — for Yokohama residents, M,W,F 10-4	045-671-7209
Assistance for Nagoya Residents (multilingual) — 9.30-4.30	052-973-0411
Kobe International Community Center (English and Chinese)	078-322-0030
Kobe Community House and Information Center	078-857-6540
AIDS Hotline — Saturdays, 7-10p.m.	03-3359-2477
AIDS Information — Saturdays, 1-6	03-5256-3002
AIDS Information, Osaka area	0720-48-2044
Alcoholics Anonymous	03-3971-1471

EMBASSIES

Finally in this section, here is a list of embassies and consulates established in Japan, with addresses and telephone numbers.

Country	*Address*	*Telephone*
Afghanistan	6-31-21 Jingu-mae, Shibuya-ku, Tokyo 150.	03-3407-7900
Algeria	2-10-67 Mita, Meguro-ku, Tokyo 153.	03-3711-2661
Argentina	2-17-8 Nagata-cho, Chiyoda-ku, Tokyo 100.	03-3592-0321
Australia	2-1-14 Mita, Minato-ku, Tokyo 108.	03-5232-4111
Austria	1-1-20 Moto Azabu, Minato-ku, Tokyo 106.	03-3451-8281
Bangladesh	2-7-45 Shirogane, Minato-ku, Tokyo 108.	03-3442-1501
Belgium	5-4 Niban-cho, Chiyoda-ku, Tokyo 102.	03-3262-0191
Bolivia	4-12-24 Nishi Azabu, Minato-ku, Tokyo 106.	03-3499-5441
Brazil	2-11-12 Kita Aoyama, Minato-ku, Tokyo 107.	03-3404-5211
Brunei	6-5-2 Kita Shinagawa, Shinagawa-ku, Tokyo.	03-3447-7997
Bulgaria	5-36-3A Yoyogi, Shibuya-ku, Tokyo 151.	03-3465-1022
Burundi	6-5-3 Kita Shinagawa, Shinagawa-ku, Tokyo.	03-3443-7321
Cameroon	9-12 Nanpeidai-cho, Shibuya-ku, Tokyo 150.	03-3496-1125
Canada	7-3-38 Akasaka, Minato-ku, Tokyo 107.	03-3408-2101
Central African Rep.	32-2 Oyama-cho, Shibuya-ku, Tokyo 151.	03-3460-8341
Chile	3-1-14 Shiba, Minato-ku, Tokyo 105.	03-3452-7561
China	3-4-33 Moto Azabu, Minato-ku, Tokyo 106.	03-3403-3379
Colombia	3-10-53 Kami Osaki, Shinagawa-ku, Tokyo.	03-3440-6491
Costa Rica	4-12-24 Nishi Azabu, Minato-ku, Tokyo 106.	03-3486-1812
Côte d'Ivoire	4-12-24 Nishi Azabu, Minato-ku, Tokyo 106.	03-3499-7022
Cuba	4-11-12 Shimo Meguro, Meguro-ku, Tokyo 153.	03-3716-3112
Denmark	29-6 Sarugaku-cho, Shibuya-ku, Tokyo 150.	03-3496-3001
Djibouti	9-12 Nanpeidai-cho, Shibuya-ku, Tokyo 150.	03-3496-6135
Dominican Rep.	4-12-24 Nishi Azabu, Minato-ku, Tokyo 106.	03-3499-6020
Ecuador	4-12-24 Nishi Azabu, Minato-ku, Tokyo 106.	03-3499-2800
Egypt	1-5-4 Aoba-dai, Meguro-ku, Tokyo 153.	03-3770-8401
El Salvador	4-12-24 Nishi Azabu, Minato-ku, Tokyo 106.	03-3499-4461
Ethiopia	1-14-15 Midorigaoka, Meguro-ku, Tokyo 152.	03-3718-1003
Fiji	2-3-5 Azabu-dai, Minato-ku, Tokyo 106.	03-3587-2038
Finland	3-5-39 Minami Azabu, Minato-ku, Tokyo 106.	03-3442-2231

France	4-11-44 Minami Azabu, Minato-ku, Tokyo 106.	03-3473-0171
Gabon	1-12-11 Kami Osaki, Shinagawa-ku, Tokyo 108.	03-3448-9540
Germany	4-5-10 Minami Azabu, Minato-ku, Tokyo 106.	03-3473-0151
Ghana	5-12-10 Shimo Meguro, Meguro-ku, Tokyo 153.	03-3710-8831
Greece	3-16-30 Nishi Azabu, Minato-ku, Tokyo 106.	03-3403-0871
Guatemala	4-12-24 Nishi Azabu, Minato-ku, Tokyo 106.	03-3400-1830
Guinea	1-12-6 Minami Azabu, Minato-ku, Tokyo 106.	03-3769-0451
Haiti	4-12-24 Nishi Azabu, Minato-ku, Tokyo 106.	03-3486-7070
Honduras	4-12-24 Nishi Azabu, Minato-ku, Tokyo 106.	03-3409-1150
Hungary	2-17-14 Mita, Minato-ku, Tokyo 108.	03-3798-8802
India	2-2-11 Kudan Minami, Chiyoda-ku, Tokyo 102.	03-3262-2392
Indonesia	5-2-9 Higashi Gotanda, Shinagawa-ku, Tokyo.	03-3441-4202
Iran	3-10-32 Minami Azabu, Minato-ku, Tokyo 106.	03-3446-8011
Iraq	8-4-7 Akasaka, Minato-ku, Tokyo 107.	03-3423-1727
Ireland	8-7 Sanban-cho, Chiyoda-ku, Tokyo 102.	03-3263-0696
Israel	3 Niban-cho, Chiyoda-ku, Tokyo 102.	03-3264-0912
Italy	2-5-4 Mita, Minato-ku, Tokyo 108.	03-3453-5292
Jordan	2-17-8 Nagata-cho, Chiyoda-ku, Tokyo 100.	03-3580-5856
Kenya	3-24-3 Yakumo, Meguro-ku, Tokyo 152.	03-3723-4007
Korea, South	1-2-5 Minami Azabu, Minato-ku, Tokyo 106.	03-3452-7611
Kuwait	4-13-12 Mita, Minato-ku, Tokyo 108.	03-3455-0362
Laos	3-6-2 Minami Magome, Ota-ku, Tokyo 143.	03-3778-1660
Lebanon	2-17-8 Nagata-cho, Chiyoda-ku, Tokyo 100.	03-3580-1206
Liberia	6-5-3 Kita Shinagawa, Shinagawa-ku, Tokyo.	03-3441-7138
Luxembourg	2-1 Niban-cho, Chiyoda-ku, Tokyo 102.	03-3265-9621
Madagascar	2-3-23 Moto Azabu, Minato-ku, Tokyo 106.	03-3446-7253
Malaysia	2-1-11 Minami Azabu, Minato-ku, Tokyo 106.	03-3280-7602
Mauritania	5-17-5 Kita Shinagawa, Shinagawa-ku, Tokyo.	03-3449-3810
Mexico	2-15-1 Nagata-cho, Chiyoda-ku, Tokyo 100.	03-3581-1132
Micronesia	1-14-2 Akasaka, Minato-ku, Tokyo 107.	03-3585-5456
Mongolia	21-4 Kamiya-cho, Shibuya-ku, Tokyo 150.	03-3469-2088
Morocco	3-16-3 Sendagaya, Shibuya-ku, Tokyo 151.	03-3478-3272
Myanmar	4-8-26 Kita Shinagawa, Shinagawa-ku, Tokyo.	03-3441-9292
Nepal	7-14-9 Todoroki, Setagaya-ku, Tokyo 158.	03-3705-5558
Netherlands	3-6-3 Shiba Koen, Minato-ku, Tokyo 105.	03-5401-0412

New Zealand	20-40 Kamiya-cho, Shibuya-ku, Tokyo 150.	03-3467-2272
Nicaragua	4-12-24 Nishi Azabu, Minato-ku, Tokyo 106.	03-3499-0400
Nigeria	2-19-7 Uehara, Shibuya-ku, Tokyo 151.	03-3468-5532
Norway	5-12-2 Minami Azabu, Minato-ku, Tokyo 106.	03-3440-2611
Oman	3-16-3 Sendagaya, Shibuya-ku, Tokyo 151.	03-3402-0877
Pakistan	2-14-9 Moto Azabu, Minato-ku, Tokyo 106.	03-3454-4862
Panama	4-12-24 Nishi Azabu, Minato-ku, Tokyo 106.	03-3499-3742
Papua New Guinea	1-4-28 Mita, Minato-ku, Tokyo 108.	03-3454-7802
Paraguay	3-5-8 Kami Osaki, Shinagawa-ku, Tokyo 141.	03-3447-7496
Peru	4-4-27 Higashi, Shibuya-ku, Tokyo 150.	03-3406-4240
Philippines	11-24 Nanpeidai-cho, Shibuya-ku, Tokyo 150.	03-3496-2731
Poland	2-13-5 Mita, Meguro-ku, Tokyo 153.	03-3711-5225
Portugal	6-31-21 Jingu-mae, Shibuya-ku, Tokyo 150.	03-3400-7908
Qatar	6-16-22 Shirogane, Minato-ku, Tokyo 108.	03-3446-7562
Romania	3-16-19 Nishi Azabu, Minato-ku, Tokyo 106.	03-3479-0311
Russia	2-1-1 Azabu-dai, Minato-ku, Tokyo 106.	03-3583-4224
Rwanda	4-12-24 Nishi Azabu, Minato-ku, Tokyo 106.	03-3486-7800
Saudi Arabia	1-53 Azabu Nagasaka-cho, Minato-ku, Tokyo.	03-3589-5241
Senegal	1-3-4 Aoba-dai, Meguro-ku, Tokyo 153.	03-3464-8451
Singapore	5-12-3 Roppongi, Minato-ku, Tokyo 106.	03-3586-9111
South Africa	2-7-9 Hirakawa-cho, Chiyoda-ku, Tokyo 102.	03-3265-3367
Spain	1-3-29 Roppongi, Minato-ku, Tokyo.	03-3583-8532
Sri Lanka	1-14-1 Akasaka, Minato-ku, Tokyo 107.	03-3585-7432
Sudan	6-6-20 Minami Aoyama, Minato-ku, Tokyo 107.	03-3406-0812
Sweden	1-10-3-100 Roppongi, Minato-ku, Tokyo 106.	03-5562-5050
Switzerland	5-9-12 Minami Azabu, Minato-ku, Tokyo 106.	03-3473-0121
Syria	6-19-45 Akasaka, Minato-ku, Tokyo 107.	03-3586-8978
Tanzania	4-21-9 Kami Yoga, Setagaya-ku, Tokyo 158.	03-3425-4531
Thailand	3-14-6 Kami Osaki, Shinagawa-ku, Tokyo 141.	03-3441-7352
Tunisia	1-18-8 Wakaba, Shinjuku-ku, Tokyo 160.	03-3353-4112
Turkey	2-33-6 Jingu-mae, Shibuya-ku, Turkey 150.	03-3470-5132
United Arab Emirates	9-10 Nanpeidai-cho, Shibuya-ku, Tokyo.	03-5489-0804
United Kingdom	1 Ichiban-cho, Chiyoda-ku, Tokyo 102.	03-3265-5511
United States	1-10-5 Akasaka, Minato-ku, Tokyo 107.	03-3224-5000
Uruguay	4-12-24 Nishi Azabu, Minato-ku, Tokyo 106.	03-3486-1888

Vatican	9-2 Sanban-cho, Chiyoda-ku, Tokyo 102.	03-3263-6851
Venezuela	4-12-24 Nishi Azabu, Minato-ku, Tokyo 106.	03-3409-1502
Vietnam	50-11 Yoyogi-cho, Shibuya-ku, Tokyo 151.	03-3466-3311
Yemen	4-12-24 Nishi Azabu, Minato-ku, Tokyo 106.	03-3499-7152
Zaire	3-53-17 Sendagaya, Shibuya-ku, Tokyo 151.	03-3423-3982
Zambia	3-9-19 Ebisu, Shibuya-ku, Tokyo 150.	03-3445-1042
Zimbabwe	5-9-10 Shirogane-dai, Minato-ku, Tokyo 108.	03-3280-0331

LIST OF TOKYO STOCK MARKET COMPANIES

FIRST SECTION

(abbreviated names)

(★ indicates that company is listed in appropriate chapter of this book.)

	Company	Address	Telephone
	AGRICULTURE AND FISHING		
	KYOKUYO	2-1-2 Marunouchi, Chiyoda-ku, Tokyo 100.	03-3211-0134
	NICHIRO	1-12-1 Yurakucho, Chiyoda-ku, Tokyo 100.	03-3240-6211
	NIPPON SUISAN	2-6-2 Otemachi, Chiyoda-ku, Tokyo 100.	03-3244-7000
	TAIYO FISHERY	1-1-2 Otemachi, Chiyoda-ku, Tokyo 100.	03-3216-0821
	HOKO FISHING	1-2-4 Tsukiji, Chuo-ku, Tokyo 104.	03-3542-5411
	HOHSUI	3-7-3 Tsukiji, Chuo-ku, Tokyo 104.	03-5565-8901
	SAKATA SEED	3-1-7 Nagata Higashi, Minami-ku, Yokohama 232.	045-715-2111
	MINING		
	MITSUI MINING	2-1-1 Nihonbashi Muro-machi, Chuo-ku, Tokyo 103.	03-3241-1334
	SUMITOMO COAL MINING	1-4-5 Marunouchi, Chiyoda-ku, Tokyo 100.	03-3216-0911
	NITTETSU MINIMG	2-3-2 Marunouchi, Chiyoda-ku, Tokyo 100.	03-3284-0516
	MITSUI MATSUSHIMA	1-1-12 Otemon, Chuo-ku, Fukuoka 810.	092-771-2171
	TEIKOKU OIL	1-31-10 Hatagaya, Shibuya-ku, Tokyo 151.	03-3466-1237
	ARABIAN OIL	3-2-3 Marunouchi, Chiyoda-ku, Tokyo 100.	03-3214-4319
	KANTO NATURAL GAS DEVELOPMENT	3-1-20 Nihonbashi Muro-machi, Chuo-ku, Tokyo 103.	03-3241-5511
	CONSTRUCTION		
	TAISEI	1-25-1 Nishi Shinjuku, Shinjuku-ku, Tokyo 163-06.	03-3348-1111
	OBAYASHI	4-33 Kitahama Higashi, Chuo-ku, Osaka 540.	06-946-4400
	SHIMIZU	1-2-3 Shibaura, Minato-ku, Tokyo 105-07.	03-5441-1111
	SATO KOGYO	1-11 Sakuragi-cho, Toyama-shi 930.	0764-31-6531
	TOBISHIMA	2 Sanban-cho, Chiyoda-ku, Tokyo 102.	03-3263-3151
	FUJITA	4-6-15 Sendagaya, Shibuya-ku, Tokyo 151.	03-3402-1911
	HASEKO	2-32-1 Shiba, Minato-ku, Tokyo 105.	03-3456-5451
	FUJIKO	2-21-46 Takanawa, Minato-ku, Tokyo 108.	03-3449-1111
	MATSUI CONSTRUCTION	1-17-22 Shinkawa, Chuo-ku, Tokyo 104.	03-3553-1151
	ZENITAKA	2-2-11 Nishi Hon-machi, Nishi-ku, Osaka 550.	06-531-6431
★	KAJIMA	1-2-7 Moto Akasaka, Minato-ku, Tokyo 107.	03-3404-3311
	FUDO CONSTRUCTION	4-2-16 Hirano-machi, Chuo-ku, Osaka 541.	06-201-1121
	DAISUE CONSTRUCTION	6-8-10 Fukushima, Fukushima-ku, Osaka 553.	06-456-3737
★	TEKKEN	2-5-3 Misaki-cho, Chiyoda-ku, Tokyo 101.	03-3262-3411
	ANDO	3-12-8 Shibaura, Minato-ku, Tokyo 108.	03-3457-0111
	KATSUMURA CONSTRUCTION	1-2-13 Negishi, Taito-ku, Tokyo 110.	03-3876-0111
	NISSAN CONSTRUCTION	1-2-6 Minami Aoyama, Minato-ku, Tokyo 107.	03-3402-8161
	TAIHEI KOGYO	2-6-2 Otemachi, Chiyoda-ku, Tokyo 100.	03-3270-8811
★	NISHIMATSU CONSTRUCTION	1-20-10 Toranomon, Minato-ku, Tokyo 105.	03-3502-0211
	MITSUI CONSTRUCTION	3-10-1 Iwamoto-cho, Chiyoda-ku, Tokyo 101.	03-5821-7001
	DAIHO CONSTRUCTION	1-24-4 Shinkawa, Chuo-ku, Tokyo 104.	03-3553-4311
	SUMITOMO CONSTRUCTION	13-4 Araki-cho, Shinjuku-ku, Tokyo 160.	03-3353-5111
	MAEDA	2-10-26 Fujimi, Chiyoda-ku, Tokyo 102.	03-3265-5551
	SATA CONSTRUCTION	1-1-7 Motosoja-machi, Maebashi-shi 371.	0272-51-1551
	NAKANO	4-2-28 Kudan Kita, Chiyoda-ku, Tokyo 102.	03-3265-4661
	OKUMURA	2-2-2 Matsuzaki-cho, Abeno-ku, Osaka 545.	06-621-1101
	ODAKYU CONSTRUCTION	4-32-22 Nishi Shinjuku, Shinjuku-ku, Tokyo 160.	03-3376-3101
	TOTETSU CONSTRUCTION	2-7 Ichigaya Sadohara-cho, Shinjuku-ku, Tokyo 162.	03-3268-4211
	DAI NIPPON CONSTRUCTION	1-6-8 Usa Minami, Gifu-shi 500.	0582-76-1111
	HAZAMA	2-5-8 Kita Aoyama, Minato-ku, Tokyo 107.	03-3405-1111
	MAGARA CONSTRUCTION	1-13-43 Hikoso-machi, Kanazawa-shi 920.	0762-31-1266
	TADA	2-8-6 Ojima, Koto-ku, Tokyo 136.	03-3683-3111
	MORIMOTO	4-11 Yuhigaoka-cho, Tennoji-ku, Osaka 543.	06-779-1451
	ICHIKEN	2-1-30 Hamabe-dori, Chuo-ku, Kobe 651.	078-252-2111
	TOKAI KOGYO	1-1-6 Yaesu, Chuo-ku, Tokyo 103.	03-5200-5141

ASANUMA	12-6 Higashi Kozu-cho, Tennoji-ku, Osaka 543.	06-768-5222
ARAI-GUMI	9-18 Ikeda-cho, Nishinomiya-shi, Hyogo 662.	0798-26-3111
TOKYU CONSTRUCTION	1-16-14 Shibuya, Shibuya-ku, Tokyo 150.	03-5466-5111
MATSUMURA-GUMI	2-1-33 Tenma, Kita-ku, Osaka 530.	06-353-1131
TODA	1-7-1 Kyobashi, Chuo-ku, Tokyo 104.	03-3562-6111
KUMAGAI-GUMI	2-6-8 Chuo, Fukui-shi 910.	0776-21-2700
ASAKAWAGUMI	3-69 Komatsubara-dori, Wakayama-shi 640.	0734-23-7161
KOMATSU CONSTRUCTION	3-5-4 Shiba Koen, Minato-ku, Tokyo 105.	03-3434-5131
KITANO CONSTRUCTION	524 Agata-machi, Nagano-shi 380.	0262-33-5111
UEKIGUMI	2-8 Shinbashi, Kashiwazaki-shi, Niigata 945.	0257-23-2200
YAHAGI CONSTRUCTION	3-19-7 Aoi, Higashi-ku, Nagoya 461.	052-935-2351
NICHIEI CONSTRUCTION	8-23-1 Nishi Kamata, Ota-ku, Tokyo 144.	03-3734-6211
DAITO TRUST CONSTRUCTION	4-7-35 Kita Shinagawa, Shinagawa-ku, Tokyo 140.	03-3473-9111
NIPPON HODO	1-19-11 Kyobashi, Chuo-ku, Tokyo 104.	03-3563-6751
TOA DORO KOGYO	7-3-7 Roppongi, Minato-ku, Tokyo 106.	03-3405-1811
MAEDA ROAD CONSTRUCTION	3-14-12 Kami Osaki, Shinagawa-ku, Tokyo 141.	03-3447-0781
NIPPON ROAD	1-6-5 Shinbashi, Minato-ku, Tokyo 105.	03-3571-4891
TOA	5 Yonban-cho, Chiyoda-ku, Tokyo 102.	03-3262-5102
AOKI	1-4-15 Oyodo Minami, Kita-ku, Osaka 531.	06-458-5851
J D C	4-9-9 Akasaka, Minato-ku, Tokyo 107.	03-3403-3311
WAKACHIKU CONSTRUCTION	2-23-18 Shimo Meguro, Meguro-ku, Tokyo 153.	03-3492-0271
SAEKI KENSETSU KOGYO	2-4-6 Bingo-machi, Chuo-ku, Osaka 541.	06-203-0161
TOYO CONSTRUCTION	3-7-1 Kanda Nishiki-cho, Chiyoda-ku, Tokyo 101.	03-3296-4611
DAITO KOGYO	1-38-6 Kameido, Koto-ku, Tokyo 136.	03-3685-2111
PENTA OCEAN CONSTRUCTION	2-2-8 Koraku, Bunkyo-ku, Tokyo 112.	03-3816-7111
TAISEI ROTEC	3-13-1 Kyobashi, Chuo-ku, Tokyo 104.	03-3567-9431
OBAYASHI ROAD CONSTRUCTION	1-2-1 Kanda Nishiki-cho, Chiyoda-ku, Tokyo 101.	03-3293-3031
SEIKITOKYU KOGYO	2-9-3 Shiba Koen, Minato-ku, Tokyo 105.	03-3434-3345
FUKUDA	3-10 Ichibanboridori-machi, Niigata-shi 951.	025-266-9111
SUMITOMO FORESTRY	14-1 Nihonbashi Koami-cho, Chuo-ku, Tokyo 103.	03-3669-1241
NISSEI BUILD KOGYO	3-16-10 Kanaiwa Kita, Kanazawa-shi 920-03.	0762-68-1111
S × L ('S-BY-L')	2-12-1 Sonezaki, Kita-ku, Osaka 530.	06-315-1131
SHOKUSAN JUTAKU SOGO	2-11-17 Yoyogi, Shibuya-ku, Tokyo 151.	03-3370-1214
TOMOEGUMI IRON WORKS	6-2-10 Ginza, Chuo-ku, Tokyo 104.	03-3571-8681
TAISEI PREFAB CONSTRUCTION	7-23-1 Nishi Gotanda, Shinagawa-ku, Tokyo 141.	03-3493-4941
MISAWA HOMES	2-4-5 Takaido Higashi, Suginami-ku, Tokyo 168.	03-3331-1111
NATIONAL HOUSE INDUSTRIAL	1-1-12 Shinsenri Nishi-machi, Toyonaka-shi, Osaka 565.	06-834-5111
DAIWA HOUSE INDUSTRY	1-5-16 Awaza, Nishi-ku, Osaka 550.	06-538-5111
RAITO KOGYO	4-2-35 Kudan Kita, Chiyoda-ku, Tokyo 102.	03-3265-2551
SEKISUI HOUSE	6-2-27 Nakanoshima, Kita-ku, Osaka 530.	06-446-3111
NITTOC CONSTRUCTION	8-14-14 Ginza, Chuo-ku, Tokyo 104.	03-3542-9126

ELECTRICAL AND OTHER ENGINEERING

YURTEC	4-1-1 Tsutsujigaoka, Miyagino-ku, Sendai 980.	022-296-2111
YONDENKO	1-11-22 Matsushima-cho, Takamatsu-shi 760.	0878-36-1111
CHUDENKO	1-15 Kami Tenma-cho, Nishi-ku, Hiroshima 733.	082-291-7411
KANDENKO	4-8-33 Shibaura, Minato-ku, Tokyo 108.	03-5476-2111
DAIMEI TELECOM ENGINEERING	6-16-5 Minami Oi, Shinagawa-ku, Tokyo 140.	03-3765-1161
KINDEN	2-3-41 Honjo Higashi, Kita-ku, Osaka 531.	03-375-6000
TOKYO DENKI KOMUSHO	6-9-7 Shinbashi, Minato-ku, Tokyo 105.	03-3434-0151
TOENEC	1-20-31 Sakae, Naka-ku, Nagoya 460.	052-221-1111
NIPPON COMSYS	3-23-14 Takanawa, Minato-ku, Tokyo 108.	03-3448-7031
NIPPON DENSETSU KOGYO	1-2-23 Ikenohata, Taito-ku, Tokyo 110.	03-3822-8811
KYOWA EXEO	4-13-13 Akasaka, Minato-ku, Tokyo 107.	03-5570-8001
NIPPON KOEI	5-4 Koji-machi, Chiyoda-ku, Tokyo 102.	03-3238-8030
TODENTSU	2-3-9 Higashi Shinbashi, Minato-ku, Tokyo 105.	03-3434-5111
NIPPON DENWA SHISETSU	2-15-18 Chiyoda, Naka-ku, Nagoya 460.	052-263-5011
KYUDENKO	1-23-35 Nanokawa, Minami-ku, Fukuoka 815.	092-523-1231
SANKI ENGINEERING	1-4-1 Yurakucho, Chiyoda-ku, Tokyo 100.	03-3502-6111
★ J G C	2-2-1 Otemachi, Chiyoda-ku, Tokyo 100.	03-3279-5441

CHUGAI RO	2-4-7 Kyomachibori, Nishi-ku, Osaka 550.	06-441-8931
TAIHEI DENGYO	2-4 Kanda Jimbo-cho, Chiyoda-ku, Tokyo 101.	03-3261-5241
TAKASAGO THERMAL ENGINEERING	4-2-8 Kanda Surugadai, Chiyoda-ku, Tokyo 101.	03-3255-8212
HITACHI PLANT ENG. & CONSTRUCT.	1-1-14 Uchi Kanda, Chiyoda-ku, Tokyo 101.	03-3292-8111
SANKO METAL INDUSTRIAL	2-9-2 Kyobashi, Chiyoda-ku, Tokyo 104.	03-3567-3551
ASAHI KOGYOSHA	1-25-7 Hamamatsu-cho, Minato-ku, Tokyo 105.	03-3432-5711
MEISEI INDUSTRIAL	1-8-5 Kyomachibori, Nishi-ku, Osaka 550.	06-447-0271
TAIKISHA	2-6-1 Nishi Shinjuku, Shinjuku-ku, Tokyo 163.	03-3344-1851
DAI-DAN	1-9-25 Edobori, Nishi-ku, Osaka 550.	06-441-8231
TOSHIBA ENG. & CONSTRUCTION	3-7-1 Nishi Shinbashi, Minato-ku, Tokyo 105.	03-3438-8009
SHO-BOND	3-18 Kanda Nishiki-cho, Chiyoda-ku, Tokyo 101.	03-3292-8101
FOODS AND BEVERAGES		
NIPPON FLOUR MILLS	5-27-5 Sendagaya, Shibuya-ku, Tokyo 151.	03-3350-2311
NISSHIN FLOUR MILLING	19-12 Nihonbashi Koami-cho, Chuo-ku, Tokyo 103.	03-3660-3111
NITTO FLOUR MILLING	4-11-2 Hatchobori, Chuo-ku, Tokyo 104.	03-3553-8781
SHOWA SANGYO	2-2-1 Uchi Kanda, Chiyoda-ku, Tokyo 101.	03-3257-2011
NIHON NOSAN KOGYO	1-11-20 Kita Saiwai, Nishi-ku, Yokohama 220.	045-323-3200
KYODO SHIRYO	2-5-12 Takashima, Nishi-ku, Yokohama 220.	045-461-5711
NIPPON FORMULA FEED MFG.	3-32-13 Tsuruya-cho, Kanagawa-ku, Yokohama 221.	045-316-7200
TAITO	7-5 Nihonbashi Odenma-cho, Chuo-ku, Tokyo 103.	03-3663-3851
TOYO SUGAR REFINING	18-20 Nihonbashi Koami-cho, Chuo-ku, Tokyo 103.	03-3668-7871
NIPPON BEET SUGAR MFG.	2-3-13 Kyobashi, Chuo-ku, Tokyo 104.	03-3273-4383
MITSUI SUGAR	3-8-3 Nihonbashi Honcho, Chuo-ku, Tokyo 103.	03-3663-3111
★ MORINAGA AND CO.	5-33-1 Shiba, Minato-ku, Tokyo 108.	03-3456-0112
MEIJI SEIKA	2-4-16 Kyobashi, Chuo-ku, Tokyo 104.	03-3272-6511
NAKAMURAYA	3-26-13 Shinjuku, Shinjuku-ku, Tokyo 160.	03-3352-6161
EZAKI GLICO	4-6-5 Utajima, Nishi Yodogawa-ku, Osaka 555.	06-477-8351
MEITO SANGYO	2-41 Sasatsuka-cho, Nishi-ku, Nagoya 451.	052-521-7111
FUJIYA	7-2-17 Ginza, Chuo-ku, Tokyo 104.	03-3572-4150
YAMAZAKI BAKING	3-2-4 Iwamoto-cho, Chiyoda-ku, Tokyo 101.	03-3864-3111
FIRST BAKING	2-18-2 Higashi Rokugo, Ota-ku, Tokyo 144.	03-3738-0131
MOROZOFF	6-11-19 Mikage Honcho, Higashi Nada-ku, Kobe 658.	078-822-5000
TAKARABUNE	Sasaya-cho, Oike-dori, Nakagyo-ku, Kyoto 604.	075-252-2111
MEIJI MILK PRODUCTS	2-3-6 Kyobashi, Chuo-ku, Tokyo 104.	03-3281-6118
SNOW BRAND MILK PRODUCTS	13 Honshio-cho, Shinjuku-ku, Tokyo 160.	03-3226-2111
MORINAGA MILK INDUSTRY	5-33-1 Shiba, Minato-ku, Tokyo 108.	03-3798-0111
YAKULT HONSHA	1-1-19 Higashi Shinbashi, Minato-ku, Tokyo 105.	03-3574-8960
PRIMA MEAT PACKERS	3-2-5 Kasumigaseki, Chiyoda-ku, Tokyo 100.	03-3593-6710
NIPPON MEAT PACKERS	3-6-14 Minami Hon-machi, Chuo-ku, Osaka 541.	06-282-3031
ITOHAM FOODS	4-27 Takahata-cho, Nishinomiya-shi, Hyogo 663.	0798-66-1231
HAYASHIKANE SANGYO	2-4-8 Yamato-machi, Shimonoseki-shi, Yamaguchi 750.	0832-66-0210
MARUDAI FOOD	21-3 Midori-cho, Takatsuki-shi, Osaka 569.	0726-75-1111
SAPPORO BREWERIES	7-10-1 Ginza, Chuo-ku, Tokyo 104.	03-3572-6111
ASAHI BREWERIES	1-23-1 Azumabashi, Sumida-ku,Tokyo 130.	03-5608-5112
KIRIN BREWERY	6-26-1 Jingu-mae, Shibuya-ku, Tokyo 150.	03-3499-6111
TAKARA SHUZO	Shijo-dori, Shimogyo-ku, Kyoto 600.	075-241-5110
GODO SHUSEI	6-2-10 Ginza, Chuo-ku, Tokyo 104.	03-3575-2711
MERCIAN	1-5-8 Kyobashi, Chuo-ku, Tokyo 104.	03-3231-3922
YOMEISHU SEIZO	16-25 Nanpeidai-cho, Shibuya-ku, Tokyo 150.	03-3462-8111
CHUKYO COCA-COLA BOTTLING	4-1-47 Sunadabashi, Higashi-ku, Nagoya 461.	052-723-3131
MIKUNI COCA-COLA BOTTLING	180 Kano, Okegawa-shi, Saitama 363.	048-774-1111
★ CALPIS FOOD INDUSTRY	2-20-3 Ebisu Nishi, Shibuya-ku, Tokyo 150.	03-3463-2111
POKKA	35-16 Daikan-cho, Higashi-ku, Nagoya 461.	052-932-1471
HONEN	1-2-3 Otemachi, Chiyoda-ku, Tokyo 100.	03-3211-6511
NISSHIN OIL MILLS	1-23-1 Shinkawa, Chuo-ku, Tokyo 104.	03-3206-5025
YOSHIHARA OIL MILL	3-6-32 Nakanoshima, Kita-ku, Osaka 530.	06-441-8851
FUJI OIL	2-1-5 Nishi Shinsaibashi, Chuo-ku, Osaka 542.	06-213-8151
KIKKOMAN	339 Noda, Noda-shi, Chiba 278.	0471-23-5111
AJINOMOTO	1-15-1 Kyobashi, Chuo-ku, Tokyo 104.	03-5250-8111

Q. P.	1-4-13 Shibuya, Shibuya-ku,Tokyo 150.	03-3486-3331
HOUSE FOOD INDUSTRIAL	1-5-7 Mikuriya Sakae-machi, Higashi Osaka 577.	06-788-1231
KAGOME	3-14-15 Nishiki, Naka-ku, Nagoya 460.	052-951-3571
NICHIREI	6-19-20 Tsukiji, Chuo-ku, Tokyo 104.	03-3248-2101
★ KATOKICHI	Ko-294-1 Kannonji-cho, Kannonji-shi, Kagawa 768.	0875-25-4781
YOKOHAMA REITO	1-1-7 Moriya-cho, Kanagawa-ku, Yokohama 221.	045-461-6611
TOYO SUISAN	2-13-40 Konan, Minato-ku, Tokyo 108.	03-3458-5111
NISSIN FOOD PRODUCTS	4-1-1 Nishi Nakajima, Yodogawa-ku, Osaka 532.	06-305-7711
NAGATANIEN-HONPO	2-36-1 Nishi Shinbashi, Minato-ku, Tokyo 105.	03-3432-2511

TEXTILES

★ KATAKURA INDUSTRIES	3-1-2 Kyobashi, Chuo-ku, Tokyo 104.	03-3281-3161
GUNZE	1-8-17 Umeda, Kita-ku, Osaka 530.	06-348-1313
SHINYEI	77-1 Kyo-machi, Chuo-ku, Kobe 651-01.	078-392-6901
KOBE KIITO	7-1-18 Onoedori, Chuo-ku, Kobe 651.	078-251-4901
KAWASHIMA TEXTILE MANUFACTS.	Ichijyo Agaru, Higashi Horikawa-dori 602.	075-414-9700
TOYOBO	2-2-8 Dojimahama, Kita-ku, Osaka 530.	06-348-3111
KANEBO	1-5-90 Tomobuchi-cho, Miyakojima-ku, Osaka 534.	06-922-8151
UNITIKA	4-1-3 Kita Kyutaro-machi, Chuo-ku, Osaka 541.	06-281-5695
FUJI SPINNING	1-18-12 Nihonbashi Nigo-cho, Chuo-ku, Tokyo 103.	03-3665-7777
NISSHINBO INDUSTRIES	3-10 Nihonbashi Yokoyama-cho, Chuo-ku, Tokyo 103.	03-3665-8833
KURABO INDUSTRIES	2-4-31 Kita Kyutaro-machi, Chuo-ku, Osaka 541.	06-266-5111
DAIWABO	1-3-7 Tosabori, Nishi-ku, Osaka 550.	06-446-5111
SHIKIBO	3-2-6 Bingo-machi, Chuo-ku, Osaka 541.	06-268-5493
NITTO BOSEKI	1-2-1 Nihonbashi Hama-cho, Chuo-ku, Tokyo 103.	03-3865-6689
TESAC	2-2-8 Nakanoshima, Kita-ku, Osaka 530.	06-227-1821
TOYODA BOSHOKU	1-1 Toyoda-cho, Kariya-shi, Aichi 448.	0566-23-6611
KOWA SPINNING	3-6-29 Nishiki, Naka-ku, Nagoya 460.	052-963-3417
JAPAN WOOL TEXTILE	3-3-10 Kawara-machi, Chuo-ku, Osaka 541.	06-205-6600
DAITO WOOLEN SPINNING & WEAVING	2-3-3 Nihonbashi Horidome-cho, Chuo-ku, Tokyo 103.	03-3665-7816
TOA WOOL SPINNING & WEAVING	3-1-4 Kawara-machi, Chuo-ku, Osaka 541.	06-203-3001
DAIDOH	3-1-16 Soto Kanda, Chiyoda-ku, Tokyo 101.	03-3257-5050
MIYUKI KEORI	1916 Nishi Shiga-machi, Nishi-ku, Nagoya 451.	052-531-1551
TEIKOKU SEN-I	2-5-13 Nihonbashi, Chuo-ku, Tokyo 103.	03-3281-3031
TEIJIN	1-6-7 Minami Hon-machi, Chuo-ku, Osaka 541.	06-268-2132
TORAY INDUSTRIES	2-2-1 Nihonbashi Muro-machi, Chuo-ku, Tokyo 103.	03-3245-5111
TOHO RAYON	3-3-9 Nihonbashi, Chuo-ku, Tokyo 103.	03-3278-7615
MITSUBISHI RAYON	2-3-19 Kyobashi, Chuo-ku, Tokyo 104.	03-3245-8662
KURARAY	1-12-39 Umeda, Kita-ku, Osaka 530.	06-348-2111
ASAHI CHEMICAL INDUSTRY	1-1-2 Yurakucho, Chiyoda-ku, Tokyo 100.	03-3507-2730
SAKAI OVEX	2-15-1 Hanadonaka, Fukui-shi 910.	0776-36-5800
SUMINOE TEXTILE	3-11-20 Minami Senba, Chuo-ku, Osaka 542.	06-251-6825
NIPPON FELT	2-2-2 Marunouchi, Chiyoda-ku, Tokyo 100.	03-3213-5611
ICHIKAWA WOOLEN TEXTILE	2-14-15 Hongo, Bunkyo-ku, Tokyo 113.	03-3816-1111
JAPAN VILENE	2-14-5 Soto Kanda, Chiyoda-ku, Tokyo 101.	03-3258-3333
NIPPON LACE	689-1 Takanna-cho, Nakagyo-ku, Kyoto 604.	075-255-1201
NITTO SEIMO	2-20-15-701 Shinbashi, Minato-ku, Tokyo 105.	03-3572-5376
ASHIMORI INDUSTRY	3-10-18 Kita Horie, Nishi-ku, Osaka 550.	06-533-9250
ATSUGI NYLON INDUSTRIAL	3905 Oya, Ebina-shi, Kanagawa 243-04.	0462-31-1111
★ DYNIC	3-1-1 Higashi Ikebukuro, Toshima-ku, Tokyo 170.	03-3987-3331
KYOWA LEATHER CLOTH	1876 Higashi-machi, Hamamatsu-shi, Shizuoka 430.	053-425-2121
★ SEIREN	1-10-1 Keya, Fukui-shi 910.	0776-35-2111
★ TOKAI SENKO	3-28-12 Mei-eki, Nakamura-ku, Nagoya 450.	052-581-8141
KOMATSU SEIREN	Nu-167 Hama-machi, Nomi-gun, Ishikawa 929-01.	0761-55-1111
FUKUSUKE	2-1-1 Minami Yasui-cho, Sakai-shi, Osaka 590.	0722-23-2111
WACOAL	29 Nakajima-cho, Kossho-in, Minami-ku, Kyoto 601.	075-682-5111

PAPER AND PULP

SANYO-KOKUSAKU PULP	1-4-5 Marunouchi, Chiyoda-ku, Tokyo 100.	03-3211-3411
TOKAI PULP	4379 Shimada-shi, Shizuoka 427.	0547-36-5151

OJI PAPER	4-7-5 Ginza, Chuo-ku, Tokyo 104.	03-3563-1111
HONSHU PAPER	5-12-8 Ginza, Chuo-ku, Tokyo 104.	03-3543-1862
JUJO PAPER	1-12-1 Yurakucho, Chiyoda-ku, Tokyo 100.	03-3211-7311
MITSUBISHI PAPER MILLS	3-4-2 Marunouchi, Chiyoda-ku, Tokyo 100.	03-3213-3751
HOKUETSU PAPER MILLS	3-2-2 Nihonbashi Hongoku-cho, Chuo-ku, Tokyo 103.	03-3245-4500
KANZAKI PAPER MFG.	4-9-8 Ginza, Chuo-ku, Tokyo 104.	03-3248-3111
TAKASAKI PAPER MFG.	2-7 Kanda Awaji-cho, Chiyoda-ku, Tokyo 101.	03-3257-0931
JAPAN PAPER INDUSTRY	1-3 Kanda Suda-cho, Chiyoda-ku, Tokyo 101.	03-3251-3101
NIPPON KAKOH SEISHI	2-5-27 Akasaka, Minato-ku, Tokyo 107.	03-3584-2671
DAISHOWA PAPER MFG.	4-1-1 Imai, Fuji-shi, Shizuoka 417.	0545-30-3000
CHUETSU PULP & PAPER	2-10-6 Ginza, Chuo-ku, Tokyo 104.	03-3544-1524
TOMOEGAWA PAPER	1-5-15 Kyobashi, Chuo-ku, Tokyo 104.	03-3272-4111
DAIO PAPER	2-7-2 Yaesu, Chuo-ku, Tokyo 104.	03-3271-1961
TOKUSHU PAPER MFG.	501 Honjuku, Nagaizumi-cho, Sunto-gun, Shizuoka 411.	0559-88-1121
KISHU PAPER	1-4-6 Dojimahama, Kita-ku, Osaka 530.	06-345-6471
SETTSU	1-4-1 Kuise Minami Shin-machi, Amagasaki, Hyogo 660.	06-488-2561
CHUO PAPERBOARD	2-3 Ogawa-cho, Nakatsugawa-shi, Gifu 508.	0573-66-1511
RENGO	3-5-12 Hirano-machi, Chuo-ku, Osaka 541.	06-202-2371
TOMOKU	2-2-2 Marunouchi, Chiyoda-ku, Tokyo 100.	03-3213-6811
CHEMICALS		
MITSUI TOATSU CHEMICALS	3-2-5 Kasumigaseki, Chiyoda-ku, Tokyo 100.	03-3592-4111
NITTO CHEMICAL INDUSTRY	1-5-1 Marunouchi, Chiyoda-ku, Tokyo 100.	03-3271-0251
CO-OP CHEMICAL	23-3 Ichiban-cho, Chiyoda-ku, Tokyo 102.	03-3230-0011
SHOWA DENKO	1-13-9 Shiba Daimon, Minato-ku, Tokyo 105.	03-5470-3111
SUMITOMO CHEMICAL	4-5-33 Kitahama, Chuo-ku, Osaka 541.	06-220-3891
NIPPON KASEI CHEMICAL	34 Takayama, Onahama, Iwaki-shi, Fukushima 971.	0246-54-3111
SUMITOMO SEIKA CHEMICALS	4-7-28 Kitahama, Chuo-ku, Osaka 541.	06-220-8508
MITSUBISHI KASEI	2-5-2 Marunouchi, Chiyoda-ku, Tokyo 100.	03-3283-6254
NISSAN CHEMICAL INDUSTRIES	3-7-1 Kanda Nishiki-cho, Chiyoda-ku, Tokyo 101.	03-3296-8111
RASA INDUSTRIES	1-1-1 Kyobashi, Chuo-ku, Tokyo 104.	03-3278-3801
KUREHA CHEMICAL INDUSTRY	1-9-11 Nihonbashi Horidome-cho, Chuo-ku, Tokyo 103.	03-3249-4666
TAYCA	3-6-1 Bakuro-cho, Chuo-ku, Osaka 541.	06-243-5811
ISHIHARA SANGYO	1-3-22 Edobori, Nishi-ku, Osaka 550.	06-444-1451
NIPPON SODA	2-2-1 Otemachi, Chiyoda-ku, Tokyo 100.	03-3245-6054
TOSOH	1-7-7 Akasaka, Minato-ku, Tokyo 107.	03-3585-3311
★ TOKUYAMA SODA	3-3-1 Shibuya, Shibuya-ku, Tokyo 150.	03-3499-8710
CENTRAL GLASS	3-7-1 Kanda Nishiki-cho, Chiyoda-ku, Tokyo 101.	03-3259-7111
TOAGOSEI CHEMICAL INDUSTRY	1-14-1 Nishi Shinbashi, Minato-ku, Tokyo 105.	03-3597-7215
DAISO	1-10-8 Edobori, Nishi-ku, Osaka 550.	06-443-5501
KATO DENKA KOGYO	1-2-1 Marunouchi, Chiyoda-ku, Tokyo 100.	03-3216-4561
DENKI KAGAKU KOGYO	1-4-1 Yurakucho, Chiyoda-ku, Tokyo 100.	03-3507-5060
IBIDEN	2-1 Kanda-cho, Ogaki-shi, Gifu 503.	0584-81-3111
SHIN-ETSU CHEMICAL	2-6-1 Otemachi, Chiyoda-ku, Tokyo 100.	03-3246-5011
NIPPON CARBIDE INDUSTRIES	3-3-1 Marunouchi, Chiyoda-ku, Tokyo 100.	03-3240-8600
SAKAI CHEMICAL INDUSTRY	1-1-23 Ebisuno-cho Nishi, Sakai-shi, Osaka 590.	0722-23-4111
TEISAN	1-15-12 Toranomon, Minato-ku, Tokyo 105.	03-3502-0551
DAIDO SANSO	1-20-16 Higashi Shinsaibashi, Chuo-ku, Osaka 542.	06-252-1757
HOXAN	1-2 Kitasanjo Nishi, Chuo-ku, Sapporo 060.	011-212-2821
OSAKA SANSO KOGYO	4-1-14 Miyahara, Yodogawa-ku, Osaka 532.	06-396-3181
TOYO SANSO	1-9-13 Koyama, Shinagawa-ku, Tokyo 142.	03-3782-1152
NIPPON SANSO	1-16-7 Nishi Shinbashi, Minato-ku, Tokyo 105.	03-3581-8200
NIPPON CHEMICAL INDUSTRIAL	9-15-1 Kameido, Koto-ku, Tokyo 136.	03-3636-8111
NIHON PARKERIZING	1-15-1 Nihonbashi, Chuo-ku, Tokyo 103.	03-3278-4333
★ KOATSU GAS KOGYO	1-5 Doyama-cho, Kita-ku, Osaka 530.	06-311-1361
TITAN KOGYO	1978-25 Kogushi, Ube-shi, Yamaguchi 755.	0836-31-4155
SHIKOKU CHEMICALS	147-1 Minato-machi, Marugame-shi, Kagawa 763.	0877-22-4111
TODA KOGYO	7-1 Yokogawa Shin-machi, Nishi-ku, Hiroshima 733.	082-231-2181
TAIYO SANSO	2-4-11 Utsubo Hon-machi, Nishi-ku, Osaka 550.	06-449-7000
TATEHO CHEMICAL INDUSTRIES	974 Kariya Kato, Ako-shi, Hyogo 678-02.	07914-2-5041

HODOGAYA CHEMICAL	1-4-2 Toranomon, Minato-ku, Tokyo 105.	03-3504-8631
NIPPON SHOKUBAI	4-1-1 Koraibashi, Chuo-ku, Osaka 541.	06-223-9111
DAINICHISEIKA COLOUR & CHEM. MFG	1-7-6 Nihonbashi Bakuro-cho, Chuo-ku, Tokyo 103.	03-3662-7111
KANEKA	3-2-4 Nakanoshima, Kita-ku, Osaka 530.	06-226-5050
KYOWA HAKKO KOGYO	1-6-1 Otemachi, Chiyoda-ku, Tokyo 100.	03-3282-0007
MITSUBISHI GAS CHEMICAL	2-5-2 Marunouchi, Chiyoda-ku, Tokyo 100.	03-3283-5000
MITSUI PETROCHEMICAL IND.	3-2-5 Kasumigaseki, Chiyoda-ku, Tokyo 100.	03-3580-2012
MITSUBISHI PETROCHEMICAL	2-5-2 Marunouchi, Chiyoda-ku, Tokyo 100.	03-3283-5700
JAPAN SYNTHETIC RUBBER	2-11-24 Tsukiji, Chuo-ku, Tokyo 104.	03-5565-6519
TOKYO OHKA KOGYO	1-403 Kosugi-cho, Nakahara-ku, Kawasaki 211.	044-722-7181
NIPPON SYNTHETIC CHEMICAL IND.	9-6 Nozaki-cho, Kita-ku, Osaka 530.	06-314-3110
DAICEL CHEMICAL INDUSTRIES	1 Teppo-cho, Sakai-shi, Osaka 590.	0722-27-3111
SUMITOMO BAKELITE	1-2-2 Uchi Saiwai-cho, Chiyoda-ku, Tokyo 100.	03-3506-7111
SEKISUI CHEMICAL	2-4-4 Nishi Tenma, Kita-ku, Osaka 530.	06-365-4122
NIPPON ZEON	2-6-1 Marunouchi, Chiyoda-ku, Tokyo 100.	03-3216-1772
AICA KOGYO	2-20-19 Marunouchi, Naka-ku, Nagoya 460.	052-202-6934
UBE INDUSTRIES	1-12-32 Nishi Hon-machi, Ube-shi, Yamaguchi 755.	0836-31-1122
TOYO CHEMICAL	2-13-1 Dai, Kamakura-shi, Kanagawa 247.	0467-45-1111
SEKISUI JUSHI	2-4-4 Nishi Tenma, Kita-ku, Osaka 530.	06-365-3204
MITSUBISHI PLASTICS INDUSTRIES	2-5-2 Marunouchi, Chiyoda-ku, Tokyo 100.	03-3283-4006
SHOWA HIGHPOLYMER	3-20 Kanda Nishiki-cho, Chiyoda-ku, Tokyo 101.	03-3293-8844
TAKIRON	2-3-13 Azuchi-machi, Chuo-ku, Osaka 541.	06-267-2800
ASAHI ORGANIC CHEMICALS IND.	2-5955 Nakanose-machi, Nobeoka-shi, Miyazaki 882.	0982-33-3311
HITACHI CHEMICAL	2-1-1 Nishi Shinjuku, Shinjuku-ku, Tokyo 163-04.	03-3346-3111
NICHIBAN	2-2-4 Kudan Minami, Chiyoda-ku, Tokyo 102.	03-3263-0151
RIKEN VINYL INDUSTRY	3-11-5 Nihonbashi Honcho, Chuo-ku, Tokyo 103.	03-3663-7991
OKURA INDUSTRIAL	1515 Nakazu-cho, Marugame-shi, Kagawa 763.	0877-23-1111
TSUTSUNAKA PLASTIC INDUSTRY	3-5-11 Dosho-machi, Chuo-ku, Osaka 541.	06-229-5000
SEKISUI PLASTICS	2-4-4 Nishi Tenma, Kita-ku, Osaka 530.	06-365-3014
GUN-EI CHEMICAL INDUSTRY	700 Shukuorui-machi, Takasaki-shi, Gunma 370.	0273-53-1818
JAPAN CARLIT	1-2-1 Marunouchi, Chiyoda-ku, Tokyo 100.	03-3287-3000
NIPPON KAYAKU	1-11-2 Fujimi, Chiyoda-ku, Tokyo 102.	03-3237-5111
NIPPON STEEL CHEMICAL	5-13-16 Ginza, Chuo-ku, Tokyo 104.	03-3248-5053
ASAHI DENKA KOGYO	2-3-14 Nihonbashi Muro-machi, Chuo-ku, Tokyo 103.	03-5255-9002
★ NIPPON OIL & FATS	1-10-1 Yurakucho, Chiyoda-ku, Tokyo 100.	03-3283-7070
MIYOSHI OIL & FAT	4-66-1 Horikiri, Katsushika-ku, Tokyo 124.	03-3603-1111
NEW JAPAN CHEMICAL	2-1-8 Bingo-machi, Chuo-ku, Osaka 541.	06-202-0624
HARIMA CHEMICALS	3-6-7 Dosho-machi, Chuo-ku, Osaka 541.	06-201-2461
KAO	1-14-10 Nihonbashi Kayaba-cho, Chuo-ku, Tokyo 103.	03-3660-7111
DAI-ICHI KOGYO SEIYAKU	Karasuma Nishiiru, Shiokoji-dori, Shimogyo-ku, Kyoto 600.	075-343-1181

PHARMACEUTICALS

SANYO CHEMICAL INDUSTRIES	11-1 Ikkyo Nomoto-cho, Higashiyama-ku, Kyoto 605.	075-541-4311
SANKYO	2-7-12 Ginza, Chuo-ku, Tokyo 104.	03-3562-0411
TAKEDA CHEMICAL INDUSTRIES	4-1-1 Dosho-machi, Chuo-ku, Osaka 541.	06-204-2111
YAMANOUCHI PHARMACEUTICAL	2-3-11 Nihonbashi Honcho, Chuo-ku, Tokyo 103.	03-3244-3000
DAIICHI PHARMACEUTICAL	3-14-10 Nihonbashi, Chuo-ku, Tokyo 103.	03-3272-0611
DAINIPPON PFARMACEUTICAL	2-6-8 Dosho-machi, Chuo-ku, Osaka 541.	06-203-5321
SHIONOGI	3-1-8 Dosho-machi, Chuo-ku, Osaka 541.	06-202-2161
TANABE SEIYAKU	3-2-10 Dosho-machi, Chuo-ku, Osaka 541.	06-205-5555
YOSHITOMI PHARMACEUTICAL IND.	2-6-9 Hirano-machi, Chuo-ku, Osaka 541.	06-201-1600
FUJISAWA PHARMACEUTICAL	3-4-7 Dosho-machi, Chuo-ku, Osaka 541.	06-202-1141
WAKAMOTO PHARMACEUTICAL	1-5-3 Nihonbashi, Muro-machi, Chuo-ku, Tokyo 103.	03-3279-0371
BANYU PHARMACEUTICAL	2-2-3 Nihonbashi Honcho, Chuo-ku, Tokyo 103.	03-3270-7551
NIPPON SHINYAKU	Hachijo Sagaru, Nishi Oji-dori, Minami-ku, Kyoto 601.	075-321-1111
TOYAMA CHEMICAL	3-2-5 Nishi Shinjuku, Shinjuku-ku, Tokyo 160.	03-3348-6611
CHUGAI PHARMACEUTICAL	2-1-9 Kyobashi, Chuo-ku, Tokyo 104.	03-3281-6611
KAKEN PHARMACEUTICAL	1 Hinode, Urayasu-shi, Chiba 279.	0473-90-6111
GREEN CROSS	1-3-3 Imabashi, Chuo-ku, Osaka 541.	06-227-4625
EISAI	4-6-10 Koishikawa, Bunkyo-ku, Tokyo 112-88.	03-3817-3700

	ROHTO PHARMACEUTICAL	1-8-1 Tatsumi Nishi, Ikuno-ku, Osaka 544.	06-758-1231
	ONO PHARMACEUTICAL	2-1-5 Dosho-machi, Chuo-ku, Osaka 541.	06-222-5551
	NIKKEN CHEMICALS	5-4-14 Tsukiji, Chuo-ku, Tokyo 104.	03-3544-8701
	HISAMITSU PHARMACEUTICAL	408 Tashiro Daikan-cho, Tosu-shi, Saga 841.	0942-83-2101
	TOKYO TANABE	2-2-6 Nihonbashi Honcho, Chuo-ku, Tokyo 103.	03-3241-5151
	MOCHIDA PHARMACEUTICAL	1-7 Yotsuya, Shinjuku-ku, Tokyo 160.	03-3358-7211
	TAISHO PHARMACEUTICAL	3-24-1 Takada, Toshima-ku, Tokyo 171.	03-3985-1111
	SANTEN PHARMACEUTICAL	3-9-19 Shimo Shinjo, Higashi Yodogawa-ku, Osaka 533.	06-321-7000
★	S S PHARMACEUTICAL	2-12-4 Nihonbashi Hama-cho, Chuo-ku, Tokyo 103.	03-3668-4511
	FUSO PHARMACEUTICAL INDUSTRIES	2-3-11 Morinomiya, Joto-ku, Osaka 536.	06-969-1131
	NIPPON CHEMIPHAR	2-2-3 Iwamoto-cho, Chiyoda-ku, Tokyo 100.	03-3863-1211
	TSUMURA & CO.	12-7 Niban-cho, Chiyoda-ku, Tokyo 102.	03-3221-0001
	TERUMO	2-44-1 Hatagaya, Shibuya-ku, Tokyo 151.	03-3374-8111
	FUJIREBIO	2-7-1 Nishi Shinjuku, Shinjuku-ku, Tokyo 163.	03-3348-0691
	INTERNATIONAL REAGENTS	2-1-30 Hamabe-dori, Chuo-ku, Kobe 651.	078-231-4151
	HOKURIKU SEIYAKU	1-3-14 Takekawa-cho, Katsuyama-shi, Fukui 911.	0779-88-5111
	KISSEI PHARMACEUTICAL	19-48 Yoshino, Matsumoto-shi, Nagano 399.	0263-25-9081
	PAINTS		
	DAI NIPPON TORYO	6-1-124 Nishi Kujo, Konohana-ku, Osaka 554.	06-466-6661
	NIPPON PAINT	2-1-2 Oyodo Kita, Kita-ku, Osaka 531.	06-458-1111
	KANSAI PAINT	4-3-6 Fushimi-machi, Chuo-ku, Osaka 541.	06-203-5531
★	TOA PAINT	2-1-29 Dojimahama, Kita-ku, Osaka 530.	06-344-1371
	SHINTO PAINT	6-10-73 Minami Tsukaguchi-cho, Amagasaki, Hyogo 661.	06-426-3355
	CHUGOKU MARINE PAINTS	1-15-2 Yoshijima Higashi, Naka-ku, Hiroshima 730.	082-248-3191
★	NIHON TOKUSHU TORYO	5-16-7 Oji, Kita-ku, Tokyo 114.	03-3913-6131
	DAINIPPON INK & CHEMICALS	3-7-20 Nihonbashi, Chuo-ku, Tokyo 103.	03-3272-4511
	SAKATA INX	1-23-37 Edobori, Nishi-ku, Osaka 550.	06-447-5811
	TOYO INK MFG.	2-3-13 Kyobashi, Chuo-ku, Tokyo 104.	03-3272-5731
	MISCELLANEOUS CHEMICALS		
	FUJI PHOTO FILM	2-26-30 Nishi Azabu, Minato-ku, Tokyo 106.	03-3406-2111
	KONICA	1-26-2 Nishi Shinjuku, Shinjuku-ku, Tokyo 163.	03-3349-5251
	SHISEIDO	7-5-5 Ginza, Chuo-ku, Tokyo 104-10.	03-3572-5111
	LION	1-3-7 Honjo, Sumida-ku, Tokyo 130.	03-3621-6211
	SUNSTAR	3-1 Asahi-machi, Takatsuki-shi, Osaka 569.	0726-82-5541
	TAKASAGO INTERNATIONAL	3-19-22 Takanawa, Minato-ku, Tokyo 108.	03-3442-1211
	S. T. CHEMICAL	1-4-10 Shimo Ochiai, Shinjuku-ku, Tokyo 161.	03-3364-2551
	IHARA CHEMICAL INDUSTRY	1-4-26 Ikenohata, Taito-ku, Tokyo 110.	03-3822-5223
	HOKKO CHEMICAL INDUSTRY	4-4-20 Nihonbashi Hongoku-cho, Chuo-ku, Tokyo 103.	03-3279-5151
	KUMIAI CHEMICAL INDUSTRY	1-4-26 Ikenohata, Taito-ku, Tokyo 110.	03-3822-5036
	NIHON NOHYAKU	1-2-5 Nihonbashi, Chuo-ku, Tokyo 103.	03-3274-3371
	PETROLEUM PRODUCTS		
	NIPPON OIL	1-3-12 Nishi Shinbashi, Minato-ku, Tokyo 105.	03-3502-1111
	SHOWA SHELL SEKIYU	3-2-5 Kasumigaseki, Chiyoda-ku, Tokyo 100.	03-3580-0123
	MITSUBISHI OIL	1-2-4 Toranomon, Minato-ku, Tokyo 105.	03-3595-7663
	TONEN	1-1-1 Hitotsubashi, Chiyoda-ku, Tokyo 100.	03-3286-5115
	KOA OIL	2-6-2 Otemachi, Chiyoda-ku, Tokyo 100.	03-3241-8611
	COSMO OIL	1-1-1 Shibaura, Minato-ku, Tokyo 105.	03-3798-3211
	FUJI KOSAN	2-4-3 Nagata-cho, Chiyoda-ku, Tokyo 100.	03-3580-3571
	NICHIREKI CHEMICAL INDUSTRY	4-3-29 Kudan Kita, Chiyoda-ku, Tokyo 102.	03-3265-1511
	GENERAL SEKIYU	2-8-6 Nishi Shinbashi, Minato-ku, Tokyo 105.	03-3595-8300
	RUBBER		
	YOKOHAMA RUBBER	5-36-11 Shinbashi, Minato-ku, Tokyo 105.	03-3432-7111
	TOYO TIRE & RUBBER	1-17-18 Edobori, Nishi-ku, Osaka 550.	06-441-8801
	BRIDGESTONE	1-10-1 Kyobashi, Chuo-ku, Tokyo 104.	03-3567-0111
	SUMITOMO RUBBER INDUSTRIES	1-1-1 Tsutsui-cho, Chuo-ku, Kobe 651.	078-231-4141
	OKAMOTO INDUSTRIES	3-27-12 Hongo, Bunkyo-ku, Tokyo 113.	03-3817-4111

	ACHILLES	22 Daikyo-cho, Shinjuku-ku, Tokyo 160.	03-3341-5111
	SEKAICHO	1-7-8 Nakatsu, Kita-ku, Osaka 531.	06-374-0071
	MITSUBOSHI BELTING	4-1-21 Hamazoe-dori, Nagata-ku, Kobe 653.	078-671-5071
	BANDO CHEMICAL INDUSTRIES	6-1-12 Goko-dori, Chuo-ku, Kobe 651.	078-232-2923
	KINUGAWA RUBBER INDUSTRIAL	330 Naganuma-cho, Inage-ku, Chiba 263.	043-259-3111
	GLASS		
	ASAHI GLASS	2-1-2 Marunouchi, Chiyoda-ku, Tokyo 100.	03-3218-5555
	NIPPON SHEET GLASS	5-11-3 Shinbashi, Minato-ku, Tokyo 105.	03-3436-8812
	ISHIZUKA GLASS	11-15 Takatsuji-cho, Showa-ku, Nagoya 466-91.	052-871-3311
	YAMAMURA GLASS	2-21 Hamamatsubara-cho, Nishinomiya-shi, Hyogo 662.	0798-32-2300
	SASAKI GLASS	2-2-6 Nihonbashi Bakuro-cho, Chuo-ku, Tokyo 103.	03-3663-1211
	TOSHIBA CERAMICS	1-26-2 Nishi Shinjuku, Shinjuku-ku, Tokyo 163.	03-3348-5825
	NIPPON ELECTRIC GLASS	2-7-1 Seiran, Otsu-shi 520.	0775-37-1700
	CEMENT AND CONCRETE PRODUCTS		
	NIHON CEMENT	1-6-1 Otemachi, Chiyoda-ku, Tokyo 100.	03-3201-1731
	SUMITOMO CEMENT	1 Kanda Mitoshiro-cho, Chiyoda-ku, Tokyo 101.	03-3296-9600
	ONODA CEMENT	6276 Onoda-shi, Yamaguchi 756.	0836-83-3331
	DAIICHI CEMENT	1-1 Asano-cho, Kawasaki-ku, Kawasaki 210.	044-322-5361
	OSAKA CEMENT	7-1-55 Minami Okashima, Taisho-ku, Osaka 551.	06-556-2111
★	CHICHIBU CEMENT	1-4-6 Marunouchi, Chiyoda-ku, Tokyo 100.	03-3281-1361
	MISCELLANEOUS CERAMICS		
	MISAWA RESORT	1-6-1 Nishi Shinjuku, Shinjuku-ku, Tokyo 160.	03-3344-8811
★	NIPPON HUME PIPE	5-33-11 Shinbashi, MInato-ku, Tokyo 105.	03-3433-4111
	DAIDO CONCRETE	2-10-14 Ryogoku, Sumida-ku, Tokyo 130.	03-5600-3311
	NIPPON CONCRETE INDUSTRIES	1-8-3 Shinbashi, Minato-ku, Tokyo 105.	03-3573-0363
	TOKAI CARBON	1-2-3 Kita Aoyama, Minato-ku, Tokyo 107.	03-3746-5100
	NIPPON CARBON	2-6-1 Hatchobori, Chuo-ku, Tokyo 104.	03-3552-6111
	NORITAKE	3-1-36 Noritake Shin-machi, Nishi-ku, Nagoya 451.	052-561-7111
	TOTO	2-1-1 Nakanoshima, Kokura Kita-ku, Kita Kyushu 802.	093-951-2111
	NGK INSULATORS	2-56 Suda-cho, Mizuho-ku, Nagoya 467.	052-872-7230
	NGK SPARK PLUG	14-18 Takatsuji-cho, Mizuho-ku, Nagoya 467.	052-872-5915
	INAX	5-1 Koie Hon-machi, Tokoname-shi, Aichi 479.	0569-35-2700
	DANTO	1-12-8 Edobori, Nishi-ku, Osaka 550.	06-448-6251
	SHINAGAWA REFRACTORIES	2-2-1 Otemachi, Chiyoda-ku, Tokyo 100.	03-3273-4511
	KROSAKI	1-1 Higashi Hamamachi, Yahata Nishi-ku, Kita Kyushu 806.	093-622-7224
	ISOLITE INSULATING PRODUCTS	1-2-6 Dojimahama, Kita-ku, Osaka 530.	06-345-7231
	HARIMA CERAMIC	1-3-1 Arai-cho Shinhama, Takasago-shi, Hyogo 676.	0794-43-1401
	T Y K	1-8-2 Marunouchi, Chiyoda-ku, Tokyo 100.	03-3201-0821
	ASK	2-5-5 Tsurumi Chuo, Tsurumi-ku, Yokohama 230.	045-503-7711
	NICHIAS	1-1-26 Shiba Daimon, Minato-ku, Tokyo 105.	03-3433-7251
	IRON AND STEEL		
	NIPPON STEEL	2-6-3 Otemachi, Chiyoda-ku, Tokyo 100-71.	03-3242-4111
	KAWASAKI STEEL	2-2-3 Uchi Saiwai-cho, Chiyoda-ku, Tokyo 100.	03-3597-3111
	N K K	1-1-2 Marunouchi, Chiyoda-ku, Tokyo 100.	03-3212-7111
	SUMITOMO METAL INDUSTRIES	4-5-33 Kitahama, Chuo-ku, Osaka 541.	06-220-5111
	KOBE STEEL	1-3-18 Wakinohama-cho, Chuo-ku, Kobe 651.	078-261-5111
	NISSHIN STEEL	3-4-1 Marunouchi, Chiyoda-ku, Tokyo 100.	03-3216-5511
	NAKAYAMA STEEL WORKS	1-1-66 Funa-machi, Taisho-ku, Osaka 551.	06-555-3028
	GODO STEEL	2-3-24 Umeda, Kita-ku, Osaka 530.	06-346-1031
	TOKYO STEEL MFG.	2-2-2 Uchi Saiwai-cho, Chiyoda-ku, Tokyo 100.	03-3501-7721
	YAMATO KOGYO	380 Kibi, Otsu-ku, Himeji-shi, Hyogo 671-11.	0792-73-1061
	TOKYO TEKKO	520 Yokokura Shinden, Oyama-shi, Tochigi 323.	0285-27-4411
	TOA STEEL	6-2 Goban-cho, Chiyoda-ku, Tokyo 102.	03-3221-7121
	YODOGAWA STEEL WORKS	4-1-1 Minami Hon-machi, Chuo-ku, Osaka 541.	06-245-1113
	TOYO KOHAN	1-4-3 Kasumigaseki, Chiyoda-ku, Tokyo 100.	03-3502-6611
	DAIDO STEEL SHEET	3-2-1 Kuise Minami Shin-machi, Amagasaki, Hyogo 660.	06-487-1717

NIPPON PIPE MFG.	3-23-1 Sugano, Ichikawa-shi, Chiba 272.	0473-22-3322
CHUBU STEEL PLATE	5-1 Ousu-dori, Nakagawa-ku, Nagoya 454.	052-661-3811
MARUICHI STEEL TUBE	3-9-10 Kita Horie, Nishi-ku, Osaka 550.	06-531-0101
MORY INDUSTRIES	1-10-4 Namba Naka, Naniwa-ku, Osaka 556.	06-648-0431
DAIDO STEEL	1-11-18 Nishiki, Naka-ku, Nagoya 460.	052-201-5111
NIPPON KOSHUHA STEEL	1-7-2 Otemachi, Chiyoda-ku, Tokyo 100.	03-3231-6761
NIPPON STAINLESS STEEL	8-2 Honshio-cho, Shinjuku-ku, Tokyo 160.	03-3358-9456
NIPPON METAL INDUSTRY	2-1-1 Nishi Shinjuku, Shinjuku-ku, Tokyo 163.	03-3345-5451
NIPPON YAKIN KOGYO	1-5-8 Kyobashi, Chuo-ku, Tokyo 104.	03-3272-1511
SANYO SPECIAL STEEL	3007 Nakajima Ichimonji, Shikama-ku, Himeji, Hyogo 672.	0792-35-6111
AICHI STEEL WORKS	1 Wanowari, Arao-machi, Tokai-shi, Aichi 476.	052-604-1111
HITACHI METALS	2-1-2 Marunouchi, Chiyoda-ku, Tokyo 100.	03-3284-4511
NIPPON KINZOKU	3-3-1 Marunouchi, Chiyoda-ku, Tokyo 100.	03-3212-8111
PACIFIC METALS	1-6-1 Otemachi, Chiyoda-ku, Tokyo 100.	03-3201-6681
YAHAGI IRON	18 Showa-cho, Minato-ku, Nagoya 455.	052-611-1511
JAPAN METALS & CHEMICALS	8-4 Nihonbashi Koami-cho, Chuo-ku, Tokyo 103.	03-3667-1331
NIPPON DENKO	2-11-8 Ginza, Chuo-ku, Tokyo 104.	03-3546-9319
KURIMOTO	1-12-19 Kita Horie, Nishi-ku, Osaka 550.	06-538-7731
KOBE CAST IRON WORKS	5-8 Ichiban-cho, Nagata-ku, Kobe 653.	078-576-5081
ASAHI TEC	547-1 Horinouchi, Kikugawa-cho, Ogasa-gun, Shizuoka 439	0537-36-3111
JAPAN STEEL WORKS	1-1-2 Yurakucho, Chiyoda-ku, Tokyo 100.	03-3501-6111
MITSUBISHI STEEL MFG.	2-6-2 Otemachi, Chiyoda-ku, Tokyo 100.	03-3270-2080
KANTO SPECIAL STEEL WORKS	1-3-1 Tsujido Kandai, Fujisawa-shi, Kanagawa 251.	0466-33-7111
NICHIA STEEL WORKS	6-74 Doi-cho, Amagasaki-shi, Hyogo 660.	06-416-1021

NON-FERROUS METALS

NIPPON LIGHT METAL	3-13-12 Mita, Minato-ku, Tokyo 108.	03-3456-9211
★ MITSUI MINING & SMELTING	2-1-1 Nihonbashi Muro-machi, Chuo-ku, Tokyo 103.	03-3246-8000
TOHO ZINC	3-12-2 Nihonbashi, Chuo-ku, Tokyo 103.	03-3272-5611
MITSUBISHI MATERIALS	1-5-1 Otemachi, Chiyoda-ku, Tokyo 100.	03-5252-5200
NIPPON MINING	2-10-1 Toranomon, Minato-ku, Tokyo 105.	03-3505-8111
SUMITOMO METAL MINING	5-11-3 Shinbashi, Minato-ku, Tokyo 105.	03-3436-7704
DOWA MINING	1-8-2 Marunouchi, Chiyoda-ku, Tokyo 100.	03-3201-1062
FURUKAWA	2-6-1 Marunouchi, Chiyoda-ku, Tokyo 100.	03-3212-6561
SHIMURA KAKO	3-1-1 Marunouchi, Chiyoda-ku, Tokyo 100.	03-3216-6431
OSAKA TITANIUM	1 Higashi, Hama-cho, Amagasaki-shi, Hyogo 660.	06-411-1121
SHOWA ALUMINUM	6-224 Kaisan-cho, Sakai-shi, Osaka 590.	0722-33-1181
TOYO ALUMINIUM	3-6-8 Kyutaro-machi, Chuo-ku, Osaka 541.	06-271-3151
SUMITOMO LIGHT METAL INDUSTRIES	5-11-3 Shinbashi, Minato-ku, Tokyo 105.	03-3436-9700
MITSUBISHI SHINDOH	1-6-2 Ginza, Chuo-ku, Tokyo 104.	03-3561-9281

WIRES AND CABLES

FURUKAWA ELECTRIC	2-6-1 Marunouchi, Chiyoda-ku, Tokyo 100.	03-3286-3001
★ SUMITOMO ELECTRIC INDUSTRIES	4-5-33 Kitahama, Chuo-ku, Osaka 541.	06-220-4141
FUJIKURA	1-5-1 Kiba, Koto-ku, Tokyo 135.	03-5606-1111
MITSUBISHI CABLE INDUSTRIES	3-4-1 Marunouchi, Chiyoda-ku, Tokyo 100.	03-3216-1551
SHOWA ELECTRIC WIRE & CABLE	1-1-18 Toranomon, Minato-ku, Tokyo 105.	03-3597-7011
TOTOKU ELECTRIC	1-3-21 Okubo, Shinjuku-ku, Tokyo 169.	03-5273-2121
TATSUTA ELECTRIC WIRE & CABLE	2-3-1 Iwata-cho, Higashi Osaka-shi 578.	06-721-3331
OPTEC DAI-ICHI DENKO	3-1-1 Marunouchi, Chiyoda-ku, Tokyo 100.	03-3212-6928
HITACHI CABLE	2-1-2 Marunouchi, Chiyoda-ku, Tokyo 100.	03-5252-3261
OKI ELECTRIC CABLE	2-12-8 Shimo Odanaka, Nakahara-ku, Kawasaki 211.	044-754-4351

DIECASTINGS

RYOBI	3-15-1 Soto Kanda, Chiyoda-ku, Tokyo 101.	03-3257-1500

METAL PRODUCTS

TOYO SEIKAN	1-3-1 Uchi Saiwai-cho, Chiyoda-ku, Tokyo 100.	03-3508-2113
HOKKAI CAN	2-2-2 Marunouchi, Chiyoda-ku, Tokyo 100.	03-3213-5111
YOKOGAWA BRIDGE	4-4-44 Shibaura, Minato-ku, Tokyo 108.	03-3453-4111

JAPAN BRIDGE	2-1-30 Fukuzaki, Minato-ku, Osaka 552.	06-576-3453
MATSUO BRIDGE	3-4-18 Tsuru-machi, Taisho-ku, Osaka 551.	06-552-1551
MIYAJI IRON WORKS	15-18 Nihonbashi Kodenma-cho, Chuo-ku, Tokyo 103.	03-3639-2111
KOMAI TEKKO	1-19-10 Ueno, Taito-ku, Tokyo 110.	03-3834-4021
SAKURADA	1-3-B-10 Nakase, Mihama-ku, Chiba 261.	043-274-8511
SANWA SHUTTER	2-1-1 Nishi Shinjuku, Shinjuku-ku, Tokyo 163.	03-3346-3019
BUNKA SHUTTER	3-26-4 Shimura, Itabashi-ku, Tokyo 174.	03-3968-6600
KAWADA INDUSTRIES	1-3-11 Takinogawa, Kita-ku, Tokyo 114.	03-3915-4321
SANKYO ALUMINIUM INDUSTRY	70 Hayakawa, Takaoka-shi, Toyama 933.	0766-20-2214
TOYO SHUTTER	1-3-8 Tokiwa-machi, Chuo-ku, Osaka 540.	06-943-6571
TOYO EXTERIOR	1-4-12 Shinjuku, Shinjuku-ku, Tokyo 160.	03-3354-3211
TOSTEM	2-1-1 Ojima, Koto-ku, Tokyo 136.	03-3638-8111
NORITZ	32 Akashi-machi, Chuo-ku, Kobe 650.	078-391-3361
RINNAI	4-1 Hirokawa-cho, Nakagawa-ku, Nagoya 454.	052-361-8211
NITTO SEIKO	20 Umegahata, Inokura-cho, Ayabe-shi, Kyoto 623.	0773-42-3111
SANYO INDUSTRIES	6-20-7 Kameido, Koto-ku, Tokyo 136.	03-3685-3451
OKABE	4-21-15 Mukojima, Sumida-ku, Tokyo 131.	03-3624-5111
NIHON KENTETSU	2-6-2 Otemachi, Chiyoda-ku, Tokyo 100.	03-3270-6511
CHUGOKUKOGYO	15-10 Hatchobori, Naka-ku, Hiroshima 730.	082-221-8111
TOPRE	3-12-2 Nihonbashi, Chuo-ku, Tokyo 103.	03-3271-0711
NETUREN	2-16-21 Higashi Gotanda, Shinagawa-ku, Tokyo 141.	03-3443-5441
TOKYO ROPE MFG.	2-3-14 Nihonbashi Muro-machi, Chuo-ku, Tokyo 103.	03-3211-2851
N H K SPRING	3-10 Fuku-ura, Kanazawa-ku, Yokohama 236.	045-786-7511
CHUO SPRING	68 Kami Shiota, Narumi-cho, Midori-ku, Nagoya 458.	052-623-1111

ENGINES

MIURA	7 Horie-cho, Matsuyama-shi 799-26.	0899-79-1111
NIIGATA ENGINEERING	1-4-1 Kasumigaseki, Chiyoda-ku, Tokyo 100.	03-3504-2111
TAKUMA	1-3-23 Dojimahama, Kita-ku, Osaka 530.	06-346-5161
ZEXEL	3-23-14 Higashi Ikebukuro, Toshima-ku, Tokyo 170.	03-3400-1551

MACHINE TOOLS

TSUGAMI	1-18-16 Shinbashi, Minato-ku, Tokyo 105.	03-3504-3451
IKEGAI	1-18-16 Shinbashi, Minato-ku, Tokyo 105.	03-3502-5701
OKUMA	5-25-1 Shimo Oguchi, Oguchi-cho, Niwa-gun, Aichi 480-01.	0587-95-7820
★ TOSHIBA MACHINE	4-2-11 Ginza, Chuo-ku, Tokyo 104.	03-3567-0511
HITACHI SEIKI	1 Abiko-shi, Chiba 270-11.	0471-84-1111
AMADASONOIKE	100 Maekawa, Odawara-shi, Kanagawa 256.	0465-48-2111
AMADA WASINO	2-158 Nakashima, Shimo Obari, Komaki-shi, Aichi 485.	0568-77-8221
AMADA	200 Ishida, Isehara-shi, Kanagawa 259-11.	0463-96-1111
★ AIDA ENGINEERING	2-10 Oyama-cho, Sagamihara-shi, Kanagawa 229.	0427-72-5231
FUJI MACHINE MFG.	19 Chausuyama, Yama-machi, Chiryu-shi, Aichi 472.	0566-81-2111
MAKINO MILLING MACHINE	2-3-19 Nakane, Meguro-ku, Tokyo 152.	03-3717-1151
O S G MFG.	450 Kami Shinkiri, Ichinomiya, Aichi 441-12.	05339-3-2181
DIJET INDUSTRIAL	2-1-18 Kamai Higashi, Hirano-ku, Osaka 547.	06-791-6781
TOSHIBA TUNGALOY	1-7 Tsukagoshi, Saiwai-ku, Kawasaki 210.	044-548-8704
ASAHI DIAMOND INDUSTRIAL	4-1 Kioi-cho, Chiyoda-ku, Tokyo 102.	03-3222-6311
MORI SEIKI	362 Idono-cho, Yamato Koriyama-shi, Nara 639-11.	07435-3-1121

INDUSTRIAL MACHINERY

TOYODA AUTOMATIC LOOM WORKS	2-1 Toyoda-cho, Kariya-shi, Aichi 448.	0566-22-2511
HOWA MACHINERY	1900 Sukaguchi, Shinkawa-cho, Nishikasugai, Aichi 452.	052-502-1111
O K K	3-21-9 Toyosaki, Kita-ku, Osaka 531.	06-376-6611
TOYODA MACHINE WORKS	1-1 Asahi-machi, Kariya-shi, Aichi 448.	0566-25-5111
ISHIKAWA SEISAKUSHO	1-2-40 Owari-cho, Kanazawa-shi 920.	0762-22-2111
TEIJIN SEIKI	1-9-1 Edobori, NIshi-ku, Osaka 550.	06-448-6001
O-M	3-5-24 Miyahara, Yodogawa-ku, Osaka 532.	06-350-1200
OKUMA & HOWA MACHINERY	1 Maeno-cho Higashi, Konan-shi, Aichi 483.	0587-55-1151
TSUDAKOMA	5-18-18 No-machi, Kanazawa-shi 921-91.	0726-42-1111
ENSHU	4888 Takatsuka-cho, Hamamatsu-shi, Shizuoka 432.	053-447-2111

	NIHON SPINDLE MFG.	4-2-30 Shioe, Amagasaki-shi, Hyogo 661.	06-499-5551
	HISAKA WORKS	3-4-6 Hirano-machi, Chuo-ku, Osaka 541.	06-201-3531
	K Y C MACHINE INDUSTRY	1-5-13 Doshin, Kita-ku, Osaka 530.	06-357-2968
	RHEON AUTOMATIC MACHINERY	2-3 Nozawa-cho, Utsunomiya-shi 320.	0286-65-1111
	S M C	1-16-4 Shinbashi, Minato-ku, Tokyo 105.	03-3502-8271
	HOSOKAWA MICRON	2-5-14 Kawara-machi, Chuo-ku, Osaka 541.	06-233-3966
	KOMATSU	2-3-6 Akasaka, Minato-ku, Tokyo 107.	03-5561-2616
	SUMITOMO HEAVY INDUSTRIES	2-2-1 Otemachi, Chiyoda-ku, Tokyo 100.	03-3245-4321
	HITACHI CONSTRUCTION MACHINERY	2-6-2 Otemachi, Chiyoda-ku, Tokyo 100.	03-3245-6305
	NIKKO	1013-1 Eigashima, Okubo-cho, Akashi-shi, Hyogo 674.	078-947-3131
	ISEKI & CO.	3-6 Kioi-cho, Chiyoda-ku, Tokyo 102.	03-3238-5261
	KIORITZ	1-7-2 Suehiro-cho, Ome-shi, Tokyo 198.	0428-32-6111
	MARUYAMA MFG.	3-4-15 Uchi Kanda, Chiyoda-ku, Tokyo 101.	03-3252-2271
	KITAGAWA IRON WORKS	77-1 Moto-machi, Fuchu-shi, Hiroshima 726.	0847-45-4560
	KUBOTA	1-2-47 Shikitsu Higashi, Naniwa-ku, Osaka 556.	06-648-2111
	TOYO ENGENEERING	3-2-5 Kasumigaseki, Chiyoda-ku, Tokyo 100.	03-3592-7411
	MITSUBISHI KAKOKI	2-6-2 Marunouchi, Chiyoda-ku, Tokyo 100.	03-3212-0611
	TSUKISHIMA KIKAI	2-17-5 Tsukuda, Chuo-ku, Tokyo 104.	03-3533-4111
	TOKYO KIKAI SEISAKUSHO	5-26-24 Shiba, Minato-ku, Tokyo 108.	03-3451-8141
	SHINTOKOGIO	4-7-23 Mei-eki, Nakamura-ku, Nagoya 450.	052-582-9211
	SHIBUYA KOGYO	Ko-58 Omameda Honcho, Kanazawa-shi 920.	0762-62-1201
	AICHI	2-15-18 Chiyoda, Naka-ku, Nagoya 460.	052-263-5191
	KOMORI	3-11-1 Azumabashi, Sumida-ku, Tokyo 130.	03-5608-7811
	TSURUMI MFG.	4-16-40 Tsurumi, Tsurumi-ku, Osaka 538.	06-911-2351
	SUMITOMO PRECISION PRODUCTS	1-10 Fuso-cho, Amagasaki-shi, Hyogo 660.	06-482-8811
	SAKAI HEAVY INDUSTRIES	1-4-8 Shiba Daimon, Minato-ku, Tokyo 105.	03-3434-3401
	EBARA	11-1 Haneda Asahi-cho, Ota-ku, Tokyo 144.	03-3743-6111
	ISHII ARON WORKS	4-2-11 Ginza, Chuo-ku, Tokyo 104.	03-3562-3211
	TORISHIMA PUMP MFG.	1-1-8 Miyata-cho, Takatsuki-shi, Osaka 569.	0726-95-0551
★	CHIYODA	2-31-19 Shiba, Minato-ku, Tokyo 105.	03-3456-1211
	DAIKIN INDUSTRIES	2-4-12 Nakazaki Nishi, Kita-ku, Osaka 530.	06-373-1201
	JAPAN ORGANO	5-5-16 Hongo, Bunkyo-ku, Tokyo 113.	03-3812-5151
	TOYO KANETSU	8-19-12 Higashi Suna, Koto-ku, Tokyo 136.	03-5690-7777
	KURITA WATER INDUSTRIES	3-4-7 Nishi Shinjuku, Shinjuku-ku, Tokyo 160.	03-3347-3111
	TSUBAKIMOTO CHAIN	4-17-96 Tsurumi, Tsurumi-ku, Osaka 538.	06-911-1221
	DAIDO KOGYO	1-197 Kumasaka-cho, Kaga-shi, Ishikawa 922.	07617-2-1234
	TOYO UMPANKI	1-15-10 Kyomachibori, Nishi-ku, Osaka 550.	06-441-9151
	NIPPON CONVEYOR	2-1-1 Midorigaoka, Daito-shi, Osaka 574.	0720-72-2151
	NIKKISO	3-43-2 Ebisu, Shibuya-ku, Tokyo 150.	03-3443-3711
	KIMURA CHEMICAL PLANTS	2-1-2 Kuisetarajima, Amagasaki-shi, Hyogo 660.	06-488-2501
	IWATA AIR COMPRESSOR MFG.	1-9-14 Ebisu Minami, Shibuya-ku, Tokyo 150.	03-3711-7231
	DAIFUKU	3-2-11 Mitejima, Nishi Yodogawa-ku, Osaka 555.	06-472-1261
	KATO WORKS	1-9-37 Higashi Oi, Shinagawa-ku, Tokyo 140.	03-3458-1111
	YUKEN KOGYO	1 Miyamae, Fujisawa-shi, Kanagawa 251.	0466-23-2111
	TADANO	Ko-34, Shinden-cho, Takamatsu-shi 761-01.	0878-39-5555
	FUJITEC	1-28-10 Sho, Ibaraki-shi, Osaka 567.	0726-22-8151
	C K D	3005 Hayasaki, Kita Toyama, Komaki-shi, Aichi 485.	0568-77-1111
	MISCELLANEOUS MACHINERY		
	AMANO	275 Omamedo-cho, Kohoku-ku, Yokohama 222.	045-401-1441
	JUKI	8-2-1 Kokuryo-cho, Chofu-shi, Tokyo 182.	03-3480-1111
	SANDEN	20 Kotobuki-cho, Isesaki-shi, Gunma 372.	0270-24-1211
	JANOME SEWING MACHINE	3-1-1 Kyobashi, Chuo-ku, Tokyo 104.	03-3277-2071
	BROTHER INDUSTRIES	15-1 Naeshiro-cho, Mizuho-ku, Nagoya 467.	052-824-2511
	SILVER SEIKO	1-51 Suzuki-cho, Kodaira-shi, Tokyo 187.	0423-43-2111
	MAX	6-6 Nihonbashi Hakizaki-cho, Chuo-ku, Tokyo 103.	03-3669-0311
	MORITA FIRE PUMP MFG.	5-5-20 Shoji Higashi, Ikuno-ku, Osaka 544.	06-758-9702
	NIPPON PISTON RING	4-2-6 Kudan Kita, Chiyoda-ku, Tokyo 102.	03-3234-4171
	RIKEN	1-13-5 Kudan Kita, Chiyoda-ku, Tokyo 102.	03-3230-3911
	N S K	1-6-3 Osaki, Shinagawa-ku, Tokyo 141.	03-3779-7111

N T N	1-3-17 Kyomachibori, Nishi-ku, Osaka 550.	06-443-5001
★ KOYO SEIKO	3-5-8 Minami Senba, Chuo-ku, Osaka 542.	06-271-8451
NACHI-FUJIKOSHI	2-4-1 Hamamatsu-cho, Minato-ku, Tokyo 105.	03-3435-5111
TSUBAKIMOTO PRECISION PRODS.	2-4 Komatsubara-cho, Kita-ku, Osaka 530.	06-313-0191
MINEBEA	1-8-1 Shimo Meguro, Meguro-ku, Tokyo 153.	03-5434-8611
NIPPON THOMPSON	2-19-19 Takanawa, Minato-ku, Tokyo 108.	03-3448-5811
EAGLE INDUSTRY	1-12-15 Shiba Daimon, Minato-ku, Tokyo 105.	03-3438-2291
KITZ	3-17-9 Minami Aoyama, Minato-ku, Tokyo 105.	03-3404-1881
ELECTRICAL MACHINERY		
HITACHI	4-6 Kanda Surugadai, Chiyoda-ku, Tokyo 101.	03-3258-1111
TOSHIBA	1-1-1 Shibaura, Minato-ku, Tokyo 105-01.	03-3457-4511
MITSUBISHI ELECTRIC	2-2-3 Marunouchi, Chiyoda-ku, Tokyo 100.	03-3218-2111
FUJI ELECTRIC	1-12-1 Yurakucho, Chiyoda-ku, Tokyo 100.	03-3211-7111
TOYO DENKI SEIZO	2-7-2 Yaesu, Chuo-ku, Tokyo 104.	03-3271-5041
YASUKAWA ELECTRIC	2-1 Kurosaki Shiroishi, Yahata-ku, Kita Kyushu 806.	093-641-3111
SHINKO ELECTRIC	3-12-2 Nihonbashi, Chuo-ku, Tokyo 103.	03-3274-1112
MEIDENSHA	2-2-1 Otemachi, Chiyoda-ku, Tokyo 100.	03-3246-7111
NIPPON ELECTRIC INDUSTRY	1-10-12 Ueno, Taito-ku, Tokyo 110.	03-3837-3711
ORIGIN ELECTRIC	1-18-1 Takada, Toshima-ku, Tokyo 171.	03-3983-7111
HITACHI KOKI	2-6-2 Otemachi, Chiyoda-ku, Tokyo 100.	03-3270-6130
MATSUSHITA REFRIGERATION	3-22 Takaida Hon-dori, Higashi Osaka-shi 577.	06-782-1121
MAKITA	3-11-8 Sumiyoshi-cho, Anjo-shi, Aichi 446.	0566-98-1711
MATSUSHITA SEIKO	6-2-61 Imafuku Nishi, Joto-ku, Osaka 536.	06-939-1161
TOKYO ELECTRIC	1-14-10 Uchi Kanda, Chiyoda-ku, Tokyo 101.	03-3292-6223
SHIBAURA ENGINEERING WORKS	1-1-12 Akasaka, Minato-ku, Tokyo 107.	03-3586-2111
MABUCHI MOTOR	430 Matsuhida, Matsudo-shi, Chiba 270.	0473-84-1111
TAKAOKA ELECTRIC MFG.	2-2-1 Otemachi, Chiyoda-ku, Tokyo 100.	03-3211-1671
DAIHEN	2-1-11 Tagawa, Yodogawa-ku, Osaka 532.	06-301-1212
AICHI ELECTRIC	1 Aichi-cho, Kasugai-shi, Aichi 486.	0568-31-1111
NISSIN ELECTRIC	47 Umezu Takase-cho, Ukyo-ku, Kyoto 615.	075-861-3151
OSAKI ELECTRIC	2-2-7 Higashi Gotanda, Shinagawa-ku, Tokyo 141.	03-3443-7171
★ OMRON	Nanajo Sagaru, Karasuma-dori, Shimogyo-ku, Kyoto 600.	075-344-7000
IDEC IZUMI	5-13-9 Nishi Nakajima, Yodogawa-ku, Osaka 532.	06-300-5500
COMMUNICATIONS EQUIPMENT		
N E C	5-7-1 Shiba, Minato-ku, Tokyo 108-01.	03-3454-1111
FUJITSU	1-6-1 Marunouchi, Chiyoda-ku, Tokyo 100.	03-3216-3211
OKI ELECTRIC INDUSTRY	1-7-12 Toranomon, Minato-ku, Tokyo 105.	03-3501-3111
IWATSU ELECTRIC	1-7-41 Kugayama, Suginami-ku, Tokyo 168.	03-5370-5111
NITSUKO	260 Kita Mikata, Takatsu-ku, Kawasaki 213.	044-811-1111
DENKI KOGYO	3-3-1 Marunouchi, Chiyoda-ku, Tokyo 100.	03-3216-1671
SANKEN ELECTRIC	3-6-3 Kitano, Niiza-shi, Saitama 352.	0484-72-1111
TOYO COMMUNICATION EQUIPMENT	3-20-4 Nishi Shinbashi, Minato-ku, Tokyo 105.	03-3459-7200
TAMURA ELECTRIC WORKS	2-2-3 Shimo Meguro, Meguro-ku, Tokyo 153.	03-3493-5113
NIPPON SIGNAL	3-3-1 Marunouchi, Chiyoda-ku, Tokyo 100.	03-3287-4500
★ KYOSAN ELECTRIC MFG.	2-29-1 Heian-cho, Tsurumi-ku, Yokohama 230.	045-501-1261
NOHMI BOSAI	4-7-3 Kudan Minami, Chiyoda-ku, Tokyo 102.	03-3265-0211
HOCHIKI	2-10-43 Kami Osaki, Shinagawa-ku, Tokyo 141.	03-3444-4111
JAPAN RADIO	2-17-22 Akasaka, Minato-ku, Tokyo 107.	03-3584-8711
CONSUMER ELECTRONICS		
MATSUSHITA ELECTRIC INDUSTRIAL	1006 Kadoma, Kadoma-shi, Osaka 571.	06-908-1121
SHARP	22-22 Nagaike-cho, Abeno-ku, Osaka 545.	06-621-1221
ANRITSU	5-10-27 Minami Azabu, Minato-ku, Tokyo 106.	03-3446-1111
FUJITSU GENERAL	1116 Suenaga, Takatsu-ku, Kawasaki 213.	044-866-1111
KOKUSAI ELECTRIC	2-3-13 Toranomon, Minato-ku, Tokyo 105.	03-3591-7292
SONY	6-7-35 Kita Shinagawa, Shinagawa-ku, Tokyo 141.	03-3448-2111
TOKIN	6-7-1 Koriyama, Taihaku-ku, Sendai 982.	022-248-4111
AIWA	1-2-11 Ikenohata, Taito-ku, Tokyo 110.	03-3827-3111

	T D K	1-13-1 Nihonbashi, Chuo-ku, Tokyo 103.	03-3278-5111
	TEIKOKU TSUSHIN KOGYO	335, Kariya-do, Nakahara-ku, Kawasaki 211.	044-422-3171
	SANYO ELECTRIC	2-18 Keihan Hon-dori, Moriguchi-shi, Osaka 570.	06-991-1181
	KENWOOD	1-2-5 Shibuya, Shibuya-ku, Tokyo 150.	03-3486-5511
	CROWN	1-19-16 Omori Kita, Ota-ku, Tokyo 143.	03-5493-8111
	MITSUMI ELECTRIC	8-8-2 Kokuryo-cho, Chofu-shi, Tokyo 182.	03-3489-5333
	TAMURA	1-19-43 Higashi Oizumi, Nerima-ku, Tokyo 178.	03-3978-2111
★	ALPS ELECTRIC	1-7 Yukigaya Otsuka-cho, Ota-ku, Tokyo 145.	03-3726-1211
★	IKEGAMI TSUSHINKI	5-6-16 Ikegami, Ota-ku, Tokyo 146.	03-5700-1111
	PIONEER ELECTRONIC	1-4-1 Meguro, Meguro-ku, Tokyo 153.	03-3494-1111
★	HITACHI ELECTRONICS	1-23-2 Kanda Suda-cho, Chiyoda-ku, Tokyo 101.	03-3255-8411
★	MATSUSHITA COMMUNICATION IND.	4-3-1 Tsunashima Higashi, Kohoku-ku, Yokohama 223.	045-531-1231
	KYUSHU MATSUSHITA ELECTRIC	4-1-62 Minoshima, Hakata-ku, Fukuoka 812.	092-431-2111
	MATSUSHITA KOTOBUKI ELECT. IND.	2-2-10 Kotobuki-machi, Takamatsu-shi 760.	0878-51-7228
	NIPPON COLUMBIA	4-14-14 Akasaka, Minato-ku, Tokyo 107-11.	03-3584-8111
	VICTOR CO. OF JAPAN	4-8-14 Nihonbashi Honcho, Chuo-ku, Tokyo 103.	03-3246-9862
	SANSUI ELECTRIC	2-14-1 Izumi, Suginami-ku, Tokyo 168.	03-3323-1111
	CLARION	2-22-3 Shibuya, Shibuya-ku, Tokyo 150.	03-3400-1121
	S M K	6-5-5 Togashi, Shinagawa-ku, Tokyo 142.	03-3785-1111
	TOKO	2-1-17 Higashi Yukigaya, Ota-ku, Tokyo 145.	03-3727-1161
	AKAI ELECTRIC	2-12-14 Higashi Kojima, Ota-ku, Tokyo 144.	03-3745-9880
	TEAC	3-7-3 Naka-machi, Musashino-shi, Tokyo 180.	0422-52-5009
	HOSIDEN	1-4-33 Kita Kyuhoji, Yao-shi, Osaka 581.	0729-93-1010
	HIROSE ELECTRIC	5-5-23 Osaki, Shinagawa-ku, Tokyo 141.	03-3491-5300
	JAPAN AVIATION ELECTRONICS IND.	1-21-6 Dogenzaka, Shibuya-ku, Tokyo 150.	03-3463-3111
	SHINTOM	2-19-1 Minowa-cho, Kohoku-ku, Yokohama 223.	045-563-3111
	HITACHI MAXELL	1-1-88 Ushitora, Ibaraki-shi, Osaka 567.	0726-23-8101
	FURUNO ELECTRIC	9-52 Ashihara-cho, Nishinomiya-shi, Hyogo 662.	0798-65-2111
	UNIDEN	8-18-11 Ginza, Chuo-ku, Tokyo 104.	03-3544-0333
	ALPINE ELECTRONICS	1-1-8 Nishi Gotanda, Shinagawa-ku, Tokyo 141.	03-3494-1101
	MEASURING INSTRUMENTS		
	YOKOGAWA ELECTRIC	2-9-32 Naka-machi, Musashino-shi, Tokyo 180.	0422-52-5555
	SHINDENGEN ELECTRIC MFG.	2-2-1 Otemachi, Chiyoda-ku, Tokyo 100.	03-3274-4431
	YAMATAKE-HONEYWELL	2-12-19 Shibuya, Shibuya-ku, Tokyo 150.	03-3486-2031
	NIHON KOHDEN	1-31-4 Nishi Ochiai, Shinjuku-ku, Tokyo 161.	03-5996-8000
★	CHINO	32-8 Kumano-cho, Itabashi-ku, Tokyo 173.	03-3956-2111
	OHKURA ELECTRIC	3-20-8 Narita Nishi, Suginami-ku, Tokyo 166.	03-3398-5111
★	HORIBA	2 Miyano Higashi-cho, Kisshoin, Minami-ku, Kyoto 601.	075-313-8121
	ADVANTEST	2-4-1 Nishi Shinjuku, Shinjuku-ku, Tokyo 163.	03-3342-7500
	ONO SOKKI	2-4-1 Nishi Shinjuku, Shinjuku-ku, Tokyo 163-08.	03-3342-9181
	TABAI ESPEC	3-5-6 Tenjinbashi, Kita-ku, Osaka 530.	06-358-4741
	KEYENCE	2-13 Aketa-cho, Takatsuki-shi, Osaka 569.	0726-84-1111
	MISCELLANEOUS ELECTRICAL PRODUCTS		
	SAWAFUJI ELECTRIC	5-29-1 Toyotama Kita, Nerima-ku, Tokyo 176.	03-5999-3355
	NIPPONDENSO	1-1 Showa-cho, Kariya-shi, Aichi 448.	0566-25-5511
	TOKO ELECTRIC	1-7-1 Yurakucho, Chiyoda-ku, Tokyo 100.	03-3214-5281
	STANLEY ELECTRIC	2-9-13 Naka Meguro, Meguro-ku, Tokyo 153.	03-3710-2222
	IWASAKI ELECTRIC	3-12-4 Shiba, Minato-ku, Tokyo 105.	03-3452-5351
	USHIO	2-6-1 Otemachi, Chiyoda-ku, Tokyo 100.	03-3242-1811
	JAPAN STORAGE BATTERY	1 Inobanba-cho, Nishinosho, Minami-ku, Kyoto 601.	075-312-1211
	YUASA BATTERY	2-4-12 Minami Senba, Chuo-ku, Osaka 542.	06-266-7611
★	SHIN-KOBE ELECTRIC MACHINERY	2-1-1 Nishi Shinjuku, Shinjuku-ku, Tokyo 163.	03-3344-2811
	FURUKAWA BATTERY	2-4-1 Hoshikawa, Hodogaya-ku, Yokohama 240.	045-331-1221
	KINSEKI	1-2-2 Manpukuji, Aso-ku, Kawasaki 215.	044-952-8101
	JEOL	3-1-2 Musashino, Akishima-shi, Tokyo 196.	0425-43-1111
	CASIO COMPUTER	2-6-1 Nishi Shinjuku, Shinjuku-ku, Tokyo 163.	03-3347-4811
	NCR JAPAN	1-2-2 Akasaka, Minato-ku, Tokyo 107.	03-3582-6111
	FANUC	Shibokusa, Oshino-mura, Yamanashi 401-05.	0555-84-5555

	FUJI ELECTROCHEMICAL	5-36-11 Shinbashi, Minato-ku, Tokyo 105.	03-3434-1271
	C M K	1106 Fujikubo, Miyoshi-machi, Iruma-gun, Saitama 354.	0492-66-7000
	AMADA METRECS	120 Maekawa, Odawara-shi, Kanagawa 256.	0465-47-8811
	DAISHINKU	1389 Kono, Shin Zaike, Kakogawa, Hyogo 675-01.	0794-26-3211
	ROHM	21 Mizozaki-cho, Sai-in, Ukyo-ku, Kyoto 615.	075-311-2121
	MITSUI HIGH-TEC	2-10-1 Komine, Yahata Nishi-ku, Kita Kyushu 806.	093-614-1111
	GRAPHTEC	503-10 Shinano-cho, Totsuka-ku, Yokohama 244.	045-825-6200
	NIPPON CONLUX	2-2-2 Uchi Saiwai-cho, Chiyoda-ku, Tokyo 100.	03-3502-1811
	KYOCERA	5-22 Kita Inoue-cho, Higashino, Yamashina-ku, Kyoto 607.	075-592-3851
	SUMITOMO SPECIAL METALS	4-7-19 Kitahama, Chuo-ku, Osaka 541.	06-220-8821
	TAIYO YUDEN	6-16-20 Ueno, Taito-ku, Tokyo 110.	03-3832-0101
	MURATA MFG.	2-26-10 Tenjin, Nagaokakyo-shi, Kyoto 617.	075-951-9111
	FUTABA	629 Oshiba, Mobara-shi, Chiba 297.	0475-24-1111
	NITTO DENKO	1-1-2 Shimo Hozumi, Ibaraki-shi, Osaka 567.	0726-22-2981
	HOKURIKU ELECTRIC INDUSTRY	3158 Shimo Okubo, Osawano-machi, Toyama 939-22.	0764-67-1111
	MATSUSHITA ELECTRIC WORKS	1048 Kadoma-shi, Osaka 571.	06-908-1131
	TOKAI RIKA	1 Noda, Toyoda, Oguchi-cho, Miwa-gun, Aichi 480-01.	0587-95-5211
	NICHICON	Karasuma Higashiiru, Oike-dori, Nakagyo-ku, Kyoto 604.	075-231-8461
	NIPPON CHEMI-CON	1-167-1 Higashi Ome, Ome-shi, Tokyo 198.	0428-22-1251
	K O A	3672 Ina, Ina-shi, Nagano 396.	0265-78-2121
	SHIPBUILDING		
	MITSUI ENGINEERING & SHIPBLDG.	5-6-4 Tsukiji, Chuo-ku, Tokyo 104.	03-3544-3147
	HITACHI ZOSEN	5-3-28 Nishi Kujo, Konohana-ku, Osaka 554.	06-466-7500
	SASEBO HEAVY INDUSTRIES	2-2-1 Otemachi, Chiyoda-ku, Tokyo 100.	03-3211-2989
★	MITSUBISHI HEAVY INDUSTRIES	2-5-1 Marunouchi, Chiyoda-ku, Tokyo 100.	03-3212-3111
	KAWASAKI HEAVY INDUSTRIES	2-1-18 Nakamachi-dori, Chuo-ku, Kobe 650.	078-371-9530
	ISHIKAWAJIMA-HARIMA HEAVY IND.	2-2-1 Otemachi, Chiyoda-ku, Tokyo 100.	03-3244-5111
	NAMURA SHIPBUILDING	3-1-1 Itachibori, Nishi-ku, Osaka 500.	06-543-3561
	SANOYAS HISHINO MEISHO	4-5-22 Dosho-machi, Chuo-ku, Osaka 541.	06-202-1221
	ROLLING STOCK		
	NIPPON SHARYO	1-1 Sanbonmatsu-cho, Atsuta-ku, Nagoya 456-91.	052-882-3316
	FUJI CAR MFG.	2-2-3 Nishi Shinsaibashi, Chuo-ku, Osaka 542.	06-213-2711
	NIPPON YUSOKI	2-1-1 Higashi Kotari, Nagaokakyo-shi, Kyoto 617.	075-951-7171
	KINKI SHARYO	3-9-60 Inada Shin-machi, Higashi Osaka-shi 577.	06-746-5222
	TOKYU CAR	1 Kamariya-cho, Kanazawa-ku, Yokohama 236.	045-701-5155
	NABCO	7-1-12 Goko-dori, Chuo-ku, Kobe 651.	078-251-8080
	MOTOR VEHICLES		
	NISSAN MOTOR	6-17-1 Ginza, Chuo-ku, Tokyo 104-23.	03-3543-5523
	ISUZU MOTORS	6-26-1 Minami Oi, Shinagawa-ku, Tokyo 140.	03-5471-1111
★	TOYOTA MOTOR	1 Toyota-cho, Toyota-shi, Aichi 471.	0565-28-2121
	KOMATSU ZENOAH	2-142-1 Sakuragaoka, Higashi Yamato-shi, Tokyo 207.	0425-61-2146
	NIHO MOTORS	3-1-1 Hinodai, Hino-shi, Tokyo 191.	0425-86-5011
	NISSAN DIESEL MOTOR	1-1 Oaza, Ageo-shi, Saitama 362.	048-781-2301
	MITSUBISHI MOTORS	5-33-8 Shiba, Minato-ku, Tokyo 108.	03-3456-1111
	TOYOTA AUTO BODY	100 Kanayama, Ichiriyama-cho, Kariya-shi, Aichi 448.	0566-36-2121
	NISSAN SHATAI	10-1 Amanuma, Hiratsuka-shi, Kanagawa 254.	0463-21-8001
	KANTO AUTO WORKS	Ta-ura Minato-machi, Yokosuka-shi, Kanagawa 237.	0468-61-5111
	SHIN MEIWA INDUSTRY	1-5-25 Kosone-cho, Nishinomiya-shi, Hyogo 663.	0798-47-0331
	KOMATSU FORKLIFT	2-3-4 Akasaka, Minato-ku, Tokyo 107.	03-3586-5111
	TOPY INDUSTRIES	5-9 Yonban-cho, Chiyoda-ku, Tokyo 102.	03-3265-0111
	TOKICO	1-6-3 Fujimi, Kawasaki-ku, Kawasaki 210.	044-244-3126
	TOYO RADIATOR	31-2 Sakuragaoka-cho, Shibuya-ku, Tokyo 150.	03-3780-2511
	AKEBONO BRAKE INDUSTRY	19-5 Nihonbashi Koami-cho, Chuo-ku, Tokyo 103.	03-3668-5171
★	N O K	1-12-15 Shiba Daimon, Minato-ku, Tokyo 105.	03-3432-4211
	FUTABA INDUSTRIAL	1 Ochaya, Hashime-cho, Okazaki-shi, Aichi 444.	0564-31-2211
	KAYABA INDUSTRY	2-4-1 Hamamatsu-cho, Minato-ku, Tokyo 105.	03-3435-3511
	SHIROKI	3-7-3 Shin Yokohama, Kohoku-ku, Yokohama 222.	045-473-4691

★ ICHIKOH INDUSTRIES	5-10-18 Higashi Gotanda, Shinagawa-ku, Tokyo 141.	03-3443-7281
PRESS KOGYO	1-1-1 Shiohama, Kawasaki-ku, Kawasaki 210.	044-266-2581
CALSONIC	5-24-15 Minamidai, Nakano-ku, Tokyo 164.	03-5385-0111
PACIFIC INDUSTRIAL	100 Kyotoku-cho, Ogaki-shi, Gifu 503.	0584-91-1111
TOCHIGI FUJI INDUSTRIAL	2388 Omiya-cho, Tochigi-shi 328.	0282-27-1111
AISIN SEIKI	2-1 Asahi-machi, Kariya-shi, Aichi 448.	0566-24-8231
MAZDA MOTOR	3-1 Shinchi, Fuchu-cho, Aki-gun, Hiroshima 730-91.	082-282-1111
DAIHATSU MOTOR	1-1 Daihatsu-cho, Ikeda-shi, Osaka 563.	0727-51-8811
AICHI MACHINE INDUSTRY	2-20 Kawanami-cho, Atsuta-ku, Nagoya 456.	052-681-1111
HONDA MOTOR	2-1-1 Minami Aoyama, Minato-ku, Tokyo 107.	03-3423-1111
SUZUKI MOTOR	300 Takatsuka-cho, Hamamatsu-shi, Shizuoka 432.	053-440-2111
FUJI HEAVY INDUSTRIES	1-7-2 Nishi Shinjuku, Shinjuku-ku, Tokyo 160.	03-3347-2111
YAMAHA MOTOR	2500 Shingai, Iwata-shi, Shizuoka 438.	0538-32-1115
SHOWA MFG.	1-14-1 Fujiwara-cho, Gyoda-shi, Saitama 361.	0485-54-1151
ATSUGI UNISIA	1370 Onna, Atsugi-shi, Kanagawa 243.	0462-25-8025
KOITO MFG.	4-8-3 Takanawa, Minato-ku, Tokyo 108.	03-3443-7111
MITSUBA ELECTRIC MFG.	1-2681 Hirosawa-cho, Kiryu-shi, Gunma 376.	0277-52-0111
KANSEI	2-1910 Nisshin-cho, Omiya-shi, Saitama 331.	048-652-5051
TOYODA GOSEI	1 Nagahata, Ochiai, Haruhi-machi, Aichi 452.	052-400-1055

BICYCLES

ARAYA INDUSTRIAL	2-12-12 Minami Senba, Chuo-ku, Osaka 542.	06-253-0221

AIRCRAFT

SHIMANO	3-77 Oimatsu-cho, Sakai-shi, Osaka 590.	0722-23-3330
JAPAN AIRCRAFT MFG.	3175 Showa-machi, Kanazawa-ku, Yokohama 236.	045-773-5100

PRECISION MACHINERY

SHIMADZU	1 Nishinokyo Kuwabara-cho, Nakagyo-ku, Kyoto 604.	075-823-1111
JAPAN MEDICAL SUPPLY	12-17 Kako-machi, Naka-ku, Hiroshima 730.	082-243-5844
STAR MICRONICS	20-10 Naka Yoshida, Shizuoka-shi 422.	054-263-1111
SOKKIA	1-1-1 Tomigaya, Shibuya-ku, Tokyo 151.	03-3465-5211
TOKIMEC	2-16-46 Minami Kamata, Ota-ku, Tokyo 144.	03-3732-2111
AICHI TOKEI DENKI	1-2-70 Chitose, Atsuta-ku, Nagoya 456-91.	052-661-5151
KIMMON MFG.	1-2-3 Shimura, Itabashi-ku, Tokyo 174.	03-3960-2151
TOKYO SEIMITSU	9-7-1 Shimo Renja-ku, Mitaka-shi, Tokyo 181.	0422-48-1011
NIKON	3-2-3 Marunouchi, Chiyoda-ku, Tokyo 100.	03-3214-5311
TOPCON	75-1 Hasunuma-cho, Itabashi-ku, Tokyo 174.	03-3966-3141
★ OLYMPUS OPTICAL	2-3-1 Nishi Shinjuku, Shinjuku-ku, Tokyo 163.	03-3340-2121
DAINIPPON SCREEN MFG.	Teranouchi Agaru, Horikawa-dori, Kamagyo-ku, Kyoto 602.	075-414-7111
HOYA	2-7-5 Naka Ochiai, Shinjuku-ku, Tokyo 161.	03-3952-1151
ASAHI OPTICAL	2-36-9 Maeno-cho, Itabashi-ku, Tokyo 174.	03-3960-5151
CANON	2-7-1 Nishi Shinjuku, Shinjuku-ku, Tokyo 163.	03-3348-2121
RICOH	1-15-5 Minami Aoyama, Minato-ku, Tokyo 107.	03-3479-3111
MINOLTA CAMERA	2-3-13 Azuchi-machi, Chuo-ku, Osaka 541.	06-271-2251
COPAL	2-16-20 Shimura, Itabashi-ku, Tokyo 174.	03-3965-1111
★ SANKYO SEIKI MFG.	1-17-2 Shinbashi, MInato-ku, Tokyo 105.	03-3502-3711
CITIZEN WATCH	2-1-1 Nishi Shinjuku, Shinjuku-ku, Tokyo 163-04.	03-3342-1231
RHYTHM WATCH	2-27-7 Taito, Taito-ku, Tokyo 110.	03-3833-7311

MISCELLANEOUS MANUFACTURING

JUKEN SANGYO	1-1 Minami Mokuzaiko, Hatsukaichi-shi, Hiroshima 738.	0829-32-3333
DAIKEN	2-3-18 Nakanoshima, Kita-ku, Osaka 530.	06-228-3321
DANTANI	2-5-12 Higashi Minato, Kokura Kita-ku, Kita Kyushu 803.	093-561-6331
TOPPAN PRINTING	1 Kanda Izumi-cho, Chiyoda-ku, Tokyo 101.	03-3835-5111
★ DAI NIPPON PRINTING	1-1-1 Ichigaya Kaga-cho, Shinjuku-ku, Tokyo 162-01.	03-3266-2111
TOSHO PRINTING	1-3-13 Takanawa, Minato-ku, Tokyo 108.	03-3473-7300
KYODO PRINTING	4-14-12 Koishikawa, Bunkyo-ku, Tokyo 112.	03-3817-2071
NISSHA PRINTING	3 Mibu Hanai-cho, Nakagyo-ku, Kyoto 601.	075-811-8111
ASICS	7-1-1 Minatojima Naka-machi, Chuo-ku, Kobe 650.	078-303-3333

YAMAHA	10-1 Nakazawa-machi, Hamamatsu-shi, Shizuoka 430.	053-460-2141
KAWAI MUSICAL INSTRUMENTS MFG.	200 Terajima-cho, Hamamatsu-shi, Shizuoka 430.	053-457-1213
CLEANUP	6-22-22 Nishi Nippori, Arakawa-ku, Tokyo 116.	03-3894-4771
TENMA	2345 Ozaki, Noda-shi, Chiba 270-02.	0471-27-2721
KANEMATSU-N N K	3-2-12 Shin Kiba, Koto-ku, Tokyo 136.	03-3521-8421
SEGA ENTERPRISES	1-2-12 Haneda, Ota-ku, Tokyo 144.	03-3743-7430
LINTEC	23-23 Honcho, Itabashi-ku, Tokyo 173.	03-5248-7711
BANDAI	2-5-4 Komagata, Taito-ku, Tokyo 111.	03-3847-5005
TAKARA	4-19-16 Aoto, Katsushika-ku, Tokyo 125.	03-3603-2131
SHIN-ETSU POLYMER	4-3-5 Nihonbashi Honcho, Chuo-ku, Tokyo 103.	03-3279-1712
TOLI	5-125 Higashi Arioka, Itami-shi, Hyogo 664.	06-492-1331
ITOKI KOSAKUSHO	1-4-18 Imafuku Higashi, Joto-ku, Osaka 536.	06-939-1421
NINTENDO	60 Kami Takamatsu-cho, Higashiyama-ku, Kyoto 605.	075-541-6111
MITSUBISHI PENCIL	5-23 Higashi Oi, Shinagawa-ku, Tokyo 140.	03-3458-6221
FRANCE BED	31-15 Sakuragaoka-cho, Shibuya-ku, Tokyo 150.	03-3463-1011
TAKARA STANDARD	1-2-1 Shigino Higashi, Joto-ku, Osaka 536.	06-962-1531
KOKUYO	6-1-1 Oimazato Minami, Higashinari-ku, Osaka 537.	06-976-1221
NAKABAYASHI	1-20 Kitakama Higashi, Chuo-ku, Osaka 540.	06-943-5555
NIFCO	184-1 Maioka-cho, Totsuka-ku, Yokohama 244.	045-825-7900
DAIWA SEIKO	3-14-16 Maesawa, Higashi Kurume-shi, Tokyo 203.	0424-75-2111
SUN WAVE	3-25-3 Yoyogi, Shibuya-ku, Tokyo 151.	03-5371-4311
OKAMURA	2-7-18 Kita Saiwai, Nishi-ku, Yokohama 220.	045-319-3401
NIPPON VALQUA INDUSTRIES	3-3-1 Marunouchi, Chiyoda-ku, Tokyo 100.	03-3212-8571
PILOT	2-8-1 Nishi Gotanda, Shinagawa-ku, Tokyo 141.	03-5487-8111
MUTOH INDUSTRIES	3-1-3 Ikejiri, Setagaya-ku, Tokyo 154.	03-5486-1111

COMMERCE

C. ITOH & CO.	4-1-3 Kyutaro-machi, Chuo-ku, Osaka 541-77.	06-241-2121
MARUBENI	2-5-7 Honmachi, Chuo-ku, Osaka 541-88.	06-266-2111
TOMEN	1-6-7 Kawara-machi, Chuo-ku, Osaka 541.	06-208-2211
NICHIMEN	1-13-1 Kyobashi, Chuo-ku, Tokyo 104.	03-3277-5111
MUTOW	672 Sato-cho, Hamamatsu-shi, Shizuoka 430.	053-464-1123
TAKASHIMA & CO.	1-15-11 Ginza, Chuo-ku, Tokyo 104.	03-3567-0211
ITOMAN	3-6-2 Honmachi, Chuo-ku, Osaka 541.	06-244-8170
SANYO SHOKAI	14 Honshio-cho, Shinjuku-ku, Tokyo 160.	03-3357-4111
NAGASE & CO.	1-1-17 Shin-machi, Nishi-ku, Osaka 550.	06-535-2114
NAIGAI	1-13-5 Uchi Kanda, Chiyoda-ku, Tokyo 101.	03-3293-1511
★ CHORI	2-4-7 Kawara-machi, Chuo-ku, Osaka 541.	06-228-5000
TOYOTA TSUSHO	4-7-23 Mei-eki, Nakamura-ku, Nagoya 450.	052-584-5015
ONWARD KASHIYAMA	3-10-5 Nihonbashi, Chuo-ku, Tokyo 103.	03-3272-2317
SANKYO SEIKO	2-5-6 Azuchi-machi, Chuo-ku, Osaka 541.	06-268-5000
ICHIDA & CO.	2-7-2 Nihonbashi Horidome-cho, Chuo-ku, Tokyo 103.	03-3663-1411
★ KANEMATSU	1-2-1 Shibaura, Minato-ku, Tokyo 105-05.	03-5440-8111
RENOWN	2-34-18 Jingu-mae, Shibuya-ku, Tokyo 150.	03-3403-2211
MIZUNO	1-12-35 Nanko Kita, Suminoe-ku, Osaka 559.	06-614-8000
TSUKAMOTO SHOJI	1-6-5 Nihonbashi Honcho, Chuo-ku, Tokyo 103.	03-3279-1310
LECIEN	Rokkaku Sagaru, Karasuma-dori, Nakagyo-ku, Kyoto 604.	075-241-6000
FAMILY MART	4-27-10 Higashi Ikebukuro, Toshima-ku, Tokyo 170.	03-3989-6600
RENOWN LOOK	2-7-7 Naka Meguro, Meguro-ku, Tokyo 153.	03-3710-7111
MITSUI & CO.	1-2-1 Otemachi, Chiyoda-ku, Tokyo 100.	03-3285-1111
JAPAN PULP & PAPER	4-6-11 Nihonbashi Hongoku-cho, Chuo-ku, Tokyo 103.	03-3270-1311
TOSHOKU	2-4-3 Nihonbashi Muro-machi, Chuo-ku, Tokyo 103.	03-3245-2211
TOKYO ELECTRON	2-3-1 Nishi Shinjuku, Shinjuku-ku, Tokyo 163-09.	03-3340-8111
NISSEI SANGYO	1-24-14 Nishi Shinbashi, Minato-ku, Tokyo 105.	03-3504-7111
KAMEI	3-1-18 Kokubun-cho, Aoba-ku, Sendai 980.	022-264-6111
TOHTO SUISAN	5-2-1 Tsukiji, Chuo-ku, Tokyo 104.	03-3541-5666
OSAKA UOICHIBA	1-1-86 Noda, Fukushima-ku, Osaka 553.	06-466-2281
NIHON MATAI	2-6-7 Moto Asakusa, Taito-ku, Tokyo 111.	03-3843-2111
ZENCHIKU	2-5-7 Konan, Minato-ku, Tokyo 108.	03-3471-5521
SEIKO	2-6-21 Kyobashi, Chuo-ku, Tokyo 104.	03-3563-2111

YAMAZEN	2-3-16 Itachibori, Nishi-ku, Osaka 550.	06-534-3021
★ TSUBAKIMOTO MACHINERY & ENG.	2-4 Komatsubara-cho, Kita-ku, Osaka 530.	06-315-5000
SUMITOMO	5-15 Kitahama, Chuo-ku, Osaka 541.	06-220-6000
OKURA & CO.	2-3-6 Ginza, Chuo-ku, Tokyo 104.	03-3566-6000
NOZAKI & CO.	1-10-11 Shiba, Minato-ku, Tokyo 105.	03-5443-5221
NIHON UNISYS	2-17-51 Akasaka, Minato-ku, Tokyo 107.	03-3585-4111
UCHIDA YOKO	2-4-7 Shinkawa, Chuo-ku, Tokyo 104.	03-3555-4031
MITSUBISHI	2-6-3 Marunouchi, Chiyoda-ku, Tokyo 100-86.	03-3210-2121
DAIICHI JITSUGYO	3-20 Kanda Nishiki-cho, Chiyoda-ku, Tokyo 101.	03-3296-6321
CANON SALES	3-11-28 Mita, Minato-ku, Tokyo 108.	03-3455-9111
SEIKA	3-3-1 Marunouchi, Chiyoda-ku, Tokyo 100.	03-3211-6811
NISSHO IWAI	2-5-8 Imabashi, Chuo-ku, Osaka 541.	06-209-2111
KINSHO-MATAICHI	1-24-1 Shinkawa, Chuo-ku, Tokyo 104.	03-3297-7111
SATO SHOJI	1-13-10 Hatchobori, Chuo-ku, Tokyo 104.	03-3553-7005
RYOYO ELECTRO	1-12-22 Tsukiji, Chuo-ku, Tokyo 104.	03-3543-7711
★ KASHO	2-14-9 Nihonbashi, Chuo-ku, Tokyo 103.	03-3276-7726
YUASA TRADING	13-10 Nihonbashi Odenma-cho, Chuo-ku, Tokyo 103.	03-3665-6511
SHINSHO	2-6-17 Kitahama, Chuo-ku, Osaka 541.	06-206-7001
KOBAYASHI METALS	2-7-4 Minami Horie, Nishi-ku, Osaka 550.	06-535-3690
HANWA	1-13-10 Tsukiji, Chuo-ku, Tokyo 104.	03-3544-2171
KANADEN	4-22-4 Shinbashi, Minato-ku, Tokyo 105.	03-3433-1211
TEC ELECTRONICS	1-11-2 Fujimi, Chiyoda-ku, Tokyo 102.	03-3239-9111
SUNTELEPHONE	1-2-2 Nihonbashi Ningyo-cho, Chuo-ku, Tokyo 103.	03-3665-1560
RYODEN TRADING	3-15-15 Higashi Ikebukuro, Toshima-ku, Tokyo 170.	03-5396-6112
NISSHO	3-9-3 Honjo Nishi, Kita-ku, Osaka 531.	06-372-2331
IWATANI INTERNATIONAL	3-4-8 Honmachi, Chuo-ku, Osaka 541.	06-267-3404
NICHIEI	4-3-1 Tsurumi Chuo, Tsurumi-ku, Yokohama 230.	045-521-6161
SHOKO	3-8-3 Nishi Shinbashi, Minato-ku, Tokyo 105.	03-3459-5111
NICHIMO	2-6-2 Otemachi, Chiyoda-ku, Tokyo 100.	03-3245-4718
KANEMATSU ELECTRONICS	2-16-1 Minami Kamata, Ota-ku, Tokyo 144.	03-5703-2111
SAN-AI OIL	5-22-5 Higashi Oi, Shinagawa-ku, Tokyo 140.	03-5479-3113
INABATA & CO.	1-15-14 Minami Senba, Chuo-ku, Osaka 542.	06-267-6051
FUJII & CO.	2-2-5 Honmachi, Chuo-ku, Osaka 541.	06-271-2311
GUNZE SANGYO	3-17 Kanda Nishiki-cho, Chiyoda-ku, Tokyo 101.	03-3294-4141
HITACHI SALES	2-15-12 Nishi Shinbashi, Minato-ku, Tokyo 105.	03-3502-2111
MEIWA TRADING	3-3-1 Marunouchi, Chiyoda-ku, Tokyo 100.	03-3240-9534
KIMURATAN	2-9-24 Kano-cho, Chuo-ku, Kobe 650.	078-241-4351
KAWASHO	2-4-1 Hamamatsu-cho, Minato-ku, Tokyo 105.	03-3578-5111
TOKYO STYLE	5-7-1 Koji-machi, Chiyoda-ku, Tokyo 102.	03-3262-8111
UNI-CHARM	3-25-23 Takanawa, Minato-ku, Tokyo 108.	03-3447-5111
DESCENTE	1-11-3 Dogashiba, Tennoji-ku, Osaka 543.	06-774-0365
D'URBAN	8-8-20 Nishi Gotanda, Shinagawa-ku, Tokyo 141.	03-5496-8111
O S G	3-22 Honnogahara, Toyokawa-shi, Aichi 442.	05338-2-1111
WAKITA & CO.	1-2-4 Nishi Shinsaibashi, Chuo-ku, Osaka 542.	06-251-1901
YAMATO INTERNATIONAL	2-3-9 Bakuro-cho, Chuo-ku, Osaka 541.	06-262-1661
SANGETSU	1-4-1 Habashita, Nishi-ku, Nagoya 451.	052-564-3311
MITSUUROKO	3-3-3 Nihonbashi Honcho, Chuo-ku, Tokyo 103.	03-3279-6311
SHINAGAWA FUEL	1-4-22 Kaigan, MInato-ku, Tokyo 105.	03-5470-7105
C. ITOH FUEL	2-17-22 Akasaka, Minato-ku, Tokyo 107.	03-3584-8521
TOKAI	1-4-12 Tokiwa-cho, Shizuoka-shi 420.	054-254-8181
SANRIO	1-6-1 Osaki, Shinagawa-ku, Tokyo 141.	03-3779-8111
RYOSAN	2-5-15 Higashi Kanda, Chiyoda-ku, Tokyo 101.	03-3862-2591
SHINKO SHOJI	1-1-5 Meguro, Meguro-ku, Tokyo 153.	03-5721-2111
TOYO	1-1-2 Nihonbashi Hongoku-cho, Chuo-ku, Tokyo 103.	03-3279-0771
GASTEC SERVICE	100 Shirakawa-cho, Toyohashi-shi, Aichi 441.	0532-32-5161
SODA NIKKA	2-3-14 Nihonbashi Muro-machi, Chuo-ku, Tokyo 103.	03-3245-1802

RETAIL STORES AND FOOD SERVICES

SATO	3-7-6 Tagawa, Yodogawa-ku, Osaka 532.	06-309-6301
CABIN	2-27-4 Nishi Gotanda, Shinagawa-ku, Tokyo 141.	03-3779-6811

	SENSHUKAI	1-4-31 Doshin, Kita-ku, Osaka 530.	06-358-1751
★	TAKA-Q	1-5-22 Shimo Ochiai, Shinjuku-ku, Tokyo 161.	03-3366-6600
	KEIYO	1-28-1 Mitsuwadai, Wakaba-ku, Chiba 264.	043-255-1111
	DAI-ICHI KATEI DENKI	6-23-15 Shinjuku, Shinjuku-ku, Tokyo 160.	03-3352-7241
	JOSHIN DENKI	1-6-5 Nipponbashi Nishi, Naniwa-ku, Osaka 556.	06-631-1221
	NIPPON GAS	3-5-2 Hatchobori, Chuo-ku, Tokyo 104.	03-3553-1281
	BEST DENKI	2-1-12 Nanotsu, Chuo-ku, Fukuoka 810.	092-781-7161
	SEIYO FOOD SYSTEMS	3-1-1 Higashi Ikebukuro, Toshima-ku, Tokyo 170.	03-3984-0662
	MARUETSU	5-51-12 Higashi Ikebukuro, Toshima-ku, Tokyo 170.	03-3590-1110
	ROYAL	3-28-5 Naka, Hakata-ku, Fukuoka 816.	092-471-2414
	SKYLARK	6-14-1 Nishi Shinjuku, Shinjuku-ku, Tokyo 160.	03-3349-7070
	TOTENKO	1-4-33 Ikenohata, Taito-ku, Tokyo 110.	03-3828-6272
	INAGEYA	6-1-1 Sakae-cho, Tachikawa-shi, Tokyo 190.	0425-37-5111
	SEVEN-ELEVEN JAPAN	4-1-4 Shiba Koen, Minato-ku, Tokyo 105.	03-3459-3711
	SHIMACHU	5-1555 Mihashi, Omiya-shi, Saitama 331.	048-623-7711
★	KYOTARU	1-36-9 Nihonbashi Kakigara-cho, Chuo-ku, Tokyo 103.	03-3665-6111
	YORK-BENIMARU	2-18-2 Asahi, Koriyama-shi, Fukushima 963.	0249-24-3111
	MATSUYADENKI	13-10 Sennichi-mae, Nanba, Chuo-ku, Osaka 542.	06-643-5461
	SUZUTAN	3-15-37 Sakae, Naka-ku, Nagoya 460.	052-263-1191
	LIFE	1-19-4 Higashi Nakajima, Higashi Yodogawa-ku, Osaka.	06-815-2600
	DENNY'S JAPAN	4-1-4 Shiba Koen, Minato-ku, Tokyo 105.	03-3459-3548
★	KASUMI	1-3 Higashi Nakanuki-machi, Tsuchiura-shi, Ibaraki 300.	0298-31-0031
	TOKYU STORE CHAIN	1-21-12 Kami Meguro, Meguro-ku, Tokyo 153.	03-3711-0109
	YAOHAN JAPAN	1256-1 Terabayashi, Okanomiya, Numazu, Shizuoka 410.	0559-23-3234
	DAIICHI	2-1-18 Kamiya-cho, Naka-ku, Hiroshima 730.	082-247-5111
	SAGAMI	3-7-1 Kyobashi, Chuo-ku, Tokyo 104.	03-3562-2231
	SOTETSU ROSEN	2-9-14 Kita Saiwai, Nishi-ku, Yokohama 220.	045-319-7064
	TOSTEM VIVA	298-1 Kami, Ageo-shi, Saitama 362.	048-773-3815
	AOKI INTERNATIONAL	6-56 Kuzugaya, Midori-ku, Yokohama 226.	045-941-1888
	CHAIN STORE OKUWA	185-3 Nakajima, Wakayama-shi 641.	0734-25-2481
	SHIMAMURA	2-19-4 Miyahara-cho, Omiya-shi, Saitama 330.	048-652-2111

DEPARTMENT STORES AND SUPERMARKETS

	MITSUKOSHI	1-4-1 Nihonbashi Muro-machi, Chuo-ku, Tokyo 103-01.	03-3241-3311
	TOKYU DEPARTMENT STORE	2-24-1 Dogenzaka, Shibuya-ku, Tokyo 150.	03-3477-3111
	TAKASHIMAYA	5-1-5 Nanba, Chuo-ku, Osaka 542.	06-631-1101
	DAIMARU	1-7-1 Shinsaibashi-suji, Chuo-ku, Osaka 542.	06-271-1231
	MATSUZAKAYA	3-16-1 Sakae, Naka-ku, Nagoya 460.	052-251-1111
★	MARUZEN	2-3-10 Nihonbashi, Chuo-ku, Tokyo 103.	03-3272-7211
	MATSUYA	3-6-1 Ginza, Chuo-ku, Tokyo 104.	03-3567-1211
	ISETAN	3-14-1 Shinjuku, Shinjuku-ku, Tokyo 160.	03-3352-1111
	YOKOHAMA MATSUZAKAYA	1-5-4 Isezaki-cho, Naka-ku, Yokohama 231.	045-261-2121
	HANSHIN DEPARTMENT STORE	1-13-13 Umeda, Kita-ku, Osaka 530.	06-345-1201
	HANKYU DEPARTMENT STORES	8-7 Kakuta-cho, Kita-ku, Osaka 530.	06-361-1381
	SOGO	1-8-3 Shinsaibashi-suji, Chuo-ku, Osaka 542.	06-281-3111
	KYOTO KINTETSU DPT. STORE	Shichijo Sagaru, Karasuma-dori, Shimogyo-ku, Kyoto 600.	075-361-1111
	MARUEI DEPARTMENT STORE	3-3-1 Sakae, Naka-ku, Nagoya 460-91.	052-264-1211
	PARCO	15-1 Udagawa-cho, Shibuya-ku, Tokyo 150.	03-3477-5731
	MARUI	3-7-18 Nakano, Nakano-ku, Tokyo 164-01.	03-3384-0101
	CREDIT SAISON	3-1-1 Higashi Ikebukuro, Toshima-ku, Tokyo 170.	03-3988-2111
	DAIEI FINANCE	7-21-1 Nishi Gotanda, Shinagawa-ku, Tokyo 141.	03-3495-8511
	JUJIYA	2-20-11 Yanagibashi, Taito-ku, Tokyo 111.	03-3864-2511
	IZUTSUYA	1-1 Senba-machi, Kokura Kita-ku, Kita Kyushu 802.	093-522-3111
	MEITETSU DEPARTMENT STORE	1-2-1 Mei-eki, Nakamura-ku, Nagoya 450.	052-585-1111
	NAGASAKIYA	3-7-14 Higashi Nihonbashi, Chuo-ku, Tokyo 103.	03-3661-3810
	DAIEI	4 -1-1 Minatojima Naka-machi, Chuo-ku, Kobe 650.	078-302-5001
	ITO-YOKADO	4-1-4 Shiba Koen, Minato-ku, Tokyo 105.	03-3459-2111
	KOTOBUKIYA	3-3-3 Honjo, Kumamoto-shi 860.	096-366-3111
	IZUMIYA	1-4-4 Hanazono Minami, Nishinori-ku, Osaka 557.	06-657-3355
	JUSCO	1-1 Kanda Nishiki-cho, Chiyoda-ku, Tokyo 101.	03-3296-7871

SEIYU	3-1-1 Higashi Ikebukuro, Toshima-ku, Tokyo 170.	03-3989-5069
NICHII	2-2-9 Awaji-machi, Chuo-ku, Osaka 541.	06-203-5071
★ UNY	2-45-19 Mei-eki, Nakamura-ku, Nagoya 450.	052-585-3111
CHUJITSUYA	2-1-11 Kabuki-cho, Shinjuku-ku, Tokyo 160.	03-3209-2760
IZUMI	2-22 Kyobashi-cho, Minami-ku, Hiroshima 732.	082-264-3211
TOBU STORE	1-4-10 Nishi Ikebukuro, Toshima-ku, Tokyo 171.	03-3989-8211
HEIWADO	31 Koizumi-cho, Hikone-shi, Shiga 522.	0749-23-3111
FUJI DENKI REIKI	6-15-12 Soto Kanda, Chiyoda-ku, Tokyo 101.	03-3832-1251
TOKYO NISSAN AUTO SALES	6-2-31 Roppongi, Minato-ku, Tokyo 106.	03-3405-2311

BANKING

INDUSTRIAL BANK OF JAPAN	1-3-3 Marunouchi, Chiyoda-ku, Tokyo 100.	03-3214-1111
LONG-TERM CREDIT BANK OF JAPAN	1-2-4 Otemachi, Chiyoda-ku, Tokyo 100.	03-3211-5111
NIPPON CREDIT BANK	1-13-10 Kudan Kita, Chiyoda-ku, Tokyo 102.	03-3263-1111
DAI-ICHI KANGYO BANK	1-1-5 Uchi Saiwai-cho, Chiyoda-ku, Tokyo 100.	03-3596-1111
HOKKAIDO TAKUSHOKU BANK	3-7 Odori Nishi, Chuo-ku, Sapporo 060.	011-271-2111
BANK OF TOKYO	1-3-2 Nihonbashi Hongoku-cho, Chuo-ku, Tokyo 103.	03-3245-1111
SAKURA BANK	1-3-1 Kudan Minami, Chiyoda-ku, Tokyo 100-91.	03-3230-3111
MITSUBISHI BANK	2-7-1 Marunouchi, Chiyoda-ku, Tokyo 100.	03-3240-1111
★ FUJI BANK	1-5-5 Otemachi, Chiyoda-ku, Tokyo 100.	03-3216-2211
SUMITOMO BANK	4-6-5 Kitahama, Chuo-ku, Osaka 541.	06-227-2111
DAIWA BANK	2-2-1 Bingo-machi, Chuo-ku, Osaka 541.	06-271-1221
SANWA BANK	3-5-6 Fushimi-machi, Chuo-ku, Osaka 541.	06-206-8111
TOKAI BANK	3-21-24 Nishiki, Naka-ku, Nagoya 460.	052-211-1111
KYOWA SAITAMA BANK	1-1-2 Otemachi, Chiyoda-ku, Tokyo 100.	03-3287-2111
DAISHI BANK	1071-1 Shichiban-cho, Higashiborimae-dori, Niigata 950-91.	025-222-4111
HOKUETSU BANK	2-2-14 Ote-dori, Nagaoka,-shi Niigata 940.	0258-35-3111
BANK OF FUKUOKA	2-13-1 Tenjin, Chuo-ku, Fukuoka 810.	092-723-2131
NISHI-NIPPON BANK	1-3-6 Hakata Eki-mae, Hakata-ku, Fukuoka 812.	092-476-2525
CHIBA BANK	1-2 Chiba Minato, Chuo-ku, Chiba 260.	043-245-1111
BANK OF YOKOHAMA	5-47 Honcho, Naka-ku, Yokohama 231.	045-201-2211
JOYO BANK	2-5-5 Minami-machi, Mito-shi 310.	0292-31-2151
GUNMA BANK	194 Motosoja-machi, Maebashi-shi 371.	0272-52-1111
ASHIKAGA BANK	4-1-25 Sakura, Utsunomiya-shi 320.	0286-22-0111
MUSASHINO BANK	1-10-8 Sakuragi-cho, Omiya -shi, Saitama 331.	048-641-6111
CHIBA KOGYO BANK	2-1-2 Saiwai-cho, Mihama-ku, Chiba 261.	043-243-2111
KANTO BANK	2-11-7 Chuo, Tsuchiura-shi, Ibaraki 300.	0298-21-8111
TOKYO TOMIN BANK	2-3-11 Roppongi, Minato-ku, Tokyo 106.	03-3582-8251
77 BANK	3-3-20 Chuo, Aoba-ku, Sendai 980.	022-267-1111
AOMORI BANK	1-9-30 Hashimoto, Aomori-shi 030.	0177-77-1111
AKITA BANK	3-2-1 Sanno, Akita-shi 010.	0188-63-1212
YAMAGATA BANK	3-1-2 Nanoka-machi, Yamagata-shi 990.	0236-23-1221
BANK OF IWATE	1-2-3 Chuo-dori, Morioka-shi 020.	0196-23-1111
TOHO BANK	3-25 O-machi, Fukushima-shi 960.	0245-23-3131
MICHINOKU BANK	1-3-1 Katsuta, Aomori-shi 030.	0177-74-1111
HOKKAIDO BANK	4-1 Odori Nishi, Chuo-ku, Sapporo 060.	011-261-7111
SHIZUOKA BANK	1-10 Gofuku-cho, Shizuoka-shi 420.	054-261-3131
JUROKU BANK	8-26 Kanda-machi, Gifu-shi 500-91.	0582-65-2111
HOKURIKU BANK	1-2-26 Tsutsumicho-dori, Toyama-shi 930.	0764-23-7111
SURUGA BANK	23 Toriyoko-cho, Numazu-shi, Shizuoka 410.	0559-62-0080
HACHIJUNI BANK	178-8 Okada, Nakagosho, Nagano-shi 380.	0262-27-1182
YAMANASHI CHUO BANK	1-20-8 Marunouchi, Kofu-shi 400.	0552-33-2111
OGAKI KYORITSU BANK	3-98 Kuruwa-machi, Ogaki-shi, Gifu 503.	0584-74-2111
FUKUI BANK	1-1-1 Junka, Fukui-shi 910.	0776-24-2030
HOKKOKU BANK	1 Shimo Tsutsumi-cho, Kanazawa-shi 920.	0762-63-1111
SHIMIZU BANK	3-1 Fujimi-cho, Shimizu-shi, Shizuoka 424.	0543-53-5151
SHIGA BANK	1-38 Hama-machi, Otsu-shi 520.	0775-24-2141
NANTO BANK	16 Hashimoto-cho, Nara-shi 630.	0742-22-1131
HYAKUGO BANK	21-27 Iwata, Tsu-shi, Mie 514.	0592-27-2151
BANK OF KYOTO	Matsubara Agaru, Karasuma-dori, Shimogyo-ku, Kyoto 600.	075-361-2211

KIYO BANK	1-35 Hon-machi, Wakayama-shi 640.	0734-23-9111
BANK OF OSAKA	1-4-1 Nishi Hon-machi, Nishi-ku, Osaka 550.	06-538-1021
SENSHU BANK	26-15 Miyamoto-cho, Kishiwada-shi, Osaka 596.	0724-23-2131
MIE BANK	7-8 Nishi Shinchi, Yokkaichi-shi, Mie 510.	0593-53-3111
★ BANK OF IKEDA	2-1-11 Jonan, Ikeda-shi, Osaka 563.	0727-51-3521
HIROSHIMA BANK	1-3-8 Kamiya-cho, Naka-ku, Hiroshima 730.	082-247-5151
YAMAGUCHI BANK	4-2-36 Takezaki-cho, Shimonoseki-shi, Yamaguchi 750.	0832-23-3411
SAN-IN GODO BANK	18 Shirakata Hon-machi, Matsue-shi, Shimane 690.	0852-26-7111
★ CHUGOKU BANK	1-15-20 Marunouchi, Okayama-shi 700.	0862-23-3111
IYO BANK	1 Minami Horibata-cho, Matsuyama-shi 790.	0899-41-1141
HYAKUJUSHI BANK	5-1 Kamei-cho, Takamatsu-shi 760.	0878-31-0114
SHIKOKU BANK	1-1-1 Minami Harimaya-cho, Kochi-shi 780.	0888-23-2111
AWA BANK	2-24-1 Nishi Senba-cho, Tokushima-shi 770.	0886-23-3131
KAGOSHIMA BANK	6-6 Kisei-cho, Kagoshima-shi 892.	0992-25-3111
SHINWA BANK	10-12 Shimanose-cho, Sasebo-shi, Nagasaki 857.	0956-24-5111
OITA BANK	3-4-1 Funai-cho, Oita-shi 870.	0975-34-1111
MIYAZAKI BANK	4-3-5 Tachibana-dori Higashi, Miyazaki-shi 880.	0985-27-3131
HIGO BANK	1 Renpei-cho, Kumamoto-shi 860.	096-325-2111
BANK OF SAGA	2-7-20 Tojin, Saga-shi 840.	0952-24-5111
EIGHTEENTH BANK	1-11 Doza-machi, Nagasaki-shi 850-91.	0958-24-1818
BANK OF OKINAWA	3-10-1 Kumoji, Naha-shi 900.	098-867-2141
BANK OF THE RYUKYUS	1-11-1 Kumoji, Naha-shi 900.	098-866-1212
MITSUI TRUST & BANKING	2-1-1 Nihonbashi Muro-machi, Chuo-ku, Tokyo 103.	03-3270-9511
MITSUBISHI TRUST & BANKING	1-4-5 Marunouchi, Chiyoda-ku, Tokyo 100.	03-3212-1211
SUMITOMO TRUST & BANKING	4-5-33 Kitahama, Chuo-ku, Osaka 541.	06-220-2121
YASUDA TRUST & BANKING	1-2-1 Yaesu, Chuo-ku, Tokyo 103.	03-3278-8111
NIPPON TRUST BANK	3-1-8 Nihonbashi, Chuo-ku, Tokyo 103.	03-3245-8111
TOYO TRUST & BANKING	1-4-3 Marunouchi, Chiyoda-ku, Tokyo 100.	03-3287-2211
CHUO TRUST & BANKING	1-7-1 Kyobashi, Chuo-ku, Tokyo 104.	03-3567-1451
JAPAN SECURITIES FINANCE	1-2-10 Nihonbashi Kayaba-cho, Chuo-ku, Tokyo 103.	03-3666-0571
OSAKA SECURITIES FINANCE	2-4-6 Kitahama, Chuo-ku, Osaka 541.	06-203-1181
BANK OF NAGOYA	3-19-17 Nishiki, Naka-ku, Nagoya 460.	052-951-5911
BANK OF KINKI	1-4-27 Shiromi, Chuo-ku, Osaka 540.	06-945-2121
NORTH PACIFIC BANK	3-11 Odori Nishi, Chuo-ku, Sapporo 060-91.	011-261-1311
FUKUTOKU BANK	1-5-9 Higashi Shinsaibashi, Chuo-ku, Osaka 542-91.	06-252-1101
AICHI BANK	3-14-12 Sakae, Naka-ku, Nagoya 460-91.	052-251-3211
GIFU BANK	1-7-1 Usa Minami, Gifu-shi 500.	0582-75-1111
DAISAN BANK	510 Kyo-machi, Matsuzaka-shi, Mie 515.	0598-23-1111
CHUKYO BANK	3-33-13 Sakae, Naka-ku, Nagoya 460-91.	052-262-6111
HYOGO BANK	1-1-2 Sannomiya-cho, Chuo-ku, Kobe 650.	078-331-8151
HIROSHIMA-SOGO BANK	1-24 Ebisu-cho, Naka-ku, Hiroshima 730.	082-241-3131
TOKYO SOWA BANK	1-6-16 Akasaka, Minato-ku, Tokyo 107.	03-3586-3111
HIGASHI-NIPPON BANK	3-11-2 Nihonbashi, Chuo-ku, Tokyo 103.	03-3273-6221
NIIGATA CHUO BANK	1176 Nanaban-cho, Kami Okawamae-dori, Niigata-shi 951.	025-229-1111
FUKUOKA CITY BANK	3-1-1 Hakata Eki-mae, Hakata-ku, Fukuoka 812.	092-441-2222
EHIME BANK	2-1 Katsuyama-cho, Matsuyama-shi 790.	0899-33-1111
TOMATO BANK	2-3-4 Ban-cho, Okayama-shi 700.	0862-21-1010
HANSHIN BANK	2-1-1 Sannomiya-cho, Chuo-ku, Kobe 651-01.	078-331-8141
KEIYO BANK	1-11-11 Fujimi, Chuo-ku, Chiba 260.	043-222-2121
BANK OF KANSAI	2-7-21 Shisaibashi-suji, Chuo-ku, Osaka 542.	06-213-0213
TAIHEIYO BANK	2-21-1 Kanda Jimbo-cho, Chiyoda-ku, Tokyo 101.	03-3230-8811
TOKUYO CITY BANK	1-5-1 Kokubun-cho, Aoba-ku, Sendai 980.	022-222-0171
KYUSHU BANK	4-24 Shimanose-cho, Sasebo-shi, Nagasaki 857.	0956-24-7111
TOCHIGI BANK	2-1-18 Nishi, Utsunomiya-shi 320.	0286-33-1241
KITA-NIPPON BANK	1-6-7 Chuo-dori, Morioka-shi 020.	0196-53-1111
BIWAKO BANK	4-5-12 Chuo, Otsu-shi 520.	0775-24-9311
KAGAWA BANK	6-1 Kamei-cho, Takamatsu-shi 760.	0878-61-3121
HANWA BANK	12 Hachiban-cho, Wakayama-shi 640.	0734-23-8181
TOWA BANK	2-12-6 Hon-machi, Maebash-shii 371.	0272-34-1111

FINANCING

	NIPPON HOUSING LOAN	1-4-2 Kasumigaseki, Chiyoda-ku, Tokyo 100.	03-3504-1031
	NICHIBOSHIN	2-1-10 Nihonbashi, Chuo-ku, Tokyo 103.	03-3271-4602
	NIPPON SHINPAN	3-33-5 Hongo, Bunkyo-ku, Tokyo 113-91.	03-3811-3111
	JACCS	1-31-1 Nishi Gotanda, Shinagawa-ku, Tokyo 141.	03-3490-0971
	ORIENT	3-1-1 Higashi Ikebukuro, Toshima-ku, Tokyo 170.	03-3989-6111
	HITACHI CREDIT	2-15-12 Nishi Shinbashi, Minato-ku, Tokyo 105.	03-3503-2111
	LIFE	2-1-1 Otemachi, Naka-ku, Hiroshima 730.	082-245-5711
★	CENTRAL FINANCE	3-20-27 Nishiki, Naka-ku, Nagoya 460.	052-203-1111
	APLUS	3-6-6 Minami Kyuhoji-machi, Chuo-ku, Osaka 541.	06-245-7771
	ORIX	2-4-1 Hamamatsu-cho, Minato-ku, Tokyo 105.	03-3435-6641
	SUMISHO LEASE	2-2-28 Dojimahama, Kita-ku, Osaka 530.	06-346-6000
	DIAMOND LEASE	2-7-2 Yaesu, Chuo-ku, Tokyo 104.	03-3274-0731

SECURITIES

	DAIWA SECURITIES	2-6-4 Otemachi, Chiyoda-ku, Tokyo 100.	03-3243-2111
	YAMAICHI SECURITIES	2-4-1 Yaesu, Chuo-ku, Tokyo 104.	03-3276-3181
	NIKKO SECURITIES	3-3-1 Marunouchi, Chiyoda-ku, Tokyo 100.	03-3283-2211
	NOMURA SECURITIES	1-9-1 Nihonbashi, Chuo-ku, Tokyo 103.	03-3211-1811
	SANYO SECURITIES	1-8-1 Nihonbashi Kayaba-cho, Chuo-ku, Tokyo 103.	03-3666-1233
★	NEW JAPAN SECURITIES	3-11 Kanda Surugadai, Chiyoda-ku, Tokyo 101-03.	03-3219-1111
	KANKAKU SECURITIES	1-6-1 Marunouchi, Chiyoda-ku, Tokyo 100.	03-3286-7111
	WAKO SECURITIES	6-1 Nihonbashi Koami-cho, Chuo-ku, Tokyo 103.	03-3667-8111
	OKASAN SECURITIES	1-17-6 Nihonbashi, Chuo-ku, Tokyo 103.	03-3272-2211
	YAMATANE SECURITIES	7-12 Nihonbashi Kabuto-cho, Chuo-ku, Tokyo 103.	03-3669-3211
	COSMO SECURITIES	1-8-12 Imabashi, Chuo-ku, Osaka 541.	06-203-2331
	DAI-ICHI SECURITIES	1-6-2 Nihonbashi Muro-machi, Chuo-ku, Tokyo 103.	03-3244-2600
★	MARUSAN SECURITIES	2-5-2 Nihonbashi, Chuo-ku, Tokyo 103.	03-3272-5211
	TOYO SECURITIES	1-20-5 Nihonbashi, Chuo-ku, Tokyo 103.	03-3274-0211
	KOKUSAI SECURITIES	2-27-1 Shinkawa, Chuo-ku, Tokyo 104.	03-3297-2111
	TOKYO SECURITIES	2-7-3 Marunouchi, Chiyoda-ku, Tokyo 100.	03-3214-3211
	KOSEI SECURITIES	4-33 Kitahama Higashi, Chuo-ku, Osaka 540.	06-943-6770
	TAIHEIYO SECURITIES	2-26-5 Nihonbashi Ningyo-cho, Chuo-ku, Tokyo 103.	03-5695-3111
	NATIONAL SECURITIES	6-7 Nihonbashi Kabuto-cho, Chuo-ku, Tokyo 103.	03-3666-0321
	MARUMAN SECURITIES	3-7-12 Sakae, Naka-ku, Nagoya 460.	052-264-1111

INSURANCE

	TOKIO MARINE & FIRE INSURANCE	1-2-1 Marunouchi, Chiyoda-ku, Tokyo 100-50.	03-3212-6211
	MITSUI MARINE & FIRE INSURANCE	3-9 Kanda Surugadai, Chiyoda-ku, Tokyo 101-11.	03-3259-3111
	SUMITOMO MARINE & FIRE INS.	2-27-2 Shinkawa, Chuo-ku, Tokyo 104.	03-3297-1111
	NIPPON FIRE & MARINE INSURANCE	2-2-10 Nihonbashi, Chuo-ku, Tokyo 103.	03-3272-8111
	YASUDA FIRE & MARINE INSURANCE	1-26-1 Nishi Shinjuku, Shinjuku-ku, Tokyo 160.	03-3349-3111
	NISSAN FIRE & MARINE INSURANCE	2-9-5 Kita Aoyama, Minato-ku, Tokyo 107.	03-3404-4111
	NISSHIN FIRE & MARINE INSURANCE	2-3-3 Shiba, Minato-ku, Tokyo 105.	03-3769-2311
	CHIYODA FIRE & MARINE INSURANCE	2-1-9 Kyobashi, Chuo-ku, Tokyo 104.	03-3281-3311
	DOWA FIRE & MARINE INSURANCE	2-3-16 Imabashi, Chuo-ku, Osaka 541.	06-363-1121
	NICHIDO FIRE & MARINE INSURANCE	5-3-16 Ginza, Chuo-ku, Tokyo 104.	03-3571-5141
	DAI-TOKYO FIRE & MARINE INS.	3-1-6 Nihonbashi, Chuo-ku, Tokyo 103.	03-3272-8811
	KOA FIRE & MARINE INSURANCE	3-7-3 Kasumigaseki, Chiyoda-ku, Tokyo 100.	03-3593-3111
	FUJI FIRE & MARINE INSURANCE	1-18-11 Minami Senba, Chuo-ku, Osaka 542.	06-271-2741
★	TAISEI FIRE & MARINE INSURANCE	4-2-1 Kudan Kita, Chiyoda-ku, Tokyo 102.	03-3234-3111

REAL ESTATE

	MITSUI FUDOSAN	2-1-1 Nihonbashi Muro-machi, Chuo-ku, Tokyo 103.	03-3246-3065
	MITSUBISHI ESTATE	2-4-1 Marunouchi, Chiyoda-ku, Tokyo 100.	03-3287-5100
	HEIWA REAL ESTATE	1-10 Nihonbashi Kabuto-cho, Chuo-ku, Tokyo 103.	03-3666-0181
	TOKYO TATEMONO	1-9-9 Yaesu, Chuo-ku, Tokyo 103.	03-3274-0111
	DAIBIRU	3-6-32 Nakanoshima, Kita-ku, Osaka 530.	06-441-1932
	SANKEI BUILDING	1-7-2 Otemachi, Chiyoda-ku, Tokyo 100.	03-3231-7171
	TOKYU LAND	1-21-2 Dogenzaka, Shibuya-ku, Tokyo 150.	03-3463-6611

HANKYU REALTY	1-1 Kakuta-cho, Kita-ku, Osaka 530.	06-313-3341
KEIHANSHIN REAL ESTATE	4-2-14 Kawara-machi, Chuo-ku, Osaka 541.	06-202-7331
L. KAKUEI	1-8-1 Shinjuku, Shinjuku-ku, Tokyo 160.	03-3350-4340
DAIWA DANCHI	1-4-12 Itachibori, Nishi-ku, Osaka 550.	06-532-6251
SUMITOMO REALTY & DEVELOPMENT	2-4-1 Nishi Shinjuku, Shinjuku-ku, Tokyo 163-08.	03-3346-1011
HANSHIN REAL ESTATE	2-2-25 Umeda, Kita-ku, Osaka 530.	06-346-1171
ODAKYU REAL ESTATE	2-7-8 Yoyogi, Shibuya-ku, Tokyo 151.	03-3370-1110
TOHO REAL ESTATE	1-5-2 Yurakucho, Chiyoda-ku, Tokyo 100.	03-3504-3333
TOWA REAL ESTATE DEVELOPMENT	2-3-13 Yaesu, Chuo-ku, Tokyo 104.	03-3272-6331
TAIHEIYO KOUHATSU	3-8-1 Kasumigaseki, Chiyoda-ku, Tokyo 100.	03-3591-1271
NICHIMO	2-6-10 Sumiyoshi, Sumiyoshi-ku, Osaka 558.	06-672-2201
DAIKYO	4-24-13 Sendagaya, Shibuya-ku, Tokyo 151.	03-3475-1111
TOC	7-22-17 Nishi Gotanda, Shinagawa-ku, Tokyo 141.	03-3494-2111
TOKYO RAKUTENCHI	4-27-14 Kotobashi, Sumida-ku, Tokyo 130.	03-3631-3121
MITSUI REAL ESTATE SALES	2-1-1 Nishi Shinjuku, Shinjuku-ku, Tokyo 163-04.	03-5381-4070

RAILWAYS

TOBU RAILWAY	1-1-2 Oshiage, Sumida-ku, Tokyo 131.	03-3621-5055
SEIBU RAILWAY	1-11-1 Kusunokidai, Tokorozawa-shi, Saitama 359.	0429-26-2035
SAGAMI RAILWAY	2-9-14 Kita Saiwai, Nishi-ku, Yokohama 220.	045-319-2111
HAKONE TOZAN RAILWAY	1-2-34 Sakae-cho, Odawara-shi, Kanagawa 250.	0465-24-2111
TOKYU	26-20 Sakuragaoka-cho, Shibuya-ku, Tokyo 150.	03-3477-6111
KEIHIN ELECTRIC EXPRESS RAILWAY	2-20-20 Takanawa, Minato-ku, Tokyo 108.	03-3280-9120
ODAKYU ELECTRIC RAILWAY	1-8-3 Nishi Shinjuku, Shinjuku-ku, Tokyo 160.	03-3349-2054
KEIO TEITO ELECTRIC RAILWAY	1-9-1 Sekido, Tama-shi, Tokyo 206.	0423-37-3112
KEISEI ELECTRIC RAILWAY	1-10-3 Oshiage, Sumida-ku, Tokyo 131.	03-3621-2242
FUJI KYUKO	5-2-1 Shin Nishihara, Fujiyoshida-shi, Yamanashi 403.	0555-22-7112
NISHI-NIPPON RAILROAD	1-11-17 Tenjin, Chuo-ku, Fukuoka 810.	092-734-1217
KINKI NIPPON RAILWAY	6-1-55 Ue Hon-machi, Tennoji-ku, Osaka 543.	06-775-3444
HANKYU	8-8 Kakuta-cho, Kita-ku, Osaka 530.	06-373-5088
HANSHIN ELECTRIC RAILWAY	1-1-24 Ebie, Fukushima-ku, Osaka 553.	06-457-2121
NANKAI ELECTRIC RAILWAY	5-1-60 Nanba, Chuo-ku, Osaka 542.	06-644-7121
KEIHAN ELECTRIC RAILWAY	1-2-27 Shiromi, Chuo-ku, Osaka 540.	06-944-2521
KOBE ELECTRIC RAILWAY	1-1-1 Daikai-dori, Hyogo-ku, Kobe 652.	078-575-2236
NAGOYA RAILROAD	1-2-4 Mei-eki, Nakamura-ku, Nagoya 450.	052-571-2111
MIE KOTSU	1-1 Chuo, Tsu-shi 514.	0592-27-3131
SANYO ELECTRIC RAILWAY	3-1-1 Oyashiki-dori, Nagata-ku, Kobe 653.	078-612-2032

TRUCKING

NIPPON EXPRESS	3-12-9 Soto Kanda, Chiyoda-ku, Tokyo 101.	03-3253-1111
YAMATO TRANSPORT	2-16-10 Ginza, Chuo-ku, Tokyo 104.	03-3541-3411
SANKYU	1-4-28 Mita, Minato-ku, Tokyo 108.	03-5484-3939
NISSIN	5 Sanban-cho, Chiyoda-ku, Tokyo 102.	03-3238-6663
★ MARUUN	1-5-11 Akasaka, Minato-ku, Tokyo 107.	03-3587-0111
MARUZEN SHOWA UNYU	2-15 Minami Naka-dori, Naka-ku, Yokohama 231.	045-671-5713
SENKO	2-7-18 Shibata, Kita-ku, Osaka 530.	06-372-1611
TONAMI TRANSPORTATION	3-2-12 Showa-machi, Takaoka-shi, Toyama 933.	0766-21-1073
JAPAN OIL TRANSPORTATION	2-2-2 Marunouchi, Chiyoda-ku, Tokyo 100.	03-3213-5511
FUKUYAMA TRANSPORTING	4-20-1 Higashi Fukatsu-cho, Fukuyama-shi, Hiroshima 721.	0849-24-2000
SEINO TRANSPORTATION	1 Taguchi-cho, Ogaki-shi, Gifu 503.	0584-81-1111
KANAGAWA CHUO KOTSU	6-18 Yaezaki-cho, Hiratsuka-shi, Kanagawa 254.	0463-22-8800
HITACHI TRANSPORT SYSTEM	3-6-3 Shibuya, Shibuya-ku, Tokyo 150.	03-3486-3111

SHIPPING

NIPPON YUSEN	2-3-2 Marunouchi, Chiyoda-ku, Tokyo 100.	03-3284-5151
MITSUI O. S. K. LINES	2-1-1 Toranomon, Minato-ku, Tokyo 105-91.	03-3587-7111
NAVIX LINE	1-1-1 Hitotsu-bashi, Chiyoda-ku, Tokyo 100.	03-3282-7500
KAWASAKI KISEN	1-2-9 Nishi Shinbashi, Minato-ku, Tokyo 105.	03-3595-5000
SHINWA KAIUN	2-2-2 Uchi Saiwai-cho, Chiyoda-ku, Tokyo 100.	03-3597-6076
INUI STEAMSHIP	8 Kaigan-dori, Chuo-ku, Kobe 650.	078-331-3367

MEIJI SHIPPING	32 Akashi-machi, Chuo-ku, Kobe 650.	078-331-3701
IINO KAIUN	2-1-1 Uchi Saiwai-cho, Chiyoda-ku, Tokyo 100.	03-3506-3033
TAIHEIYO KAIUN	2-4-1 Marunouchi, Chiyoda-ku, Tokyo 100.	03-3201-2166
SHOWA LINE	2-2-3 Uchi Saiwai-cho, Chiyoda-ku, Tokyo 100.	03-3581-8535
KYOEI TANKER	3-1-17 Nihonbashi, Chuo-ku, Tokyo 103.	03-3271-7371
DAIICHI CHUO KISEN	3-5-15 Nihonbashi, Chuo-ku, Tokyo 103.	03-3278-6800
KANSAI KISEN	6-7-15 Benten, Minato-ku, Osaka 552.	06-574-9131
AIRLINES AND AERIAL SURVEYING		
JAPAN AIRLINES	2-7-3 Marunouchi, Chiyoda-ku, Tokyo 100.	03-3284-2511
ALL NIPPON AIRWAYS	3-2-5 Kasumigaseki, Chiyoda-ku, Tokyo 100.	03-3592-3065
★ KOKUSAI KOGYO	2 Rokuban-cho, Chiyoda-ku, Tokyo 102.	03-3262-6221
PASCO	7-10-20 Akasaka, Minato-ku, Tokyo 107.	03-3586-0671
WAREHOUSING AND PORT TRANSPORTATION		
MITSUBISHI WAREHOUSE & TRANSPT.	1-19-1 Nihonbashi, Chuo-ku, Tokyo 103.	03-3278-6611
MITSUI-SOKO	1-13-12 Nihonbashi Kayaba-cho, Chuo-ku, Tokyo 103.	03-3667-5331
SUMITOMO WAREHOUSE	2-1-5 Kawaguchi, Nishi-ku, Osaka 550.	06-581-1181
SHIBUSAWA WAREHOUSE	1-13-16 Nihonbashi Kayaba-cho, Chuo-ku, Tokyo 103.	03-3660-4040
YAMATANE	1-2-21 Etchujima, Koto-ku, Tokyo 135.	03-3820-1111
TOYO WAREHOUSE	2-6-17 Mei-eki Minami, Nakamura-ku, Nagoya 450.	052-581-0251
JAPAN TRANSCITY	6-6 Chitose-cho, Yokkaichi-shi, Mie 510.	0593-53-5211
KEIHIN	3-4-20 Kaigan, Minato-ku, Tokyo 108.	03-3456-7801
TOYO WHARF & WAREHOUSE	1-1-15 Nishi Shinbashi, Minato-ku, Tokyo 105.	03-3503-5351
UTOKU EXPRESS	6-85 Benten-dori, Naka-ku, Yokohama 231.	045-201-6609
KAMIGUMI	4-1-11 Hamabe-dori, Chuo-ku, Kobe 651.	078-271-5119
MASS MEDIA AND COMMUNICATIONS		
TOKYO BROADCASTING SYSTEM	5-3-6 Akasaka, Minato-ku, Tokyo 107-06.	03-3584-3111
CHUBU-NIPPON BROADCASTING	1-2-8 Shin Sakae, Naka-ku, Nagoya 460.	052-241-8111
NIPPON TELEVISION NETWORK	14 Niban-cho, Chiyoda-ku, Tokyo 102-40.	03-5275-1111
K D D	2-3-2 Nishi Shinjuku, Shinjuku-ku, Tokyo 163.	03-3347-7111
NIPPON TELEGRAPH AND TELEPHONE	1-1-6 Uchi Saiwai-cho, Chiyoda-ku, Tokyo 100.	03-3509-5111
GAKKEN	4-40-5 Kami Ikedai, Ota-ku, Tokyo 145.	03-3726-8111
ELECTRICITY AND GAS		
TOKYO ELECTRIC POWER	1-1-3 Uchi Saiwai-cho, Chiyoda-ku, Tokyo 100.	03-3501-8111
CHUBU ELECTRIC POWER	1 Higashi Shin-cho, Higashi-ku, Nagoya 461-91.	052-951-8211
KANSAI ELECTRIC POWER	3-3-22 Nakanoshima, Kita-ku, Osaka 530-70.	06-441-8821
CHUGOKU ELECTRIC POWER	4-33 Ko-machi, Naka-ku, Hiroshima 730-91.	082-241-0211
HOKURIKU ELECTRIC POWER	15-1 Ushijima-cho, Toyama-shi 930.	0764-41-2511
TOHOKU ELECTRIC POWER	3-7-1 Ichiban-cho, Aoba-ku, Sendai 980.	022-225-2111
SHIKOKU ELECTRIC POWER	2-5 Marunouchi, Takamatsu-shi 760-91.	0878-21-5061
KYUSHU ELECTRIC POWER	2-1-82 Watanabe-dori, Chuo-ku, Fukuoka 810.	092-761-3031
HOKKAIDO ELECTRIC POWER	1-2 Odori Higashi, Chuo-ku, Sapporo 060-91.	011-251-1111
TOKYO GAS	1-5-20 Kaigan, Minato-ku, Tokyo 105.	03-3433-2111
OSAKA GAS	4-1-2 Hirano-machi, Chuo-ku, Osaka 541.	06-202-2221
TOHO GAS	19-18 Sakurada-cho, Atsuta-ku, Nagoya 456.	052-871-3511
HOKKAIDO GAS	5-373 Kita Shijo Higashi, Chuo-ku, Sapporo 060-00.	011-231-9511
SAIBU GAS	1-17-1 Chiyo, Hakata-ku, Fukuoka 812.	092-633-2211
SERVICES		
SHOCHIKU	1-13-5 Tsukiji, Chuo-ku, Tokyo 104.	03-3542-5551
TOHO	1-2-1 Yurakucho, Chiyoda-ku, Tokyo 100.	03-3591-1221
TOEI	3-2-17 Ginza, Chuo-ku, Tokyo 104.	03-3535-4641
NIKKATSU	3-28-12 Hongo, Bunkyo-ku, Tokyo 113.	03-5689-1002
SUBARU ENTERPRISE	1-10-1 Yurakucho, Chiyoda-ku, Tokyo 100.	03-3213-2861
TOKYO THEATRES	1-16-1 Ginza, Chuo-ku, Tokyo 104.	03-3561-8531
YOSHIMOTO KOGYO	11-6 Sennichi-mae, Nanba, Chuo-ku, Osaka 542.	06-643-1122
NIPPON DREAM KANKO	4-3-25 Nanba, Chuo-ku, Osaka 542.	06-631-2120

YOMIURI LAND	3294 Yanokuchi, Inagi-shi, Tokyo 206.	044-966-1111
TOKYOTOKEIBA	3-3-9 Nihonbashi, Chuo-ku, Tokyo 103.	03-3271-9105
JOBAN KOSAN	3-7-19 Higashi Nihonbashi, Chuo-ku, Tokyo 103.	03-3663-3411
TOKYO DOME	1-3-61 Koraku, Bunkyo-ku, Tokyo 112.	03-3811-2111
CHISAN-TOKAN	6-12-18 Jingu-mae, Shibuya-ku, Tokyo 150.	03-3400-7101
TOKAI KANKO	2-1-17 Takanawa, Minato-ku, Tokyo 108.	03-5488-1010
★ GAJOEN KANKO	1-8-1 Shimo Meguro, Meguro-ku, Tokyo 153.	03-3495-9501
JAPAN AIRPORT TERMINAL	1-5-1 Marunouchi, Chiyoda-ku, Tokyo 100.	03-3201-7111
DAI-ICHI HOTEL	1-2-6 Shinbashi, Minato-ku, Tokyo 105.	03-3501-4411
SUMISHO COMPUTER SERVICE	2-10-14 Ryogoku, Sumida-ku, Tokyo 130.	03-5624-1600
FUJITA KANKO	1-9-15 Kaigan, Minato-ku, Tokyo 105.	03-3433-5151
HOTEL NEW HANKYU	1-1-35 Shibata, Kita-ku, Osaka 530.	06-372-5101
TOKYU HOTEL CHAIN	6-6 Koji-machi, Chiyoda-ku, Tokyo 102.	03-3264-0111
★ KINKI NIPPON TOURIST	19-2 Kanda Matsunaga-cho, Chiyoda-ku, Tokyo 101.	03-3255-7116
TOKYU TOURIST	3-8-1 Higashiyama, Meguro-ku, Tokyo 153.	03-5704-3750
HAKUYOSHA	4-14 Kamiyama-cho, Shibuya-ku, Tokyo 150.	03-3460-1111
SECOM	1-26-2 Nishi Shinjuku, Shinjuku-ku, Tokyo 163.	03-3348-7511
C S K	2-6-1 Nishi Shinjuku, Shinjuku-ku, Tokyo 163.	03-3344-1811
INTEC	2-11 Okuda-cho, Toyama-shi 930.	0764-32-5511
INES	6-11-1 Akasaka, Minato-ku, Tokyo 107.	03-3505-6131
ASATSU	1-9-6 Shinbashi, Minato-ku, Tokyo 105.	03-3575-3001
TOYO INFORMATION SYSTEMS	1-13-33 Esaka-cho, Suita-shi, Osaka 564.	06-385-0888
NAMCO	2-1-21 Yaguchi, Ota-ku, Tokyo 146.	03-3756-2311
DAIWA KOSHO LEASE	5-20 Honmachi-bashi, Chuo-ku, Osaka 540.	06-942-8011
KONAMI	4-3-1 Toranomon, Minato-ku, Tokyo 105.	03-3432-5678

SECOND SECTION
(abbreviated names)

(★ indicates that company is listed in appropriate chapter of this book.)

	Company	Address	Telephone
	MINING		
	CHUGAI MINING	2-4-1 Marunouchi, Chiyoda-ku, Tokyo 100.	03-3201-1541
	SHOWA MINING	2-14-2 Nagata-cho, Chiyoda-ku, Tokyo 100.	03-3581-7101
	KYORITSU CERAMIC MATERIALS	2-41 Tsukisan-cho, Minato-ku, Nagoya 455.	052-661-3180
	CONSTRUCTION		
★	ISHIHARA CONSTRUCTION	25 Shinano-machi, Shinjuku-ku, Tokyo 160.	03-3355-2411
	DAIWA CONSTRUCTION	1-5-34 Yushima, Bunkyo-ku, Tokyo 113.	03-5689-4111
	KOKUNE	3-3-1 Iidabashi, Chiyoda-ku, Tokyo 102.	03-3222-8600
	SUZUNUI INDUSTRY	1-11-31 Jonan-cho, Hitachi, Ibaraki 317.	0294-22-5311
	NANKAI CONSTRUCTION	3-5-19 Nanba Naka, Naniwa-ku, Osaka 556.	06-644-7802
	OHKI	1-23-2 Kanda Suda-cho, Choyoda-ku, Tokyo 101.	03-3255-4111
	MORI-GUMI	4-5-17 Dosho-machi, Chuo-ku, Osaka 541.	06-201-2761
	INOUE KOGYO	2-3 Wada-machi, Takasaki, Gunma 370.	0273-22-5841
	TATSUMURA GUMI	5-4-35 Minami Aoyama, Minato-ku, Tokyo 107.	03-3406-3111
	NIPPON TETRAPOD	2-7-1 Nishi Shinjuku, Shinjuku-ku, Tokyo 163-07.	03-3342-0151
	MEIKO CONSTRUCTION	1-1-17 Mei-eki, Nishi-ku, Nagoya 451.	052-589-1501
	P. S.	3-4-1 Marunouchi, Chiyoda-ku, Tokyo 100.	03-3216-1981
	AOKI MARINE	6-13-7 Fukushima, Fukushima-ku, Osaka 553.	06-455-7158
	TOKURA CONSTRUCTION	3-13-5 Nishiki, Naka-ku, Nagoya 460.	052-961-3271
	KANESHITA CONSTRUCTION	471-1 Suzu, Miyazu, Kyoto 629-22.	0772-46-3151
	NIPPON DRY-CHEMICAL	2-3-12 Higashi Shinagawa, Shinagawa-ku, Tokyo 140.	03-5460-6013
	MISAWA CERAMICS	2-1 Maeno-cho Higashi, Konan, Aichi 483.	0587-55-1177
	JAPAN FOUNDATION ENGINEERING	6-22 Matsugae-cho, Kita-ku, Osaka 530.	06-351-5621
	NISSEKI HOUSE INDUSTRY	1-4 Nihonbashi Kodenma-cho, Chuo-ku, Tokyo 103.	03-3663-0431
	SEKISUI HOUSE-W	3-5-24 Miyahara, Yodogawa-ku, Osaka 532.	06-391-7571
	CHUBU ENGINEERING	28 Tonowari, Jinno Shinden-cho, Toyohashi, Aichi 441.	0532-31-1111
	ELECTRICAL AND OTHER ENGINEERING		
	HOKURIKU ELECTRICAL CONSTRUCT.	1-1-1 Higashi Denjigata-machi, Toyama 930.	0764-31-6551
★	NIPPON DENTSU KENSETSU	2-21-1 Isoji, Minato-ku, Osaka 552.	06-575-3881
	K T K TELECOMMUNICATIONS ENG.	3-3-15 Edobori, Nishi-ku, Osaka 550.	06-446-3331
	TOHOKU TELECOM. CONSTRUCTION	1-2-23 Shintera, Wakabayashi-ku, Sendai 980.	022-297-5111
	CHUBU COMMUNICATION CONSTR.	1-6-7 Habashita, Nishi-ku, Nagoya 451.	052-563-5000
	SEIBU ELECTRIC INDUSTRIAL	2-1-42 Tsuboi, Kumamoto 860.	096-344-1111
	CHITOSE ELECTRICAL CONSTRUCT.	1-52-10 Nishigahara, Kita-ku, Tokyo 114.	03-3917-8151
	KODENSHA	6-12-10 Ginza, Chuo-ku, Tokyo 104.	03-3571-4351
	SUMITOMO DENSETSU	2-1-4 Awaza, Nishi-ku, Osaka 550.	06-537-3400
	SHIN NIPPON AIR CONDITIONING ENG.	4-4-20 Hongoku-cho, Nihonbashi, Chuo-ku, Tokyo 103.	03-3279-5671
	SHIN NIPPON AIR CONDITIONING ENG.	4-4-20 Hongoku-cho, Nihonbashi, Chuo-ku, Tokyo 103.	03-3279-5671
	HOAN KOGYO	1-6-14 Yaesu, Chuo-ku, Tokyo 103.	03-3271-4855
	SANWA-DAIEI ELECTRIC CONSTRUCT.	5-18-1 Shinbashi, Minato-ku, Tokyo 105.	03-3436-3111
	SANYO ENGINEERING & CONSTRUCT.	9 Niban-cho, Chiyoda-ku, Tokyo 102.	03-3265-6181
	TOYOKO RIKEN	89-6 Yamashita-cho, Naka-ku, Yokohama 231.	045-663-3111
	YAMATO SETUBI CONSTRUCTION	118 Furuichi-machi, Maebashi 371.	0272-26-3111
	CHUO BUILD INDUSTRY	1-10-12 Nihonbashi Horidome-cho, Chuo-ku, Tokyo 103.	03-3661-9631
	NEC SYSTEM INTEGRATION & CONST.	3-9-4 Nishi Shinbashi, Minato-ku, Tokyo 105.	03-3436-3311
	MIYAJI CONSTRUCTION & ENG.	2-11-1 Sugamo, Toshima-ku, Tokyo 170.	03-3917-7711
	ATAKA CONSTRUCTION & ENG.	2-1-9 Itachibori, Nishi-ku, Osaka 550.	06-533-5011
	HIBIYA ENGINEERING	5-37-8 Shiba, Minato-ku, Tokyo 108.	03-3454-1385
	FOODS AND BEVERAGES		
	TOFUKU FLOUR MILLS	4-9-20 Nanotsu,Chuo-ku, Fukuoka 810.	092-781-1661
★	FUJI FLOUR MILLING	3-1-18 Seikai, Shimizu-shi, Shizuoka 424.	0543-34-2311
	MASUDA FLOUR MILLING	1-1-10 Umagaka-cho, Nagata-ku, Kobe 653.	078-681-6703

TORIGOE FLOUR MILLING	1-40 Gion-cho, Hakata-ku, Fukuoka 812.	092-281-8910
CHUBU SHIRYO	14-6 Kitahama-cho, Chita-shi, Aichi 478.	0562-33-2102
NICHIWA SANGYO	19-5 Sumiyoshi Hama-cho, Higashi Nada-ku, Kobe 658.	078-811-1221
FUJI SEITO	1-4-10 Seikai, Shimizu-shi, Shizuoka 424.	0543-34-5353
ENSUIKO SUGAR REFINING	13-46 Daikoku-cho, Tsurumi-ku, Yokohama 230.	045-501-1251
NIHON SUGAR REFINING	1-4-9 Nihonbashi Kayaba-cho, Chuo-ku, Tokyo 103.	03-3667-7811
NISSIN SUGAR MFG.	14-1 Nihonbashi Koami-cho, Chuo-ku, Tokyo 103.	03-3668-2229
SURUGAYA	6 Suruga-machi, Wakayama-shi 640.	0734-22-1151
IMURAYA CONFECTIONERY	3730 Komori-cho, Takachaya, Tsu-shi 514.	0592-34-2131
NAGASAKIYA	Karasuma Higashiiru, Shijo-dori, Shimogyo-ku, Kyoto 600.	075-231-5366
KANRO	2-3-18 Shimo Ochiai, Shinjuku-ku, Tokyo 161.	03-3950-8811
ROKKO BUTTER	1-3-13 Sakaguchi-dori, Chuo-ku, Kobe 651.	078-231-4681
SNOW BRAND FOOD	2-15-4 Nihonbashi Kayaba-cho, Chuo-ku, Tokyo 103.	03-5640-8611
YONEKYU	1259 Terabayashi, Okanomiya, Numazu-shi, Shizuoka 410.	0559-22-5321
FUKUTOME MEAT PACKERS	2-6-75 Kusatsuko, Nishi-ku, Hiroshima 733.	082-278-6161
CHUYU	4-1-1 Minami-machi, Shinzaike, Nada-ku, Kobe 657.	078-882-0001
NIKKA WHISKY DISTILLING	5-4-31 Minami Aoyama, Minato-ku, Tokyo 107.	03-3498-0331
HOKKAIDO COCA-COLA BOTTLING	1-2-1 Ichijo, Kiyota, Toyohira-ku, Sapporo 004.	011-888-2001
SANYO COCA-COLA BOTTLING	2-11-20 Higashi Chida-cho, Naka-ku, Hiroshima 730.	082-245-8111
MIKASA COCA-COLA BOTTLING	1-1-15 Omiya-cho, Nara-shi 630.	0742-27-0111
KINKI COCA-COLA BOTTLING	7-9-31 Senrigaoka, Settsu-shi, Osaka 566.	06-330-2222
KUMAZAWA SEIYU SANGYO	2-2 Suehiro-cho, Yokkaichi-shi, Mie 510.	0593-51-1221
BOSO OIL & FAT	1-1-8 Nihonbashi Honcho, Chuo-ku, Tokyo 103.	03-3241-4226
SETTSU OIL MILL	6-5-77 Noda, Fukushima-ku, Osaka 553.	06-461-0531
MARUKIN SHOYU	Naeba, Utsumi-cho, Shozu-gun, Kagawa 761-44.	0879-82-1221
BULL-DOG SAUCE	11-5 Nihonbashi Kabuto-cho, Chuo-ku, Tokyo 103.	03-3668-6811
S & B SHOKUHIN	18-6 Nihonbashi Kabuto-cho, Chuo-ku, Tokyo 103.	03-3668-0551
YUTAKA SHOYU	34-1 Kawawaki, Taketoyo-cho, Chita-gun, Aichi 470-23.	0569-72-1231
SANBISHI	53 Wakamiya, Shinotaba, Kazakai-cho, Aichi 441-01	05337-2-3111
ORIENTAL YEAST	10-11 Nihonbashi Kodenma-cho, Chuo-ku, Tokyo 103.	03-3663-8205
NIHON SHOKUHIN KAKO	3-4-1 Marunouchi, Chiyoda-ku, Tokyo 100.	03-3212-2081
MIHIRO SHOKUHIN	6-12-18 Jingu-mae, Shibuya-ku, Tokyo 150.	03-3498-9911
ISHII FOOD	2-9-24 Honcho, Funabashi-shi, Chiba 273.	0474-35-0141
SONTON FOOD INDUSTRY	2-9-4 Nihonbashi Kayaba-cho, Chuo-ku, Tokyo 103.	03-3669-7371
★ MYOJO FOODS	3-50-11 Sendagaya, Shibuya-ku, Tokyo 151.	03-3470-1691
★ TAIYO KAGAKU	9-5 Akahori Shin-machi, Yokkaichi-shi, Mie 510.	0593-52-2555
SHINOBU FOODS PRODUCTS	3-13-14 Himejima, Nishi Yodogawa-ku, Osaka 555.	06-473-7383
FUJICCO	6-13-4 Minatojima Naka-machi, Chuo-ku, Kobe 650.	078-303-5911
ROCK FIELD	48 Akashi-cho, Chuo-ku, Kobe 650.	078-331-1021

TEXTILES

SHOEI	1-2-1 Kanda Nishiki-cho, Chiyoda-ku, Tokyo 101.	03-3292-3381
JOMO TWISTING THREAD	370 Rokku-machi, Maebashi-shi 371.	0272-24-2111
SAITAMA SENI KOGYO	1-102 Ishihara, Kumagaya-shi, Saitama 360.	0485-23-2018
OMIKENSHI	3-5-13 Awaji-machi, Chuo-ku, Osaka 541.	06-205-7300
HIRABO	6-12-18 Jingu-mae, Shibuya-ku, Tokyo 150.	03-3406-6511
DOKO SPINNING	Maru-2-36 Oguchi-cho, Niwa-gun, Aichi 480-01.	0587-95-6211
DAIICHIBO	3-6-2 Bingo-machi, Chuo-ku, Osaka 541.	06-264-3541
SHIN NIPPON SPINNING	3-1 Hinode-cho, Kasuga-shi, Fukuoka 816.	092-581-0031
SAIBO	1-1-70 Maekawa, Kawaguchi-shi, Saitama 333.	0482-67-5151
SHINNAIGAI TEXTILE	4-2-7 Koraibashi, Chuo-ku, Osaka 541.	06-202-0471
TERADA COTTON SPINNING	28-55 Tsuda Minami-cho, Kaizuka-shi, Osaka 597.	0724-31-2424
TOYAMA SPINNING	1-7-13 Azuchi-machi, Chuo-ku, Osaka 541.	06-261-7077
NANKAI WORSTED SPINNING	2-5-28 Kyutaro-machi, Chuo-ku, Osaka 541.	06-252-8855
CHUO WOOLLEN MILLS	1-5-13 Nishiki, Naka-ku, Nagoya 460.	052-202-3571
KANEMATSU WOOLEN MILLS	2-2-7 Kawara-machi, Chuo-ku, Osaka 541.	06-227-6500
BISAI WOOL YARN SPINNING	3-15-1 Nishi-machi, Inazawa-shi, Aichi 492.	0587-21-3111
TOSCO	1-1-10 Nihonbashi, Ningyo-cho, Chuo-ku, Tokyo 103.	03-3667-3321
NIHON SEIMA	3-1-8 Azumadori, Chuo-ku, Kobe 651.	078-251-8271
KITANIHON SPINNING	1-2-40 Owari-cho, Kanazawa-shi 920.	0762-22-2131

Company	Address	Telephone
OHTORI	1-8-9 Minami Kyutaro-machi, Chuo-ku, Osaka 541.	06-261-4541
ORIX INTERIOR	1-17-5 Shin-machi, Nishi-ku, Osaka 550.	06-536-3681
★ TOWA ORIMONO	737 Nishi Itamochi, Tondabayashi-shi, Osaka 584.	0721-34-1234
CAROLINA	1310-1 Inami-machi, Higashi Tonami-gun, Toyama 932-02.	0763-82-1620
HOTTA TEXTILE INDUSTRY	556-1 Hakari-cho, Ashikaga-shi, Tochigi 326-03.	0284-71-1181
TOYO CLOTH	2-2-7 Hon-machi, Chuo-ku, Osaka 541.	06-271-5051
NIPPON ORIMONO KAKO	1-1 Kosuna-machi, Kosei-cho, Koga-gun, Shiga 520-32.	0748-75-1411
SOTO KOGYO	5-1-1 Kagoya, Bisai-shi, Aichi 494.	0586-45-1121
DAIDO-MARUTA FINISHING	12 Minami Ochiai-cho, Kisshoin, Minami-ku, Kyoto 601.	075-681-4151
KANBO PRAS	1-3-9 Azuchi-machi, Chuo-ku, Osaka 541.	06-262-1277
SOKO SEIREN	4-111 Tamaboko, Kanazawa-shi 921.	0762-91-3811
GISEN	1941-1 Honjo Kumano-mae, Gifu-shi 500.	0582-52-2318
AUBEX	5-1-12 Narihira, Sumida-ku, Tokyo 130.	03-3625-3151
KYOKUICHI	3-11-23 Nishiki, Naka-ku, Nagoya 460.	052-971-2011
HOGY MEDICAL	1-12-4 Yushima, Bunkyo-ku, Tokyo 113.	03-3833-1541

PAPER AND PULP

Company	Address	Telephone
MISHIMA PAPER	506 Harada, Fuji-shi, Shizuoka 417.	0545-52-4060
SANKO PAPER MFG.	1180-1 Denpo, Fuji-shi, Shizuoka 417.	0545-52-4070
CHUETSU	2-8-6 Kami Akae-machi, Toyama 930.	0764-42-2851
TAIHEI PAPER MFG.	2-10-12 Uchi Kanda, Chiyoda-ku, Tokyo 101.	03-3252-7331
GENERAL	2-14-37 Chuo, Joto-ku, Osaka 536.	06-933-1801
CHIYODA SHIGYO	1-7-8 Shibuya, Shibuya-ku, Tokyo 150.	03-3407-8481
FURUBAYASHI SHIKO	3-1-12 Otedori, Chuo-ku, Osaka 540.	06-941-8561
SUPERBAG	5-18-11 Nishi Ikebukuro, Toshima-ku, Tokyo 171.	03-3987-9201
DAINIPPON SHIGYO	3-14-15 Nishiki, Naka-ku, Nagoya 460.	052-971-2651
NIPPON HI-PACK	5-7-1 Nyoisaru-cho, Kasugai-shi, Aichi 486.	0568-33-1311
THE PACK	2-9-9 Higashi Obase, Higashinari-ku, Osaka 537.	06-972-1221
TOKYO SEROFAN	1-5-15 Kyobashi, Chuo-ku, Tokyo 104.	03-3272-3461

CHEMICALS

Company	Address	Telephone
★ TAKI CHEMICAL	2 Midori-machi, Beppu-cho, Kakogawa-shi, Hyogo 675-01.	0794-37-2111
KATAKURA CHIKKARIN	1-2-3 Otemachi, Chiyoda-ku, Tokyo 100.	03-3213-2511
TSURUMI SODA	1-7 Suehiro-cho, Tsurumi-ku, Yokohama 230.	045-503-7300
KIBUN FOODS CHEMIFA	2-12-11 Minato, Chuo-ku, Tokyo 104.	03-3206-0778
FUJI TITANIUM INDUSTRY	3-6-32 Nakanoshima, Kita-ku, Osaka 530.	06-441-6856
TOHO ACETYLENE	3-2-9 Kyobashi, Chuo-ku, Tokyo 104.	03-3274-1012
NIHON KAGAKU SANGYO	2-20-5 Shitaya, Taito-ku, Tokyo 110.	03-3876-3131
SHOWA TANSAN	3-3-23 Misaki-cho, Chiyoda-ku, Tokyo 101.	03-3237-2360
MARUO CALCIUM	1455 Nishioka, Uozumi-cho, Akashi-shi, Hyogo 674.	078-942-2112
ISE CHEMICALS	2-7-12 Yaesu, Chuo-ku, Tokyo 104.	03-3281-0141
TAOKA CHEMICAL	4-2-11 Nishi Mikuni, Yodogawa-ku, Osaka 532.	06-394-1221
HONSHU CHEMICAL INDUSTRY	1-5-3 Yaesu, Chuo-ku, Tokyo 103.	03-3272-1481
KAWASAKI KASEI CHEMICALS	3-8-2 Nihonbashi, Chuo-ku, Tokyo 103.	03-3272-3811
NIPPON PIGMENT	1-9-14 Kaji-cho, Chiyoda-ku, Tokyo 101.	03-3258-1411
SUGAI CHEMICAL INDUSTRY	4-4-6 Uzu, Wakayama-shi 640.	0734-22-1171
YAMAMOTO CHEMICALS	1-43 Yuge-cho Minami, Yao-shi, Osaka 581.	0729-49-4561
OSAKA ORGANIC CHEMICAL IND.	1-7-20 Azuchi-machi, Chuo-ku, Osaka 541.	06-264-5071
FUDOW	4-11-26 Nishi Rokugo, Ota-ku, Tokyo 144.	03-3737-0611
PLAS-TECH	3-2-4 Kyobashi, Chuo-ku, Tokyo 104.	03-3272-5561
KODAMA CHEMICAL INDUSTRY	1-1-12 Ueno, Taito-ku, Tokyo 110.	03-3834-0511
LONSEAL	4-15-3 Midori, Sumida-ku, Tokyo 130.	03-5600-1811
MISAWA CERAMIC CHEMICAL	3-7-1 Kyobashi, Chuo-ku, Tokyo 104.	03-3562-2451
TIGERS POLYMER	1-4-1 Shin Senri Higashi-machi, Toyonaka-shi, Osaka 565.	06-834-1551
TOSHIBA CHEMICAL	3-3-9 Shinbashi, Minato-ku, Tokyo 105.	03-3502-3212
KAWAGUCHI CHEMICAL INDUSTRY	2-8-4 Uchi Kanda, Chiyoda-ku, Tokyo 101.	03-3254-8481
NIPPON FINE CHEMICAL	2-4-9 Bingo-machi, Chuo-ku, Osaka 541.	06-231-4781
★ TOHO CHEMICAL INDUSTRY	1-2-5 Nihonbashi Ningyo-cho, Chuo-ku, Tokyo 103.	03-3668-2271
ISHIHARA CHEMICAL	5-26 Nishi Yanagihara-cho, Hyogo-ku, Kobe 652.	078-681-4801

PHARMACEUTICALS

TEIKOKU HORMONE MFG.	2-5-1 Akasaka, Minato-ku, Tokyo 107.	03-3583-8361
BIOFERMIN PHARMACEUTICAL	2-1 Niban-cho, Nagata-ku, Kobe 653.	078-575-5501
WAKODO	4-20 Kanda Sakuma-cho, Chiyoda-ku, Tokyo 101.	03-3861-8521
MORISHITA JINTAN	1-1-30 Tamatsukuri, Chuo-ku, Osaka 540.	06-761-1131
RIKEN VITAMIN	2-9-18 Misaki-cho, Chiyoda-ku, Tokyo 101.	03-5275-5111
★ YUKI GOSEI KOGYO	2-3-24 Hirakawa-cho, Chiyoda-ku, Tokyo 102.	03-5275-5061
NIHON IYAKUHIN KOGYO	1-6-21 Sogawa, Toyama-shi 930.	0764-32-2121
EIKEN CHEMICAL	1-33-8 Hongo, Bunkyo-ku, Tokyo 113.	03-3813-5401
NISSUI PHARMACEUTICAL	2-11-1 Sugamo, Toshima-ku, Tokyo 170.	03-3918-8161

PAINTS

KAWAKAMI PAINT MFG.	2-41-1 Tsukaguchi Honcho, Amagasaki-shi, Hyogo 661.	06-421-6325
★ FUJIKURA KASEI	2-6-15 Shiba Koen, Minato-ku, Tokyo 105.	03-3436-1101
ROCK PAINT	3-1-47 Himejima, Nishi Yodogawa-ku, Osaka 555.	06-473-1551
ASAHIPEN	4-1-12 Tsurumi, Tsurumi-ku, Osaka 538.	06-930-5001
ISAMU PAINT	2-15-24 Sagizu, Fukushima-ku, Osaka 553.	06-458-0036
TOKYO PRINTING INK MFG.	2-7-15 Tabata Shin-machi, Kita-ku, Tokyo 114.	03-3893-5151

MISCELLANEOUS CHEMICALS

ORIENTAL PHOTO INDUSTRIAL	1-11-3 Okubo, Shinjuku-ku, Tokyo 169.	03-3205-3521
TERAOKA SEISAKUSHO	1-4-22 Hiro-machi, Shinagawa-ku, Tokyo 140.	03-3491-1141
SHOWA CHEMICAL INDUSTRY	2-23-18 Shimo Meguro, Meguro-ku, Tokyo 153.	03-3494-0491
FUMAKILLA	11 Kanda Mikura-cho, Chiyoda-ku, Tokyo 101.	03-3252-5941
CEMEDINE	4-5-9 Higashi Gotanda, Shinagawa-ku, Tokyo 141.	03-3442-1331

PETROLEUM PRODUCTS

TOA OIL	2-2-1 Otemachi, Chiyoda-ku, Tokyo 100.	03-3211-1451
NIPPON SEIRO	2-8-7 Kyobashi, Chuo-ku, Tokyo 104.	03-3561-5931
YUSHIRO CHEMICAL INDUSTRY	2-34-16 Chidori, Ota-ku, Tokyo 146.	03-3750-6761

RUBBER

DAIKI ENGINEERING	2-16-1 Shinbashi, Minato-ku, Tokyo 105.	03-3503-4331
SHOWA RUBBER	32-1 Senju Asahi-cho, Adachi-ku, Tokyo 120.	03-3888-8201
NITTO KAKO	6-1-3 Ichinomiya, Samukawa-machi, Kanagawa 253-01.	0467-74-3111
OHTSU TIRE & RUBBER	9-1 Kawara-machi, Izumi Otsu-shi, Osaka 595.	0725-21-1111
FUJIKURA RUBBER	2-11-20 Nishi Gotanda, Shinagawa-ku, Tokyo 141.	03-3490-2111
TOYO BOSUIFU MFG.	1-27-13 Wakagi, Itabashi-ku, Tokyo 174.	03-3933-3151
SAKURA RUBBER	1-21-17 Sasazuka, Shibuya-ku, Tokyo 151.	03-3466-2171
TOKAI RUBBER INDUSTRIES	3600 Utazu, Kita Toyama, Komaki-shi, Aichi 485.	0568-77-2121
HEISEI POLYMER	1-3-15 Nihonbashi Horidome-cho, Chuo-ku, Tokyo 103.	03-3639-0351
SAGAMI RUBBER INDUSTRIES	2-1 Moto-machi, Atsugi-shi, Kanagawa 243.	0462-21-2311

GLASS

NIPPON MUKI	3-1 Kanda Nishiki-cho, Chiyoda-ku, Tokyo 101.	03-3295-1515
ARISAWA MFG.	1-5-5 Minami Hon-machi, Joetsu-shi, Niigata 943.	0255-24-5126
IWAKI GLASS	3-2-3 Marunouchi, Chiyoda-ku, Tokyo 100.	03-3211-5441

CEMENT AND CONCRETE PRODUCTS

NOZAWA	15 Naniwa-cho, Chuo-ku, Kobe 651-01.	078-333-4111

MISCELLANEOUS CERAMICS

TEIHYU	4-30-5 Ryogoku, Sumida-ku, Tokyo 130.	03-5600-9111
HANEDA HUME PIPE	1-22-2 Nishi Shinjuku, Shinjuku-ku, Tokyo 160.	03-3345-7831
ASAHI CONCRETE WORKS	1-8-2 Tsukiji, Chuo-ku, Tokyo 104.	03-3542-1201
Z•R•CONCRETE	1000 Shimo Imaizumi, Ebina-shi, Kanagawa 243-04.	0462-33-3363
TOYO PILE HUME PIPE PRODUCTION	315-2 Ichihara, Numazu-shi, Shizuoka 410-03.	0559-67-3535
ASANO SLATE	2-12-10 Shiba Daimon, Minato-ku, Tokyo 108.	03-3434-1211
MITANI SEKISAN	1-3-B-16 Nakase, Mihama-ku, Chiba 261.	043-296-4100
ISHIKAWAJIMA CONSTR. MATERIALS	2-6-21 Yaesu, Chuo-ku, Tokyo 104.	03-3277-4170

S E C	5, Misono-machi, Amagasaki-shi, Hyogo 660.	06-413-3811
DAITO	3-4-38 Matsubara, Izumi Sano-shi, Osaka 598.	0724-64-5881
ASAHI EITO	451 Kobirao, Mihara-cho, Minami Kawachi-gun, Osaka 587.	0723-62-5235
JANIS	2-88 Karasaki-cho, Tokoname-shi, Aichi 479.	0569-35-3150
NIKKO	383 Ainoki-machi, Matsuo-shi, Ishikawa 924.	0762-76-2121
★ NIPPON CRUCIBLE	1-21-3 Ebisu, Shibuya-ku, Tokyo 150.	03-3443-5551
MINO CERAMIC	719 Terakado-cho, Mizunami-shi, Gifu 509-61.	0572-68-2106
YOTAI REFRACTORIES	1-4-12 Sonezaki Shinchi, Kita-ku, Osaka 530.	06-341-3821
TOKAI KONETSU KOGYO	6-14-1 Nishi Shinjuku, Shinjuku-ku, Tokyo 160.	03-3340-1511
KYUSHU REFRACTORIES	1175 Uraibe, Bizen-shi, Okayama 705.	0869-64-3321
★ NIPPON RESIBON	1-22-10 Kita Horie, Nishi-ku, Osaka 550.	06-538-0136
UBE CHEMICAL INDUSTRIES	1985 Kogushi, Ube-shi, Yamaguchi 755.	0836-31-0156
RIKEN CORUNDUM	547-1 Miya-mae, Konosu-shi, Saitama 365.	0485-96-3550
MIE HORO	1001 Hoshikawa, Kuwana-shi, Mie 511.	0594-31-3131
NIHON KENSHI	2-12-9 Minami Horie, Nishi-ku, Osaka 550.	06-536-3511
IRON AND STEEL		
TOYO STEEL	1-18-14 Shinbashi, Minato-ku, Tokyo 105.	03-3508-0151
TAKASAGO TEKKO	1-1-1 Shingashi, Itabashi-ku, Tokyo 175.	03-5399-8111
TOSHIBA STEEL TUBE	12-1 Minato-cho, Kawasaki-ku, Kawasaki 210.	044-222-5391
CHUO DENKI KOGYO	272 Taguchi, Myoko Kogen-machi, Niigata 949-21.	0255-86-3101
AUTOMOBILE FOUNDRY	25-25 Egasaki-cho, Tsurumi-ku, Yokohama 230.	045-575-3500
CHUO MALLEABLE IRON	3-1-1 Tomikawa-cho, Nakagawa-ku, Nagoya 454.	052-361-3141
KAWAGUCHI METAL INDUSTRIES	18-19 Miya-machi, Kawaguchi-shi, Saitama 332.	0482-59-1111
JAPAN CASTING	2-1 Shiraishi-cho, Kawasaki-ku, Kawasaki 210.	044-322-3751
DAIWA HEAVY INDUSTRY	1-21-23 Kabe, Asakita-ku, Hiroshima 731-02.	082-814-2101
NIPPON CHUTETSUKAN	3-16-9 Uchi Kanda, Chiyoda-ku, Tokyo 101.	03-3252-4661
T D F	3-43-1 Omori Kita, Ota-ku, Tokyo 143.	03-3766-8621
JAPAN DROP FORGE	2-1 Ohama-cho, Amagasaki-shi, Hyogo 660.	06-416-1051
METALART	1350 Noji-cho, Kusatsu-shi, Shiga 525.	0775-63-2111
KOKOKU STEEL WIRE	2-15-1 Kyobashi, Chuo-ku, Tokyo 104.	03-3561-2171
SUZUKI METAL INDUSTRY	1-8-2 Marunouchi, Chiyoda-ku, Tokyo 100.	03-3214-4111
NIPPON SEISEN	4-2-7 Koraibashi, Chuo-ku, Osaka 541.	06-222-5431
SHINKO WIRE	10-1 Nakahama-cho, Amagasaki-shi, Hyogo 660.	06-411-1051
TOKYO SHEARING	2-12-8 Shinkawa, Chuo-ku, Tokyo 104.	03-3553-5111
DAIKI ALUMINIUM INDUSTRY	1-4-8 Tosabori, Nishi-ku, Osaka 550.	06-444-2751
TOHO TITANIUM	2-13-31 Konan, Minato-ku, Tokyo 108.	03-3458-4411
NON-FERROUS METALS		
TOKYO TUNGSTEN	2-6-1 Kaji-cho, Chiyoda-ku, Tokyo 101.	03-3258-5325
NIHON SEIKO	3-2 Shimo Miyabi-cho, Shinjuku-ku, Tokyo 162.	03-3235-0021
NIPPON FOIL MFG.	5-13-9 Nishi Nakajima, Yodogawa-ku, Osaka 532.	06-309-1285
NIPPON SHINDO	3-1-1 Minami Shima-machi, Sakai-shi, Osaka 590.	0722-29-0346
TOHO KINZOKU	2-6-17 Kitahama, Chuo-ku, Osaka 541.	06-202-3376
WIRES AND CABLES		
RIKEN ELECTRIC WIRE	1-12-22 Tsukiji, Chuo-ku, Tokyo 104.	03-3542-3711
ONAMBA	3-1-27 Fukae Kita, Higashinari-ku, Osaka 537.	06-976-6101
NIHON ELECTRIC WIRE & CABLE	2-2-302 Suminodo, Daito-shi, Osaka 574.	0720-71-0364
DIECASTINGS		
AHRESTY	3-19 Kanda Nishiki-cho, Chiyoda-ku, Tokyo 101.	03-3293-2881
KYOTO DIE-CASTING	3-5-26 Zuiko, Higashi Yodogawa-ku, Osaka 533.	06-328-1321
TOKYO RIKA MFG.	3-1-1 Maeno-cho, Itabashi-ku, Tokyo 174.	03-3960-6111
METAL PRODUCTS		
NIHON SEIKAN	2-275 Yoshino-cho, Omiya-shi, Saitama 330.	048-665-1251
TATEYAMA ALUMINIUM INDUSTRY	550 Hayakawa, Takaoka-shi, Toyama 933.	0766-20-3131
HARUMOTO IRON WORKS	4-1-4 Hongo, Bunkyo-ku, Tokyo 113.	03-5684-0521
TAKIGAMI STEEL CONSTRUCTION	1-9-9 Minato, Chuo-ku, Tokyo 104.	03-3552-6681

	Company	Address	Telephone
	JAPAN STEEL TOWER	1-6-27 Shin Suna, Koto-ku, Tokyo 136.	03-3645-3181
	KAWAGISHI BRIDGE WORKS	1-2-13 Higashi Shinbashi, Minato-ku, Tokyo 105.	03-3572-5401
	NASU DENKI TEKKO	1-1-14 Shinjuku, Shinjuku-ku, Tokyo 160.	03-3351-6131
	TAKADA KIKO	2-1-12 Shikitsu Nishi, Naniwa-ku, Osaka 556.	06-649-5100
★	SHIN NIKKEI	2-7-23 Kiba, Koto-ku, Tokyo 135.	03-3820-2100
	SAKAI IRON WORKS	3-1 Dejima Nishi-machi, Sakai-shi, Osaka 590.	0722-44-1515
	AG AJIKAWA	4-11-88 Takeshima, Nishi Yodogawa-ku, Osaka 555.	06-474-2050
	ALMETAX MANUFACTURING	7-1-26 Nishi Nakashima, Yodogawa-ku, Osaka 532.	06-305-3151
	NIPPON ALUMINIUM	3-9-39 Mikuni Hon-machi, Yodogawa-ku, Osaka 532.	06-394-6211
★	NIPPON FILCON	3-27-24 Ikejiri, Setagaya-ku, Tokyo 154.	03-3421-5131
	HITACHI POWDERED METALS	520 Minoridai, Matsudo-shi, Chiba 271.	0473-62-1171
	KDK	363 Shimonouchi, Yasuragawa, Takahagi-shi, Ibaraki 318.	0293-23-2511
	NISCO	8-24 Hiroshiba-cho, Suita-shi, Osaka 564.	06-384-1541
	AMATEI	9 Nishi Takasu-cho, Amagasaki-shi, Hyogo 660.	06-411-1231
	TOPURA	201 Soya, Hadano-shi, Kanagawa 257.	0463-82-2711
	YAMASHINA SEIKO-SHO	16 Kitsuneyabu-cho, Higashino, Yamashina-ku, Kyoto 607.	075-591-2131
	ASAKA INDUSTRIAL	2-117 Kaisan-cho, Sakai-shi, Osaka 590.	0722-29-1101
	HITACHI TOOL ENGINEERING	4-1-13 Toyo, Koto-ku, Tokyo 135.	03-3615-5471
	TOYO KNIFE	4-15-1 Minato, Miyagino-ku, Sendai 983.	022-258-2233
	KYOTO TOOL	128 Sayama Shinkaichi, Kumiyama-cho, Kuze, Kyoto 613.	0774-46-3700
	MAEDA METAL INDUSTRIES	3-14-3 Fukae Kita, Higashinari-ku, Osaka 537.	06-976-5561
	"LOBSTER" TOOL	116-1 Naka Shinkai, Higashi Osaka-shi 578.	0729-62-1600
	SUNCALL	14 Umezu Nishiura-cho, Ukyo-ku, Kyoto 615.	075-881-5280
	MOLITEC STEEL	6-18-31 Tani-machi, Chuo-ku, Osaka 542.	06-762-2721
	CHITA KOGYO	84 Otsuka, Sakamaki, Jimokuji-cho, Ama-gun, Aichi 490-11	052-444-9251
	TOKYO SINTERED METALS	2-30-11 Minami Ikebukuro, Toshima-ku, Tokyo 171.	03-3971-2121
	NEW TACHIKAWA AIRCRAFT	1-100 Takamatsu-cho, Tachikawa--shi, Tokyo 190.	0425-29-1111
	KATO SPRING WORKS	1-1-3 Higashi Tabata, Kita-ku, Tokyo 114.	03-3800-8076
	ENGINES		
	KOBE DIESEL	3-2-2 Takatsukadai, Nishi-ku, Kobe 651-22.	078-991-1801
	HANSHIN DIESEL WORKS	8 Kaigan-dori, Chuo-ku, Kobe 650.	078-332-2081
	SHINKO ENGINEERING	1682-2 Motoima-cho, Ogaki-shi, Gifu 503.	0584-89-3121
	FUJI ROBIN INDUSTRIES	35 O-oka, Numazu-shi, Shizuoka 410.	0559-63-1111
	AKASAKA DIESELS	3-2-5 Kasumigaseki, Chiyoda-ku, Tokyo 100.	03-3581-9781
	DAIHATSU DIESEL MFG.	2-4-14 Tokui-cho, Chuo-ku, Osaka 540.	06-945-5314
	NIPPON CARBURETER	3029 Uenohara, Kami Ichi, Atsugi-shi, Kanagawa 243.	0462-85-0227
	MACHINE TOOLS		
	ASAHI-SEIKI MFG.	5050-1 Shindenbora, Owari Asahi-shi, Aichi 488.	0561-53-3111
	KOJIMA IRON WORKS	8 Utagawa-cho, Takasaki-shi, Gunma 370.	0273-22-2021
	SUMIKURA INDUSTRIAL	1-9-6 Shinbashi, Minato-ku, Tokyo 105.	03-3572-4321
	SHOUN MACHINE TOOL	1-39 Kamisu-cho, Toyonaka-shi, Osaka 561.	06-331-6401
	ISHII PRECISION TOOL	8-10-5 Ginza, Chuo-ku, Tokyo 104.	03-3573-4866
	TAKISAWA MACHINE TOOL	983 Natsukawa, Okayama-shi 701-01.	0862-93-6111
	WAKAYAMA PRECISION	5-2-1 Kishibe Naka, Suita-shi, Osaka 564.	06-389-3581
	OKAMOTO MACHINE TOOL WORKS	2-7-3 Minowa-cho, Kohoku-ku, Yokohama 223.	045-562-3126
	OSAKA DIAMOND INDUSTRIAL	2-80 Otori Kita-machi, Sakai-shi, Osaka 593.	0722-62-1061
	NIPPEI TOYAMA	2-4-1 Hamamatsu-cho, Minato-ku, Tokyo 105.	03-3435-4701
	HAMAI	5-5-15 Nishi Gotanda, Shinagawa-ku, Tokyo 141.	03-3491-0131
	KOIKE SANSO KOGYO	3-4-8 Taihei, Sumida-ku, Tokyo 130-91.	03-3624-3111
	FUJI SEIKO	26 Hirako, Yoshihara-cho, Toyota-shi, Aichi 473.	0565-53-6611
	SODICK	1-5-1 Shin Yokohama, Kohoku-ku, Yokohama 222.	045-942-3111
	SEIBU ELECTRIC & MACHINERY	868-1 Kubo, Koga-machi, Kasuya-gun, Fukuoka 811-31.	092-943-7071
	INDUSTRIAL MACHINERY		
	KIRIU MACHINE MFG.	1-124 Aioi-cho, Kiryu-shi, Gunma 376.	0277-54-3101
	TOYO MACHINERY & METAL	523 Fukusato, Futami-cho, Akashi-shi, Hyogo 674.	078-942-2345
	KURAKI	1-2-1 Shiro-oka, Nagaoka-shi, Niigata 940.	0258-35-3040
	KOTOBUKI INDUSTRY	680 Omandokoro, Bukkoji Sagaru, Shimogyo-ku, Kyoto 600	075-343-4811

DAITO SEIKI	2-27-4 Higashi Nihonbashi, Chuo-ku, Tokyo 103.	03-3862-6423
SHIMA SEIKI MFG.	85 Sakata, Wakayama-shi 641.	0734-71-0511
HIRANO TECSEED	101-1 Kawai, Kawai-machi, Kita Katsuragi-gun, Nara 636.	07455-7-0681
INOUE KINZOKU KOGYO	1-10-10 Nishi Hon-machi, Nishi-ku, Osaka 550.	06-534-0231
NISSEI INDUSTRIES	1-1 Inoue, Izumi-cho, Anjo-shi, Aichi 444-12.	0566-92-1151
SHINKAWA	2-51-1 Inadaira, Musashi Murayama-shi, Tokyo 208.	0425-60-1231
ZUIKO	15-21 Minami Befu-cho, Settsu-shi, Osaka 566.	06-340-2215
MEIKI	2 One, Kitazaki-cho, Obu-shi, Aichi 474.	0562-48-2111
HAMADA PRINTING PRESS	2-15-28 Mitejima, Nishi Yodogawa-ku, Osaka 555.	06-472-1152
NISSEI PLASTIC INDUSTRIAL	2110 Minami Jo, Sakai-machi, Nagano 389-06.	0268-82-3000
SEIREI INDUSTRY	428 Enami, Okayama-shi 702.	0862-76-8111
COMSON	5-3-41 Asahi-cho, Takamatsu-shi 760.	0878-21-8161
S N T	1-2-8 Hatchobori, Chuo-ku, Tokyo 104.	03-3553-8351
SHIN-DAIWA KOGYO	35 Shin Ujigami, Chiyoda-cho, Hiroshima 731-15.	082672-6021
TAKAKITA	2828 Natsumi, Nabari-shi, Mie 518-04.	05956-3-3111
HITACHIZOSEN ENG. & CONSTR.	1-4-6 Sakurajima, Konohana-ku, Osaka 554.	06-466-4811
MEIJI MACHINE	2-3-13 Kyobashi, Chuo-ku, Tokyo 104.	03-3281-3551
HITACHI ZOSEN TOMIOKA MACHINE.	1-1-27 Motogo, Kawaguchi-shi, Saitama 332.	0482-22-5191
TAIHEI MACHINERY WORKS	900 Shindo, Irukade Shinden, Komaki-shi, Aichi 485.	0568-73-6411
MACROSS	3-6-7 Kudan Minami, Chiyoda-ku, Tokyo 102.	03-3265-6236
KIKUKAWA IRON WORKS	85 Ominato-cho, Ise-shi, Mie 516.	0596-36-2181
SHIN NIPPON MACHINERY	2-1-28 Shiba, Minato-ku, Tokyo 105.	03-3454-1211
NAKASHIMA MFG.	19-28 Kajigashima, Amagasaki-shi, Hyogo 660.	06-489-1511
HITACHI KIDEN KOGYO	3-11-1 Shimosakabe, Amagasaki-shi, Hyogo 661.	06-499-4021
NIPPON GEAR	7 Kirihara-cho, Fujisawa-shi, Kanagawa 252.	0466-45-2100
SANSEI YUSOKI	1-13-18 Esaka-cho, Suita-shi, Osaka 564.	06-385-5621
AWAMURA MFG.	1-3-1-500 Umeda, Kita-ku, Osaka 530.	06-341-1751
TOKYO AUTOMATIC MACHINERY WKS.	3-10-7 Iwamoto-cho, Chiyoda-ku, Tokyo 101.	03-3866-7171
D M W	1-5-1 Omori Kita, Ota-ku, Tokyo 143.	03-3298-5132
OSAKA CHAIN AND MACHINERY	4-16-1 Wakihama, Kaizuka-shi, Osaka 597.	0724-31-3021
KOYO IRON WORKS & CONSTRUCT.	1-27-2 Nishi Gotanda, Shinagawa-ku, Tokyo 141.	03-3495-2221
SANKO ENGINEERING	4-6-29 Namamugi, Tsurumi-ku, Yokohama 230.	045-509-7331
ORIENTAL CHAIN MFG.	485 Miyanaga Ichi-machi, Matsuto-shi, Ishikawa 924.	0762-76-1155
TRINITY INDUSTRIAL	2-4-1 Marunouchi, Chiyoda-ku, Tokyo 100.	03-3201-2201
FUSO LEXEL	2-4-1 Marunouchi, Chiyoda-ku, Tokyo 100.	03-3216-4741
MISAWA-VAN	3-24-1 Shinjuku, Shinjuku-ku, Tokyo 160.	03-3350-1911
UCHIDA OIL HYDRAULICS MFG.	18 Yamato-cho, Itabashi-ku, Tokyo 173.	03-3962-8111
KAJI TECHNOLOGY	6 Bodai, Mihara-cho, Minami Kawachi-gun, Osaka 587.	0723-61-0881
YAMADA	1-1-3 Minami Magome, Ota-ku, Tokyo 143.	03-3777-5101
OYE KOGYO	4-6-7 Minami Oi, Shinagawa-ku, Tokyo 140.	03-3763-5171
UNOZAWA-GUMI IRON WORKS	1-19-15 Ebisu, Shibuya-ku, Tokyo 150.	03-3444-5111
GO IRON WORKS	58-2 Omochino, Osa, Tarui-cho, Fuwa-gun, Gifu 503-21.	0584-22-1122
SHIMPO INDUSTRIAL	338 Kuze Tonoshiro-cho, Minami-ku, Kyoto 601.	075-921-7151
MISCELLANEOUS MACHINERY		
HEIWA	2-3014-8 Hirosawa-cho, Kiryu-shi, Gunma 376.	0277-52-0121
NIPPON TYPEWRITER	1-11-2 Kyobashi, Chuo-ku, Tokyo 104.	03-3562-4161
SANJO MACHINE WORKS	Inokoba Shinden, Sakae-cho, Niigata 959-11	0256-45-3131
NAKANIPPON CASTING	7-53 Takahata-cho, Nishio-shi, Aichi 445.	0563-56-2121
COPYER	6-3-3 Shimo Renja-ku, Mitaka-shi, Tokyo 181.	0422-47-7151
TOYO ENGINEERING WORKS	4-11-34 Higashi Shinagawa, Shinagawa-ku, Tokyo 140.	03-3474-2111
GLORY	1-3-1 Shimo Teno, Himeji-shi, Hyogo 670.	0792-97-3131
SHINKO KOGYO	1-4-5 Minami Mori-machi, Kita-ku, Osaka 541.	06-367-1811
DAIWA INDUSTRIES	2-3-13 Azuchi-machi, Chuo-ku, Osaka 541.	06-271-8171
TEIKOKU PISTON RING	1-9-9 Yaesu, Chuo-ku, Tokyo 103.	03-3272-1811
AMATSUJI STEEL BALL MFG.	1-1 Kami Noguchi-cho, Kadoma-shi, Osaka 571.	06-908-2261
OSAKA BEARING	9-510 Otori Kita-machi, Sakai-shi, Osaka 593.	0722-62-1125
SEKISUI MACHINERY	62-1 Nomura Naka-machi, Hirakata-shi, Osaka 573-01.	0720-58-1121
NIPPON PILLAR PACKING	2-11-48 Nonaka Minami, Yodogawa-ku, Osaka 532.	06-305-1781
★ TOA VALVE	5-12-1 Nishi Tachibana-cho, Amagasaki-shi, Hyogo 660.	06-416-1152

OKANO VALVE MFG.	1-14 Naka-machi, Moji-ku, Kita Kyushu 800.	093-372-1131
NITTAN VALVE	2-7-2 Yaesu, Chuo-ku, Tokyo 104.	03-3271-4821
MIYAIRI VALVE MFG.	1-2 Ginza Nishi, Chuo-ku, Tokyo 104.	03-3535-5575
NAKAKITA SEISAKUSHO	1-1 Fukano Minami-machi, Daito-shi, Osaka 574.	0720-71-1331
OKUMA ENGINEERING	1-32 Tsuji-machi, Kita-ku, Nagoya 462.	052-915-3911
ELECTRICAL MACHINERY		
SANYO DENKI	1-15-1 Kita Otsuka, Toshima-ku, Tokyo 170.	03-3917-5151
DENYO	2-13-4 Shiba, Minato-ku, Tokyo 105.	03-5484-3001
SANOH INDUSTRIAL	1-1 Kanda Nishiki-cho, Chiyoda-ku, Tokyo 101.	03-3294-6121
JAPAN SERVO	7 Kanda Mitoshiro-cho, Chiyoda-ku, Tokyo 101.	03-3292-3501
NISHISHIBA ELECTRIC	1000 Hamada, Aboshi-ku, Himeji-shi, Hyogo 671-12.	0792-74-2111
NIPPON DENSAN	552 Nijoden-cho, Oike Agaru, Karasuma-dori, Kyoto 604.	075-211-1161
TABUCHI ELECTRIC	1-12-22 Mitejima, Nishi Yodogawa-ku, Osaka 555.	06-475-5111
TOGAMI ELECTRIC MFG.	1-1 Otakara Kita-machi, Saga-shi 840.	0952-24-4111
ENERGY SUPPORT	1 Kami Kobari, Inuyama-shi, Aichi 484.	0568-67-0851
MORIO DENKI	4-34-1 Tateishi, Katsushika-ku, Tokyo 124.	03-3691-3181
KAWASAKI ELECTRIC	225 Koiwasawa, Nanyo-shi, Yamagata 999-22.	0238-49-2011
KASUGA ELECTRIC WORKS	8-3-11 Shimo Renjaku, Mitaka-shi, Tokyo 181.	0422-47-5881
NITTO ELECTRIC WORKS	1 Nagakute, Kanihara, Nagakute-cho, Aichi 480-11.	0561-62-3111
COMMUNICATIONS EQUIPMENT		
MEISEI ELECTRIC	2-5-7 Koishikawa, Bunkyo-ku, Tokyo 112.	03-3814-5115
TAIKO ELECTRIC WORKS	6-10-13 Nakanobu, Shinagawa-ku, Tokyo 142.	03-3788-9050
TAKAMISAWA ELECTRIC	3-18-7 Kamiuma, Setagaya-ku, Tokyo 154.	03-3424-5111
KANDA TSUSHIN KOGYO	2-23-2 Nishi Gotanada, Shinagawa-ku, Tokyo 141.	03-3490-2232
NAKAYO TELECOMMUNICATIONS	24-4 Sakuragaoka-cho, Shibuya-ku, Tokyo 150.	03-3496-1151
FUJITSU DENSO	1-17-3 Sakato, Takatsu-ku, Kawasaki 213.	044-822-2121
AIPHONE	2-18 Jinno-cho, Atsuta-ku, Nagoya 456.	052-682-6191
DAIDO SIGNAL	2-20-2 Naka Ikegami, Ota-ku, Tokyo 146.	03-3754-1122
SONY CHEMICALS	1-6-3 Nihonbashi Muro-machi, Chuo-ku, Tokyo 103.	03-3279-0441
KOITO INDUSTRIES	3-5-23 Takanawa, Minato-ku, Tokyo 108.	03-3443-6171
SEIWA ELECTRIC	36 Terada Shinike, Joyo-shi, Kyoto 610-01.	07745-5-8181
MASPRO DENKOH	80 Jono, Asada, Nisshin-cho, Aichi-gun, Aichi 470-01.	052-802-2222
CONSUMER ELECTRONICS		
TOKYO COSMOS ELECTRIC	1387 Tobuki-cho, Hachioji-shi, Tokyo 192.	0426-91-2511
TOWA MECCS	3-5-5 Hongo, Bunkyo-ku, Tokyo 113.	03-5684-2321
TENSHO ELECTRIC INDUSTRIES	1-3-3 Koyama, Shinagawa-ku, Tokyo 142.	03-3492-0731
NIHON DEMPA KOGYO	3-2-4 Nishi Shinjuku, Shinjuku-ku, Tokyo 160.	03-3346-8151
FOSTER ELECTRIC	512 Miyazawa-cho, Akishima-shi, Tokyo 196.	0425-46-2311
UNIDEN 21	8-18-11 Ginza, Chuo-ku, Tokyo 104.	03-3544-0335
MARANTZ JAPAN	7-35-1 Sagami Ono, Sagamihara-shi, Kanagawa 228.	0427-48-1251
YOKOWO	7-5-11 Takinogawa, Kita-ku, Tokyo 114.	03-3916-3111
YAGI ANTENNA	1-6-10 Uchi Kanda, Chiyoda-ku, Tokyo 101.	03-3292-2371
T O A	7-2-1 Minatojima Naka-machi, Chuo-ku, Kobe 650.	078-303-5620
NAKAMICHI	1-153 Suzuki-cho, Kodaira-shi, Tokyo 187.	0423-42-1111
S P C ELECTRONICS	2-1-3 Shibasaki, Chofu-shi, Tokyo 182.	0424-81-8510
ICOM	6-9-16 Kami Higashi, Hirano-ku, Osaka 547.	06-793-5301
MEASURING INSTRUMENTS		
TOKO SEIKI	3-14-40 Senrigaoka, Settsu-shi, Osaka 556.	06-387-1181
CHUO SEISAKUSHO	24-1 Uchihama-cho, Mizuho-ku, Nagoya 467.	052-821-6111
ANDO ELECTRIC	4-19-7 Kamata, Ota-ku, Tokyo 144.	03-3733-1151
TOA ELECTRONICS	1-29-10 Takadanobaba, Shinjuku-ku, Tokyo 169.	03-3202-0211
KYOWA ELECTRONIC INSTRUMENTS	3-5-1 Chofugaoka, Chofu-shi, Tokyo 182.	0424-88-1111
SUNX	2431-1 Ushiyama-cho, Kasugai-shi, Aichi 486.	0568-33-7211
MISCELLANEOUS ELECTRICAL PRODUCTS		
NIKKO ELECTRIC INDUSTRY	1-12-11 Higashi Rokugo, Ota-ku, Tokyo 144.	03-3739-9111

HITACHI MEDICAL	1-1-14 Uchi Kanda, Chiyoda-ku, Tokyo 101.	03-3292-8111
OKAYA ELECTRIC INDUSTRIES	1-8-3 Shibuya, Shibuya-ku, Tokyo 150.	03-3400-8511
NIPPON CERAMIC	15-2 Nanei-cho, Tottori 689-11.	0857-53-3600
ENDO LIGHTING	1-2-17 Nishimoto-cho, Nishi-ku, Osaka 550.	06-533-9150
JAPAN DIGITAL LABORATORY	2-1-1 Nishi Shinjuku, Shinjuku-ku, Tokyo 163-04.	03-3348-6751
TOYO TAKASAGO DRY BATTERY	4-10-3 Higashi Ueno, Taito-ku, Tokyo 110.	03-3843-2177
FUJITSU KIDEN	1776 Yanokuchi, Inagi-shi, Tokyo 206.	0423-77-5111
NIPPON AVIONICS	1-15-1 Nishi Shinbashi, Minato-ku, Tokyo 105.	03-3501-7351
ZUKEN	2-25-1 Eda Higashi, Midori-ku, Yokohama 225.	045-942-1511
★ SUMITOMO WIRING SYSTEMS	1-14 Nishi Suehiro-cho, Yokkaichi-shi, Mie 510.	0593-54-6200
Y E DATA	182 Shinko, Iruma-shi, Saitama 358.	0429-32-2211
ENPLAS	2-30-1 Namiki, Kawaguchi-shi, Saitama 332.	0482-53-3131
SHINKO ELECTRIC INDUSTRIES	80 Oshimada-cho, Nagano-shi 381-22.	0262-83-1000
★ MATSUO ELECTRIC	3-5-3 Sennari-cho, Toyonaka-shi, Osaka 561.	06-332-0871
E L N A	2-2-1 Tsujido Shin-machi, Fujisawa-shi, Kanagawa 251.	0466-35-1606
KYOEI SANGYO	2-20-4 Shoto, Shibuya-ku, Tokyo 150.	03-3481-2111
NIHON INTER ELECTRONICS	1204 Soya, Hadano-shi, Kanagawa 257.	0463-82-1111
JAPAN RESISTOR MFG.	2315 Kitano, Joana-machi, Toyama 939-18.	0763-62-1180
WAKO ELECTRIC	100 Tomioka, Kasaoka-shi, Okayama 714.	08656-7-0111
HITACHI A I C	1-31-1 Nishi Gotanada, Shinagawa-ku, Tokyo 141.	03-3490-6481
LEAD	578 Yatogo, Menuma-machi, Osato-gun, Saitama 360-02.	0485-88-1121
ASAHI NATIONAL LIGHTING	1 Hishie, Higashi Osaka-shi 578.	0729-62-1121
U-SHIN	1-7-2 Nishi Shinbashi, Minato-ku, Tokyo 105.	03-3502-5241
TOWA ELECTRON	2-44 Muro-machi, Hadano-shi, Kanagawa 257.	0463-82-1022
KOKUSAN DENKI	3744 O-oka, Numazu-shi, Shizuoka 410.	0559-21-5930
MORI DENKI MFG.	3-11-22 Omori Nishi, Ota-ku, Tokyo 143.	03-3763-3131
SHIZUKI ELECTRIC	10-45 Daisha-cho, Nishinomiya-shi, Hyogo 662.	0798-74-5821
NIPPON TUNGSTEN	2-20-31 Shimizu, Minami-ku, Fukuoka 815.	092-511-1111

SHIPBUILDING

NAIKAI SHIPBUILDING & ENGINEERING	226-6 Sawa, Setoda-cho, Toyota-gun, Hiroshima 722-24.	08452-7-2111
NITCHITSU	1-3-6 Uchi Saiwai-cho, Chiyoda-ku, Tokyo 100.	03-3502-6641

ROLLING STOCK

YUSOKI KOGYO	102 Kamihama-cho, Handa-shi, Aichi 475.	0569-21-3311

MOTOR VEHICLES

HINO AUTO BODY	1-1-25 Shitte, Tsurumi-ku, Yokohama 230.	045-581-1231
KYOKUTO KAIHATSU KOGYO	6-1-45 Koshien-guchi, Nishinomiya-shi, Hyogo 663.	0798-66-1000
JIDOSHA BUHIN KOGYO	2400 Kamigo, Ebina-shi, Kanagawa 243.	0462-31-3111
HASHIMOTO FORMING INDUSTRY	320 Kami Yabe-machi, Totsuka-ku, Yokohama 245.	045-811-1211
TOKYO RADIATOR MFG.	3-5-1 Fujisaki, Kawasaki-ku, Kawasaki 210.	044-288-3501
JIDOSHA KIKI	2-10-12 Yoyogi, Shibuya-ku, Tokyo 151.	03-3379-2211
TACHI-S	568-1 Tanaka-cho, Akishima-shi, Tokyo 196.	0425-46-8111
DAIDO METAL	2 Sanage-cho, Kita-ku, Nagoya 462.	052-913-1161
MIKUNI	6-13-11 Soto Kanda, Chiyoda-ku, Tokyo 101.	03-3833-0392
OWARI PRECISE PRODUCTS	2-148 Yada-cho, Higashi-ku, Nagoya 461.	052-721-7131
KEIHIN SEIKI MFG.	4-3-17 Shinjuku, Shinjuku-ku, Tokyo 160.	03-3341-8588
NIPPON GASKET	248 Kano, Higashi Osaka-shi 578.	0729-62-4024
FUJI UNIVANCE	2418 Washizu, Kosai-shi, Shizuoka 431-04.	053-576-1311
KASAI KOGYO	2-3-18 Nihonbashi, Chuo-ku, Tokyo 103.	03-3271-5411
JIDOSHA DENKI KOGYO	1760 Higashi Matano, Totsuka-ku, Yokohama 245.	045-853-7500
FUJI KIKO	2028 Washizu, Kosai-shi, Shizuoka 431-04.	053-575-2711
TOKYO BUHIN KOGYO	1-6-1 Tsukimino, Yamato-shi, Kanagawa 242.	0462-74-2351
DAIKIN MFG.	1-1-1 Kida Motomiya, Neyagawa-shi, Osaka 572.	0720-22-1152
NIPPON CABLE SYSTEM	1-12-28 Sakae-cho, Takarazuka-shi, Hyogo 665.	0797-85-2500
★ AISAN INDUSTRY	1-1-1 Kyowa-cho, Obu-shi, Aichi 474.	0562-47-1131
MEIWA INDUSTRY	33 Onna, Atsugi-shi, Kanagawa 243.	0462-23-7611
IKEDA BUSSAN	771 Kozono, Ayase-shi, Kanagawa 252.	0467-70-0512
NIPPON SEIKI	2-2-34 Higashi Zao, Nagaoka-shi, Niigata 940.	0256-24-3311

BICYCLES

MIYATA INDUSTRY	1-1-1 Shimo Machiya, Chigasaki-shi, Kanagawa 253.	0467-85-1211
NICHIBEI FUJI CYCLE	2-2-36 Morino, Machida-shi, Tokyo 194.	0427-26-7111
MARUISHI CYCLE INDUSTRIES	1-10-4 Kaji-cho, Chiyoda-ku, Tokyo 101.	03-3252-0161
TSUNODA	4-142 Horinouchi, Komaki-shi, Aichi 485.	0568-72-2331

AIRCRAFT

SHOWA AIRCRAFT INDUSTRY	1-13-12 Nishi Shinjuku, Shinjuku-ku, Tokyo 160.	03-3347-0600

PRECISION MACHINERY

KAWASUMI LABORATORIES	3-28-15 Minami Oi, Shinagawa-ku, Tokyo 140.	03-3763-1155
SONY MAGNESCALE	3-9-17 Nishi Gotanda, Shinagawa-ku, Tokyo 141.	03-3490-3151
TOKYOKOKI SEIZOSHO	2-6-10 Iwamoto-cho, Chiyoda-ku, Tokyo 101.	03-5687-9331
KURODA PRECISION INDUSTRIES	239 Shimo Hirama, Saiwai-ku, Kawasaki 211.	044-555-3800
OVAL ENGINEERING	3-23-14 Higashi Ikebukuro, Toshima-ku, Tokyo 170.	03-3360-5061
TOSOK	2-215 Sobudai, Zama-shi, Kanagawa 228.	0462-52-3110
RIKEN KEIKI	2-7-6 Azusawa, Itabashi-ku, Tokyo 174.	03-3966-1121
UNION OPTICAL	2-20-9 Shimura, Itabashi-ku, Tokyo 174.	03-3966-2201
CHINON INDUSTRIES	1-21-17 Takashima, Suwa-shi, Nagano 392.	0266-52-2700
CANON ELECTRONICS	1248 Shimo Kagemori, Chichibu-shi, Saitama 369-18.	0494-23-3111
SEKONIC	7-24-14 Oizumi Gakuen-machi, Nerima-ku, Tokyo 178.	03-3978-2323
ORIENT WATCH	2-4-4 Soto Kanda, Chiyoda-ku, Tokyo 101.	03-3255-1451
RICOH ELEMEX	2-28-24 Izumi, Higashi-ku, Nagoya 461.	052-931-6181
JECO	1-4-1 Fujimi-cho, Gyoda-shi, Saitama 361.	0485-56-7111

MISCELLANEOUS MANUFACTURING

SEVEN INDUSTRY	1107 Naka Aso, Hichiso-cho, Kamo-gun, Gifu 509-04.	0574-48-2277
HOKUSHIN	17-2 Mokuzai-cho, Kishiwada-shi, Osaka 596.	0724-38-0141
NAGOYA LUMBER	2-6-41 Sanno, Nakagawa-ku, Nagoya 454.	052-321-1526
TENRYU LUMBER	38 Zaimoku-cho, Hamamatsu-shi, Shizuoka 435.	053-421-1188
DAINIHON WOOD-PRESERVING	1-3-17 Chidori, Minato-ku, Nagoya 455.	052-661-1501
MITSUMURA PRINTING	1-15-9 Osaki, Shinagawa-ku, Tokyo 141.	03-3492-1181
NOZAKI INSATSU SHIGYO	54-5 Koyama Shimo Fusa-cho, Kita-ku, Kyoto 603.	075-441-6965
MIURA PRINTING	2-3-9 Chitose, Sumida-ku, Tokyo 130.	03-3632-1111
SONY MUSIC ENTERTAINMENT (JPN.)	1-4 Ichigaya Tamachi, Shinjuku-ku, Tokyo 162.	03-3266-5995
MIRAI INDUSTRY	1695-1 Niremata, Wanouchi-cho, Anpachi-gun, Gifu 503-02	0584-69-2323
MELX	4-24-3 Midori, Sumida-ku, Tokyo 130.	03-3635-2641
J S P	2-1-1 Uchi Saiwai-cho, Chiyoda-ku, Tokyo 100.	03-3503-4919
NICHIHA	4-8-10 Mei-eki, Nakamura-ku, Nagoya 450.	052-582-9411
ROLAND	3-7-13 Shin Kitajima, Suminoe-ku, Osaka 559.	06-681-5431
COMANY	1-93 Kogyo Danchi, Komatsu-shi, Ishikawa 923.	0761-21-1144
KOYOSHA	4-5-8 Tani-machi, Chuo-ku, Osaka 540.	06-944-5014
F P	1-105 Akebono-cho, Fukuyama-shi, Hiroshima 721.	0849-53-1145
NIHON DECOLUXE	10 Maeyashiki, Kashiwamori, Fuso-cho, Aichi 480-01.	0587-93-2411
KIKUSUI CHEMICAL INDUSTRIES	3-14-16 Mei-eki, Nakamura-ku, Nagoya 450.	052-581-6311
FUJICOPIAN	4-8-43 Utajima, Nishi Yodogawa-ku, Osaka 555.	06-471-7071
OLIVER	1-1-12 Yabuta, Okazaki-shi, Aichi 444-21.	0564-21-6663
ZOJIRUSHI	1-20-5 Tenma, Kita-ku, Osaka 530.	06-356-2311
TASAKI SHINJU	6-3-2 Minatojima Naka-machi, Chuo-ku, Kobe 650.	078-302-3321
HOUTOKU	3509 Higashiyama, Kamizue, Komaki-shi, Aichi 485.	0568-79-3581
LIHIT LAB.	1-1-12 Noninbashi, Chuo-ku, Osaka 540.	06-946-2525
SHOFU	11 Kami Takamatsu-cho, Higashiyama-ku, Kyoto 605.	075-561-1112
MIROKU FIREARMS MFG.	537-1 Shinohara, Nangoku-shi, Kochi 783.	0888-63-3310
NEPON	1-4-2 Shibuya, Shibuya-ku, Tokyo 150.	03-3409-3131
TACHIKAWA	1-11-1 Kaigan, Minato-ku, Tokyo 105.	03-5404-4500
OLYMPIC	1294 Shimo Fujisawa, Iruma-shi, Saitama 358.	0429-64-5110
SAILOR PEN	1-15-4 Ueno, Taito-ku, Tokyo 110.	03-3837-2901
KUROGANE KOSAKUSHO	1-4-26 Shin-machi, Nishi-ku, Osaka 550.	06-538-1010
TAKASHIMAYA KOSAKUSHO	1-1-25 Shikitsu Higashi, Naniwa-ku, Osaka 556.	06-644-4611

COMMERCE		
★ KAIGEN	2-5-14 Dosho-machi, Chuo-ku, Osaka 541.	06-202-8971
YUASA FUNASHOKU	3-10-3 Miyamoto, Funabashi-shi, Chiba 273.	0474-33-1211
SHINKO SANGYO	2-4-27 Kita Kyutaro-machi, Chuo-ku, Osaka 541.	06-266-6271
HANKYU KYOEI BUSSAN	7-1-10 Tenjinbashi, Kita-ku, Osaka 531.	06-358-1131
DAIKO DENSHI TSUSHIN	2-1 Ageba-cho, Shinjuku-ku, Tokyo 162.	03-3266-8111
NAIGAI CLOTHES	1-12-23 Minami Senba, Chuo-ku, Osaka 542.	06-263-8100
TACHIKAWA	13-5 Nihonbashi Odenma-cho, Chuo-ku, Tokyo 103.	03-3663-2311
CHUO GYORUI	5-2-1 Tsukiji, Chuo-ku, Tokyo 104.	03-3541-2500
G-NET	3-6-21 Itachibori, Nishi-ku, Osaka 550.	06-537-2626
TSUKIJI UOICHIBA	5-2-1 Tsukiji, Chuo-ku, Tokyo 104.	03-3541-6312
TOKYO SOIR	1-1-1 Minami Aoyama, Minato-ku, Tokyo 107.	03-3475-1251
DAITO GYORUI	5-2-1 Tsukiji, Chuo-ku, Tokyo 104.	03-5565-8114
MARUFUJI SHEET PILING	1-6-5 Nihonbashi Honcho, Chuo-ku, Tokyo 103.	03-3242-7641
MITANI	1-3-1 Toyoshima, Fukui-shi, 910.	0776-20-3111
TOMIYA APPAREL	1-7-15 Minami Hon-machi, Chuo-ku, Osaka 541.	06-266-9020
TOKYO SANGYO	3-3-1 Marunouchi, Chiyoda-ku, Tokyo 100.	03-3212-7611
TOKAI BUSSAN	3-34-14 Sakae, Naka-ku, Nagoya 460.	052-261-3211
CANOX	1-1-12 Nakono, Nishi-ku, Nagoya 451.	052-564-3511
SHOEI FOODS	5-7 Akihabara, Taito-ku, Tokyo 110.	03-3253-1211
NARASAKI SANGYO	2-7-1 Nihonbashi Honcho, Chuo-ku, Tokyo 103.	03-3666-2341
FURUSATO INDUSTRIES	2-1-9 Itachibori, Nishi-ku, Osaka 550.	06-533-3391
FUJITSU BUSINESS SYSTEMS	4-1-4 Roppongi, Minato-ku, Tokyo 106.	03-3584-0231
KYOKUTO BOEKI	2-2-1 Otemachi, Chiyoda-ku, Tokyo 100.	03-3244-3511
IWAKI & CO.	4-8-2 Nihonbashi Honcho, Chuo-ku, Tokyo 103.	03-3279-0481
MARUSHO	1-11-1 Nihonbashi Horidome-cho, Chuo-ku, Tokyo 103.	03-3662-8111
GOLDWIN	210 Kiyosawa, Oyabe-shi, Toyama 932-01.	0766-61-4800
MOONBAT	Shijo Minamiiru, Muromachi-dori, Shimogyo-ku, Kyoto 600.	075-361-0381
CENTRAL AUTOMOTIVE PRODUCTS	4-2-30 Nakanoshima, Kita-ku, Osaka 530.	06-443-5181
KING	2-1 Takakura-cho, Higashi Shiokoji, Kyoto 600.	075-681-9111
LONGCHAMP	369 Gokuishi-machi, Karasuma Nishiiru, Kyoto 600.	075-344-7777
F-ONE	3-1-6 Bisho-en, Abeno-ku, Osaka 545.	06-629-6621
ZETT	1-2-16 Karasugatsuji, Tennoji-ku, Osaka 543.	06-779-1171
SANKYO KASEI	1-9-8 Kita Kyuhoji-cho, Chuo-ku, Osaka 541.	06-262-2881
NAGAHORI	1-15-3 Ueno, Taito-ku, Tokyo 110.	03-3832-8266
TOHO	85 Fukae Hama-cho, Higashi Nada-ku, Kobe 658.	078-452-0841
LAPINE	1-5-7 Tenma, Kita-ku, Osaka 530.	06-358-2251
DENKYOSHA	2-1-3 Nipponbashi Higashi, Naniwa-ku, Osaka 556.	06-644-6711
CHUBU SUISAN	2-22 Kawanami-cho, Atsuta-ku, Nagoya 456.	052-683-3110
KOSUGI SANGYO	2-8-5 Nihonbashi Horidome-cho, Chuo-ku, Tokyo 103.	03-3662-3111
UEHARA SEI SHOJI	Nakabori, Karasuma Higashiiru, Oike-dori, Kyoto 604.	075-211-0161
SANSHIN ELECTRONICS	4-4-12 Shiba, Minato-ku, Tokyo 108.	03-3453-5111
SOMAR	4-11-2 Ginza, Chuo-ku, Tokyo 104.	03-3542-2151
MOS FOOD SERVICES	22 Tansu-machi, Shinjuku-ku, Tokyo 162.	03-3266-7141
KAGA ELECTRONICS	1-26-1 Otowa, Bunkyo-ku, Tokyo 112.	03-3942-6211
TSUZUKI DENKI	1-6-4 Osaki, Shinagawa-ku, Tokyo 141.	03-3779-7511
TACHIBANA SHOKAI	2-3-2 Utsubo Hon-machi, Nishi-ku, Osaka 550.	06-444-8600
RETAIL STORES AND FOOD SERVICES		
KISOJI	3-18-13 Shiragane, Showa-ku, Nagoya 466.	052-872-1811
EIDENSHA	4-22-21 Mei-eki, Nakamura-ku, Nagoya 450.	052-583-9111
BROTHER SALES	15-1 Naeshiro-cho, Mizuho-ku, Nagoya 467.	052-824-3311
MARUKYU	1935 Mure Ukino, Hofu-shi, Yamaguchi 747.	0835-38-1511
ADERANS	1-6-3 Shinjuku, Shinjuku-ku, Tokyo 160.	03-3350-3111
★ FREX	185-1 Okuchi-cho, Matsusaka-shi, Mie 515.	0598-51-3125
CHIYODA	4-39-8 Narita Higashi, Suginami-ku, Tokyo 166.	03-3316-4131
YAMANAKA	3-15-31 Aoi, Higashi-ku, Nagoya 461.	052-937-9300
NAKAGAWA MUSEN	7-20-23 Tsukumodai, Suita-shi, Osaka 565.	06-831-1261
RINGER HUT	5-20-3 Mugino, Hakata-ku, Fukuoka 816.	092-573-6655
MR MAX	1-5-7 Matsuda, Higashi-ku, Fukuoka 812.	092-623-1111

	ELLEME	1-6-10 Kawara-machi, Chuo-ku, Osaka 541.	06-201-3243
★	FRIENDLY	3-5-24 Miyahara, Yodogawa-ku, Osaka 532.	06-397-0101
	FOOTWORK INTERNATIONAL	4-14-3 Nishi Tenma, Kita-ku, Osaka 530.	06-312-2109
	OAK & CO.	6-3-2 Kiba, Koto-ku, Tokyo 135.	03-3649-3111
	VOLKS	9-1 Toyotsu-cho, Suita-shi, Osaka 564.	06-380-3099
	AOYAMA TRADING	1-3-5 Oji-cho, Fukuyama-shi, Hiroshima 721.	0849-20-0050
	RIKEI	1-26-2 Nishi Shinjuku, Shinjuku-ku, Tokyo 163.	03-3345-2151
	MARUICHI	3-48 Ichiba, Nagano-shi 381-22.	0262-85-4101
	KIMISAWA	13-4 Hirokoji-machi, Mishima-shi, Shizuoka 411.	0559-72-4888
	SAPPORO LION	6-10-12 Ginza, Chuo-ku, Tokyo 104.	03-3572-2291
	DAIWA	2-2-5 Kata-machi, Kanazawa-shi 920.	0762-20-1111
	NISSEN	79 Nishinochaya-cho, Kisshoin, Minami-ku, Kyoto 601.	075-682-2000
	TOYO BUSSAN	2-7-16 Sakuragawa, Naniwa-ku, Osaka 556.	06-561-8651
	DEPARTMENT STORES AND SUPERMARKETS		
	SAIKAYA	8 Ogawa-cho, Kawasaki-ku, Kawasaki 210.	044-211-3153
	UNEED DAIEI	7-20 Gion-cho, Hakata-ku, Fukuoka 812.	092-261-3098
	SHINSHU JUSCO	4-10 Takamiya Kita, Matsumoto-shi, Nagano 390.	0263-27-3811
	FUJI	1-2-1 Miya Nishi, Matsuyama-shi 790.	0899-26-7111
	XEBIO	3-7-35 Asahi, Koriyama-shi, Fukushima 963.	0249-38-1111
	MITANI SANGYO	16-1 Showa-machi, Kanazawa-shi 920.	0762-33-2151
	AUTOMOBILE SALES		
	TOKYO ISUZU MOTOR	2-4-12 Nagata-cho, Chiyoda-ku, Tokyo 100.	03-3581-5211
	AICHI TOYOTA MOTOR	6-8 Takatsuji-cho, Showa-ku, Nagoya 466.	052-871-4511
	CHUO SUBARU MOTORS	1-20-8 Ebisu, Shibuya-ku, Tokyo 150.	03-3448-4411
	TOKYO TOYOTA MOTOR	3-11-34 Mita, Minato-ku, Tokyo 108.	03-3455-1211
	DAIEI TAIGEN	1-22-25 Nipponbashi, Chuo-ku, Osaka 542.	06-641-7660
	FINANCING		
	CHUBU SECURITIES FINANCING	3-3-17 Sakae, Naka-ku, Nagoya 460.	052-251-1301
	TOKUSHIMA BANK	1-16 Tomidahama, Tokushima 770.	0886-23-3111
	HYOGIN FACTORS	1-4-3 Ikuta-cho, Chuo-ku, Kobe 651.	078-261-2222
	NICHIEI FINANCE	4-33-1 Tsurumi Chuo, Tsurumi-ku, Yokohama 230.	045-521-4311
	DAIICHI HOUSING LOAN	1-26-2 Nishi Shinjuku, Shinjuku-ku, Tokyo 163-05.	03-3343-5111
	TOKYO LEASING	7-15-7 Roppongi, Minato-ku, Tokyo 106.	03-3475-7111
	CENTRAL LEASING	1-24-15 Sakae, Naka-ku, Nagoya 460.	052-221-1531
	SECURITIES		
★	UNIVERSAL SECURITIES	3-4-2 Marunouchi, Chiyoda-ku, Tokyo 100.	03-3284-3511
	MITO SECURITIES	3-13-5 Nihonbashi, Chuo-ku, Tokyo 103.	03-3274-6111
	MEIKO SECURITIES	1-7-18 Imabashi, Chuo-ku, Osaka 541.	06-202-2341
	ICHIYOSHI SECURITIES	3-1-3 Koraibashi, Chuo-ku, Osaka 541.	06-231-9771
	TAKAGI SECURITIES	1-3-1-400 Umeda, Kita-ku, Osaka 530 .	06-345-1221
	JAPAN SECURITIES AGENTS	1-2-4 Nihonbashi Kayaba-cho, Chuo-ku, Tokyo 103.	03-3668-9211
	OSAKA SHOKEN DAIKO	2-4-6 Kitahama, Chuo-ku, Osaka 541.	06-203-1751
	REAL ESTATE		
	TACHIHI ENTERPRISE	841 Izumi-machi, Tachikawa-shi, Tokyo 190.	0425-36-1111
	YURAKU REAL ESTATE	3-13-1 Kyobashi, Chuo-ku, Tokyo 104.	03-3567-9411
	CÉSAR	3-3-1 Kami Osaki, Shinagawa-ku, Tokyo 141.	03-5420-5420
	URBAN LIFE	4-4-3 Minami Senba, Chuo-ku, Osaka 542.	06-244-1011
	KANSAI SEKIWA REAL ESTATE	2-4-5 Sonezaki, Kita-ku, Osaka 530.	06-361-0351
	DIAMOND CITY	2-4-11 Kyutaro-machi, Chuo-ku, Osaka 541.	06-261-9600
	JAPAN LIVING SERVICE	1-11-4-300 Umeda, Kita-ku, Osaka 532.	06-343-1841
	ANA REAL ESTATE	2-6-23 Shibata, Kita-ku, Osaka 530.	06-372-3071
★	DIA KENSETSU	6-28-7 Shinjuku, Shinjuku-ku, Tokyo 160.	03-3205-5555
	ISUZU CONSTRUCTION	5-2-17 Higashi Naniwa-cho, Amagasaki-shi, Hyogo 660.	06-488-3388
	FUJI	2236-1 Habu-cho, Kishiwada-shi, Osaka 596.	0724-37-8700
	CHUBU SEKIWA REAL ESTATE	4-10-25 Mei-eki, Nakamura-ku, Nagoya 450.	052-541-2101

RAILWAYS

IZU HAKONE RAILWAY	300 Daiba, Mishima-shi, Shizuoka 411.	0559-77-1201
SHIN-KEISEI ELECTRIC RAILWAY	4-1-12 Kunugiyama, Kamagaya-shi, Chiba 273-01.	0473-89-1111
IZUKYU	1151 Yahatano, Ito-shi, Shizuoka 413-02.	0557-53-1111
KEIFUKU ELECTRIC RAILROAD	3-20 Mibu Kayo Gosho-machi, Nakagyo-ku, Kyoto 604.	075-841-9385

TRUCKING

NIPPON KONPO UNYU SOKO	6-17 Akashi-cho, Chuo-ku, Tokyo 104.	03-3541-5331
MEITETSU TRANSPORT	2-12-8 Aoi, Higashi-ku, Nagoya 461.	052-935-5721
S LINE GIFU	4-68 Heisei, Ginan-cho, Hashima-gun, Gifu 501-61.	0582-45-3131
SOTETSU TRANSPORTATION	2-19-11 Aobadai, Meguro-ku, Tokyo 153.	03-3791-3311
DAIWA MOTOR TRANSPORTATION	1-9-7 Ginza, Chuo-ku, Tokyo 104.	03-3561-7161
SHINKI BUS	1 Nishi Ekimae-cho, Himeji-shi, Hyogo 670.	0792-23-1241
NOHI SEINO TRANSPORTATION	2348 Oze, Seki-shi, Gifu 501-32.	0575-23-1711

SHIPPING

SHIN YEI STEAMSHIP	3-1-20 Nihonbashi Muro-machi, Chuo-ku, Tokyo 103.	03-3241-5186
NIHONKAI STEAMSHIP	1-10-7 Shinbashi, Minato-ku, Tokyo 105.	03-5568-2611
HINODE KISEN	2-3-3 Shiba, Minato-ku, Tokyo 105.	03-3457-1741
SEA-COM	1-11-30 Nagata-cho, Chiyoda-ku, Tokyo 100.	03-3593-8471
TAMAI SHOSEN	3-13-12 Mita, Minato-ku, Tokyo 108.	03-3456-8568
TAIYO KAIUN	18-2 Akashi-machi, Chuo-ku, Kobe 650.	078-332-8081
TOKYO SENPAKU	2-7-3 Marunouchi, Chiyoda-ku, Tokyo 100.	03-3282-0723
KURIBAYASHI STEAMSHIP	2-4-1 Marunouchi, Chiyoda-ku, Tokyo 100.	03-3201-1651
TOKAI KISEN	1-11-1 Kaigan, Minato-ku, Tokyo 105.	03-3436-1131
FUJI KISEN	3-1-20 Nihonbashi Muro-machi, Chuo-ku, Tokyo 103.	03-3246-1891
AWAJI FERRY BOAT	4-1-1 Sotohama-cho, Suma-ku, Kobe 654.	078-733-0001
TOKYO KISEN	2 Yamashita-cho, Naka-ku, Yokohama 231.	045-671-7711

AERIAL SURVEYING

ASIA AIR SURVEY	4-2-18 Shinjuku, Shinjuku-ku, Tokyo 160.	03-5379-2151

WAREHOUSING AND PORT TRANSPORTATION

SUGIMURA WAREHOUSE	1-1-57 Fukuzaki, Minato-ku, Osaka 552.	06-571-1221
INUI TATEMONO	5-9-9 Ginza, Chuo-ku, Tokyo 104.	03-3572-4561
KEISHIN WAREHOUSE	21-1 Wake-cho, Shimogyo-ku, Kyoto 600.	075-371-3165
ASAGAMI	2-8-12 Nihonbashi Honcho, Chuo-ku, Tokyo 103.	03-3639-8411
MARUHACHI WAREHOUSE	2-31-10 Morishita, Koto-ku, Tokyo 135.	03-3846-5146
ONAMI UNYU SOKO	2-3-81 Kizugawa, Naniwa-ku, Osaka 556.	06-561-1071
NIHONBASHI WAREHOUSE	2-7 Nihonbashi Odenma-cho, Chuo-ku, Tokyo 103.	03-3661-3261
CHUO WAREHOUSE	41 Sujaku Uchihata-cho, Shimogyo-ku, Kyoto 600.	075-313-6151
SANWA SOKO	1-5-2 Kita Shinjuku, Shinjuku-ku, Tokyo 169.	03-3366-8111
MITSUI WHARF	9-1 Ogi-machi, Kawasaki-ku, Kawasaki 210.	044-333-5311
SAKURAJIMA FUTO	1-1-11 Ume-machi, Konohana-ku, Osaka 554.	06-461-5331
RINKO	5-11-30 Bandai, Niigata-shi 950.	025-245-4113
MEIKO TRANS	2-4-6 Irifune, Minato-ku, Nagoya 455.	052-661-8135
ISEWAN TERMINAL SERVICE	1-7-40 Irifune, Minato-ku, Nagoya 455.	052-661-2121
SINWART	4-8-8 Higashi Shinagawa, Shinagawa-ku, Tokyo 140.	03-5479-5011
FUSHIKI KAIRIKU UNSO	5-1 Fushiki Minato-cho, Takaoka-shi, Toyama 933-01.	0766-45-1111
HYOKI KAIUN	2-4-14 Sakaemachi-dori, Chuo-ku, Kobe 650.	078-321-7131
DAIUN	1-10-10 Nishi Honmachi, Nishi-ku, Osaka 550.	06-532-4101
DAINICHI TSUUN	1-2-22 Kaigan-dori, Chuo-ku, Kobe 650.	078-391-7170

MASS MEDIA AND COMMUNICATIONS

ASAHI BROADCASTING	2-2-48 Oyodo Minami, Kita-ku, Osaka 531-01.	06-458-5321
BUNKEIDO	2801 Egira-cho, Hashima-shi, Gifu 501-62.	0583-98-4411

ELECTRICITY AND GAS

OKINAWA ELECTRIC POWER	5-2-1 Maki Minato, Urasoe-shi, Okinawa 901-21.	098-877-2341
KEIYO GAS	2-8-8 Ichikawa Minami, Ichikawa-shi, Chiba 272.	0473-25-1121

CHUBU GAS	100 Shirakawa-cho, Toyohashi-shi, Aichi 441.	0532-31-7141

SERVICES

TOKYU RECREATION	2-9 Sakuragaoka-cho, Shibuya-ku, Tokyo 150.	03-3462-8888
MUSASHINO KOGYO	3-37-12 Shinjuku, Shinjuku-ku, Tokyo 160.	03-3352-0052
KINKI EIGA GEKIJO	1-5-31 Abeno-suji, Abeno-ku, Osaka 545.	06-632-4551
O S	1-1 Kakuta-cho, Kita-ku, Osaka 530.	06-361-3554
KOMA STADIUM	5-14 Kakuta-cho, Kita-ku, Osaka 530.	06-312-0821
NAKANIHON THEATRICAL	4-7-23 Mei-eki, Nakamura-ku, Nagoya 450.	052-551-0272
KABUKIZA	4-12-15 Ginza, Chuo-ku, Tokyo 104.	03-3541-3131
MISONOZA THEATRICAL	1-6-14 Sakae, Naka-ku, Nagoya 460.	052-211-1451
KOSHIEN TOCHI KIGYO	1-8-33 Minami Koshien, Nishinomiya-shi, Hyogo 663.	0798-40-4600
KAGETSUENKANKO	1-7-6 Kita Saiwai, Nishi-ku, Yokohama 220.	045-311-7441
OSAKA STADIUM	5-1-60 Nanba, Chuo-ku, Osaka 542.	06-632-6256
TOYO TEC	1-7-18 Sakuragawa, Naniwa-ku, Osaka 556.	06-563-2111
COMPUTER ENG. & CONSULTING	3-15-6 Shibuya, Shibuya-ku, Tokyo 150.	03-3407-8561
HITACHI SOFTWARE ENGINEERING	6-81 Onoe-cho, Naka-ku, Yokohama 231.	045-681-2111
S R L	2-4-1 Nishi Shinjuku, Shinjuku-ku, Tokyo 163.	03-3344-6511
TOKYO KAIKAN	3-2-1 Marunouchi, Chiyoda-ku, Tokyo 100.	03-3215-2111
IMPERIAL HOTEL	1-1-1 Uchi Saiwai-cho, Chiyoda-ku, Tokyo 100.	03-3504-1111
NIPPON COMPUTER SYSTEM	3-2-18 Nakanoshima, Kita-ku, Osaka 530.	06-444-1901
ROYAL HOTEL	5-3-68 Nakanoshima, Kita-ku, Osaka 530.	06-448-1121
NOMURA	4-6-4 Shibaura, Minato-ku, Tokyo 108.	03-3455-1171
TOKAI	9-16 Wakamiya-cho, Gifu-shi 500.	0582-63-5111
TOEI CHEMICAL INDUSTRY	8-9-1 Kokuryo-cho, Chofu-shi, Tokyo 182.	03-3430-3331
CENTRAL SECURITY PATROLS	2-4-1 Nishi Shinjuku, Shinjuku-ku, Tokyo 163.	03-3344-1711
HITACHI INFORMATION SYSTEMS	1-16-5 Dogenzaka, Shibuya-ku, Tokyo 150.	03-3464-5110
TANSEISHA	5-2-2 Ueno, Taito-ku, Tokyo 110.	03-3836-7221
MEITEC	2-3-1 Sakae, Naka-ku, Nagoya 460.	052-212-1711
T K C	2-1 Ageba-cho, Shinjuku-ku, Tokyo 162.	03-3235-5511
O Y O	4-2-6 Kudan Kita,Chiyoda-ku, Tokyo 102.	03-3234-0811
FUNAI CONSULTING	5-15 Taiyuji-cho, Kita-ku, Osaka 530.	06-314-3901
NIPPON SYSTEM DEVELOPMENT	4-1-21 Kitahama, Chuo-ku, Osaka 541.	06-201-2701
TOKAI LEASE	2-Kita 2-6 Tenjinbashi, Kita-ku, Osaka 530.	03-352-0001
MARUBENI CONST. MATERIAL LEASE	1-23-4 Shinkawa, Chuo-ku, Tokyo 104.	03-3206-0111
GIKEN KOGYO	13-10 Sakuragaoka-cho, Shibuya-ku, Tokyo 150.	03-3464-4391
O H B A	2-4-9 Yoyogi, Shibuya-ku, Tokyo 151.	03-3374-0121
NIKKEN KOGAKU	2-6-1 Nishi Shinjuku, Shinjuku-ku, Tokyo 163.	03-3344-6811

MISCELLANEOUS ADDITIONS

NITTETSU SHOJI	1-1-1 Shibaura, Minato-ku, Tokyo 105.	03-3798-2111
ASICS TRADING	5-2-10 Hosoda-cho, Nagata-ku, Kobe 653.	078-641-6111
★ CATENA	2-10-24 Shiomi, Koto-ku, Tokyo 135.	03-3615-3211
DAIMARU INDUSTRIAL	1-4-39 Midorigi, Suminoe-ku, Osaka 559.	06-685-5101
SENSHU ELECTRIC	1-4-21 Minami Kaneden, Suita-shi, Osaka 564.	06-384-1101
NIPPON SHOJI	2-2-9 Koku-machi, Chuo-ku, Osaka 540.	06-942-6300
JEUGIA	Kawara-machi, Sanjo-dori, Nakagyo-ku, Kyoto 604.	075-255-1566
AUTOBACS SEVEN	1-23-5 Esaka-cho, Suita-shi, Osaka 564.	06-338-1752
★ NISHIMOTO SANGYO	1-15 Higashi Koraibashi, Chuo-ku, Osaka 540.	06-942-4901
RIO CHAIN	2-2-1 Shin Sakae, Naka-ku, Nagoya 460.	052-241-2622
JUNTENDO	206-5 Shimo Hongo-cho, Masuda-shi, Shimane 698.	0856-24-2400
MORITO	4-2-4 Minami Hon-machi, Chuo-ku, Osaka 541.	06-252-3551
TENMAYA STORE	13-16 Oka-machi, Okayama-shi 700.	0862-32-7265
TOYOTA COROLLA GIFU	4-1-3 Omizo, Rokujo, Gifu-shi 500.	0582-72-3111
GOURMET KINEYA	3-4-7 Kita Kagawa, Suminoe-ku, Osaka 559.	06-683-1222
AIGAN	4-9-12 Daido, Tennoji-ku, Osaka 543.	06-772-3383
EIWA	4-6-6 Kita Horie, Nishi-ku, Osaka 550.	06-538-1851
U. STORE	2267-1 Go-hyoiri, Shobata, Saori-cho, Ama-gun, Aichi 496.	0567-26-1322
GIFU HINO MOTOR	5-57 Kita Uzura, Gifu-shi 500.	0582-71-8811
MARUTOMI GROUP	2-7-28 Kakeage, Minami-ku, Nagoya 457.	052-821-9631

★ NAKAI	3-62 Okihama Higashi, Tokushima-shi 770.	0886-55-0001
NISSHO ELECTRONICS	7-3-1 Tsukiji, Chuo-ku, Tokyo 104.	03-3544-8311
TORII	1-21-17 Sakae, Naka-ku, Nagoya 460.	052-231-0429
KATO SANGYO	9-20 Matsubara-cho, Nishinomiya-shi, Hyogo 662.	0798-33-7650
HANATEN	3-3-21 Suwa, Joto-ku, Osaka 536.	06-968-0101
ITOKI	1-5-18 Dosho-machi, Chuo-ku, Osaka 541.	06-223-3031
KITAKEI	3-6-14 Minami Hon-machi, Chuo-ku, Osaka 541.	06-251-1161
KENTUCKY FRIED CHICKEN JAPAN	1-1-1 Ebisu Minami, Shibuya-ku, Tokyo 150.	03-3719-0231
FUTATA	3-1-1 Tenjin, Chuo-ku, Fukuoka 810.	092-712-2003
SAGAMI CHAIN	1-1709 Moritaka, Moriyama-ku, Nagoya 463.	052-771-2126
JUEL VÉRITÉ OHKUBO	1-13-9 Shibuya, Shibuya-ku, Tokyo 150.	03-3486-1511
ASAHI BEER SYSTEM	1-5-5 Kitahama, Chuo-ku, Osaka 541.	06-231-6441
DAIWA RAKUDA INDUSTRY	2-1-9 Itachibori, Nishi-ku, Osaka 550.	06-536-6111
KANSAI SUPER MARKET	5-3-38 Chuo, Itami-shi, Hyogo 664.	0727-72-0341
HITACHI METALS TECHNO	4-1-13 Toyo, Koto-ku, Tokyo 135.	03-3615-5411
DOMY	11 Hon-machi, Nishio-shi, Aichi 445.	0563-56-3321

LOCAL MARKET COMPANIES

(abbreviated names)

These companies are not listed on the Tokyo Stock Market, but appear on other local markets within Japan.

(★ indicates that a company is listed in the appropriate chapter of this book.)

	Company	Address	Telephone
	NISHINIPPON SYSTEM INSTAL. & CON.	3-15-7 Kuhonji, Kumamoto-shi 862.	096-372-1111
	TSUKEN	7-2-19 Nijuyonken Sanjo, Nishi-ku, Sapporo 063.	011-621-1161
	TAKADA	1-1 Tsukiji-cho, Yahata Nishi-ku, Kita Kyushu 806.	093-632-2631
	HIROSHIMA KENSETSU TELE. CONST.	2-32 Higashi-machi, Minami Senda, Hiroshima 730.	082-246-2661
	BURUBON	4-2-14 Matsunami, Kashiwazaki-shi, Niigata 945.	0257-23-2333
	NICHIRYO BAKING	18-5-1 Higashi Ichijo, Tsukisappu, Toyohira-ku 062.	011-851-8111
	KAMEDA SEIKA	2871-8 Oaza Hayadori, Kameda-cho, Niigata 950-01.	025-382-2111
	NIIGATA REFRIGERATOR	3347 Yonno-cho, Minatomachi-dori, Niigata-shi 951.	025-229-1261
	AHJIKAN	7-3-9 Shoko Center, Nishi-ku, Hiroshima 733.	082-277-7010
	OHISHI SANGYO	2-7-1 Momozono, Yahata Higashi-ku, Kita Kyushu 805.	093-661-6511
	MANAC	2-10-1 Nishi-machi, Fukuyama-shi, Hiroshima 720.	0849-26-0433
	SANKEI CHEMICALS	880 Korimoto-cho, Kagoshima-shi 890.	0992-54-1161
	NISHIKAWA RUBBER	2-2-8 Misasa-cho, Nishi-ku, Hiroshima 733.	082-237-9371
★	FUKAGAWA PORCELAIN	1362 Arita-cho, Nishi Matsuura-gun, Saga 844.	0955-43-2151
	HOKUETSU METAL	3-3-1 Zao, Nagaoka-shi, Niigata 940.	0258-24-5111
	CHOFU SEISAKUSHO	2-1 Ogi-cho, Chofu, Shimonoseki-shi, Yamaguchi 752.	0832-48-1111
	SHOWA MANUFACTURING	3-1-35 Hakozaki Futo, Higashi-ku, Fukuoka-shi 812.	092-651-2932
	HOKUETSU INDUSTRIES	113-1 Oaza Otake Shinden, Bunsui-cho, Niigata 959-01.	0256-97-3201
	SEIKO ELECTRIC	2-7-25 Toko, Hakata-ku, Fukuoka 812.	092-473-8831
	APOLLO ELECTRONICS	883 Oaza Kami Kitajima, Chikugo-shi, Fukuoka 833.	0942-53-6111
	AS'TY	2-15-1 Shoko Center, Nishi-ku, Hiroshima 733.	082-278-1111
	NAKAMICHI MACHINERY	3-3 Higashi, Kita Ichijo, Chuo-ku, Sapporo 060.	011-241-4191
	KUWAZAWA TRADING	7-1-1 Chuo Nijo, Shiroishi-ku, Sapporo 003.	011-864-1111
	HAKODATE SEIMO SENGU	6-1 Oiwake-cho, Hakodate-shi, Hokkaido 040.	0138-45-4811
	YAMAE HISANO	2-13-34 Hakata Eki Higashi, Hakata-ku, Fukuoka 812.	092-474-0711
	SOGO DENKI	3-11 Odori Nishi, Chuo-ku, Sapporo 060.	011-214-2923
	KOMERI	4-1-28 Yoneyama, Niigata-shi 950.	025-247-3111
	HASEGAWA	3-2-1 Hakata Eki-mae, Hakata-ku, Fukuoka 812.	092-472-1621
	IWATAYA DEPARTMENT STORE	2-11-1 Tenjin, Chuo-ku, Fukuoka 810.	092-721-1111
	HARASHIN	18-2 Nakagoya, Nakanoshima-machi, Niigata 954-01.	0258-66-6711
	CHIKUHO BANK	2456-1 Suwano-machi, Kurume-shi, Fukuoka 830.	0942-32-5331
	SAPPORO BANK	4-1 Odori Nishi, Chuo-ku, Sapporo 060-91.	011-251-2111
	FUKUOKA CHUO BANK	2-12-1 Daimyo, Chuo-ku, Fukuoka 810.	092-751-4431
	SETOUCHI BANK	2-3-7 Hondori, Kure-shi, Hiroshima 737.	0823-22-2222
	KUMAMOTO FAMILY BANK	6-29-20 Suizenji, Kumamoto-shi 862.	096-385-1111
	MINAMI-NIPPON BANK	1-1 Yamashita-cho, Kagoshima-shi 892.	0992-26-1111
	HOWA BANK	4-10 Oji Naka-machi, Oita-shi 870.	0975-34-2611
	MIYAZAKI TAIYO BANK	3-3-27 Tachibana-dori Nishi, Miyazaki-shi 880.	0985-24-2111
	NAKAMICHI LEASING	10-4 Odori Nishi, Chuo-ku, Sapporo 060.	011-271-1022
	KYUSHU LEASING SERVICE	4-1-1 Hakata Eki-mae, Hakata-ku, Fukuoka 812.	092-431-2530
	HOKKAIDO SHINKO	11-16 Nishi, Kita Gojo, Chuo-ku, Sapporo 060.	011-271-9111
	NIIGATA KOTSU	1-6-1 Bandai, Niigata-shi 950.	025-244-2111
	HIROSHIMA ELECTRIC RAILWAY	2-9-29 Higashi Senda-machi, Naka-ku, Hiroshima 730.	082-241-1191
	SAPPORO EXPRESS	6-2 Nishi, Kita Gojo, Chuo-ku, Sapporo 060.	011-251-4112
	HOKKAIDO CHUO BUS	1-8-6 Ironai, Otaru-shi, Hokkaido 047.	0134-24-1111
	RKB MAINICHI BROADCASTING	4-1-10 Watanabe-dori, Chuo-ku, Fukuoka 810.	092-713-2111
	HIROSHIMA GAS	2-7-1 Minami-machi, Minami-ku, Hiroshima 734.	082-251-2151
	HOKURIKU GAS	1-2-23 Higashi Odori, Niigata-shi 950.	025-245-2211
★	MITSUI GREENLAND	1616 Shimoide, Arao-shi, Kumamoto 864.	0968-66-2111
	KANAMOTO	1-6-11 Konan-cho, Muroran-shi, Hokkaido 051.	0143-23-3324
	SUN RIVER	13-14 Yoshino-cho, Suita-shi, Osaka 564.	06-384-4314
	KYOTO HOTEL	537-4 Ichino Funairi-cho, Nakagyo-ku, Kyoto 604.	075-211-5111
	SUPER DAIEI	1-1-7 Nakasu, Yawata Nishi-ku, Kita Kyushu 807.	093-602-2770

NITORI	1-1152 Shin Hassamu Rokujo, Teine-ku, Sapporo 006.	011-664-6611
HOSHI ITO	14-3-15 Nishi, Minami Hachijo, Chuo-ku, Sapporo 064.	011-561-6111
MARUKYO	285-1 Oaza Yamada, Onojo-shi, Fukuoka 816.	092-501-5221
MARUWA	10-10 Ote-cho, Kokura Kita-ku, Kita Kyushu 803.	093-582-7100
KOKURA ENTERPRISE	2-15-1 Asano, Kokura Kita-ku, Kita Kyushu 802.	093-511-4101
HOME Y. DO	3291-1 Oaza Shimogori, Oita-shi 870.	0975-69-1188
KYUKO PHARMACEUTICAL	2-2-5 Handobashi, Hakata-ku, Fukuoka 816.	092-451-8771
SUNDAY'S SUN	1-21 Fukukawa Minami-cho, Nanyo-shi, Yamaguchi 746.	0834-64-1234
SHINDEN	2-3-16 Bandai, Niigata-shi 950.	025-245-8211

'OVER THE COUNTER' COMPANIES

(abbreviated names)

The shares of these companies are not listed, but are traded on an 'over the counter' basis.

(★ indicates that a company is listed in the appropriate chapter of this book.)

	Company	Address	Telephone
	KANEKO SEEDS	1-50-12 Furuichi-machi, Maebashi-shi, Gunma 371.	0272-51-1617
	SANYU CONSTRUCTION	2-17-7 Minami Yukigaya, Ota-ku, Tokyo 145.	03-3727-5751
	HIGASHI NIHON HOUSE	2-20 Nagata-cho, Morioka-shi, Iwate 020.	0196-24-3261
★	SATOHIDE CONSTRUCTION	5-6-11 Shinjuku, Shinjuku-ku, Tokyo 160.	03-3225-0314
	KABUTO DECOM	8-6-3 Yamanote Shichijo, Nishi-ku, Sapporo 063.	011-644-9111
	KAWADA CONSTRUCTION	1-3-9 Takinogawa, Kita-ku, Tokyo 114.	03-3915-5321
	SHINNIHON CORP.	2-15-6 Miyako-machi, Chuo-ku, Chiba-shi 260.	043-232-1111
	SURUGA CONSTRUCTION	3-33-7 Tsuruya-machi, Kanagawa-ku, Yokohama 221.	045-314-0361
	ROYAL CONSTRUCTION	2-16-1 Nihonbashi Hama-cho, Chuo-ku, Tokyo 103.	03-3639-2100
	SHIRAISHI	1-14 Iwamoto-cho, Kanda, Chiyoda-ku, Tokyo 101.	03-3253-9111
	NITTO LIFE	8-4-14 Akasaka, Minato-ku, Tokyo 107.	03-3423-3111
	TAISEI ONCHO	1-47-1 Oi, Shinagawa-ku, Tokyo 140.	03-3774-1111
	TENOX	2-4-1 Akasaka, Minato-ku, Tokyo 107.	03-3582-1873
	HOSODA	3-35-21 Asagaya Minami, Suginami-ku, Tokyo 166.	03-3220-1111
	TOHOKU MISAWA HOMES	3-7-33 Hinode-cho, Miyagino-ku, Sendai 983.	022-284-8711
	SAMPEI CONSTRUCTION	1-1-1 Moto Asakusa, Taito-ku, Tokyo 111.	03-3847-3311
	FUDO BUILDING RESEARCH	1-38-9 Taito, Taito-ku, Tokyo 110.	03-3835-2665
	ASAHI HOMES	1-19-5 Nishi Shinjuku, Shinjuku-ku, Tokyo 160.	03-3344-9415
	TOKYO MISAWA HOMES	2-46-5 Kabuki-cho, Shinjuku-ku, Tokyo 160.	03-5272-6221
	KOKUSAI DENSETSU	4-11 Yotsuya, Shinjuku-ku, Tokyo 160.	03-3355-1011
	TECHNO RYOWA	2-3-6 Minami Aoyama, Minato-ku, Tokyo 107.	03-3402-7231
	J-COS	1-1-6 Meguro, Meguro-ku, Tokyo 153.	03-3711-6161
	KYOWA KENKO	1-8-10 Jinnan, Shibuya-ku, Tokyo 150.	03-3464-0121
	SANSHIN	1-2-7 Koraku, Bunkyo-ku, Tokyo 112.	03-3816-2151
	DAIWA DENSETSU	2-5-1 Omachi, Aoba-ku, Sendai 980.	022-216-3111
	NISSHO INTER LIFE	2-11-1 Higashi Tabata, Kita-ku, Tokyo 114.	03-3810-7111
	HOKURIKU DENWA KOHJI	2-3 Otemachi, Kanazawa-shi, Ishikawa 920.	0762-21-6116
	TOHOKEN SYSTEM ENGINEERING	2-1 Takahagi-cho, Sano-shi, Tochigi 327.	0283-24-5556
	TSUZUKI TSUSHIN GIJUTSU	2-1-18 Hamamatsu-cho, Minato-ku, Tokyo 105.	03-3434-2181
	KANDA TSUSHINKI	24, Tomiyama-cho, Kanda, Chiyoda-ku, Tokyo 101.	03-3252-7731
	NITTAN	1-11-6 Hatagaya, Shibuya-ku, Tokyo 151.	03-3468-1111
	TAKAHASHI CURTAIN WALL	3-6-6 Nihonbashi, Chuo-ku, Tokyo 103.	03-3271-1711
	IWATSUKA CONFECTIONERY	1264 Oaza Iizuka, Koshiji-machi, Mishima-gun, Niigata 949.	0258-92-4111
	B-R31 ICE CREAM	2-13-38 Kami Osaki, Shinagawa-ku, Tokyo 141.	03-3449-0331
	SAGAMI HAM	59 Shobusawa, Fujisawa-shi, Kanagawa 252.	0466-48-8111
	STAMINA FOODS	1-22-13 Naruohama, Nishinomiya-shi, Hyogo 663.	0798-43-1065
	TAKIZAWA HAM	556 Izumigawa-machi, Tochigi-shi 328.	0282-23-5640
★	ITO EN	2-31-11 Kabuki-cho, Shinjuku-ku, Tokyo 160.	03-3200-9911
	YAIZU SUISANKAGAKU INDUSTRY	5-8-13 Ogawa Shin-machi, Yaizu, Shizuoka 425.	054-628-6388
	WAKOU SHOKUHIN	2-22-1 Inaho, Okaru-shi, Hokkaido 047.	0134-33-1915
★	SATO FOODS INDUSTRIES	4-154 Horinouchi, Komaki-shi, Aichi 485.	0568-77-7316
	ARIAKE JAPAN	2-14-14 Shimo Meguro, Meguro-ku, Tokyo 153.	03-3494-7031
	ISHIGAKI FOODS	1-9-17 Kudan Kita, Chiyoda-ku, Tokyo 102.	03-3263-4444
	ICHIMASA KAMABOKO	7-77 Tsushimaya, Niigata-shi 950.	025-270-7111
	O K FOOD INDUSTRY	1080-1 Oaza Oda, Amagi-shi, Fukuoka 838.	0946-22-7131
	HOKKOKU	3-11-10 Nihonbashi Ningyo-cho, Chuo-ku, Tokyo 103.	03-5695-2005
	TOKATSU FOODS	6-1-8 Hiyoshi, Kohoku-ku, Yokohama 223.	045-564-5100
	TAIYO WOOLEN SPINNING	5-5-9 Kami Aoki, Kawaguchi-shi, Saitama 333.	0482-65-2412
	HOKOKU SANGYO	1-9-4 Misuji, Taito-ku, Tokyo 111.	03-3851-9171
	MARUYAMA KOGYO	700 Oaza, Yasutsugu, Godo-cho, Anpachi-gun, Gifu 503-23	0584-27-4146
	CHOYA	15-2 Odenma-cho, Nihonbashi, Chuo-ku, Tokyo 103.	03-3662-2281
	HIKARI BUSINESS FORM	553 Higashi Asakawa-cho, Hachioji-shi, Tokyo 193.	0426-63-1631

KONOSHIMA CHEMICAL	4-3-7 Koraibashi, Chuo-ku, Osaka 541.	06-226-1201
NITTOH BION	68-1 Omachi, Kitami-shi, Hokkaido 090.	0157-24-7549
HAKUSUI CHEMICAL INDUSTRIES	3-9-7 Toyosaki, Kita-ku, Osaka 531.	06-373-0231
NIKKO SANSO	3-10-10 Tsukiji, Chuo-ku, Tokyo 104.	03-3542-4011
MELTEX	4-5-14 Nihonbashi Honcho, Chuo-ku, Tokyo 103.	03-3241-1070
N.E.CHEMCAT	2-4-1 Hamamatsu-cho, Minato-ku, Tokyo 105.	03-3435-5490
TESCO	1-12-17 Kami Renjaku, Mitaka-shi, Tokyo 181.	0422-56-2411
GUNZE KOBUNSHI	3-17-1 Sakuradai, Isehara-shi, Kanagawa 259-11.	0463-94-3711
HOSOYA FIREWORKS	2510 Kusabana, Akikawa-shi, Tokyo 197.	0425-58-5111
MATSUMOTO YUSHI-SEIYAKU	2-1-3 Shibukawa-cho, Yao-shi, Osaka 581.	0729-91-1001
MIKASA SEIYAKU	2-3-1 Toyotama Kita, Nerima-ku, Tokyo 176.	03-3992-0141
SEIKAGAKU	3-1-11 Nihonbashi Honcho, Chuo-ku, Tokyo 103.	03-3270-0966
TORII & CO.	3-4-1 Nihonbashi Honcho, Chuo-ku, Tokyo 103.	03-3231-6811
UNION PAINT	50-1 Shin-machi, Yashio-shi, Saitama 340.	0489-31-9141
ATOM CHEMICAL PAINT	3-9-2 Funato, Itabashi-ku, Tokyo 174.	03-3969-3111
TAIYO INK MFG.	2-7-1 Hazawa, Nerima-ku, Tokyo 176.	03-5999-1511
AVON PRODUCTS	2-12-19 Shibuya, Shibuya-ku, Tokyo 150.	03-3797-8300
NOEVIR	1-1-1 Minami Aoyama, Minato-ku, Tokyo 107.	03-3403-3351
MANDOM	4-33 Kitahama Higashi, Chuo-ku, Osaka 540.	06-943-7221
SDS BIOTECH	2-12-7 Higashi Shinbashi, Minato-ku, Tokyo 105.	03-3436-3811
TAIHO INDUSTRIES	2-21-44 Takanawa, Minato-ku, Tokyo 108.	03-3445-8111
MARKTEC	2-3-10 Sanno, Ota-ku, Tokyo 143.	03-3777-1852
AIKOH	2-1-39 Ikenohata, Taito-ku, Tokyo 110.	03-3823-1111
★ NITTA INDUSTRIES	1-8-12 Honcho, Chuo-ku, Osaka 541.	06-266-1771
CREATE MEDIC	3-18-14 Shin Yokohama, Kohoku-ku, Yokohama 222.	045-474-4711
TEITO RUBBER	2-26-5 Minami Ikebukuro, Toshima-ku, Tokyo 171.	03-3983-1101
FUJI LATEX	3-19-1 Kanda Nishiki-cho, Chiyoda-ku, Tokyo 101.	03-3293-5686
FUJI GLASS	2-15-9 Bunka, Sumida-ku, Tokyo 131.	03-3617-5111
NIPPON ZENITH PIPE	2-24-14 Higashi Nihonbashi, Chuo-ku, Tokyo 103.	03-3865-2618
SPANCRETE	2-27-8 Hongo, Bunkyo-ku, Tokyo 113.	03-5689-6311
EBATA	1-38-2 Higashi Kanamachi, Katsushika-ku, Tokyo 125.	03-3600-1161
NIKKATO	3-2-24 Oriono-cho, Sakai-shi, Osaka 590.	0722-38-3641
CHIYODA UTE	15-2 Sumiyoshi-machi, Yokkaichi-shi, Mie 512.	0593-64-5215
KUNIMINE INDUSTRIES	1-10-5 Iwamoto-cho, Chiyoda-ku, Tokyo 101.	03-3866-7255
TOKYO KOHTETSU	3-7 Kanda Kaji-cho, Chiyoda-ku, Tokyo 101.	03-3254-5201
SHINHOKOKU STEEL	5-13-1 Arajuku-machi, Kawagoe-shi, Saitama 350.	0492-42-1950
DAIWA KOTAI	5-4-14 Tsukiji, Chuo-ku, Tokyo 104.	03-5565-8255
POWDERTECH	217 Toyofuta, Kashiwa-shi, Chiba 277.	0471-45-2126
KAWATETSU GALVANIZING	2-4-1 Shiba Koen, Minato-ku, Tokyo 105.	03-3578-6411
TOKAI ALUMINUM FOIL	1 Tomiya-cho, Kanagawa-ku, Yokohama 221.	045-434-3111
TOYOKUNI ELECTRIC CABLE	2-30-11 Minami Ikebukuro, Toshima-ku, Tokyo 171.	03-3985-7511
TONICHI CABLE	1-1 Aragane, Ishioka-shi, Ibaraki 315.	0299-23-7111
CANARE ELECTRIC	1201-10 Aza Okuhazama, Oaza Fujieda, Aichi 470.	05617-2-3011
SHIBAZAKI SEISAKUSHO	1-3-1 Tajiri, Ichikawa-shi, Chiba 272.	0473-79-2345
MK SEIKO	1825 Oaza Amamiya, Koshoku-shi, Nagano 387.	0262-72-0601
SUZUKI SHUTTER MANUFACTURING	1-1-4 Minami Otsuka, Toshima-ku, Tokyo 170.	03-3944-1111
HORY	1-7-10 Nihonbashi, Ningyo-cho, Chuo-ku, Tokyo 103.	03-3664-3631
OTANI SAKURAI IRON WORKS	5-4-14 Kita Shinagawa, Shinagawa-ku, Tokyo 141.	03-3280-3951
TENRYU SAW MFG.	3711 Asaba, Asaba-cho, Iwata-gun, Shizuoka 437-11.	0538-23-6111
YAMAKAWA INDUSTRIAL	19-1 Gomijima, Fuji-shi, Shizuoka 416.	0545-61-1800
DAINICHI	651 Oaza Izumi, Shirane-shi, Niigata 950-12.	025-362-1101
KITAZAWA SANGYO	2-23-10 Higashi, Shibuya-ku, Tokyo 150.	03-5485-5111
IHARA HIGH PRESSURE FITTINGS	6-17-20 Shinbashi, Minato-ku, Tokyo 105.	03-3434-3474
UOZU MFG.	1-12-35 Shin Kanaya, Uozu-shi, Toyama 937.	0765-24-1200
ASAHINA MACHINE	2-14-21 Yanagisawa, Hoya-shi, Tokyo 188.	0424-61-3611
MITACHI ELECTRIC MACHINE	6-28-10 Nishi Nippori, Arakawa-ku, Tokyo 116.	03-3810-3101
NITTOKU ENGINEERING	10-18-3 Tajima, Urawa-shi, Saitama 336.	048-837-2011
DISCO	2-14-3 Higashi Kojiya, Ota-ku, Tokyo 144.	03-3743-0111
★ YAMAZAKI	489-23 Aritama Kita-machi, Hamamatsu-shi 431-31.	053-434-3011
USHIO	1-24-25 Sakae, Naka-ku, Nagoya 460.	052-222-0100

ODAWARA ENGINEERING	4289 Yoshidajima, Kaisei-cho, Kanagawa 258.	0465-83-1122
TAKEDA MACHINERY	To-78 Yoshimitsu, Terai-machi, Nomi-gun, Ishikawa 923-11	0761-58-5665
ISEKI POLY-TECH	4-31-6 Yoyogi, Shibuya-ku, Tokyo 151.	03-3299-6411
NAVITAS	1-5-15 Ishizu-cho Higashi, Hamadera, Sakai-shi 592.	0722-44-1231
UNION TOOL	2-23-1 Chuo, Ota-ku, Tokyo 143.	03-3777-4443
MAEDA SEISAKUSHO	1095 Shinonoi Goheigawa, Nagano-shi 388.	0262-92-2221
★ OILES	1-3-2 Shiba Daimon, Minato-ku, Tokyo 105.	03-3433-1371
ORII	6 Suzukawa, Isehara-shi, Kanagawa 259-11.	0463-93-0811
NISSEI A S B MACHINE	4586-3 Ko, Komoro-shi, Nagano 384.	0267-23-1560
HANIX INDUSTRY	1478-1 Oaza Kamitomi, Miyoshi-machi, Saitama 354.	0492-58-5840
SEIKO	2-8-1 Tenjin, Shimizu-shi, Shizuoka 424.	0543-66-0111
SATO	1-15-5 Shibuya, Shibuya-ku, Tokyo 150.	03-3797-9201
GIKEN SEISAKUSHO	3948-1 Nunoshida, Kochi-shi 781-51.	0888-46-2933
★ SANKYO ENGINEERING	1-25-12 Akebono-cho, Tachikawa-shi, Tokyo 190.	0425-23-6687
★ AIRTECH JAPAN	3-17-8 Higashi Ueno, Taito-ku, Tokyo 110.	03-3832-1731
KAWATA MFG.	1-15-15 Awaza, Nishi-ku, Osaka 550.	06-531-8214
PLACO	550 Sasakubo Shinden, Iwatsuki-shi, Saitama 339.	048-798-0222
DOVER JAPAN	3-27 Kioi-cho, Chiyoda-ku, Tokyo 102.	03-3230-2211
TOYO KOKEN	2418 Kanahorizuka, Kamiyabe-cho, Yokohama 245.	045-812-1551
SHIMAZAKI MIXING EQUIPMENT	2-24-2 Nishi Nippori, Arakawa-ku, Tokyo 116.	03-3802-3741
SUIDO KIKO	1-9-9 Yaesu, Chuo-ku, Tokyo 103.	03-3281-0151
OGURA CLUTCH	2-678 Aioi-cho, Kiryu-shi, Gunma 376.	0277-54-7101
K I T O	2000 Tsukiji Arai, Showa-machi, Yamanashi 409-38.	0552-75-7521
NAKANO REFRIGERATORS	2-15-4 Shibaura, Minato-ku, Tokyo 108.	03-3455-1311
★ RISO KAGAKU	2-20-15 Shinbashi, Minato-ku, Tokyo 105.	03-3572-8501
KAWASAKI THERMAL ENGINEERING	1000 Aochi-machi, Kusatsu-shi, Shiga 525.	0775-63-1111
NISCA	430-1 Kobayashi, Mashiho-machi, Yamanashi 400-05.	0556-22-6600
KATSURAGAWA ELECTRIC	1-5-1 Yaguchi, Ota-ku, Tokyo 146.	03-3758-0181
SANKYO	6-460 Sakaino-cho, Kiryu-shi, Gunma 376.	0277-44-3161
T H K	3-6-4 Kami Osaki, Shinagawa-ku, Tokyo 141.	03-3440-1431
MAEZAWA KYUSO INDUSTRIES	2-13-5 Takaban, Meguro-ku, Tokyo 152.	03-3716-1511
YOSHITAKE	7-3 Nino-cho, Mizuho-ku, Nagoya 467.	052-881-7146
MAEZAWA INDUSTRIES	1-3-3 Kyobashi, Chuo-ku, Tokyo 104.	03-3281-5521
NIPPON FURNACE KOGYO	2-1-53 Shitte, Tsurumi-ku, Yokohama 230.	045-575-8111
HAMAI INDUSTRIES	5-22-13 Nishi Gotanda, Shinagawa-ku, Tokyo 141.	03-3492-6655
ROYAL ELECTRIC	5-10-18 Higashi Gotanda, Shinagawa-ku, Tokyo 141.	03-3449-6281
CHUO-MUSEN	1-9-12 Omori Nishi, Ota-ku, Tokyo 143.	03-3762-5151
LUX	1-1-8 Nishi Gotanda, Shinagawa-ku, Tokyo 141.	03-3493-4381
JALCO	5-28-2 Higashi Yukigaya, Ota-ku, Tokyo 145.	03-3720-5181
SUMIDA ELECTRIC	2-4-8 Kanamachi, Katsushika-ku, Tokyo 125.	03-3607-5111
BODYSONIC	1-19-3 Kami Ochiai, Shinjuku-ku,Tokyo 161.	03-3950-3321
YAESU MUSEN	1-20-2 Shimo Maruko, Ota-ku, Tokyo 146.	03-3759-7111
TECHNOL SEVEN	1-3-10 Kamoi, Midori-ku, Yokohama 226.	045-931-3321
RIKADENKI KOGYO	1-17-11 Kakinoki-zaka, Meguro-ku, Tokyo 152.	03-3724-5411
MINATO ELECTRIC	4105 Minami Yamada-cho, Kohoku-ku, Yokohama 223.	045-591-5611
NIRECO	2951-4 Ishikawa-cho, Hachioji-shi, Tokyo 192.	0426-42-3111
NF CORP.	6-3-20 Tsunashima Higashi, Kohoku-ku, Yokohama 223.	045-545-8101
TESCON	3138-3 Tana, Sagamihara-shi, Kanagawa 229.	0427-63-3355
HIOKI E. E.	81 Oaza Koizumi, Ueda-shi, Nagano 386-11.	0268-28-0555
LEADER ELECTRONICS	2-6-33 Tsunashima Higashi, Kohoku-ku, Yokohama 223.	045-541-2121
★ NEW JAPAN RADIO	1-8-1 Shimo Meguro, Meguro-ku, Tokyo 153.	03-5434-8222
KIKUSUI ELECTRONICS	3-1175 Shin Maruko Higashi, Nakahara-ku, Kawasaki 211.	044-411-0111
MELCO	4-11-50 Osu, Naka-ku, Nagoya 460.	052-251-6891
OPTEX	4-7-5 Nionohama, Otsu-shi, Shiga 520.	0775-24-6990
CHIYODA INTEGRE	4-5 Akashi-cho, Chuo-ku, Tokyo 104.	03-3542-3410
I•O DATA DEVICE	24 Gaiku 1, Sakurada-cho, Kanazawa-shi, Ishikawa 920.	0762-60-3377
NEMIC-LAMBDA	1-11-5 Higashi Gotanada, Shinagawa-ku, Tokyo 141.	03-3447-4411
AVAL DATA	1041 Kaneda, Atsugi-shi, Kanagawa 243.	0462-22-0111
K E L	6-17-7 Nagayama, Tama-shi, Tokyo 206.	0423-74-5810
LESERTEC	4-10-4 Tsunashima Higashi, Kohoku-ku, Yokohama 223.	045-544-4111

SHOWA INFORMATION SYSTEMS	8-1-19 Akasaka, Minato-ku, Tokyo 107.	03-3403-7101
PHOENIX ELECTRIC	100-1 Minamino-oka, Hanjo-machi, Kasai-shi 675-21.	0790-49-2377
★ ENOMOTO	2222 Uenohara, Uenohara-machi, Yamanashi 409-01.	0554-62-5111
★ NIPPON ANTENNA	7-49-8 Nishi Ogu, Arakawa-ku, Tokyo 116.	03-3893-5221
SOSHIN ELECTRIC	1-18-18 Naka Magome, Ota-ku, Tokyo 143.	03-3775-2111
NMB SEMICONDUCTOR	1580 Yamamoto, Tateyama-shi, Chiba 294.	0470-23-3121
TAMA ELECTRIC	2-15-12 Nakane, Meguro-ku, Tokyo 152.	03-3723-1211
YAMAICHI ELECTRONICS	3-28-7 Naka Magome, Ota-ku, Tokyo 143.	03-3778-6111
SOPHIA SYSTEMS	2-4-1 Nishi Shinjuku, Shinjuku-ku, Tokyo 163-08.	03-3348-7000
NIHON KAIHEIKI INDUSTRY	1-5-14 Minami Magome, Ota-ku, Tokyo 143.	03-3774-0611
AIREX	280 Kawawa-cho, Midori-ku, Yokohama 226.	045-934-1111
SHINMEI ELECTRIC	1-16 Shinmei-cho, Saiwai-ku, Kawasaki 210.	044-555-1211
SHIBAURA ELECTRONICS	2-7-18 Machiya, Urawa-shi, Saitama 338.	048-852-6661
FUKUDA DENSHI	3-39-4 Hongo, Bunkyo-ku, Tokyo 113.	03-3815-2121
SANKO	959 Hiro Okano-mura, Shiojiri-shi, Nagano 399-07.	0263-52-2918
HAMAMATSU PHOTONICS	325-6 Sunayama-cho, Hamamatsu-shi, Shizuoka 430.	053-452-2141
SHIGI SHIPBUILDING	2-1 Ishizu Nishi-machi, Sakai-shi, Osaka 592.	0722-41-2033
FUJI MACHINERY	2-24-3 Iwagami-machi, Maebashi-shi, Gunma 371.	0272-31-3111
SAKURAI	830 Sukenobu-cho, Hamamatsu-shi, Shizuoka 430.	053-463-2111
IZUMI INDUSTRIES	620 Onakai, Kawagoe-shi, Saitama 350.	0492-35-1111
TECHNOL EIGHT	1 Akatsuki-cho, Seto-shi, Aichi 489.	0561-48-5311
TSUCHIYA MANUFACTURING	4-6-3 Higashi Ikebukuro, Toshima-ku, Tokyo 170.	03-3989-8484
NHK PRECISION	56 Suzukawa, Isehara-shi, Kanagawa 259-11.	0463-94-5235
NIHON PLAST	218 Aoshima-cho, Fuji-shi, Shizuoka 417.	0545-52-0481
MURAKAMI	12-25 Miyamoto-cho, Shizuoka-shi, Shizuoka 422.	054-286-2161
OHI SEISAKUSHO	1-14-7 Maruyama, Isogo-ku, Yokohama 235.	045-757-7000
YOROZU	3-7-60 Taru-machi, Kohoku-ku, Yokohama 222.	045-543-6800
I.S.PRESISION MACHINERY	8 Kozawatari-cho, Hamamatsu-shi, Shizuoka 432.	053-447-1511
SAKAE RINGYO	2-16-5 Aoi, Adachi-ku, Tokyo 120.	03-3889-3405
JAMCO	6-11-25 Osawa, Mitaka-shi, Tokyo 181.	0422-31-9111
ALOKA	6-22-1 Mure, Mitaka -shi, Tokyo 181.	0422-45-5111
SUKEGAWA ELECTRIC	3-19-5 Namekawa Honcho, Hitachi-shi, Ibaraki 317.	0294-21-5181
CABIN INDUSTRIAL	2-2-10 Hatagaya, Shibuya-ku, Tokyo 151.	03-3376-2311
TAMRON	1385 Oaza Hasunuma, Omiya-shi, Saitama 330.	048-684-9111
NORITA KOGAKU	477 Oaza Shimo Hiroya, Kawagoe-shi, Saitama 350.	0492-31-1814
S E E D	2-40-2 Hongo, Bunkyo-ku, Tokyo 113.	03-3813-1110
ODE SANGYO	4-12-8 Toyo, Koto-ku, Tokyo 135.	03-3645-9181
AKATSUKI PRINTING	1-44-1 Sekiguchi, Bunkyo-ku, Tokyo 112.	03-3268-3151
TAKARA PRINTING	3-28-8 Takada, Toshima-ku, Tokyo 171.	03-3971-3101
SANKO SANGYO	2-7-25 Kita Aoyama, Minato-ku, Tokyo 107.	03-3403-8134
T O I N	4-5-5 Hatchobori, Chuo-ku, Tokyo 104.	03-3297-6314
SHINKIGOSEI	2-14-10 Nishi Gotanda, Shinagawa-ku, Tokyo 141.	03-3495-2251
NIPPI	1-1-1 Senju Midori-cho, Adachi-ku, Tokyo 120.	03-3888-5111
NIPPON FILING	1-6 Kanda Surugadai, Chiyoda-ku, Tokyo 101.	03-3294-1751
COMBI	3-16-9 Uchi Kanda, Chiyoda-ku, Tokyo 101.	03-3256-8131
TSUTSUMI JEWELRY	4-24-21 Chuo, Warabi-shi, Saitama 335.	0484-31-5111
REGAL	2-16 Tamachi, Ichigaya, Shinjuku-ku, Tokyo 162.	03-3266-9111
KENSOH	448 Kami Fukawa-cho, Asakita-ku, Hiroshima-shi 739-17.	082-840-1001
JAPAN WAVELOCK	1-13-10 Tsukiji, Chuo-ku, Tokyo 104.	03-3543-8161
TOKAI	2181-7 Enokiyato, Kita Hassaku, Midori-ku, Yokohama 226.	045-933-2111
EMOTO INDUSTRY	1-26 Hondori 14, Shiraishi-ku, Sapporo 003.	011-863-1115
KOMATSU WALL INDUSTRY	1-72 Kogyo Danchi, Komatsu-shi, Ishikawa 923.	0761-21-3131
JALECO	2-19-7 Yoga, Setagaya-ku, Tokyo 158.	03-3708-4811
PIGEON	5-1 Kanda Tomiyama-cho, Chiyoda-ku, Tokyo 101.	03-3252-4111
PARAMOUNT BED	2-14-5 Higashi Suna, Koto-ku, Tokyo 136.	03-3648-1111
KING JIM	2-10-18 Higashi Kanda, Chiyoda-ku, Tokyo 101.	03-3862-2231
KOKEN	7 Yonban-cho, Chiyoda-ku, Tokyo 102.	03-5276-1911
SHIGEMATSU WORKS	3-13-8 Soto Kanda, Chiyoda-ku, Tokyo 101.	03-3255-0251
KING INDUSTRIAL	2-7-13 Moto Asakusa, Taito-ku, Tokyo 110.	03-3833-9651
YOKOHAMA MARUUO	1 Yamanouchi-machi, Kanagawa-ku, Yokohama 221.	045-459-2921

AM JAPAN	5-3 Koji-machi, Chiyoda-ku, Tokyo 102.	03-3230-4611
ELECTRONIC & INDUSTRIAL ENTERP.	5-1-7 Ginza, Chuo-ku, Tokyo 104.	03-3572-3204
ADO ELECTRONIC INDUSTRIAL	2-4-6 Soto Kanda, Chiyoda-ku, Tokyo 101.	03-3257-2630
SANYO KOGYO	1-1 Minami-cho, Kawasaki-ku, Kawasaki 210.	044-233-0271
SANYEI	4-1-2 Kotobuki, Taito-ku, Tokyo 111.	03-3847-3500
O H K I	2-1-4 Otowa, Bunkyo-ku, Tokyo 112.	03-3947-2232
KOKOKU HAUSING	1-3-22 Mejiro, Toshima-ku, Tokyo 171.	03-3987-1211
T. KAWABE & CO.	1-28-14 Shinjuku, Shinjuku-ku, Tokyo 160.	03-3352-7111
SANKO JUNYAKU	1-10-6 Iwamoto-cho, Chiyoda-ku, Tokyo 101.	03-3865-4311
TOHO PHARMACEUTICAL	5-2-1 Daisawa, Setagaya-ku, Tokyo 155.	03-3419-7811
YAMADA KOGYO	3-4-12 Ginza, Chuo-ku, Tokyo 104.	03-3563-4211
TOMITA	8-3-10 Ginza, Chuo-ku, Tokyo 104.	03-3572-8261
MIMATSU SEMICONDUCTOR IND.	762 Ashikado, Gunma-machi, Gunma-gun, Gunma 370-35.	0273-73-1662
TAKARABUNE	3-2-10 Takasago, Urawa-shi, Saitama 336.	048-824-8181
OTSUKA KAGU	1-5-1 Yurakucho, Chiyoda-ku, Tokyo 100.	03-3508-4321
HIKARI FURNITURE	4-7-1 Higashi Ogu, Arakawa-ku, Tokyo 116.	03-3800-0111
LAOX	3-2-14 Soto Kanda, Chiyoda-ku, Tokyo 101.	03-3251-9061
JONAS & CO.	1-6-14 Nishikubo, Musashino-shi, Tokyo 180.	0422-55-1611
SHAKLEE JAPAN	3-2-6 Nishi Azabu, Minato-ku, Tokyo 106.	03-3478-1061
TEN ALLIED	1-7-3 Nihonbashi Bakuro-cho, Chuo-ku, Tokyo 103.	03-3661-0666
ENCHO	10-7 Hinode-cho, Shizuoka-shi 420.	054-273-0800
GINZA YAMAGATAYA	3-5-4 Tsukiji, Chuo-ku, Tokyo 104.	03-3545-4731
KOMATSU STORE	6-9-5 Ginza, Chuo-ku, Tokyo 104.	03-3571-5051
MARUMITSU	2-1-1 Minami Kyuhoji-machi, Chuo-ku, Osaka 541.	06-262-0303
SANYO DEPARTMENT STORE	1 Minami-machi, Himeji-shi, Hyogo 670.	0792-23-1231
FORVAL	5-52-2 Jingu-mae, Shibuya-ku, Tokyo 150.	03-3476-1541
YAOKO	460 Oaza Ogawa, Ogawa-machi, Hiki-gun, Saitama 355-03	0493-73-1111
KATO DENKI	1-13-20 Yanagi-machi, Mito-shi, Ibaraki 310.	0292-24-9600
PALTAC	1-5-9 Minami Kyuhoji-machi, Chuo-ku, Osaka 541.	06-262-1286
ATSUGI NYLON SHOJI	3905 Otani, Ebina-shi, Kanagawa 243-04.	0462-31-1111
AIYA & CO.	1-19-18 Naka-cho, Musashino-shi, Tokyo 180.	0422-55-4111
WELL MART	76 Hojo Ishii, Himeji-shi, Hyogo 670.	0792-88-6966
NIPPON DATA KIKI	3-24-9 Higashi Ueno, Taito-ku, Tokyo 110.	03-3835-0542
OLYMPIC	4-12-25 Honcho, Kokubunji-shi, Tokyo 185.	0423-27-8711
DENKODO	1-7-10 Tsutsujigaoka, Miyagino-ku, Sendai 980.	022-291-3434
CANON COPYER SALES	2-2-4 Higashi Shinagawa, Shinagawa-ku, Tokyo 140.	03-5479-7878
J A X	3-7-5 Oyama-dai, Setagaya-ku, Tokyo 158.	03-3704-9999
FAMILY	2-8-15 Higashi Chiba, Chuo-ku, Chiba 260.	043-284-1111
TAIKO BANK	1-5-6 Otedori, Nagaoka-shi, Niigata 940.	0258-36-4111
NICHIEI	50-2 Shijo Hatake-machi, Nishinoin, Ukyo-ku, Kyoto 616.	075-321-6161
FIRST CREDIT	3-2-17 Nihonbashi, Chuo-ku, Tokyo 103.	03-3281-2281
EQUION	1-7-20 Yaesu, Chuo-ku, Tokyo 103.	03-3277-2700
JAPAN ASSOCIATED FINANCE	1-1-1 Shibaura, Minato-ku, Tokyo 105.	03-3456-5101
SHOHKOH FUND	3-2-4 Nihonbashi Hongoku-cho, Chuo-ku, Tokyo 103.	03-3271-9123
ALL CORP.	1-12-1 Shibuya, Shibuya-ku, Tokyo 150.	03-5466-0365
TAIYO FIRE & MARINE INSURANCE	3-18 Kanda Nishiki-cho, Chiyoda-ku, Tokyo 101.	03-3293-6511
JAPAN CENTRAL REAL ESTATE	1-5-3 Nihonbashi, Chuo-ku, Tokyo 103.	03-3271-2641
OSAKA PORT DEVELOPMENT	3-7-15 Chikko, Minato-ku, Osaka 552.	06-571-0861
HUNET	2-20-7 Oji, Kita-ku, Tokyo 114.	03-3913-4601
RECRUIT COSMOS	7-3-5 Ginza, Chuo-ku, Tokyo 104.	03-3571-1111
SEKIWA REAL ESTATE	1-20-3 Nishi Shinjuku, Shinjuku-ku, Tokyo 160.	03-3348-3366
DAIICHI	1-17-1 Nishi Shinjuku, Shinjuku-ku, Tokyo 160.	03-3342-4111
M D I	2-54-11 Honcho, Nakano-ku, Tokyo 164.	03-5350-0017
MINOWA REAL ESTATE	3-21-16 Ayase, Adachi-ku, Tokyo 120.	03-3620-8111
STARTS	3-37-4 Naka Kasai, Edogawa-ku, Tokyo 134.	03-3686-1011
MORINAGA DEVELOPMENT	5-33-1 Shiba, Minato-ku, Tokyo 108.	03-3451-1933
SENKO SANGYO	1-7 Furu Shin-machi, Takamatsu-shi, Kagawa 760.	0878-35-7000
HINOKI REAL ESTATE	7-7-26 Nishi Shinjuku, Shinjuku-ku, Tokyo 160.	03-3363-3111
CHICHIBU RAILWAY	1-1 Akebono-cho, Kumagaya-shi, Saitama 360.	0485-23-3311
KYOGOKU UNYU SHOJI	2-15-5 Shinkawa, Chuo-ku, Tokyo 104.	03-5566-8001

KATO SEINO TRANSPORTATION	16-1 Itahana, Annaka-shi, Gunma 379-01.	0273-82-3311
TAKASE	1-10-9 Shinbashi, Minato-ku, Tokyo 105.	03-3571-4151
BANDAI TRUCKING & WAREHOUSING	4-42-5 Higashi Yotsugi, Katsushika-ku, Tokyo 124.	03-3695-5151
★ TOEI REEFER LINE	1-9-18 Kaigan, Minato-ku, Tokyo 105.	03-3431-0336
SADO STEAMSHIP	353 Oaza Minato, Ryotsu-shi, Niigata 952.	02592-7-5174
JAPAN AIR SYSTEM	3-5-1 Toranomon, Minato-ku, Tokyo 105.	03-5473-4100
SHINAGAWA SOKO TATEMONO	3-6-17 Osaki, Shinagawa, Tokyo 141.	03-3492-7171
SANRITSU	2-4-7 Konan, Minato-ku, Tokyo 108.	03-5461-1185
BROADCASTING SYSTEM OF NIIGATA	3-18 Kawagishi-cho, Niigata-shi 951.	025-267-4111
ESCOM	1-2-10 Hirakawa-cho, Chiyoda-ku, Tokyo 102.	03-3264-1911
ASCII	6-11-1 Minami Aoyama, Minato-ku, Tokyo 107-24.	03-3486-7111
INTERNATIONAL TELEVISION FILMS	5-7-1 Kinuta, Setagaya-ku, Tokyo 157.	03-3749-7213
AOI ADVERTISING PROMOTION	1-6-1 Osaki, Shinagawa-ku, Tokyo 141.	03-3779-8000
JAPAN PROCESS DEVELOPMENT	1-5-1 Omori Kita, Ota-ku, Tokyo 143.	03-3768-5601
BUNKAHOSO BRAINS	3-2-1 Yotsuya, Shinjuku-ku, Tokyo 160.	03-3355-2111
KOEI	1-23-3 Minowa-cho, Kohoku-ku, Yokohama 223.	045-561-6888
STAT	2-37-5 Minami Otsuka, Toshima-ku, Tokyo 170.	03-3943-5911
COMTEC	3-1-12 Mita, Minato-ku, Tokyo 108.	03-3798-9711
BUSINESS BRAIN – SHOWA OTA	2-2-3 Uchi Saiwai-cho, Chiyoda-ku, Tokyo 100.	03-3595-1581
I X	2-8-15 Ginza, Chuo-ku, Tokyo 104.	03-3567-5211
CRC RESEARCH INSTITUTE	3-6-2 Honcho, Nihonbashi, Chuo-ku, Tokyo 103.	03-3665-9711
EYEFUL HOME TECHNOLOGY	2-10-14 Ryogoku, Sumida-ku, Tokyo 130.	03-5624-1525
NAGAWA	1-41 Yoshiki-cho, Omiya-shi, Saitama 330.	048-648-6111
HORIPRO	1-2-5 Shimo Meguro, Meguro-ku, Tokyo 153.	03-3490-4601
SOTETSU KIGYO	2-9-14 Kita Saiwai, Nishi-ku, Yokohama 220.	045-319-2361
AUCNET	2-7-26 Kita Aoyama, Minato-ku, Tokyo 107.	03-3423-6111
I G S	27-5 Saka-machi, Shinjuku-ku, Tokyo 160.	03-3353-2201
MATSUDO KOUSAN	594 Kami Hongo, Matsudo-shi, Chiba 271.	0473-63-5458
NIHON JAMBO	27-1 Izumi Yamashita, Atami-shi, Shizuoka 413.	0465-62-6121
HORAI	1-20-2 Nishi Shinjuku, Shinjuku-ku, Tokyo 160.	03-3344-2921
KYOSEI RENTEMU	1-14 Kita, Nishi Juhachi-jo, Obihiro-shi, Hokkaido 080.	0155-33-2211
DATA COMMUNICATION SYSTEM	5-23-4 Shinbashi, Minato-ku, Tokyo 105.	03-3437-5488
ENIX	7-5-25 Nishi Shinjuku, Shinjuku-ku, Tokyo 160.	03-3367-1916
KYODO COMPUTER	1-2-7 Suda-cho, Kanda, Chiyoda-ku, Tokyo 101.	03-3254-5491
KOKUSAI SYSTEM	2-4-1 Nishi Shinjuku, Shinjuku-ku, Tokyo 163.	03-3343-0701
★ GREEN HOUSE	1-36-4 Yoyogi, Shibuya-ku, Tokyo 151.	03-3379-1211
CORNET	1-10 Ogawa-machi, Kanda, Chiyoda-ku, Tokyo 101.	03-3251-1717
RYOMO SYSTEMS	3-4025 Hirosawa-cho, Kiryu-shi, Gunma 376.	0277-53-3131
KAMOGAWA GRAND HOTEL	2-8-18 Kyobashi, Chuo-ku, Tokyo 104.	03-3563-6491
DAIICHI KYOKEN	4-7-5 Awaji-machi, Chuo-ku, Osaka 541.	06-202-2776
CAPCON	1-4-12 Ote-dori, Chuo-ku, Osaka 540.	06-946-6622
CREO	4-9-25 Shibaura, Minato-ku, Tokyo 108.	03-3456-4611
★ NISHIO RENT ALL	3-4-26 Minami Senba, Chuo-ku, Osaka 542.	06-251-7302
I S B	1-1-8 Nishi Gotanda, Shinagawa-ku, Tokyo 141.	03-3490-1761
KANTO BIOMEDICAL LABORATORY	3-673 Tenjin, Konosu-shi, Saitama 365.	0485-42-3171
NIPPON COMPUTER SYSTEMS	2-1-1 Nishi Shinjuku, Shinjuku-ku, Tokyo 163.	03-3346-2001
NIPPON MIC	545-9 O-oka, Numazu-shi, Shizuoka 410.	0559-51-5700
SOFTWARE RESEARCH ASSOCIATES	1-1-1 Hirakawa-cho, Chiyoda-ku, Tokyo 102.	03-3234-2611
TRANS COSMOS	3-3-3 Akasaka, Minato-ku, Tokyo 107.	03-3586-2880
JASTEC	3-5-23 Takanawa, Minato-ku, Tokyo 108.	03-3446-0295
KOKUSAI KANKO KAIKAN	1-8-3 Marunouchi, Chiyoda-ku, Tokyo 100.	03-3215-1181
HOTEL NEW GRAND	10 Yamashita-cho, Naka-ku, Yokohama 231.	045-681-1841
BIWAKO HOTEL	5-35 Yanagasaki, Otsu-shi, Shiga 520.	0775-24-1255
NIPPON KANZAI	5-23 Matsubara-machi, Nishinomiya-shi, Hyogo 662.	0798-35-2200
INSTITUTE OF GENERAL EDUCATION	2-1-61 Shiromi, Chuo-ku, Osaka 540.	06-949-0571
NAGASE BROTHERS	1-29-2 Kichijoji Minami-cho, Musashino-shi, Tokyo 180.	0422-45-7011
SEIYOKEN	4-58 Ueno Koen, Taito-ku, Tokyo 110.	03-3821-2181
HAKUSEISHA	1-10-2 Kyobashi, Chuo-ku, Tokyo 104.	03-3567-4401
ABC	1-13-10 Tsukiji, Chuo-ku, Tokyo 104.	03-3546-7777
NJK	2-22-3 Shibuya, Shibuya-ku, Tokyo 150.	03-3499-2871

FUJI SOFTWARE	2-13-18 Okamoto, Kamakura-shi, Kanagawa 247.	0467-45-2811
MKC	3-10-12 Nagisa, Matsumoto-shi, Nagano 390.	0263-26-8220
JAPAN KNOWLEDGE INDUSTRY	7-22-17 Nishi Gotanda, Shinagawa-ku, Tokyo 141.	03-3494-5441
T.S.D	1-32-4 Takadanobaba, Shinjuku-ku, Tokyo 169.	03-3205-4321
ASK PLANNING CENTER	1-2-9 Yariya-machi, Chuo-ku, Osaka 540.	06-944-1181
JAPAN SYSTEMS	3-7-1 Higashiyama, Meguro-ku, Tokyo 153.	03-3760-1311
SHINGAKUKAI	Kita 1-15 Hongo-dori 1-chome, Shiraishi-ku, Sapporo 003.	011-863-5557
SHIN-NIPPON MET. & OCEAN. CONSLT	3-14-5 Tamagawa, Setagaya-ku, Tokyo 158.	03-3708-1161
GAKKYUSHA	1-4 Higashi, Kunitachi-shi, Tokyo 186.	0425-74-1161
EIWA	67-173 Aza Higashihama, Takihama, Niihama, Ehime 792.	0897-46-2500
T.O. OGASAWARA	3-18-15 Minato-machi, Hakodate-shi, Hokkaido 041.	0138-45-3911
TOKKI	7-15-5 Ginza, Chuo-ku, Tokyo 104.	03-3543-8841
LEASE ELECTRONICS	8 Mikura-cho, Kanda, Chiyoda-ku, Tokyo 101.	03-3256-0362
GOTO	10-1 Midorigaoka, Numazu-shi, Shizuoka 410.	0559-23-5100
KOGURE	1-19-9 Ningyo-cho, Nihonbashi, Chuo-ku, Tokyo 103.	03-3667-5054
AMWAY (JAPAN)	2-8-12 Minami Azabu, Minato-ku, Tokyo 106.	03-3769-5741
FR	2-17 Nanpeidai-cho, Shibuya-ku, Tokyo 150.	03-3770-1411
MAMMY MART	5-1-1 Chiyoda, Sakado-shi, Saitama 350-02.	0492-84-5811
LILYCOLOR	7-5-20 Nishi Shinjuku, Shinjuku-ku, Tokyo 160.	03-3366-7845
GENKI SUSHI	2-1-5 Odori, Utsunomiya-shi, Tochigi 320.	0286-32-5711
NAGANO TOKYU DEPART. STORE	1-1-1 Minami Chitose, Nagano-shi 380.	0262-26-8181
NAKAYAMA KIKO	2-73-8 Honjo Nishi, Higashi Osaka-shi 578.	06-747-5478
YAMADA DENKI	4-12-10 Hiyoshi-cho, Maebashi-shi, Gunma 371.	0272-33-5522
LEVI STRAUSS JAPAN	3-1-30 Minami Aoyama, Minato-ku, Tokyo 107.	03-5410-8700
TRAVELER	1-10 Koji-machi, Chiyoda-ku, Tokyo 102.	03-3234-7911
GETZ BROS	3-1-30 Minami Aoyama, Minato-ku, Tokyo 107.	03-3423-6451
ISHIGURO HOMA	9-3 Nakasono-cho, Kushiro-shi, Hokkaido 085.	0154-25-0801
NIKKODO	3-12-1 Kita Horie, Nishi-ku, Osaka 550.	06-533-1121
ARCLAND SAKAMOTO	445 Oaza Kamisugoro, Sanjo-shi, Niigata 955.	0256-33-6000
USC	7-19-1 Nishi Gotanda, Shinagawa-ku, Tokyo 141.	03-3491-8571
PARKER	2-12-6 Nihonbashi, Chuo-ku, Tokyo 103.	03-3273-7461
TOKYO DEN-ON	3-8-12 Soto Kanda, Chiyoda-ku, Tokyo 101.	03-3251-3377
KAWACHIYA PAPER	7-48-18 Takinogawa, Kita-ku, Tokyo 114.	03-3916-0261
CHUO BUSSAN	2-2-3 Minami Aoyama, Minato-ku, Tokyo 107.	03-3402-7211
GINZA RENOIR	2-2-1 Koenji Kita, Suginami-ku, Tokyo 166.	03-3336-1251
KUROGANEYA	1-13-18 Naka Kogawara, Kofu-shi, Yamanashi 400.	0552-41-2472
KEIYU	1670 Tsuruma, Machida-shi, Tokyo 194.	0427-96-6111
MEIKO SHOKAI	1-1 Goban-cho, Chiyoda-ku, Tokyo 102.	03-3262-1611
YOSHINOYA D & C	4-3-17 Shinjuku, Shinjuku-ku, Tokyo 160.	03-5269-5111
MEMOREX TELEX JAPAN	6-26-2 Minami Oi, Shinagawa-ku, Tokyo 140.	03-5471-4030
KOBADEN ELECTRONICS	8-3-3 Nishi Kamata, Ota-ku, Tokyo 144.	03-3732-1131
MATSUMOTOKIYOSHI	44 Kogane, Matsudo-shi, Chiba 270.	0473-44-5111
COX	320-23 Kaji-cho, Hamamatsu-shi, Shizuoka 430.	053-455-0160
MARUFURU	4932 Funatsu, Kawaguchiko-machi, Yamanashi 401-03.	0555-72-1980
SEKIDO	1685-1 Hazama-machi, Hachioji-shi, Tokyo 193.	0426-66-1111
INNOTECH	2-5-1 Kita Aoyama, Minato-ku, Tokyo 107.	03-3497-4400
HI-MART	381-1 Shimo Nakayama, Shimodate-shi, Ibaraki 308.	0296-24-1222
ROYAL	2-26-11 Kita Senzoku, Ota-ku, Tokyo 145.	03-3726-1316
FUJI ELECTRONICS	3-2-12 Hongo, Bunkyo-ku, Tokyo 113.	03-3814-1411
TSUZUKI DENSAN	3-11-6 Nishi Shinbashi, Minato-ku, Tokyo 105.	03-3433-2171
CHARLE	3-1-2 Yasakadai, Suma-ku, Kobe 654-01.	078-792-7000
MAKE	2-4-12 Ryutsu Center Minami, Yakin-cho, Iwate 020.	0196-37-0088
MATSUYA FOODS	4-1-7 Shimo Shakujii, Nerima-ku, Tokyo 177.	03-3904-1121
UENO METALEX	3-7-8 Kyobashi, Chuo-ku, Tokyo 104.	03-3562-5511
JAPAN BUSINESS COMPUTER	1368 Futo-o-cho, Kohoku-ku, Yokohama 222.	045-544-6611
MAKIYA	709-1 Aza Takenomisaki, Numazu-shi, Shizuoka 410.	0559-23-1171
HIMIKO	6-17-10 Jingu-mae, Shibuya-ku, Tokyo 150.	03-5485-3711
CONSEC	4-6-8 Shoko Center, Nishi-ku, Hiroshima-shi 733.	082-277-5451
MARUYOSHI	3-2-6 Hirano, Koto-ku, Tokyo 135.	03-3820-0441
UNIDAX	5-1-21 Kyonan-cho, Musashino-shi, Tokyo 180.	0422-32-4111

HOHRIN	8 Dai-machi, Ichigaya, Shinjuku-ku, Tokyo 162.	03-3353-7272
STEAK MIYA	2-7-24 Ichijo, Utsunomiya-shi, Tochigi 320.	0286-34-3815
NICHIDEN	2-73-1 Honjo Nishi, Higashi Osaka-shi 578.	06-746-5700
KANSEKI	3-1-1 Nishi Kawada Honmachi, Utsunomiya-shi 321-01.	0286-58-8123
KOJITU	2-1-1 Nishi Tamon-dori, Hyogo-ku, Kobe 652.	078-578-0766
FUJII SANGYO	41-3 Hirade Kogyo Danchi, Utsunomiya-shi, Tochigi 321.	0286-62-6060
DAIDENSHA	1-6-17 Nipponbashi Nishi, Naniwa-ku, Osaka 556.	06-632-6111
NIHON DENKEI	5-14-12 Ueno, Taito-ku, Tokyo 110.	03-3834-6330
AIKO	205-2 Nishi Otomo, Odawara-shi, Kanagawa 250-02.	0465-37-2111
OLYMPIC SPORTS	80 Aza Irigome, Miai-cho, Okazaki-shi, Aichi 444.	0564-53-3111
DAIWABO INFORMATION SYSTEM	3-2-5 Hon-machi, Chuo-ku, Osaka 541.	06-281-1161
NIPPO	5-27-12 Sakae, Naka-ku, Nagoya 460.	052-263-1281
UEMATSU SHOKAI	3-7-5 Oroshi-machi, Wakabayashi-ku, Sendai 983.	022-232-5171
SUN-S	1-1 Otemachi, Aoba-ku, Sendai 980.	022-266-4511
MATSUMOTO DENKI	2662 Oaza Tsuruma, Fujimi-shi, Saitama 354.	0492-51-3111
JAPAN CBM	1-1-48 Okubo, Shinjuku-ku, Tokyo 169.	03-3200-6294
KANSAIDENPA	328 Kikuwa-cho, Yokkaichi-shi, Mie 510.	0593-31-1000
DAITO MECHATRONICS	2-1 Tashiro Hondori, Chikusa-ku, Nagoya 464.	052-761-7171